THE COMPLETE INSTANT POT FOR TWO COOKBOOK

by: Lara Green

Contents

VEGETABLES **14**
1. Braised Cabbage with Mediterranean Herbs 14
2. Green Autumn Soup 14
3. Classic Spanish Pisto 14
4. Southern Sweet Potato Casserole 15
5. Fall Harvest Soup 15
6. Country-Style Turkey and Brussels Sprouts.................. 15
7. Colby Cheese and Cabbage Bake 16
8. Rich and Easy Potato Chowder............................... 16
9. Rutabaga Salad with Apples and Dijon Mustard 16
10. Italian-Style Zucchini Casserole 17
11. Greek Eggplant with Chickpeas 17
12. Chinese Bok Choy 17
13. Italian Crunchy and Cheesy Cauliflower Salad 18
14. Harvest Vegetable Soup 18
15. Easy Glazed Baby Carrots...................................... 18
16. Caprese Asparagus with Gorgonzola Cheese 19
17. Beetroot Thoran Onam Sadhya 19
18. Traditional Ratatouille with Pinot Noir 19
19. Pumpkin Pie Oats 20
20. Creamy Broccoli and Spinach Soup 20
21. Carrot Salad with Dijon Mustard and Honey 20
22. Traditional Italian Wedding Soup............................ 21
23. Warm Vegetable Salad with Tahini Sauce 21
24. Authentic Persian Khoreshe Karafs 21
25. Classic Cuban Sofregit.. 22
26. Turkey Noodle Soup with Herbs 22
27. Steamed Vegetables with Cilantro 22
28. Mixed Buttered Vegetables 23
29. Vegetarian Medley with Cream Cheese 23
30. Artichokes with Garlic-Mayo Dipping Sauce 23
31. Broccoli Salad with Seeds and Mayo 24
32. Traditional Pozole with Hominy 24
33. Indian Curry with Kale 24
34. Potato Salad with Eggs 25
35. Rich Yellow Bean Salad 25
36. Braised Collard Greens with Bacon 25
37. German Cabbage Soup with Sausage 26
38. Italian-Style Endive with Salami and Cheese 26
39. Old-Fashioned Bhindi Masala................................ 26

SOUPS **27**
40. Indian Tomato Soup 27
41. Mexican Chicken Enchilada Soup 27
42. Old-Fashioned Chicken Noodle Soup 27
43. Hearty Squash and Leek Soup 28
44. Mediterranean Fish Soup 28
45. Habanero Chicken Soup with Beans 28
46. Mom's Barley Soup 29
47. Classic Stroganoff Soup 29
48. Rich Meatball Soup 29
49. Vegetables, Corn and Chicken Soup 30
50. Ground Pork and Tomato Soup 30
51. Traditional Minestrone Soup.................................. 30
52. Chipotle Beef Soup 31

53. Masala Turkey and Rice Soup 31
54. Classic French Bouillabaisse 31
55. Creamed Potato Soup with Corn............................ 32
56. Lima Bean Soup 32
57. Swiss-Style Fish Chowder 32
58. Dad's Duck Soup with Millet 33
59. Colorful Seafood Bisque Soup 33
60. Thai Oxtail Soup (Hang Wuao)............................... 33
61. Quinoa Soup with Zucchini 34
62. Easy Lentil Soup with Spinach 34
63. Nutty Sweet Potato Soup...................................... 34
64. French Onion-Bread Soup 35
65. Cheesy Broccoli Soup 35
66. Ham Bone Soup with Vegetables 35
67. Lentil and Tomato Soup 36
68. Wild Rice Soup with Root Vegetable 36
69. Hearty Beef and Vegetable Soup 36
70. French Bouillabaisse with Pinot Grigio 37
71. Creamed Clam Chowder 37
72. Classic New England Clam Chowder 37
73. Country-Style Vegetable Chicken Soup 38
74. Vegetable Soup with Mediterranean Herbs 38
75. Creamy Asparagus Soup with Yogurt and Mint 38
76. Creamed Tomato Soup 39
77. Easy Ukrainian Borscht 39
78. Ditalini Soup with Chicken 39
79. Decadent Burger Soup 40
80. Italian-Style Sausage and Cabbage Soup 40

SIDE DISHES **41**
81. Couscous Florentine with Yogurt and Tahini 41
82. Buttery Garlicky Mushrooms with Herbs 41
83. French-Style Peppers 41
84. Restaurant-Style Mexican Rice............................... 42
85. Zingy Kamut with Spinach and Lime 42
86. Spicy Kashmiri Eggplant 42
87. Fettuccine Pasta alla Parmigiana............................ 43
88. Sweet Potato Mash 43
89. Black Eyed Peas with Spinach and Bacon 43
90. Zingy Garlicky Kale with Lemon 44
91. Cauliflower Rice with Butter and Parsley 44
92. Hearty Cabbage Bowl 44
93. Mediterranean Saucy Eggplant 45
94. Indian Rice with Yogurt 45
95. Cholula Baked Beans 45
96. Tex-Mex Chili with Rice 46
97. Crunchy Brussels Sprouts with Parmesan 46
98. Steamed Sweet Potatoes with Butter....................... 46
99. Curried Chickpea with Avocado 47
100. Sausage and Cheese Stuffed Mushrooms.................. 47
101. Tangy Glazed Root Vegetables 47
102. Aromatic Baby Potatoes with Herbs 48
103. Easy Okra with Tomato and Shallots 48
104. Decadent Balsamic Brussels Sprouts with Cranberries 48
105. Steamed Spicy and Cheesy Potatoes 49

106. Sesame Crispy Asparagus 49
107. Creamy Au Gratin Potatoes.................... 49
108. Spicy Corn on the Cob with Aioli 50
109. Italian-Style Creamy Broccoli 50
110. Creamed Ranch Potatoes 50
111. Bucatini alla Puttanesca 51
112. Green Beans with Garlic and Chives 51
113. Warm Millet Salad with Roasted Tomatoes 51
114. Kidney Bean Curry.................... 52
115. Corn Chaat (Masala Corn) 52
116. Aromatic Cauliflower Kurma 52
117. Classic Italian Caponata 53
118. Peppery Red Lentils.................... 53
119. Sticky Cauliflower with Tahini 53
120. Fall Vegetable Mash 54

PASTA & GRAINS

PASTA & GRAINS 55
121. Lasagna with Sausage and Italian Cheese 55
122. Philadelphia Spaghetti Carbonara 55
123. Creamed Corn with Cottage Cheese.................... 55
124. Za'atar Oatmeal with Eggs and Peppers 56
125. Bulgur Pilau with Shallots 56
126. Cheesy Farro with Mushrooms 56
127. Truffle and Parmesan Popcorn.................... 57
128. Spicy Buckwheat with Manchego 57
129. Strawberries and Coconut Milk Bread Pudding 57
130. Hungarian Cornmeal Squares (Kukoricaprósza) 58
131. Squash and Quinoa Pilaf 58
132. Cheese Pie with Pancetta and Scallions 58
133. Buckwheat Porridge with Blueberries.................... 59
134. Three-Grain Porridge 59
135. Hearty Chicken Soup with Couscous 59
136. Chicken and Kamut Soup Provençale.................... 60
137. Pasta al' Arrabbiata 60
138. Macaroni and Cheese Pot Pie 60
139. Basic Breakfast Oatmeal 61
140. Creamy and Cheesy Baked Ziti.................... 61
141. Breakfast Millet Porridge with Nuts 61
142. Sweet Buttermilk Cornbread 62
143. Quinoa and Chickpea Salad 62
144. Cheesy Chicken Bake 62
145. Breakfast Amaranth Porridge.................... 63
146. Traditional Moroccan Couscous 63
147. Wheat Berry Salad 63
148. Korean Sorghum Pudding 64
149. Old-Fashioned Spaghetti with Ground Meat Sauce..... 64
150. Peppery Pearl Barley with Chives.................... 64
151. Paprika Creamed Grits.................... 65
152. Corn with Cilantro Butter 65
153. Chocolate Croissant Breakfast Bake 65
154. Indian Spicy Bulgur with Chicken 66
155. Cheesy Porridge with Kale 66
156. Amaranth Pilaf with Eggs and Cheese.................... 66
157. Spelt Grains with Spinach and Mushrooms 67
158. Polenta with Feta Cheese and Herbs 67

BEANS, LEGUMES & LENTILS

BEANS, LEGUMES & LENTILS....................68
159. Kidney Bean and Vegetable Soup 68
160. Indian Aromatic Chili 68
161. The Best Minestrone Soup Ever 68
162. Spicy and Herby Chickpea Stew 69
163. Tangy Lentil Curry 69
164. Indian Tarka Dal 69
165. Authentic Greek Fasolakia 70
166. Lebanese Lentils with Rice (Mujadara).................... 70
167. Mexican Vegetarian Tacos 70
168. Split Pea Soup with Ham 71
169. Creole Boiled Peanuts.................... 71
170. Green Pea and Mushroom Soup 71
171. Mom's Lentil Salad 72
172. Classic Spicy Hummus 72
173. Scarlet Runner with Turkey and Herbs 72
174. Mediterranean Lima Beans with Ham 73
175. Oriental Bean and Cheese Dip 73
176. Country-Style Anasazi Bean Soup 73
177. Green Lentil Stew 74
178. Traditional Japanese Kuromame.................... 74
179. Traditional Indian Matar 74
180. Thanksgiving Beans with Turkey 75
181. Indian Sorakkai Sambar 75
182. Pinto Beans with Turkey Sausage and Tomato 75
183. Italian-Style Heirloom Beans 76
184. Spicy Pea Dip with Herbs 76
185. Vegetarian Chili with Sour Cream 76
186. Bean Soup with Potatoes and Parmesan 77
187. Wax Bean Salad with Peanut Butter 77
188. Summer Bean Salad.................... 77
189. Snap Pea and Chicken Medley 78
190. Dad's Lima Beans with Bacon 78
191. Balsamic Lentils with Brown Rice 78
192. Mom's Black-Eyed Peas 79
193. Baked Beans with Colby Cheese 79

CHICKEN

CHICKEN 80
194. Mexican-Style Chicken Sandwiches 80
195. Roast Chicken with Garlic and Herbs 80
196. Classic Chicken Gumbo 80
197. Spicy Chicken Bake with Beans 81
198. Traditional Locrio de Pollo 81
199. Chicken Medley with Garden Vegetables 81
200. Spicy Chicken and Root Vegetable Mélange 82
201. Chicken Drumsticks with Millet and Green Beans..... 82
202. Chicken and Pasta Bake with Ricotta Cheese 82
203. Saucy Chicken Fillets with Olives 83
204. Hot Chicken Tacos.................... 83
205. Cholula Chicken Wings 83
206. Meatloaf with Parmesan and Peppers 84
207. Classic Teriyaki Chicken with Broccoli 84
208. Cheesy Chicken Tenders 84
209. Creamy Dijon Chicken.................... 85
210. Asian Glazed Chicken Drumsticks.................... 85

211. Creamed Chicken Salad 85
212. Zingy Ranch Chicken with Butter 86
213. Chicken Drumsticks with Lemon Sauce 86
214. Greek-Style Chicken with Haloumi and Couscous...... 86
215. Summer Chicken Sandwiches 87
216. Spicy Chicken Meatballs 87
217. Chicken Tenders with Cheese and Potatoes 87
218. Chicken and Bacon in Orange Sauce 88
219. Marsala Chicken Wings with Cream Cheese 88
220. Mexican Chicken Casserole 88
221. Chicken Cutlets in Herb Sauce 89
222. Mexican Taco Meat 89
223. Easy Chicken Congee 89

DUCK 90
224. Indian Duck Masala 90
225. Duck with Curried Cherry Sauce 90
226. Thai Duck Breasts 90
227. Spicy Glazed Duck Breast 91
228. Japanese Duck with Rice and Eggs 91
229. The Best Duck Ragù 91
230. Chinese-Style Duck Salad 92
231. Duck with Apricot and Orange Sauce 92
232. Chinese-Style Saucy Duck 92
233. Balsamic Duck with Mixed Vegetables 93
234. Traditional Szechuan Duck 93
235. Decadent Duck in Cranberry Sauce 93

TURKEY 94
236. Holiday Turkey Breasts with Herbs 94
237. Turkey Sandwich with Mustard and Cheese 94
238. Caribbean-Style Turkey with Beer 94
239. Creamed Turkey Salad with Apples 95
240. Herby Turkey with Gravy 95
241. Spicy Turkey Meatballs 95
242. Festive Roast Turkey 96
243. Italian Turkey with Garden Vegetables 96
244. The Best Thanksgiving Meatloaf Ever 96
245. Turkey and Barley Bowl 97
246. Fontina Meatballs with Herbed Sauce........................ 97
247. Sticky Orange Turkey Thighs 97
248. Country-Style Turkey and Cabbage Bake 98
249. Mediterranean Turkey Salad with Cheese 98
250. Turkey with Bacon and Sherry Gravy 98

FISH & SEAFOOD 99
251. Tangy Haddock with Green Beans 99
252. South Indian Fish Curry (Meen Kulambu) 99
253. Mexican-Style Haddock Tacos 99
254. Sea Bass in Orange Sauce 100
255. Cheesy Tuna and Asparagus Bake 100
256. Buttery Codfish with Scallions 100
257. Southern California Fish Stew 101
258. Exotic and Saucy Thai Prawns........................ 101
259. Rich and Easy Creole Gumbo 101
260. Seafood Hot Pot with Jasmine Rice 102
261. Fish en Papillote 102
262. Lemony Sole with Fennel 102
263. Blue Crab with Lemon and Herbs 103
264. Salmon Salad Sandwich 103

265. Glazed Sea Bass Fillets 103
266. Mussels with Butter-Scallion Sauce 104
267. Greek-Style Seafood Tart 104
268. Traditional Japanese Yosenabe 104
269. Shrimp with Feta Cheese and Mint 105
270. Tangy Cheese and Crab Dip 105
271. Fish Masala Curry 105
272. Parmesan and Prawn Dip 106
273. Spanish Paella with White Wine 106
274. Buttery Lobster Tails 106
275. Spicy Shrimp Salad 107
276. French-Style Fish Packets 107
277. Tilapia with Lemon and Peppers 107
278. Indian Biryani with Halibut 108
279. Old Bay Crab Salad Rolls 108
280. Spicy Red Snapper 108
281. Crabs with Garlic Sauce 109
282. Tuna Fillets with Tarragon and Onion 109
283. Cheesy Cod Fish with Potatoes 109
284. Seafood Stew with Sausage 110
285. Cheese and Spinach-Stuffed Salmon Fillets 110
286. Tilapia with Spinach 110
287. Easy Teriyaki Salmon 111
288. Halibut with Mayo Sauce 111
289. Greek-Style Cod with Olives 111
290. Saucy Shrimp Scampi with Wine........................ 112

PORK 113
291. Saucy Pork Loin Roast 113
292. Barbecued Pork with Ketchup 113
293. Pork Medallions with Lemon-Butter Sauce 113
294. Pork Chops with Tomato and Parmesan 114
295. Orange and Bourbon Glazed Ham 114
296. Ground Pork Goulash with Sweet Corn 114
297. Spicy Ground Pork Omelet 115
298. Asian-Style Pork 115
299. Authentic Pork Carnitas........................ 115
300. Spicy Roasted Pork Sandwich 116
301. Saucy Boston-Style Butt 116
302. Winter Pork Burgers 116
303. Pineapple Glazed Pork 117
304. Indian-Style Pork Curry 117
305. Traditional Arepas with Pork Roast 117
306. Picnic Ham with Peppers 118
307. Pork Cutlets with Ricotta Sauce 118
308. Country-Style Huevos Rancheros 118
309. Mexican Chile Verde 119
310. Sicily Pork and Vegetable Bake 119
311. Family Roast Pork 119
312. Pork with Italian Mushroom Sauce 120
313. Classic Pork with Garlic Mayo 120
314. Pork Meatballs with Marinara Sauce 120
315. Winter Pork and Sauerkraut........................ 121
316. Pork Steak and Pepper Bake 121
317. Japanese Buta Niku No Mushimono 121
318. Pork Stew with Polenta 122
319. Sausage Bake with Bacon and Herbs 122
320. Pork with Port and Root Vegetables 122
321. Pork Loin with Garlic Sauce 123
322. Italian-Style Meatloaf with Bacon 123

323. Pork Chops and Potatoes and Onion 123
324. Spicy Cheesy Pork Frittata..........124
325. Grandma's Stuffed Peppers 124
326. Pork Liver Mousse 124
327. Easy Dad's Pork Chops 125
328. Barbecued Pork Ribs 125
329. Oaxacan Pork Fajitas 125
330. Broiled St. Louis-Style Ribs..........126

BEEF..........**127**
331. Cheesy Beef Enchilada Pasta..........127
332. Japanese-Style Beef Shanks..........127
333. New York Strip with Sauce 127
334. Mustard and Parmesan Meatballs..........128
335. Steak Salad with Peppers and Olives 128
336. BBQ Back Ribs with Beer 128
337. Beef Stroganoff with a Twist 129
338. Short Ribs with Leek and Herbs 129
339. Beef Round Roast with veggies 129
340. Sticky Beef with Syrah Reduction 130
341. Boozy Tequila Ribs 130
342. Bœuf à la Bourguignonne 130
343. Delmonico Steak with Gorgonzola Cheese 131
344. Châteaubriand with Red Wine Reduction..........131
345. Hearty Ground Beef Chili..........131
346. Rump Steak in Tomato Sauce 132
347. Chunky Beef Frittata 132
348. Boozy Glazed Roast Beef 132
349. Classic Homemade Cheeseburgers 133
350. Korean Beef Bulgogi 133
351. Crustless Beef Mince Pie 133
352. Rosemary and Cheeseburger Dip 134
353. Homemade Philly Cheese Steaks..........134
354. Festive Beef with Gravy 134
355. Moussaka with Ground Beef and Potatoes 135
356. Japanese-Style Beef Bowl 135
357. Sticky Sloppy Joes 135
358. Decadent Filet Mignon 136
359. Classic Corned Beef Brisket 136
360. Mexican Beef Tacos 136
361. Ground Beef and Cheese Bowl 137
362. Beer Braised Chuck Roast 137
363. Italian Spaghetti Bolognese 137
364. Paprika Pot Roast with Vegetables 138
365. Traditional Beef Peperonata 138
366. Fall-Apart Beef Brisket with Broccoli 138
367. Cheesy Beef Stuffed Peppers 139
368. Mexican-Style Meatloaf 139
369. Pot Roast with Harvest Vegetables 139
370. Breakfast Cheeseburger Cups 140

STEWS **141**
371. Bean and Beef Steak Chili 141
372. French Beef Bourguignon 141
373. Mediterranean Pottage with Oats 141
374. Irish-Style Barley and Cabbage Stew..........142
375. Almond and Lentil Pottage 142
376. Spanish Zarzuela de Mariscos 142
377. Indian Lentil Curry..........143
378. Spicy Mulligan Stew (Burgoo)..........143

379. Pot-Au-Feu (Traditional French Stew)..........143
380. Vegetable Barley Medley 144
381. Olla Podrida Burgalesa..........144
382. Thai Coconut and Cauliflower Curry 144
383. Easy Creole Jambalaya 145
384. Jamaican Beef Stew 145
385. Bosnian Hot Pot 145
386. Fisherman's Stew with Potatoes 146
387. Traditional Hungarian Gulyás..........146
388. Traditional Polish Bigos 146
389. Winter Pinto Bean and Sausage Stew 147
390. Spanish Stew with Chorizo 147
391. Pork Chile Verde 147
392. Creole Brunswick Stew 148
393. Catalan Seafood Stew 148
394. Authentic Beef Ragout 148
395. Curried Lentil Stew 149
396. Fricassee De Poulet a L'Ancienne 149
397. Irish Garden Stew (Slumgullion) 149
398. Spicy Provençal Ratatouille 150
399. Traditional Liverpool Scouse 150
400. Traditional Indian Rajma 150
401. Italian Boiled Beef 151
402. Spicy Chickpea Stew 151
403. Hearty Squash and Chicken Stew 151
404. Easy Kentucky Burgoo 152
405. Southern Style Chicken Perlo 152
406. Harvest Vegetables and Lentil Stew 152
407. Hearty Seafood Cassoulet 153
408. Greek-Style Chicken Mélange 153
409. Hungarian Famous Paprikás Csirke 153
410. Country-Style Beef and Potato Hash 154

RICE **155**
411. Spanish Paella with Green Peas 155
412. Winter Sichuan Congee 155
413. Rice Salad with Fruits and Nuts 155
414. Chop Suey Rice Bowls 156
415. Smoked Salmon Pilau 156
416. Late Summer Risotto 156
417. Risotto with Petite Peas and Peanuts..........157
418. Old-Fashioned Chicken and Rice Soup 157
419. Risotto with Shrimp and Peppers 157
420. Mexican Cheesy Rice 158
421. Spicy Beef Stew with Brown Rice 158
422. Chicken, Pea and Rice Bowl 158
423. Japanese Rice with Potatoes and Tonkatsu Sauce 159
424. Thai Rice with Sage and Peppers 159
425. Chicken and Broccoli Moussaka 159
426. Red Fisherman's Risotto 160
427. Hearty Louisiana-Style Gumbo..........160
428. Spanish Lentejas Caseras 160
429. Pakistani-Style Corn Pilaf 161
430. Mushroom Risotto with Romano Cheese..........161
431. Rizogalo (Greek Rice Pudding) 161
432. Pakistani Jeera Rice 162
433. Authentic Sushi Rice..........162
434. Rice and Chicken Gratin 162
435. Mexican Arroz Rojo with Peppers 163
436. Easy Chicken Feijoada..........163

437. Kidney Beans with Rice and Marinara Sauce............ 163
438. One-Pot Kinoko Gohan 164
439. Classic Spanish Rice Pudding............................. 164
440. Easy Egg Drop Soup 164
441. One-Pot Indian Khichri 165
442. Easy Korean Bowl 165
443. Rice with Cheese and Vegetables 165
444. Spicy Enchilada Rice with Cheese 166
445. Old-Fashioned Pork Pilaf 166
446. One-Pot Wild Rice Pilaf 166

EGGS & DAIRY 167
447. Easy Hash Brown Casserole 167
448. Deviled Eggs with Paprika and Cheese 167
449. Eggs with Cheese and Chanterelles 167
450. Queso Fundido Dip 168
451. Silver Dollar Pancakes 168
452. Home-Style Cheese... 168
453. Dilled Cheese Dip.. 169
454. Keto Mac n' Cheese.. 169
455. Macaroni and Cheese 169
456. Breakfast Muffins with Ham 170
457. Hard-Boiled Eggs 170
458. Breakfast Cheese and Egg Frittatas 170
459. Greek-Style Stuffed Eggs 171
460. Spanish Tortilla with Manchego Cheese............... 171
461. The Best Homemade Yogurt Ever 171
462. Frittata with Mushrooms and Asiago Cheese 172

SNACKS & APPETIZERS 173
463. Sticky Little Smokies 173
464. Tangy Chicken Wings with Cilantro 173
465. Chinese-Style Baby Carrots 173
466. Cocktail Mushrooms with Herbs 174
467. Herby Ribs with Port Wine 174
468. Greek-Style Dipping Sauce 174
469. Candied Nuts, Seeds and Chickpeas 175
470. Easy Buffalo Dip 175
471. Light Lettuce Wraps 175
472. Mediterranean-Style Polenta Bites 176
473. Italian Pizza Dipping Sauce 176
474. Mexican Nacho Dip 176
475. Sticky Cocktail Meatballs 177
476. Coconut Cinnamon Popcorn 177
477. Fava Dip with Olives 177
478. Garlicky Party Shrimp 178
479. Taco Stuffed Pepper Bites 178

STOCKS & SAUCES 179
480. French Court-Bouillon 179
481. Mediterranean Tomato Sauce 179
482. Grandma's Berry Sauce..................................... 179
483. Sicilian Sauce with Pork and Wine 180
484. Classic French Bouillon 180
485. Vegetable Stock with White Wine 180
486. Fall Applesauce with Cinnamon and Dates 181
487. Pork Bone Broth 181
488. Classic Chicken and Veggie Stock 181
489. Easy Shrimp Consommé 182
490. Tikka Masala Sauce.. 182
491. Spaghetti Meat Sauce 182

492. Velvety Caramel Sauce 183
493. Classic Marinara Sauce 183
494. Vanilla Cranberry Sauce 183
495. Harvest Pear Butter 184
496. Hot Peppery Sauce 184
497. Classic Beef Bone Stock 184
498. Easy Festive Gravy 185
499. Home-Style Mexican Salsa 185
500. American-Style BBQ Sauce 185
501. Black Bean Dipping Sauce 186
502. Herbed Chicken Broth 186
503. Chicken Ragù with Wine 186
504. Spicy Chorizo Sauce 187
505. Nana's Raspberry Coulis 187
506. Mediterranean Eggplant Sauce 187
507. Two-Cheese and Bacon Sauce 188
508. Goat Cheese and Artichoke Dip 188
509. Classic Chicken and Leek Stock 188
510. Home-Style Fumet 189

DESSERTS & DRINKS... 190
511. Cinnamon Stewed Apples 190
512. Easy Dulce de Leche 190
513. Coconut Banana Bread 190
514. Lemon Pound Cake 191
515. Molten Lava Cake 191
516. Stuffed Apples with Walnuts and Currants 191
517. Old-Fashioned Mixed Berry Jam 192
518. Double Chocolate Fudge................................... 192
519. New York-Style Cheesecake................................ 192
520. Butternut and Coconut Pudding......................... 193
521. Greek Hosafi (Stewed Dried Fruits) 193
522. Nut Butter Brownies 193
523. Hot Mulled Apple Cider.................................... 194
524. Hungarian Golden Dumpling Cake (Aranygaluska) . 194
525. Dutch Baby 194
526. White Hot Chocolate with Chai Syrup 195
527. Rice Pudding with Cranberries............................ 195
528. Home-Style Horchata 195
529. Summer Blueberry Sauce 196
530. Jamaican Hibiscus Tea...................................... 196
531. Skinny Mini Cheesecakes 196
532. Mixed Berry Compote 197
533. Cinnamon Coffee Cake 197
534. Rum Caramel Pudding...................................... 197
535. Autumn Pear and Pecan Pie 198
536. Classic Vanilla Cupcakes 198
537. Winter Hot Apple Cider 198
538. Easter Chocolate Cake with Apricots 199
539. Greek Compote with Honey Yogurt..................... 199
540. Traditional Polish Szarlotka 199
541. Classic French Souffle....................................... 200
542. Almond Cream Pie 200
543. Chocolate Mini Clafoutis.................................. 200
544. Orange Spritzer with Cranberries........................ 201
545. Traditional Budín Puertorriqueño....................... 201
546. Hazelnut Jumble Bread 201
547. Granny's Pinch-Me Cake 202
548. French Pots de Créme au Chocolate.................... 202
549. Traditional Arroz Con Leche 202
550. Old-Fashioned Peach Crumble 203

INTRODUCTION

People often find it difficult to cook smaller portions. Meal planning, bulk buying, and budgeting can be daunting when it's just the two of you. I think differently – if you don't have an army to feed, you can be more creative and relaxed. Moreover, you can save your time with meal prepping; in other words, simply freeze leftovers until you're ready to eat. I've got to tell you – I prefer the relaxed approach to cooking; I love to cook homemade meals for my family of two. My husband and I have been married for almost seven years. Previously, I had been cooking for me and my sister for years before I got married. Therefore, I've got some solid experience cooking for two. In my opinion, with quality kitchen tools and some knowledge, anyone can cook basic meals, and with time, even become a great cook!

As I said before, I love cooking but I don't always have enough time to do it. So I thought – wouldn't it be nice if I could find a simpler way to cook dinner every night? I did some research on the Internet and realized – it is perfectly possible if you have a good and reliable multi-cooker. Then, I discovered the Instant Pot. Its versatility and flexibility are fascinating! The Instant pot makes cooking fast, convenient, satisfying and in the first place – healthy. I felt like I discover the secret to the best, grandma-approved recipes!

When it comes to the small portions, the Instant Pot is the perfect kitchen appliance. For instance, the Instant Pot Duo Mini with 3-quart capacity is perfect for individuals and families of two people. However, if you prefer big-batch cooking, you should purchase DUO60 which is twice as large as Mini. If you are looking for Instant Pot recipes for your family of two, this collection is ready to be your reliable kitchen companion. Moreover, the Instant Pot and this recipe collection may help you to take your cooking routine up a notch!

What Can You Do with Your Instant Pot?

The Instant Pot is a versatile electric pressure cooker that can perform multiple tasks in the kitchen – from pressure cooking and slow cooking to steaming and baking. In fact, the Instant Pot utilizes high temperature and pressure to cook food inside the sealed inner pot. If you take a look at the control panel of your device, you can notice different cooking program keys as well as operation keys (Keep Warm and Cancel). You can also notice pressure indicators (Less, Normal, More) and +/- keys (to adjust time). Unlike the DUO60, the Duo Mini does not have the "Multigrain" and "Poultry" buttons.

The Instant Pot can replace multiple kitchen tools; it can sear or sauté your food like a pan, steam delicate vegetables, and bake a cake like a conventional oven. How does it work? You should place the ingredients along with water or another liquid in the inner pot. Then, the machine raises the temperature of the cooking liquid above boiling point, turning the liquid into super-heated steam. It contains a smart microprocessor that speeds up cooking time and uses less energy than conventional cooking methods. In this way, you can cook one-pot meals in less than 30 minutes that otherwise would take hours.

The Instant Pot doesn't work without liquid; the amount of liquid depends on the food you cook. Generally, one cup of liquid is sufficient for most dishes (it is obvious that you will need much more liquid if you cook soup or broth). You can use water, broth or alcohol. The Instant Pot has multiple fully automated cooking settings, which may be available depending on the model. These programs offer lots of flexibility in the kitchen and make your cooking routine much easier.

Sauté – You can use your Instant Pot as a regular skillet or frying pan; you can sauté the vegetables, caramelize onions or brown the meat to enhance the flavor. Plus, you can thicken the sauce or simmer the liquid under low temperature. The maximum operation duration is 30 minutes but you can cancel the program at any time by using the "Cancel" key. You can add a splash wine or broth to deglaze the pot after browning since these bits are full of flavor!

Slow Cooker – this function works as a regular slow cooker. You can cook a wide range of foods, from root vegetables and dried grains to tough cuts of meat and carcass. The cooking duration is 30 minutes to 20 hours while cooking modes include Normal, More and Less.

Steam – you can steam delicate items such as vegetables and seafood. You can cook them straight from the freezer. This is an exceptionally healthy cooking method since the foods cook in the steam loaded with their own juices. If you cook the vegetables in a conventional way, you can easily end up with a pile of tasteless mush. On the other hand, steaming is the perfect method that can shorten the cooking time of your veggies and produce that crisp-tender texture!

Manual – use this mode if you want to adjust parameters to suit your recipe and preference. Maximum operation time is 2 hours but you can press the "Cancel" button whenever you want.

Soup – you can cook hearty soups and chowders in no time. If you have leftovers and carcass on hand, make a big batch of homemade soup and then, freeze it for a quick meal during busy weeknights.

Porridge – you can cook risotto, pilaf, and grains just like your grandma used to make. This button comes in handy when you want to make healthy breakfast for busy mornings, requiring just a little bit of add-ins.

Rice – you can cook all types of rice. As for the water to grain ratio, you should follow the instructions, since it's not the same as it is for the traditional cooking techniques. The cooking times depend on the amount and type of rice you plan to cook. Jasmine rice takes 3 to 5 minutes, white basmati 4-8 minutes, wild rice 25-30 minutes, brown rice 22-28 minutes. Cook's pro tip: add a tablespoon of butter or olive oil to the cooking liquid. It will give your rice a little something special.

Bean/Chili – here is the secret to the best old-fashioned chili – always use a homemade broth. If you want to add little something-something, pour your favorite beer or wine into the inner pot. Fish sauce or Worcestershire sauce are excellent umami amplifiers too.

Meat/Stew – when it comes to the comforting dishes, the Instant Pot is a real game changer. You can cook a big batch of meat or chicken stew and keep it in your freezer.

Yogurt – you can make amazing, home-style yogurt in your Instant Pot but keep in mind that the whole process can take from 12 to 24 hours. You can keep it in your refrigerator for up to 10 days.

Keep Warm/Cancel – keep your food warm until you are ready to eat.

Last but not least, there are two ways to release the pressure once cooking is complete – Quick pressure release and Natural pressure release.

Top 8 Benefits of the Instant Pot

The Instant Pot revamps one-pot meals. In fact, you can cook an entire meal in your Instant Pot. First things first, you can sauté the onions and sear the meat by pressing the "Sauté" button on the Instant Pot. Then, you can add the other ingredients, seal the cooker's lid and wait for your meal to cook. Lastly, you can remove the cooker's lid and thicken the liquid by pressing the "Sauté" button one more time. We know the fact – you don't have to clean up another cookware!

The grandma's secret recipes. Pressure cooking is all about getting amazing results by using the next-generation technology. The Instant Pot and this recipe collection promote natural food and clean eating, minimizing processed foods.

It's easy to use. Once you master small tasks with your Instant pot, you will be able to adapt every recipe for the Instant Pot.

The Instant Pot can significantly cut cooking time. It can cook your food up to 5 times faster than other cooking methods. It is a little fuss for you but lots of deep flavors and distinct aromas!

Butch cooking. Prepare big-batch recipes on Sunday and eat well for days. If you are new to the Instant Pot, start small and pick a simple recipe like a chicken stew. Once you unlock the mystery of a successful pressure cooking, you can make an endless variety of delicious meals with a touch of a button!

A well-balanced diet. The Instant Pot has that great ability to preserve important vitamins and minerals in your food. The super-heated steam cooks your food faster, allowing it to retain its natural nutrients. In addition, pressure cooking requires less oil. The Instant Pot cooks lean meats to perfection so you will be able to avoid greasy food without compromising taste. The Instant pot promotes good eating habits and they are certainly linked to a healthier and happier life.

It saves you money. A ton of money! The Instant Pot can cook almost everything so you can eat well and still stay on budget. Pressure cooking is one of the most affordable ways to cook a large amount of budget-friendly foods such as cheap cuts of meat and grains. Further, your Instant Pot is a durable kitchen appliance so it will last for years! Plus, you do not have to waste your money on other kitchen tools and gadgets such as additional pans, rice cooker, steamer or slow cooker.

Go green! The Instant Pot is an eco-friendly appliance since it uses less electricity (up to 70 %). It is versatile multi-cooker so you can finally declutter your cupboards and counter. This is an excellent way to get started with minimalism, simplify your life, and save the Mother Earth. Remember, there is no Planet B!

Cooking for Two: Why We Need to Rethink Home-Cooked Meals?

Cooking at home is inexpensive, fun and creative way to eat better and healthier. Nobody can resist a bowl of warming stew or homey porridge! Plus, instead of spending time and money in restaurants, I can do meal prep and save my time. Learning to cook may seem difficult but there are many benefits of home-cooked meals – health benefits, financial benefits, and social benefits. Home-cooked meals are closely linked to ideal body weight and health in general, so it is a huge motivation for me. Look at it this way: your body deserves the best!

The Instant Pot redefines one-pot meals so it's almost impossible to mess them up. With your Instant Pot, you can save natural flavorings and get amazing results in no time! From juicy poultry and succulent fish to decadent desserts, the Instant Pot allows you to cook almost everything. Plus, you do not need particular culinary skills. I am fascinated by home-cooked meals. They can significantly lower the chances to order take-outs; thus, I found a great way to balance my diet. Whether I'm cooking for my dinner guests or just whipping up a light dinner for me and my husband, there is the secret behind these old-fashioned dishes. That secret ingredient is a pinch of love! You can't find it in a can or takeout box. Do you still think that spending some time cooking family meal is a waste of time?

When it comes to pressure cooking, I like to put storage containers and jars into use. I am doing my best to purchase local and quality ingredients. I like to buy in bulk and look for cheap vegetables and meat since the Instant pot can cook everything to perfection. Here is my basic list of Instant Pot staple ingredients.

Refrigerated items – milk, eggs, cheese, butter, mayonnaise, meat, poultry, and fish.

Frozen items – vegetables, fruits, meat, poultry, seafood, and fish.

Dry goods – rice, grains, legumes (beans, lentils, chickpeas), and flour.

Canned goods – vegetables, fish, pumpkin purée, sauces, tomato paste, applesauce, and stock.

Condiments – mustard, fish sauce, ketchup, hot sauce, soy sauce, vinegar, and Worcestershire sauce.

Herbs and Spices – fresh or dried.

I prefer to plan a weekly menu since the preparation is half the battle! Trust me, with a good plan and your Instant Pot, you can get dinner on the table every night. Leftovers, such as chicken breasts or vegetables, can make hearty salads for dinner. For those days when you feel so freaking busy, these nutritious meals can balance everything out. This habit can help you lose weight in the long run. Recent studies have found that cooking at home has both short- and long-term benefits. Other studies have shown that people who eat as a family are less likely to be sick and overweight. These families tend to be healthier and consume less processed foods, which can result in better physical and mental health.

In this way, you can have an insight into calorie intake so you will be less likely to overeat. With the Instant Pot, I can finally control my eating. I found out that a regular restaurant meal can contain more than 1000 calories per portion! The reality is, it contains much more sugar and salt than an average homemade meal. Doubtlessly, if you make time to sit down at the dinner table, you will set a great example for your children. Moreover, cooking can reduce stress and encourage creativity; therapists suggest coking therapy to give people a new and creative way to cope with stress and feel better.

Make sure to keep your staple ingredients at your fingertips and prepare them ahead of time. Making a hearty stew for lunch of a refreshing healthy smoothie for breakfast may become much faster when your vegetables and fruits are chopped in advance. Plus, it is less expensive than buying pre-cut ingredients. Add the leftover vegetables, tofu or fish to the cooked rice or other grains; then, freeze the portions and serve throughout the week. Therefore, preparing multiple servings all at once is the key to successful home-cooked meals! It can reduce your time and minimize food waste. Take advantage of your Instant Pot and prepare an extra-large casserole or a huge pot of soup. Choose the foods that reheat well; it seems like a great way of cutting down on food waste, right?! Did you notice that a pork stew really tastes better when you reheat it the next day? And it's going to taste good on the third days as well!

How You Can Benefit From this Recipe Collection

With its possibilities for pressure cooking, steaming, sautéing, baking, simmering, and thickening, the Instant Pot is one of the best things I have in my kitchen. I've collected these 550 recipes for years and finally, I designed this collection. These hand-picked recipes offer a lot of inspiration for pressure cooking and they will give you the guidelines to get the most out of your Instant Pot. Each recipe includes the number of servings, cooking time, the ingredient list, detailed directions, and nutritional analysis. As for the cooking time, I didn't count the time it takes the Instant Pot to get to the pressure (it is between 5 and 20 minutes).

Whether you plan to cook a hearty soup for cold winter night or whip up the best birthday cake for your special one, this collection is designed to make cooking a great, enjoyable experience for you. It offers proven strategies on how to maximize the use of your Instant Pot. If you are an expert cook, just looking for new ideas and motivation, this cookbook may come in handy. On the other hand, if you are an absolute beginner in pressure cooking, this collection is a good place to start your Instant Pot adventure. Get started cooking with the top Instant Pot recipes that follow and enjoy!

VEGETABLES

1. Braised Cabbage with Mediterranean Herbs

(Ready in about 15 minutes)

Per serving: 200 Calories; 13.8g Fat; 21.5g Carbs; 3.5g Protein; 11.2g Sugars; 6g Fiber

INGREDIENTS

2 tablespoons olive oil

1 pound head of cabbage, cut into wedges

1 carrot, chopped

1 bell pepper, chopped

1 cup roasted vegetable broth

1/2 teaspoon cayenne pepper

Sea salt and ground black pepper, to taste

1 bay leaf

1 sprig thyme

1 sprig rosemary

DIRECTIONS

Add all ingredients to the inner pot of your Instant Pot. Stir to combine.

Secure the lid. Choose the "Manual" mode and cook for 6 minutes at High pressure. Once cooking is complete, use a quick pressure release; carefully remove the lid.

Ladle into individual bowls and serve warm. Bon appétit!

2. Green Autumn Soup

(Ready in about 20 minutes)

Per serving: 262 Calories; 2.7g Fat; 41g Carbs; 8.5g Protein; 10.9g Sugars; 10g Fiber

INGREDIENTS

1 teaspoons butter, at room temperature

1/2 onion, chopped

1 garlic clove, minced

2 cups chicken broth

1/2 teaspoon dried basil

1/2 teaspoon dried oregano

Kosher salt and ground black pepper, to taste

1 medium potato, chopped

1 carrot, chopped

1/2 cup turnip, chopped

1 cup tomato puree

1 ½ cups kale, torn into pieces

DIRECTIONS

Press the "Sauté" button and melt the butter. Once hot, cook the onion until tender and translucent.

Then, add the garlic and continue to sauté an additional 30 seconds, stirring continuously. Add a splash of chicken broth to deglaze the pan.

Now, stir in the basil, oregano, salt, black pepper, potatoes, carrots, turnip, and tomato puree; stir to combine.

Secure the lid. Choose the "Manual" mode and cook for 5 minutes at High pressure. Once cooking is complete, use a natural pressure release for 10 minutes; carefully remove the lid.

Stir in the kale and seal the lid; let it sit in the residual heat until thoroughly warmed. Adjust the seasonings to taste and serve immediately.

3. Classic Spanish Pisto

(Ready in about 20 minutes)

Per serving: 206 Calories; 14.7g Fat; 18.2g Carbs; 11.4g Protein; 9.6g Sugars; 8.6g Fiber

INGREDIENTS

1 tablespoon olive oil

1/2 onion, diced

2 cloves garlic, sliced

1/4 cup Spanish wine

1 cup cream of mushrooms soup

1 bell pepper, diced

1 Guajillo chili pepper, minced

1 pound zucchini, cut into 1-inch cubes

1/2 can (14-ounce) tomatoes with juice

Sea salt and cracked black pepper, or to taste

DIRECTIONS

Press the "Sauté" button and heat the olive oil. Now, cook the onion until just tender and translucent.

Then, stir in the garlic; continue to cook until fragrant. Add a splash of wine to deglaze the pan.

Stir in the remaining ingredients; stir to combine well.

Secure the lid. Choose the "Manual" mode and cook for 10 minutes at High pressure. Once cooking is complete, use a quick pressure release; carefully remove the lid. Serve immediately.

4. Southern Sweet Potato Casserole

(Ready in about 30 minutes)

Per serving: 580 Calories; 28.9g Fat; 77g Carbs; 18.2g Protein; 41.1g Sugars

INGREDIENTS

3 medium-sized sweet potatoes, peeled and cut into 1-inch pieces
1/2 cup water
1/4 cup granulated sugar
3 tablespoons butter softened
1/2 teaspoon vanilla paste
1/2 cup milk
1 egg, whisked

Topping:
1/3 cup brown sugar
1/4 cup all-purpose flour
1/4 teaspoon cinnamon, or to taste
1/8 teaspoon salt
1/4 cup chopped pecans
2 tablespoons butter, at room temperature
1/2 cup mini marshmallows

DIRECTIONS

Add the sweet potatoes and water to the Instant Pot.

Secure the lid. Choose the "Manual" mode and cook for 8 minutes at High pressure. Once cooking is complete, use a quick pressure release; carefully remove the lid.

Drain the potatoes and transfer them to a mixing bowl. Now, add the granulated sugar, butter, vanilla, milk, and egg to the bowl.

Mash the potatoes using a potato masher or your food processor. Scrape the mashed potatoes into a lightly greased baking dish.

Mix all ingredients for the topping; top your casserole with the pecan/marshmallow mixture. Place a metal trivet and 1 cup of water in the inner pot. Lower the baking dish onto the trivet; make a foil sling if needed.

Secure the lid. Choose the "Manual" mode and cook for 15 minutes at High pressure. Once cooking is complete, use a quick pressure release; carefully remove the lid. Bon appétit!

5. Fall Harvest Soup

(Ready in about 25 minutes)

Per serving: 149 Calories; 7.4g Fat; 16.1g Carbs; 2.9g Protein; 7.3g Sugars; 4.2g Fiber

INGREDIENTS

1 tablespoon olive oil
1/2 onion, diced
1 garlic clove, minced
2 cups chicken broth

1 teaspoon Italian seasoning mix
Sea salt and ground black pepper, to taste
1 carrot, chopped

1 parsnip, chopped
1 celery rib, chopped
1 green bell pepper, chopped
1 cup fresh green beans, cut in thirds

DIRECTIONS

Press the "Sauté" button and heat the olive oil until sizzling. Then, cook the onion until tender and fragrant. Stir in the garlic and continue to sauté an additional 2 minutes.

Add a splash of chicken broth to scrape the bottom to remove any left behind bits. Add the seasonings, carrots, parsnip, celery, and bell pepper.

Secure the lid. Choose the "Manual" mode and cook for 10 minutes at High pressure. Once cooking is complete, use a natural pressure release for 10 minutes; carefully remove the lid.

Stir in the green beans and press the "Sauté" button again. Let it cook on the lowest setting until thoroughly warmed. Enjoy!

6. Country-Style Turkey and Brussels Sprouts

(Ready in about 15 minutes)

Per serving: 270 Calories; 10.1g Fat; 23.8g Carbs; 24.1g Protein; 6.6g Sugars; 9.2g Fiber

INGREDIENTS

1 pound Brussels sprouts, cut into halves
1 tablespoon sesame oil
1 teaspoon garlic, minced

1 shallot, chopped
4 ounces smoked turkey, boneless and shredded

Kosher salt and freshly cracked black pepper, to taste
1 teaspoon red pepper flakes

DIRECTIONS

Add 1 cup of water and a steamer basket to the inner pot. Place the Brussels sprouts in the steamer basket.

Secure the lid. Choose the "Steam" mode and cook for 3 minutes at High pressure. Once cooking is complete, use a quick pressure release; carefully remove the lid.

Drain the water out of the inner pot.

Press the "Sauté" button and heat the oil until sizzling. Then, cook the garlic and shallot for 2 minutes or until tender and aromatic.

Add the smoked turkey and cook an additional 2 minutes. Add the Brussels sprouts, salt, and black pepper, and stir for a few minutes more or until everything is heated through.

Serve garnished with red pepper flakes. Bon appétit!

7. Colby Cheese and Cabbage Bake

(Ready in about 30 minutes)

Per serving: 433 Calories; 35.5g Fat; 22.2g Carbs; 17.5g Protein; 6.7g Sugars; 4.2g Fiber

INGREDIENTS

1 tablespoon olive oil
1/2 pound green cabbage, shredded
1 onion, thinly sliced
1 garlic clove, sliced
1 sweet pepper, thinly sliced

1 serrano pepper, chopped
Sea salt and ground black pepper, to taste
1 teaspoon paprika
1 cup cream of mushroom soup
4 ounces Colby cheese, shredded

DIRECTIONS

Grease a casserole dish with 1/2 tablespoon of olive oil. Add the cabbage, onion, garlic, and peppers to the casserole dish.
Drizzle with remaining oil and season with salt, black pepper, and paprika. Next, pour in the mushroom soup.
Top with the shredded cheese and cover with a piece of aluminum foil.
Add 1 cup of water and a metal trivet to the inner pot. Lower the casserole dish onto the trivet.
Secure the lid. Choose the "Manual" mode and cook for 25 minutes at High pressure. Once cooking is complete, use a quick pressure release; carefully remove the lid. Serve warm.

8. Rich and Easy Potato Chowder

(Ready in about 20 minutes)

Per serving: 528 Calories; 26g Fat; 49.5g Carbs; 25.5g Protein; 5.8g Sugars; 3.6g Fiber

INGREDIENTS

1 tablespoon butter
1 shallot, chopped
1 clove garlic, minced
2 cups chicken broth
1 pound russet potatoes, peeled and chopped
Kosher salt and ground black pepper, to taste

1 teaspoon cayenne pepper
1/2 teaspoon dried basil
1/2 teaspoon dried oregano
1/2 cup milk
1 cup Swiss cheese, shredded

DIRECTIONS

Press the "Sauté" button and melt the butter. Once hot, cook the shallot for 3 to 4 minutes or until tender.
Now, stir in the garlic and continue to cook for 30 seconds more, stirring frequently.
Add the broth, potatoes, salt, black pepper, cayenne pepper, basil, and oregano to the inner pot; stir well to combine.
Secure the lid. Choose the "Manual" mode and cook for 10 minutes at High pressure. Once cooking is complete, use a quick pressure release; carefully remove the lid.
Press the "Sauté" button and pour in the milk. Let it simmer approximately 4 minutes. Add in the Swiss cheese and stir until it has melted.
Bon appétit!

9. Rutabaga Salad with Apples and Dijon Mustard

(Ready in about 15 minutes)

Per serving: 325 Calories; 19.9g Fat; 32.2g Carbs; 3.2g Protein; 16.6g Sugars; 6.6g Fiber

INGREDIENTS

1/2 pound rutabaga, peeled and cut into 1/4-inch chunks
1/3 pound cabbage, shredded
1 Granny Smith apple, cored and diced
4 tablespoons almonds, slivered

3 tablepsoons olive oil
1 tablespoon fresh lemon juice
1 teaspoon Dijon mustard
1/2 tablespoon agave syrup

DIRECTIONS

Add 1 cup of water and a steamer basket to the inner pot of your Instant Pot. Now, place the rutabaga in the steamer basket.
Secure the lid. Choose the "Manual" mode and cook for 6 minutes at High pressure. Once cooking is complete, use a quick pressure release; carefully remove the lid.
Toss the rutabaga chunks with the cabbage, apple, and almonds. Mix the remaining ingredients to prepare the salad dressing.
Dress your salad and serve chilled. Enjoy!

10. Italian-Style Zucchini Casserole

(Ready in about 20 minutes)

Per serving: 587 Calories; 39.2g Fat; 21.2g Carbs; 40.4g Protein; 7.7g Sugars; 4.1g Fiber

INGREDIENTS

1/2 tablespoon canola oil
1/2 pound ground chuck
2 ounces Italian sausage, crumbled
1/2 onion, chopped
1 garlic clove, minced

1/3 cup parmesan cheese, grated
1/2 cup cream cheese
Sea salt and ground black pepper, to taste
1 teaspoon cayenne pepper

1 teaspoon Italian seasoning blend
1/2 cup tomato puree
1/3 pound zucchini, cut into long slices

DIRECTIONS

Press the "Sauté" button and heat the oil. Then, cook the ground chuck, sausage, and onion for 3 to 4 minutes; stir in the garlic and cook an additional minute.

In a mixing bowl, thoroughly combine the cheese and seasonings.

Place a layer of the zucchini strips on the bottom of a lightly greased baking pan. Spoon 1/3 of the meat mixture onto the zucchini layer. Place 1/2 of the cheese mixture and tomato puree on the meat layer.

Repeat the layers, ending with a cheese layer. Add 1 cup of water and a metal rack to the inner pot. Lower the baking pan onto the rack.

Secure the lid. Choose the "Manual" mode and cook for 6 minutes at High pressure. Once cooking is complete, use a quick pressure release; carefully remove the lid. Bon appétit!

11. Greek Eggplant with Chickpeas

(Ready in about 15 minutes)

Per serving: 401 Calories; 10.4g Fat; 53.4g Carbs; 14g Protein; 17.4g Sugars; 17g Fiber

INGREDIENTS

1 pound eggplant, cut into cubes
1 tablespoon sea salt
1 tablespoon olive oil
1 red onion, chopped
2 bell peppers, deseeded and diced

1 garlic clove, sliced
1/2 teaspoon oregano
1 teaspoon basil
1/3 teaspoon ground turmeric
1/4 teaspoon sea salt

1/4 teaspoon ground black pepper. or more to taste
1/2 teaspoon paprika
4 vine-ripened tomatoes, pureed
6 ounces chickpeas, boiled and rinsed

DIRECTIONS

Toss the eggplant with 1 tablespoon of sea salt in a colander. Let it sit for 30 minutes; then squeeze out the excess liquid.

Press the "Sauté" button and heat the olive oil. Now, cook the onion until tender and translucent; add the reserved eggplant, peppers and garlic and continue to cook an additional 2 minutes or until they are fragrant.

Add the remaining ingredients to the inner pot. Stir to combine well.

Secure the lid. Choose the "Manual" mode and cook for 3 minutes at High pressure.

Once cooking is complete, use a quick pressure release; carefully remove the lid. Ladle into individual bowls and serve immediately.

12. Chinese Bok Choy

(Ready in about 15 minutes)

Per serving: 92 Calories; 5.4g Fat; 8.1g Carbs; 3.8g Protein; 5.1g Sugars; 2.6g Fiber

INGREDIENTS

1 teaspoon sesame oil
1 clove garlic, pressed
1 pound Bok choy

1/2 cup water
1 tablespoon rice wine vinegar
2 tablespoons soy sauce

DIRECTIONS

Press the "Sauté" button and heat the oil. Now, cook the garlic for 1 minute or until it is fragrant but not browned.

Add the Bok choy and water to the inner pot.

Secure the lid. Choose the "Manual" mode and cook for 5 minutes at High pressure. Once cooking is complete, use a quick pressure release; carefully remove the lid.

Meanwhile, in a mixing bowl, whisk the rice vinegar and soy sauce. Drizzle this sauce over the Bok choy and serve immediately.

13. Italian Crunchy and Cheesy Cauliflower Salad

(Ready in about 10 minutes + chilling time)

Per serving: 188 Calories; 8.4g Fat; 14.8g Carbs; 16.3g Protein; 6.2g Sugars; 3.9g Fiber

INGREDIENTS

1/2 pound cauliflower florets
1 bell pepper, thinly sliced
1/2 red onion, thinly sliced
1/4 cup fresh flat-leaf parsley, coarsely chopped
1/4 cup green olives, pitted and coarsely chopped

3 tablespoons extra-virgin olive oil
2 tablespoons fresh lime juice
1 teaspoon hot mustard
Sea salt and ground black pepper, to taste
2 ounces mozzarella cheese, crumbled

DIRECTIONS

Add 1 cup of water and steamer basket to the inner pot. Place the cauliflower in the steamer basket.

Secure the lid. Choose the "Steam" mode and cook for 2 minutes at High pressure. Once cooking is complete, use a quick pressure release; carefully remove the lid.

Toss the cooked cauliflower with peppers, onion, parsley, and olives. In a small bowl, prepare the salad dressing by mixing the olive oil, lime juice, mustard, salt, and black pepper.

Dress your salad and serve garnished with the crumbled mozzarella cheese. Bon appétit!

14. Harvest Vegetable Soup

(Ready in about 15 minutes)

Per serving: 166 Calories; 7.9g Fat; 12.3g Carbs; 3.8g Protein; 9.2g Sugars; 6.2g Fiber

INGREDIENTS

1 tablespoon olive oil
1 shallot, chopped
Kosher salt and ground black pepper, to taste
1 cup cabbage, shredded
1 carrot, thinly sliced
1 celery stalk, thinly sliced

1 medium zucchini, chopped
1/2 (15-ounce) can tomatoes, diced with their juice
1 ½ cups vegetable broth
1/2 teaspoon cayenne pepper
1/2 teaspoon dried sage
1/2 teaspoon dried parsley flakes

DIRECTIONS

Press the "Sauté" button and heat the oil. Now, sauté the shallot until tender and translucent.

Add the remaining ingredients; stir to combine well.

Secure the lid. Choose the "Manual" mode and cook for 10 minutes at High pressure. Once cooking is complete, use a quick pressure release; carefully remove the lid.

Ladle into soup bowls and serve with garlic croutons if desired. Bon appétit!

15. Easy Glazed Baby Carrots

(Ready in about 10 minutes)

Per serving: 210 Calories; 11.8g Fat; 22.5g Carbs; 1.8g Protein; 15.5g Sugars; 6.8g Fiber

INGREDIENTS

1 pound baby carrots
2 tablespoons butter
1 tablespoon molasses

1/4 teaspoon kosher salt
1/8 teaspoon white pepper
1/3 teaspoon cayenne pepper

DIRECTIONS

Add water and a steamer basket to the inner pot of your Instant Pot. Place the carrots in the steamer basket.

Secure the lid. Choose the "Steam" mode and cook for 3 minutes at High pressure. Once cooking is complete, use a quick pressure release; carefully remove the lid.

Discard the water and press the "Sauté" button. Once hot, melt the butter. Stir in the cooked carrots, molasses, salt, white pepper, and cayenne pepper.

Sauté approximately 2 minutes, stirring frequently. Serve warm.

16. Caprese Asparagus with Gorgonzola Cheese

(Ready in about 20 minutes)

Per serving: 414 Calories; 22.3g Fat; 46g Carbs; 13.1g Protein; 40.1g Sugars; 5g Fiber

INGREDIENTS

1 pound asparagus, trimmed
1 tablespoon balsamic vinegar
4 tablespoons honey
1/4 teaspoon dried dill
4 tablespoons extra-virgin olive oil

Sea salt and freshly ground black pepper, to taste
1 tomato, sliced
1/2 cup Gorgonzola cheese, crumbled
1 tablespoon fresh chives, chopped

DIRECTIONS

Add 1 cup of water and a steamer basket to the inner pot. Place the asparagus in the steamer basket.

Secure the lid. Choose the "Steam" mode and cook for 3 minutes at High pressure. Once cooking is complete, use a quick pressure release; carefully remove the lid.

In the meantime, make the balsamic glaze. Heat a small pan over a moderate flame. Simmer the balsamic vinegar, honey and dried dill for about 15 minutes or until it is reduced by half.

Transfer the cooked asparagus to a serving bowl. Add the oil, salt, pepper, and tomatoes. Drizzle with the balsamic glaze; garnish with cheese and chives and serve immediately.

17. Beetroot Thoran Onam Sadhya

(Ready in about 20 minutes)

Per serving: 177 Calories; 13.2g Fat; 12.8g Carbs; 2.8g Protein; 8.4g Sugars; 3.5g Fiber

INGREDIENTS

1/2 pound small beets
2 tablespoons olive oil
1/2 cup shallots, chopped
1 garlic clove, minced

1/2 chili pepper, chopped
5 curry leaves
1/3 teaspoon turmeric powder
Sea salt and ground black pepper, to taste

DIRECTIONS

Add 1 cup of water and a steamer basket to the inner pot. Place the beets in the steamer basket.

Secure the lid. Choose the "Steam" mode and cook for 15 minutes at High pressure. Once cooking is complete, use a quick pressure release; carefully remove the lid.

Once your beets are cool enough to touch, transfer them to a cutting board; peel and chop them into small pieces.

Press the "Sauté" button and heat the olive oil until sizzling. Then, cook the shallots, garlic, chili pepper, and curry leaves for about 4 minutes, or until they have softened.

Add the turmeric, salt, and black pepper; add the cooked beets to the inner pot and press the "Cancel" button. Serve warm.

18. Traditional Ratatouille with Pinot Noir

(Ready in about 40 minutes)

Per serving: 228 Calories; 7.7g Fat; 30.4g Carbs; 8g Protein; 8.8g Sugars; 8.4g Fiber

INGREDIENTS

1/2 pound eggplant, sliced
1 teaspoon sea salt
1/2 pound zucchini, sliced
2 sweet peppers, seeded and sliced
1 onion, sliced

2 cloves garlic, pressed
1/2 pound tomatoes, pureed
1/2 cup vegetable broth
Sea salt and ground red pepper, to taste

1/3 teaspoon oregano
1/2 teaspoon basil
1/2 teaspoon rosemary
2 tablespoons extra-virgin olive oil
2 tablespoons Pinot Noir

DIRECTIONS

Toss the eggplant with 1 teaspoon of salt in a colander. Let it sit for 30 minutes; then squeeze out the excess liquid. Transfer the eggplant to the inner pot of your Instant Pot.

Add the other ingredients to the inner pot

Secure the lid. Choose the "Manual" mode and cook for 6 minutes at High pressure. Once cooking is complete, use a quick pressure release; carefully remove the lid.

Season to taste with salt and pepper and serve warm. Enjoy!

19. Pumpkin Pie Oats

(Ready in about 25 minutes)

Per serving: 92 Calories; 7.8g Fat; 6.7g Carbs; 1.4g Protein; 2.8g Sugars; 8.4g Fiber

INGREDIENTS

3/4 cup steel cut oats
1 ½ cups water
1/2 cup pumpkin puree
1 tablespoon pumpkin pie spice
A pinch of salt

A pinch of grated nutmeg
2 tablespoons honey
1 teaspoon ground cinnamon
1 teaspoon vanilla essence

DIRECTIONS

Add all ingredients to the inner pot of your Instant Pot.
Secure the lid. Choose the "Manual" mode and cook for 4 minutes at High pressure. Once cooking is complete, use a natural pressure release for 15 minutes; carefully remove the lid
Ladle the oatmeal into serving bowls and serve immediately. Enjoy!

20. Creamy Broccoli and Spinach Soup

(Ready in about 15 minutes)

Per serving: 218 Calories; 15.4g Fat; 16.1g Carbs; 10.4g Protein; 8g Sugars; 6.4g Fiber

INGREDIENTS

1 teaspoon sesame oil
1 clove garlic, minced
1 shallot, finely chopped
1/2 piri piri pepper, minced
1/4 teaspoon ground cumin
1/2 pound broccoli florets

2 cups vegetable broth, preferably homemade
Sea salt and ground black pepper, to taste
1/2 teaspoon cayenne pepper
6 ounces spinach
1/2 cup coconut milk
1/4 cup coconut cream

DIRECTIONS

Press the "Sauté" button and heat the oil until sizzling. Now, cook the garlic, shallot, pepper, and cumin until they are just softened and aromatic.
Then, stir in the broccoli, broth, salt, black pepper, and cayenne pepper.
Secure the lid. Choose the "Manual" mode and cook for 5 minutes at High pressure. Once cooking is complete, use a quick pressure release; carefully remove the lid.
Afterwards, stir in the spinach, coconut milk, and cream. Seal the lid again and let it sit in the residual heat until the spinach wilts.
Now, puree the soup with an immersion blender and serve warm. Bon appétit!

21. Carrot Salad with Dijon Mustard and Honey

(Ready in about 10 minutes + chilling time)

Per serving: 141 Calories; 7.3g Fat; 18.9g Carbs; 1.4g Protein; 9.9g Sugars; 6.8g Fiber

INGREDIENTS

1 pound carrots, sliced to 2-inch chunks
1/2 teaspoon Himalayan salt
1/2 tablespoon Dijon mustard
1/2 tablespoon lime juice
1 tablespoon olive oil

1 teaspoon honey
1/4 teaspoon ground white pepper, to taste
1/4 teaspoon red pepper flakes
1 scallion, finely sliced

DIRECTIONS

Add 1 cup of water and a steamer basket to the inner pot of your Instant Pot.
Place the carrots in the steamer basket.
Secure the lid. Choose the "Steam" mode and cook for 3 minutes at High pressure. Once cooking is complete, use a quick pressure release; carefully remove the lid.
Toss your carrots with the remaining ingredients and serve chilled. Enjoy!

22. Traditional Italian Wedding Soup

(Ready in about 25 minutes)

Per serving: 485 Calories; 30.2g Fat; 32.4g Carbs; 25.4g Protein; 9g Sugars; 12.2g Fiber

INGREDIENTS

2 cups chicken broth
1/2 onion, chopped
1 carrot, chopped
1/2 teaspoon Italian seasoning mix
8 ounces Italian-style meatballs, frozen

2 tablespoons tomato paste
1 bay leaf
1/2 cup tubettini pasta
2 cups escarole, chopped

DIRECTIONS

Add the broth, onion, carrots, Italian seasoning mix, meatballs, tomato paste, and bay leaves to the inner pot of your Instant Pot.

Secure the lid. Choose the "Manual" mode and cook for 15 minutes at High pressure. Once cooking is complete, use a quick pressure release; carefully remove the lid.

Next, sit in the tubettini pasta and escarole.

Secure the lid. Choose the "Manual" mode and cook for 5 minutes at High pressure. Once cooking is complete, use a quick pressure release; carefully remove the lid. Bon appétit!

23. Warm Vegetable Salad with Tahini Sauce

(Ready in about 10 minutes)

Per serving: 506 Calories; 32g Fat; 48.5g Carbs; 11.2g Protein; 4.3g Sugars; 13g Fiber

INGREDIENTS

2 carrots, sliced
2 medium potatoes, diced
1/2 pound cauliflower florets
1 tablespoon olive oil
1/4 teaspoon sea salt
1/2 cup vegetable broth

1/4 cup tahini
2 tablespoons olive oil
1/4 cup water
1 clove garlic, pressed
1 tablespoons fresh lime juice
1 tablespoon fresh parsley, finely chopped

DIRECTIONS

Place the vegetables, olive oil, salt, and vegetable broth in the inner pot of your Instant Pot.

Secure the lid. Choose the "Manual" mode and cook for 4 minutes at High pressure. Once cooking is complete, use a quick pressure release; carefully remove the lid.

Meanwhile, make the tahini sauce by mixing the remaining ingredients. Serve the warm vegetables with the tahini sauce on the side. Bon appétit!

24. Authentic Persian Khoreshe Karafs

(Ready in about 40 minutes)

Per serving: 293 Calories; 8g Fat; 45.3g Carbs; 8.9g Protein; 4.1g Sugars; 11g Fiber

INGREDIENTS

1 tablespoon unsalted butter
1 garlic clove, minced
1/2 onion, chopped
Sea salt and ground black pepper, to taste
1/2 teaspoon cayenne pepper
1/2 teaspoon mustard seeds

1/2 pound celery stalks, diced
1 tablespoon fresh mint, finely chopped
1 tablespoon fresh cilantro, roughly chopped
2 cups vegetable broth
1 Persian lime, prick a few holes
1 cup basmati rice, steamed

DIRECTIONS

Press the "Sauté" button and melt the butter. Once hot, cook the garlic and onions for about 3 minutes or until tender and fragrant. Stir in the spices, celery, herbs, broth, and Persian lime.

Secure the lid. Choose the "Manual" mode and cook for 18 minutes at High pressure. Once cooking is complete, use a natural pressure release for 15 minutes; carefully remove the lid.

Taste for seasoning and add more salt as needed.

Serve with hot basmati rice and enjoy!

25. Classic Cuban Sofregit

(Ready in about 20 minutes)

Per serving: 118 Calories; 3.7g Fat; 19g Carbs; 3.4g Protein; 7.1g Sugars; 4.3g Fiber

INGREDIENTS

1 tablespoon extra-virgin olive oil
1 onion, chopped
1 clove garlic, minced
1 sweet pepper, chopped

3 tomatoes, pureed
1/4 bunch parsley leaves, roughly chopped
1 teaspoon paprika

DIRECTIONS

Press the "Sauté" button and heat 2 tablespoons of olive oil until sizzling. Now, sauté the onion until just tender and fragrant.

Add the garlic and peppers and continue to sauté an additional minute or until fragrant. Add the other ingredients.

Secure the lid. Choose the "Manual" mode and cook for 4 minutes at High pressure. Once cooking is complete, use a natural pressure release for 10 minutes; carefully remove the lid.

Let your sofrito cool completely and store in the refrigerator for a week. Enjoy!

26. Turkey Noodle Soup with Herbs

(Ready in about 3 hours 15 minutes)

Per serving: 436 Calories; 7.3g Fat; 60g Carbs; 30.5g Protein; 10.2g Sugars; 11.3g Fiber

INGREDIENTS

1/2 pound turkey thighs, boneless and chopped
2 ½ cups vegetable broth
1/2 shallot finely diced
1 carrot, diced
1 parsnip, sliced
1 celery stalk, sliced

Kosher salt and ground black pepper, to taste
1 teaspoon dried parsley flakes
1/2 teaspoon dried basil
1/2 teaspoon dried sage
1/2 teaspoon granulated garlic
1 cup wheat noodles

DIRECTIONS

Place all ingredients, except for the noodles, in the inner pot.

Secure the lid. Choose the "Slow Cook" mode and cook for 3 hours at High pressure. Once cooking is complete, use a quick pressure release; carefully remove the lid.

Now, stir in the noodles. Secure the lid. Choose the "Manual" mode and cook for 10 minutes at High pressure. Once cooking is complete, use a quick pressure release; carefully remove the lid.

Serve warm and enjoy!

27. Steamed Vegetables with Cilantro

(Ready in about 10 minutes)

Per serving: 153 Calories; 13.8g Fat; 6.6g Carbs; 2g Protein; 2.2g Sugars; 2.5g Fiber

INGREDIENTS

1/3 pound cauliflower florets
1 carrot, sliced
1 celery rib, sliced
2 tablespoons olive oil

2 cloves garlic, minced
1/2 teaspoon cayenne pepper
Sea salt and freshly ground black pepper, to taste
1 tablespoon fresh cilantro, chopped

DIRECTIONS

Add 1 cup water and a steamer basket to the inner pot of your Instant Pot. Place the vegetables in the steamer basket.

Secure the lid. Choose the "Steam" mode and cook for 3 minutes at High pressure. Once cooking is complete, use a quick pressure release; carefully remove the lid; reserve the steamed vegetables.

Press the "Sauté" button and heat the oil. Now, sauté the garlic until tender. Add the steamed vegetables back to the inner pot.

Season generously with cayenne pepper, salt, and black pepper. Garnish with fresh cilantro and serve.

28. Mixed Buttered Vegetables

(Ready in about 10 minutes)

Per serving: 329 Calories; 7.3g Fat; 60g Carbs; 9.8g Protein; 8.5g Sugars; 16g Fiber

INGREDIENTS

1 tablespoon butter, at room temperature
1 clove garlic, minced
1 carrot, cut into 1-inch pieces
1 parsnip, cut into 1-inch pieces

1/2 pound broccoli florets
2 medium waxy potatoes, peeled and cubed
2 cups acorn squash
1 cup roasted vegetable broth

DIRECTIONS

Press the "Sauté" button and melt the butter. Once hot, sauté the garlic until aromatic but not browned.
Stir in the remaining ingredients.
Secure the lid. Choose the "Manual" mode and cook for 4 minutes at High pressure. Once cooking is complete, use a quick pressure release; carefully remove the lid.
Add some extra butter if desired and serve warm. Bon appétit!

29. Vegetarian Medley with Cream Cheese

(Ready in about 10 minutes)

Per serving: 330 Calories; 27.3g Fat; 16.8g Carbs; 8.2g Protein; 7.7g Sugars; 5.9g Fiber

INGREDIENTS

1/2 pound cauliflower florets
2 carrots
1 cup broccoli florets
1 tablespoon olive oil
1/2 teaspoon garlic, minced

1/2 cup cream cheese
1 tablespoon lemon juice
1/2 teaspoon oregano
1/2 teaspoon dried basil
Sea salt and ground black pepper, to taste

DIRECTIONS

Add 1 cup of water and a steamer basket to the inner pot. Place the cauliflower, carrots, and broccoli in the steamer basket.
Secure the lid. Choose the "Steam" mode and cook for 2 minutes at High pressure. Once cooking is complete, use a quick pressure release; carefully remove the lid; reserve the steamed vegetables.
Press the "Sauté" button and heat the olive oil until sizzling. Then, cook the garlic until just tender and fragrant.
Add the remaining ingredients and press the "Cancel" button. Add the reserved vegetables to the inner pot. Stir to combine and serve warm. Bon appétit!

30. Artichokes with Garlic-Mayo Dipping Sauce

(Ready in about 20 minutes)

Per serving: 270 Calories; 20.7g Fat; 19.9g Carbs; 5.7g Protein; 2.3g Sugars; 8.9g Fiber

INGREDIENTS

1 cup water
1 bay leaf
1 lemon wedge
2 medium artichokes, trimmed
Sea salt, to taste

1/4 cup mayonnaise
1/2 teaspoon garlic, pressed
1 tablespoon fresh parsley, minced

DIRECTIONS

Place water and bay leaf in the inner pot. Rub the lemon wedge all over the outside of the prepared artichokes. Season them with salt.
Place the artichokes in the steamer basket; lower the steamer basket into the inner pot.
Secure the lid. Choose the "Manual" mode and cook for 11 minutes at High pressure. Once cooking is complete, use a quick pressure release; carefully remove the lid.
Meanwhile, mix the mayonnaise with the garlic and parsley. Serve the artichokes with the mayo dip on the side. Bon appétit!

31. Broccoli Salad with Seeds and Mayo

(Ready in about 10 minutes)

Per serving: 407 Calories; 33.8g Fat; 20.1g Carbs; 11.3g Protein; 5.2g Sugars; 5.6g Fiber

INGREDIENTS

1/2 pound broccoli florets
Sea salt and ground black pepper, to taste
2 scallion stalks, chopped

2 tablespoons raisins
2 tablespoons sunflower seeds, to toasted
2 tablespoons sesame seeds, toasted

1 tablespoon balsamic vinegar
1 tablespoon fresh lemon juice
1/3 cup mayonnaise
1/3 cup sour cream

DIRECTIONS

Add 1 cup of water and steamer basket to the inner pot. Place the broccoli florets in the steamer basket.

Secure the lid. Choose the "Manual" mode and cook for 1 minute at High pressure. Once cooking is complete, use a quick pressure release; carefully remove the lid.

Transfer the chilled broccoli florets to a nice salad bowl. Add the salt, black pepper, scallions, raisins, and seeds to the salad bowl.

Next, stir in the balsamic vinegar, lemon juice, mayo, and sour cream. Bon appétit!

32. Traditional Pozole with Hominy

(Ready in about 1 hour)

Per serving: 233 Calories; 3.3g Fat; 45.8g Carbs; 5.8g Protein; 8.7g Sugars; 4.9g Fiber

INGREDIENTS

1 dried pasilla chili peppers, seeded and minced
1/2 teaspoon cumin seeds
1/2 teaspoon garlic, sliced
Kosher salt and ground black pepper, to taste
1/2 onion, chopped
1/3 pound dried hominy, soaked overnight and rinsed

2 cups water
1 Roma tomato, chopped
1/2 tablespoon bouillon granules
1 bay leaf
1/2 cup radishes, sliced

DIRECTIONS

Put the chilis in a bowl with hot water; let them soak for 15 minutes until soft. Transfer the chilis to your food processor; add the cumin seeds, garlic, salt, and black pepper.

Add 1 cup of water to the food processor and puree the mixture until well blended. Transfer the mixture to your Instant Pot.

Add the onion, hominy, water, tomatoes, bouillon granules, and bay leaves to the inner pot.

Secure the lid. Choose the "Soup/Broth" mode and cook for 40 minutes at High pressure. Once cooking is complete, use a quick pressure release; carefully remove the lid.

Serve warm, garnished with fresh radishes. Bon appétit!

33. Indian Curry with Kale

(Ready in about 20 minutes)

Per serving: 355 Calories; 16.7g Fat; 47.7g Carbs; 8.4g Protein; 5.8g Sugars; 6.6g Fiber

INGREDIENTS

1/2 tablespoon grapeseed oil
1/2 onion, chopped
1 teaspoon ginger-garlic paste
1 teaspoon ground cumin
1/2 tablespoon ground coriander
1/2 teaspoon ground turmeric

Sea salt and freshly ground black pepper, to taste
1 cinnamon stick
1 tablespoon tomato paste
1/2 cup vegetable broth
2 medium-sized sweet potatoes, diced

1/2 cup tomatoes juice
1/2 cup coconut milk
2 cups kale, torn into pieces
1 tablespoon fresh cilantro, chopped

DIRECTIONS

Press the "Sauté" button and heat the oil until sizzling. Now, sauté the onion until just tender and fragrant.

Now, stir in the ginger-garlic paste, spices, tomato paste, vegetable broth, sweet potatoes, and tomato juice.

Secure the lid. Choose the "Manual" mode and cook for 6 minutes at High pressure. Once cooking is complete, use a quick pressure release; carefully remove the lid.

After that, add the coconut milk and kale. Press the "Sauté" button and let it simmer for 5 to 6 minutes or until thoroughly heated.

Ladle into soup bowls and serve garnished with fresh cilantro. Enjoy!

34. Potato Salad with Eggs

(Ready in about 20 minutes + chilling time)

Per serving: 448 Calories; 21.5g Fat; 55.4g Carbs; 9.7g Protein; 11.8g Sugars; 6.6g Fiber

INGREDIENTS

1 pound small Yukon Gold potatoes
1/3 cup mayonnaise
1/4 cup pickle relish
1/2 tablespoon yellow mustard
1/3 teaspoon cayenne pepper
2 boiled eggs, peeled and chopped

1 celery rib, diced
1/2 yellow onion, sliced
1 garlic clove, minced
1/2 teaspoon fresh rosemary, chopped
Sea salt and ground black pepper, to taste

DIRECTIONS

Place a metal trivet and 1 cup of water in the inner pot of your Instant Pot. Place the Yukon Gold potatoes in a steamer basket. Lower the steamer basket onto the trivet.

Secure the lid. Choose the "Manual" mode and cook for 12 minutes at High pressure. Once cooking is complete, use a quick pressure release; carefully remove the lid.

Peel and slice the potatoes; place them in a large bowl and toss with the other ingredients. Gently stir to combine. Serve well chilled and enjoy!

35. Rich Yellow Bean Salad

(Ready in about 15 minutes)

Per serving: 232 Calories; 9g Fat; 33.3g Carbs; 8g Protein; 3.7g Sugars; 4.6g Fiber

INGREDIENTS

1 tablespoon olive oil
1 tablespoon freshly squeezed lemon juice
1/3 cup coconut milk
1 pound yellow beans
1 sweet pepper, seeded and sliced
1/2 red chili pepper, seeded and minced

2 scallion stalks, chopped
1 stalk green garlic, sliced
1 tablespoon fresh cilantro, roughly chopped
Coarse sea salt, to taste
1/2 cup smoked tofu cubes

DIRECTIONS

Mix the olive oil, lemon juice, and coconut milk in your blender or food processor. Reserve.

Place 1 cup of water and a steamer basket in the inner pot of your Instant Pot. Place the yellow beans in the steamer basket.

Secure the lid. Choose the "Manual" mode and cook for 3 minutes at High pressure. Once cooking is complete, use a quick pressure release; carefully remove the lid.

Toss the chilled yellow beans with the other ingredients, including the reserved dressing; toss to combine well. Serve well chilled and enjoy!

36. Braised Collard Greens with Bacon

(Ready in about 10 minutes | Servings 4)

Per serving: 304 Calories; 19.3g Fat; 19.8g Carbs; 17.8g Protein; 2.9g Sugars; 14g Fiber

INGREDIENTS

3 smoked bacon slices, chopped
1/2 onion, chopped
2 garlic cloves, chopped
1 cup chicken broth
1 ½ pounds fresh collard greens

4 tablespoons dry white wine
1/2 teaspoon paprika
1 bay leaf
Kosher salt and ground black pepper, to taste

DIRECTIONS

Press the "Sauté" button to preheat your Instant Pot. Then, cook the bacon until crisp and set aside.

Add the remaining ingredients to the inner pot and stir to combine.

Secure the lid. Choose the "Manual" mode and cook for 5 minutes at High pressure. Once cooking is complete, use a quick pressure release; carefully remove the lid.

Serve garnished with the reserved bacon. Bon appétit!

37. German Cabbage Soup with Sausage

(Ready in about 20 minutes)

Per serving: 472 Calories; 34g Fat; 20.5g Carbs; 21.4g Protein; 8.9g Sugars; 7.4g Fiber

INGREDIENTS

1 teaspoon chicken schmaltz
1/2 pound smoked sausage, sliced
1/2 onion, chopped
1 garlic clove, minced
1 carrot, chopped

1/2 celery stalk, chopped
1 fresh tomato, chopped
2 cups chicken broth
1/3 teaspoon basil
1/3 teaspoon dried thyme

1/3 teaspoon dried oregano
1/2 teaspoon paprika
3/4 pound cabbage, cored and shredded
Salt and ground black pepper, to taste

DIRECTIONS

Press the "Sauté" button and melt the chicken schmaltz. Then, cook the sausage and onion for about 3 minutes. Now, stir in the garlic and continue to sauté for 30 seconds more, stirring frequently.

Add the remaining ingredients; stir to combine.

Secure the lid. Choose the "Manual" mode and cook for 10 minutes at High pressure. Once cooking is complete, use a quick pressure release; carefully remove the lid.

Serve in individual bowls. Bon appétit!

38. Italian-Style Endive with Salami and Cheese

(Ready in about 15 minutes)

Per serving: 393 Calories; 26.2g Fat; 21.3g Carbs; 20.4g Protein; 5.6g Sugars; 8.2g Fiber

INGREDIENTS

1 tablespoon extra-virgin olive oil
4 ounces Italian dry salami, cut into 1/2-inch chunks
1/2 shallot, sliced
1 garlic clove, minced
1 pound endive, coarsely chopped
1 tomato, chopped

1/2 tablespoon Italian seasoning mix
1/2 teaspoon cayenne pepper
Sea salt and freshly ground pepper, to taste
1/2 cup chicken broth
3 tablespoons Romano cheese, preferably freshly grated

DIRECTIONS

Press the "Sauté" button and heat the olive oil until sizzling. Now, cook the Italian salami for 3 minutes; add the shallot and garlic and cook an additional 2 minutes or until they have softened.

Add the endive, tomatoes, spices, and broth to the inner pot.

Secure the lid. Choose the "Manual" mode and cook for 2 minutes at High pressure. Once cooking is complete, use a quick pressure release; carefully remove the lid.

Divide between serving bowls and serve garnished with the grated Romano cheese. Bon appétit!

39. Old-Fashioned Bhindi Masala

(Ready in about 10 minutes)

Per serving: 253 Calories; 16.8g Fat; 24.9g Carbs; 5.4g Protein; 9.5g Sugars; 5g Fiber

INGREDIENTS

1 tablespoon coconut oil, at room temperature
1/2 yellow onion, sliced
1 teaspoon ginger garlic paste

1/2 pound okra, cut into small pieces
1/2 cup tomato puree
1/3 teaspoon jeera (cumin seeds)
1/3 teaspoon ground turmeric

1/2 teaspoon Gram masala
1/2 teaspoon amchur (mango powder)
1/2 teaspoon Sriracha sauce
Himalayan salt, to taste

DIRECTIONS

Press the "Sauté" button and heat the oil until sizzling. Now, cook the onion until it is tender and translucent.

Stir in the ginger-garlic paste and continue to cook for 30 to 40 seconds. Stir the remaining ingredients into the inner pot.

Secure the lid. Choose the "Manual" mode and cook for 4 minutes at High pressure. Once cooking is complete, use a quick pressure release; carefully remove the lid. Serve warm.

SOUPS

40. Indian Tomato Soup

(Ready in about 15 minutes)

Per serving: 92 Calories; 7.8g Fat; 6.7g Carbs; 1.4g Protein; 2.8g Sugars; 1.9g Fiber

INGREDIENTS

1/2 tablespoon cumin seeds
1/2 tablespoon whole black pepper
1 clove garlic
1 dry red chili pepper

1 tablespoon coconut oil
1/3 teaspoon mustard seeds
1 medium tomato, diced
4 curry leaves

1/3 teaspoon turmeric
1 tablespoon tamarind
Himalayan salt, to taste
2 cups water

DIRECTIONS

Grind the cumin seeds, whole black pepper, garlic, and red chili pepper to a coarse paste.

Press the "Sauté" button and heat the oil until sizzling. Now, cook the mustard seeds for a minute or so. Once they splutter, add chopped tomatoes and curry leaves. Cook for 3 to 4 minutes more.

Add the ground paste, turmeric powder, and freshly squeezed tamarind juice; add salt and the water and stir to combine.

Secure the lid. Choose the "Manual" mode and cook for 4 minutes at High pressure. Once cooking is complete, use a quick pressure release; carefully remove the lid. Serve hot and enjoy!

41. Mexican Chicken Enchilada Soup

(Ready in about 25 minutes)

Per serving: 438 Calories; 34.2g Fat; 23.7g Carbs; 20.6g Protein; 6.6g Sugars; 7.9g Fiber

INGREDIENTS

1 tablespoon olive oil
1/2 cup shallots, chopped
1 sweet pepper, chopped
1/2 Poblano chili pepper, chopped
1/2 pound chicken thighs, boneless and skinless
1 ripe tomato, chopped

5 ounces red enchilada sauce
1 teaspoon ground cumin
1 teaspoon ground coriander
Seasoned salt and freshly cracked pepper, to taste
2 cups roasted vegetable broth
1 bay leaf

6 ounces black beans, drained and rinsed
2 (6-inch) corn tortillas, cut crosswise into 1/4-inch strips
1/2 avocado, cut into 1/2-inch dice
1/2 cup cheddar cheese, shredded

DIRECTIONS

Press the "Sauté" button and heat the olive oil. Once hot, sauté the shallots and peppers until tender and aromatic.

Add the chicken thighs, tomatoes, enchilada sauce, cumin, coriander, chili powder, salt, black pepper, vegetable broth, and bay leaf to the inner pot.

Secure the lid. Choose the "Manual" mode and cook for 8 minutes at High pressure. Once cooking is complete, use a natural pressure release for 10 minutes; carefully remove the lid.

Stir in the canned beans and seal the lid; let it sit in the residual heat until everything is heated through.

Divide your soup between individual bowls and serve garnished with tortilla strips, avocado, and cheddar cheese.

42. Old-Fashioned Chicken Noodle Soup

(Ready in about 20 minutes)

Per serving: 426 Calories; 18.4g Fat; 18.6g Carbs; 40.5g Protein; 2.7g Sugars; 1.9g Fiber

INGREDIENTS

1 tablespoon olive oil
1 carrot, diced
1 parsnip, diced
1/2 yellow onion, chopped

1 clove garlic, minced
3 cups chicken bone broth
1 bay leaf
Salt and freshly ground black pepper

1 pound chicken thighs drumettes
1 cup wide egg noodles
2 tablespoons fresh cilantro, roughly chopped

DIRECTIONS

Press the "Sauté" button and heat the oil. Once hot, cook the carrots, parsnips, and onions until they are just tender.

Add the minced garlic and continue to cook for a minute more.

Add the chicken bone broth, bay leaf, salt, black pepper, and chicken to the inner pot.

Secure the lid. Choose the "Manual" mode and cook for 9 minutes at High pressure. Once cooking is complete, use a quick pressure release; carefully remove the lid.

Shred the cooked chicken and set aside. Stir in noodles and press the "Sauté" button. Cook approximately 5 minutes or until thoroughly heated. Afterwards, add the chicken back into the soup. Serve garnished with fresh cilantro. Bon appétit!

43. Hearty Squash and Leek Soup

(Ready in about 20 minutes)

Per serving: 152 Calories; 6.1g Fat; 27.4g Carbs; 2.8g Protein; 3.6g Sugars; 5.2g Fiber

INGREDIENTS

1 tablespoon butter, softened
1 clove garlic, sliced
1/2 medium-sized leek, chopped
1/2 turnip, chopped

1 carrot, chopped
1 pound acorn squash, chopped
1 cup vegetable broth
1 cup water

1/2 teaspoon ground allspice
1 sprig fresh thyme
Himalayan salt and black pepper, to taste

DIRECTIONS

Press the "Sauté" button and melt the butter. Once hot, cook the garlic and leek until just tender and fragrant.

Add the remaining ingredients to the inner pot.

Secure the lid. Choose the "Manual" mode and cook for 10 minutes at High pressure. Once cooking is complete, use a quick pressure release; carefully remove the lid.

Puree the soup in your blender until smooth and uniform. Serve warm and enjoy!

44. Mediterranean Fish Soup

(Ready in about 12 minutes)

Per serving: 324 Calories; 22.4g Fat; 7.3g Carbs; 20.3g Protein; 4.1g Sugars; 1.6g Fiber

INGREDIENTS

4 tablespoons butter, at room temperature
1/2 onion, chopped
1 garlic clove, minced
1 ripe tomato, pureed
1 tablespoon tomato paste

1/2 cup shellfish stock
1/4 cup cooking wine
1/2 pound cod fish, cut into bite-sized pieces
1/4 teaspoon basil
1/4 teaspoon dried dill weed

1/3 teaspoon dried oregano
1/4 teaspoon hot sauce
1/2 teaspoon paprika
Sea salt and freshly ground black pepper, to taste

DIRECTIONS

Press the "Sauté" button and melt the butter; once hot, cook the onion and garlic for about 2 minutes or until they are just tender.

Add the remaining ingredients.

Secure the lid. Choose the "Manual" mode and cook for 5 minutes at High pressure. Once cooking is complete, use a quick pressure release; carefully remove the lid.

Ladle into serving bowls and serve immediately.

45. Habanero Chicken Soup with Beans

(Ready in about 20 minutes)

Per serving: 505 Calories; 26.8g Fat; 39g Carbs; 27.7g Protein; 3.5g Sugars; 6.1g Fiber

INGREDIENTS

1 tablespoon butter, softened
1/2 onion, chopped
1 sweet pepper, deseeded and chopped
1 habanero pepper, deseeded and chopped
1 clove garlic, minced

Sea salt and ground black pepper, to taste
1/2 teaspoon dried basil
1/2 teaspoon dried oregano
1/2 teaspoon cayenne pepper
2 cups vegetable broth

1/2 pound chicken thighs
5 ounces red kidney beans
2 tablespoons fresh cilantro, chopped
2 ounces tortilla chips

DIRECTIONS

Press the "Sauté" button and melt the butter. Once hot, cook the onion until tender and translucent.

Stir in the peppers and sauté for a few minutes more. Add the minced garlic and continue to sauté for another minute.

Add the spices, vegetable broth, and chicken thighs to the inner pot.

Secure the lid. Choose the "Manual" mode and cook for 13 minutes at High pressure. Once cooking is complete, use a quick pressure release; carefully remove the lid.

Remove the chicken to a cutting board. Add the kidney beans to the inner pot and seal the lid again. Let it sit in the residual heat until thoroughly heated.

Shred the chicken and discard the bones; put it back into the soup. Serve with fresh cilantro and tortilla chips. Enjoy!

46. Mom's Barley Soup

(Ready in about 25 minutes)

Per serving: 300 Calories; 5.7g Fat; 52.6g Carbs; 11.6g Protein; 5.9g Sugars; 9.3g Fiber

INGREDIENTS

1/2 tablespoon canola oil
1 shallot, chopped
1 garlic clove, minced
1 celery stalk, chopped

1 parsnip, chopped
1/2 cup tomato puree
2 cups beef broth
1/2 cup pearl barley

1 sprig thyme
Sea salt and white pepper, to taste
1/2 teaspoon red pepper flakes, crushed

DIRECTIONS

Press the "Sauté" button and heat the canola oil. Once hot, sauté the shallots, garlic, celery, and parsnip until tender and aromatic.
Add the remaining ingredients and stir to combine.
Secure the lid. Choose the "Soup/Broth" mode and cook for 20 minutes at High pressure. Once cooking is complete, use a quick pressure release; carefully remove the lid.
Serve in individual bowls. Bon appétit!

47. Classic Stroganoff Soup

(Ready in about 1 hour)

Per serving: 267 Calories; 9.6g Fat; 11.4g Carbs; 34.2g Protein; 2.2g Sugars; 1.4g Fiber

INGREDIENTS

1/2 pound beef stew meat, cubed
2 cups beef bone broth
1/2 teaspoon dried basil
1/2 teaspoon dried oregano
1/2 teaspoon dried rosemary

1/2 teaspoon dried sage
1/2 teaspoon shallot powder
1/2 teaspoon porcini powder
1/2 teaspoon garlic powder
Sea salt and ground black pepper, to taste

4 ounces button mushrooms, sliced
1/2 cup sour cream
1 tablespoon potato starch, mixed with
2 tablespoons of cold water

DIRECTIONS

In the inner pot, place the stew meat, broth, and spices.
Secure the lid. Choose the "Manual" mode and cook for 50 minutes at High pressure. Once cooking is complete, use a quick pressure release; carefully remove the lid.
Add the mushrooms and sour cream to the inner pot.
Choose the "Soup/Broth" mode. Bring to a boil and add the potato starch slurry. Continue to simmer until the soup thickens.
Ladle into serving bowls and serve immediately. Bon appétit!

48. Rich Meatball Soup

(Ready in about 30 minutes)

Per serving: 487 Calories; 21.9g Fat; 30.1g Carbs; 40.8g Protein; 4.7g Sugars; 2.3g Fiber

INGREDIENTS

Meatballs:
1/4 pound ground beef
1/4 pound ground turkey
1/4 cup panko crumbs
4 tablespoons Pecorino Romano cheese, grated

1 egg, beaten
1 clove garlic, crushed
1 tablespoon cilantro, chopped
Sea salt and ground black pepper, to taste
Soup:
1/2 tablespoon olive oil

1/2 onion, chopped
1/2 celery stalk, chopped
1 tomato, crushed
2 cups chicken broth
1 bay leaf
3 ounces noodles

DIRECTIONS

In a mixing bowl, thoroughly combine all ingredients for the meatballs.
Form the mixture into 20 meatballs. Press the "Sauté" button and heat the oil. Now, brown the meatballs in batches; reserve.
Heat the olive oil; sauté the onion and celery for 3 to 4 minutes or until they are fragrant.
Add the tomatoes, broth, and bay leaves to the inner pot.
Secure the lid. Choose the "Manual" mode and cook for 12 minutes at High pressure. Once cooking is complete, use a quick pressure release; carefully remove the lid.
Next, sit in the noodles and secure the lid again.
Choose the "Manual" mode and cook for 5 minutes at High pressure. Once cooking is complete, use a quick pressure release; carefully remove the lid. Bon appétit!

49. Vegetables, Corn and Chicken Soup

(Ready in about 20 minutes)

Per serving: 313 Calories; 15.5g Fat; 19.4g Carbs; 24.7g Protein; 4.6g Sugars; 1.7g Fiber

INGREDIENTS

1/2 tablespoon olive oil
1/2 yellow onion, chopped
1/2 celery stalk, diced
1/2 carrot, finely diced
1/2 turnip, diced
2 cups roasted vegetable broth

1/2 pound chicken breasts, skinless, boneless and diced
1/2 teaspoon garlic powder
1/2 teaspoon mustard powder
4 ounces canned creamed corn
1 egg, whisked
Kosher salt and ground black pepper, to taste

DIRECTIONS

Press the "Sauté" button and heat the oil. Now, sauté the onion until just tender and translucent.

Add the celery, carrot, turnip, vegetable broth, chicken, garlic powder, and mustard powder.

Secure the lid. Choose the "Manual" mode and cook for 9 minutes at High pressure. Once cooking is complete, use a quick pressure release; carefully remove the lid.

Press the "Sauté" button and use the lowest setting. Stir in the creamed corn and egg; let it simmer, stirring continuously for about 5 minutes or until everything is thoroughly heated.

Season with salt and pepper to taste and serve warm. Bon appétit!

50. Ground Pork and Tomato Soup

(Ready in about 30 minutes)

Per serving: 382 Calories; 26.2g Fat; 10.5g Carbs; 26.3g Protein; 2.4g Sugars; 2.3g Fiber

INGREDIENTS

1/2 pound ground pork
1 teaspoon Italian seasoning
1/2 teaspoon garlic powder
Sea salt and ground black pepper, to taste

1 sweet pepper, seeded and sliced
1/2 jalapeno pepper, seeded and minced
1 ripe tomato, pureed
2 cups chicken stock

DIRECTIONS

Press the "Sauté" button to preheat your Instant Pot. Then, brown the ground pork until no longer pink or about 3 minutes.

Add the remaining ingredients to the inner pot and stir.

Secure the lid. Choose the "Manual" mode and cook for 10 minutes at High pressure. Once cooking is complete, use a natural pressure release for 10; carefully remove the lid.

Serve warm. Bon appétit!

51. Traditional Minestrone Soup

(Ready in about 10 minutes)

Per serving: 413 Calories; 21.1g Fat; 39.5g Carbs; 19.8g Protein; 10.6g Sugars; 8.3g Fiber

INGREDIENTS

1 tablespoon canola oil
1/2 onion, chopped
1 stalks celery, diced
1 carrot, diced
1 clove garlic, pressed

1 pound tomatoes, pureed
1 cup chicken broth
1/2 cup pasta, uncooked
1 teaspoon Italian seasoning
Sea salt and ground black pepper, to taste

1/3 cup fresh corn kernels
1 cup cannellini beans, canned and rinsed
2 ounces Parmesan cheese, grated

DIRECTIONS

Press the "Sauté" button and heat oil until sizzling, Then, sauté the onion, celery, and carrots for 3 to 4 minutes or until tender.

Add the garlic, tomatoes, broth, pasta, Italian seasoning, salt, and black pepper.

Secure the lid. Choose the "Manual" mode and cook for 5 minutes at High pressure. Once cooking is complete, use a quick pressure release; carefully remove the lid.

Lastly, stir in the corn kernels and beans. Seal the lid and let it sit in the residual heat for 5 to 8 minutes. Ladle into individual bowls and serve topped with Parmesan cheese. Bon appétit!

52. Chipotle Beef Soup

(Ready in about 45 minutes)

Per serving: 343 Calories; 17.5g Fat; 10.9g Carbs; 34.7g Protein; 3.3g Sugars; 6.5g Fiber

INGREDIENTS

1/2 tablespoon canola oil
1/2 pound ground beef
1 clove garlic, smashed
1/2 medium leek, chopped

1 chipotle chili in adobo sauce, roughly chopped
1/2 (14 ½ -ounce) can tomatoes, diced
1 cup vegetable broth

6 ounces pinto beans, undrained
1/2 teaspoon cumin powder
1/2 teaspoon stone-ground mustard
1/2 teaspoon chili powder

DIRECTIONS

Press the "Sauté" button and heat the oil. Brown the ground beef for 2 to 3 minutes, stirring frequently.

Add the remaining ingredients and stir to combine well.

Secure the lid. Choose the "Bean/Chili" mode and cook for 30 minutes at High pressure. Once cooking is complete, use a natural pressure release for 10 minutes; carefully remove the lid. Bon appétit!

53. Masala Turkey and Rice Soup

(Ready in about 15 minutes)

Per serving: 254 Calories; 9.7g Fat; 36.3g Carbs; 7.1g Protein; 10.9g Sugars; 7g Fiber

INGREDIENTS

1/2 tablespoon sesame oil
1/2 onion, chopped
1 thumb-sized piece fresh ginger, peeled and grated
1/2 pound turkey breast, boneless and cut into chunks

1 carrot, sliced
1 celery stalk, sliced
2 cups chicken broth
1/2 teaspoon garlic powder
1/2 teaspoon cumin seeds
1/2 teaspoon garam masala

1/2 teaspoon turmeric powder
1/2 cup basmati rice, rinsed
2 heaping tablespoons fresh coriander, roughly chopped

DIRECTIONS

Press the "Sauté" button and heat the sesame oil until sizzling. Now, sauté the onion and ginger until tender and aromatic.

Add the turkey, carrot, and celery to the inner pot; continue to cook for 3 to 4 minutes more or until the turkey is no longer pink.

Add the chicken broth and spices to the inner pot. Secure the lid. Choose the "Manual" mode and cook for 5 minutes at High pressure. Once cooking is complete, use a quick pressure release; carefully remove the lid.

After that, stir in the basmati rice.

Secure the lid. Choose the "Manual" mode and cook for 4 minutes at High pressure. Once cooking is complete, use a quick pressure release; carefully remove the lid.

Ladle into serving bowls and serve with fresh coriander. Enjoy!

54. Classic French Bouillabaisse

(Ready in about 15 minutes)

Per serving: 433 Calories; 21.6g Fat; 37g Carbs; 22g Protein; 10.9g Sugars; 3g Fiber

INGREDIENTS

1/2 pound lump lobster meat
1 tablespoon olive oil
1/2 yellow onion, chopped
1/2 celery stalk, diced
1/2 carrot, diced
1 clove garlic, minced
1/2 teaspoon rosemary

1/2 teaspoon basil
1/2 teaspoon thyme
1/4 teaspoon turmeric powder
1/2 tomato, pureed
2 tablespoons cooking sherry
2 cups clam juice
1/2 tablespoon soy sauce

1/2 teaspoon smoked paprika
Sea salt and ground white pepper, to taste
1/2 teaspoon Tabasco sauce
1/2 cup heavy cream

DIRECTIONS

In the inner pot of your Instant Pot, place the lobster meat, olive oil, onion, celery, carrot, garlic, rosemary, basil, thyme, turmeric, tomato puree, cooking sherry, and clam juice.

Secure the lid. Choose the "Manual" mode and cook for 4 minutes at High pressure. Once cooking is complete, use a quick pressure release; carefully remove the lid. Set the lobster meat aside and chop into small chunks.

Now, add in the soy sauce, smoked paprika, salt, white pepper, Tabasco sauce, and heavy cream; continue to stir and simmer until it's all blended together and heated through.

Lastly, put the lobster meat back into your bisque. Serve in individual bowls and enjoy!

55. Creamed Potato Soup with Corn

(Ready in about 25 minutes)

Per serving: 439 Calories; 20.4g Fat; 56.2g Carbs; 12.8g Protein; 9.3g Sugars; 8.1g Fiber

INGREDIENTS

1 tablespoon butter
1/2 sweet onion, chopped
1 garlic clove, minced
1 sweet pepper, deveined and sliced
1/2 jalapeno pepper, deveined and sliced

2 tablespoons all-purpose flour
2 cups vegetable broth
1/2 pound potatoes, cut into bite-sized pieces
2 cups creamed corn kernels

1/2 cup double cream
Kosher salt and ground black pepper, to taste
1/3 teaspoon cayenne pepper

DIRECTIONS

Press the "Sauté" button and melt the butter. Once hot, sauté the sweet onions, garlic, and peppers for about 3 minutes or until they are tender and fragrant.

Sprinkle the flour over the vegetables; continue stirring approximately 4 minutes or until your vegetables are coated.

Add the broth and potatoes and gently stir to combine.

Secure the lid. Choose the "Manual" mode and cook for 5 minutes at High pressure. Once cooking is complete, use a quick pressure release; carefully remove the lid.

Press the "Sauté" button and use the lowest setting. Stir in the creamed corn, double cream, salt, black pepper, and cayenne pepper.

Let it simmer, stirring continuously for about 5 minutes or until everything is thoroughly heated. Taste and adjust the seasonings. Bon appétit!

56. Lima Bean Soup

(Ready in about 25 minutes)

Per serving: 217 Calories; 8.2g Fat; 32.7g Carbs; 12g Protein; 11.7g Sugars; 11g Fiber

INGREDIENTS

1 tablespoon sesame oil
1/2 pound cremini mushrooms, thinly sliced
1/2 eggplant, sliced into rounds
1/2 red onion, chopped
1 garlic clove, chopped

1 carrot, sliced
1 sweet potato, peeled and diced
1/2 teaspoon red curry paste
1/2 teaspoon cayenne pepper
Sea salt and ground black pepper, to taste

1 sprig thyme
1 sprig rosemary
1 medium-sized tomatoes, pureed
2 cups roasted vegetable broth
5 ounces lima beans, soaked overnight
Juice of 1 fresh lemon

DIRECTIONS

Press the "Sauté" button and heat the oil until sizzling. Now, cook the mushrooms, eggplant, onion, and garlic until just tender and fragrant.

Add the carrots, sweet potatoes, curry paste, spices, tomatoes, broth, and lima beans.

Secure the lid. Choose the "Manual" mode and cook for 13 minutes at High pressure. Once cooking is complete, use a quick pressure release; carefully remove the lid.

Divide your soup between individual bowls; add a few drizzles of lemon juice to each serving and enjoy!

57. Swiss-Style Fish Chowder

(Ready in about 15 minutes)

Per serving: 456 Calories; 20.2g Fat; 15.7g Carbs; 50.2g Protein; 7.7g Sugars; 1.7g Fiber

INGREDIENTS

1 tablespoon butter
1/2 leek, sliced
1/2 carrot, shredded
1 celery stalk, shredded
1 clove garlic, minced

2 cups chicken bone broth
1 ripe tomato, chopped
1/2 pound halibut, cut into small cubes
Kosher salt and cracked black pepper, to taste

1/2 cup milk
1/3 cup double cream
1/2 cup Swiss cheese, shredded

DIRECTIONS

Press the "Sauté" button and melt the butter. Once hot, sauté the leeks, carrot, celery, and garlic until they are just tender and fragrant.

Then, add the chicken bone broth, tomatoes, halibut, salt, and black pepper.

Secure the lid. Choose the "Manual" mode and cook for 5 minutes at High pressure. Once cooking is complete, use a quick pressure release; carefully remove the lid.

Press the "Sauté" button and use the lowest setting. Stir in the milk and double cream. Allow it to simmer for about 3 minutes or until heated through.

Ladle your chowder into serving bowls; top with the shredded Swiss cheese and serve immediately.

58. Dad's Duck Soup with Millet

(Ready in about 20 minutes)

Per serving: 427 Calories; 21.3g Fat; 25g Carbs; 31.3g Protein; 0.3g Sugars; 3.2g Fiber

INGREDIENTS

1 tablespoon olive oil
1/2 pound duck portions with bones
1 garlic clove, minced

2 cups water
1 tablespoon chicken bouillon granules
1/3 cup millet, rinsed

Salt and freshly cracked black pepper, to taste
2 scallion stalks, chopped

DIRECTIONS

Press the "Sauté" button and heat the oil. Once hot, brown your duck for 4 to 5 minutes; stir in the garlic and cook an additional 30 seconds or until aromatic.

Add the remaining ingredients.

Secure the lid. Choose the "Manual" mode and cook for 12 minutes at High pressure. Once cooking is complete, use a quick pressure release; carefully remove the lid.

Remove the cooked duck to a cutting board. Shred the meat and discard the bones. Put your duck back into the inner pot. Stir and serve immediately. Bon appétit!

59. Colorful Seafood Bisque Soup

(Ready in about 15 minutes)

Per serving: 362 Calories; 18.9g Fat; 20.3g Carbs; 29.6g Protein; 7.8g Sugars; 2.8g Fiber

INGREDIENTS

1 tablespoon butter
1/3 cup white onion, chopped
1/2 celery rib, chopped
1 parsnip, chopped

1/2 carrot, chopped
1 tablespoon all-purpose flour
1/4 cup sherry wine
Sea salt and ground black pepper

1/2 cup tomato puree
1 ½ cups chicken bone broth
8 ounces shrimp, deveined
1/2 cup heavy whipping cream

DIRECTIONS

Press the "Sauté" button and melt the butter. Once hot, cook the onion, celery, parsnip, and carrot until softened.

Add the flour and cook for 3 minutes more or until everything is well coated. Pour in sherry wine to deglaze the pot.

Now, add the salt, pepper, tomato puree, and broth.

Secure the lid. Choose the "Manual" mode and cook for 5 minutes at High pressure. Once cooking is complete, use a quick pressure release; carefully remove the lid.

Now, add the shrimp and heavy cream and cook on the "Sauté" function for a further 2 to 3 minutes or until everything is heated through. Bon appétit!

60. Thai Oxtail Soup (Hang Wuao)

(Ready in about 1 hour 10 minutes)

Per serving: 428 Calories; 14.4g Fat; 37.9g Carbs; 33g Protein; 3.8g Sugars; 5.5g Fiber

INGREDIENTS

1/2 pound oxtails
2 cloves garlic, sliced
1 bay leaf
1 thyme sprig
1 rosemary sprig
1/2 tablespoon soy sauce

1/2 teaspoon cumin powder
1 teaspoon paprika
1 potato, peeled and diced
1 carrot, diced
1 parsnip, diced
1 cup vegetable broth

1 bird's eye chilis, pounded in a mortar and pestle
1 star anise
Sea salt and ground black pepper, to taste

DIRECTIONS

Place the oxtails in the inner pot. Cover the oxtails with water. Stir in the garlic, bay leaves, thyme, rosemary, soy sauce, cumin, and paprika.

Secure the lid. Choose the "Manual" mode and cook for 50 minutes at High pressure. Once cooking is complete, use a natural pressure release for 10 minutes; carefully remove the lid.

After that, add the other ingredients to the inner pot.

Secure the lid. Choose the "Manual" mode and cook for 4 minutes at High pressure. Once cooking is complete, use a quick pressure release; carefully remove the lid.

Serve with crusty bread and enjoy!

61. Quinoa Soup with Zucchini

(Ready in about 10 minutes)

Per serving: 252 Calories; 9.2g Fat; 33g Carbs; 9.6g Protein; 1.1g Sugars; 4.7g Fiber

INGREDIENTS

1 tablespoon olive oil
1 shallot, diced
1 teaspoon fresh garlic, minced
Sea salt and ground black pepper, to your liking

1/2 pound zucchini, cut into rounds
1/2 cup quinoa
2 cups vegetable broth
1 tablespoon fresh parsley leaves

DIRECTIONS

Press the "Sauté" button and heat the oil. Once hot, sweat the shallot for 2 to 3 minutes. Stir in the garlic and continue to cook for another 30 seconds or until aromatic.
Stir in the salt, black pepper, zucchini, quinoa, and vegetable broth.
Secure the lid. Choose the "Manual" mode and cook for 3 minutes at High pressure. Once cooking is complete, use a quick pressure release; carefully remove the lid.
Ladle into soup bowls; serve garnished with fresh parsley leaves. Enjoy!

62. Easy Lentil Soup with Spinach

(Ready in about 10 minutes)

Per serving: 295 Calories; 1.9g Fat; 52.7g Carbs; 19.2g Protein; 1.6g Sugars; 11.7g Fiber

INGREDIENTS

1 cup red lentils, rinsed
1/2 onion, chopped
1 clove garlic, minced
1/2 teaspoon cumin
1/2 teaspoon smoked paprika

Sea salt and ground black pepper, to taste
1 carrot, sliced
2 cups water
1 bay leaf
1 cups fresh spinach leaves, torn into small pieces

DIRECTIONS

Place all ingredients, except for the fresh spinach, in the inner pot.
Secure the lid. Choose the "Manual" mode and cook for 3 minutes at High pressure. Once cooking is complete, use a quick pressure release; carefully remove the lid.
Stir in the spinach and seal the lid again; let it sit until the spinach just starts to wilt.
Serve in individual bowls and enjoy!

63. Nutty Sweet Potato Soup

(Ready in about 15 minutes)

Per serving: 254 Calories; 9.7g Fat; 36.3g Carbs; 7.1g Protein; 10.9g Sugars; 5.7g Fiber

INGREDIENTS

1 tablespoon butter, softened at room temperature
1/2 white onion, chopped
1 sweet pepper, deveined and chopped
1 clove garlic, pressed
1/2 pound sweet potatoes, peeled and diced
1 ripe tomato, pureed

1 cup chicken bone broth
1 cup water
Kosher salt and freshly ground black pepper, to taste
2 tablespoons peanut butter
1 cup Swiss chard, torn into pieces

DIRECTIONS

Press the "Sauté" button and melt the butter. Once hot, cook the onion, pepper, and garlic until tender and fragrant.
Add the sweet potatoes and continue to sauté for about 3 minutes longer. Now, stir in the tomatoes, broth, water, salt, and black pepper.
Secure the lid. Choose the "Manual" mode and cook for 4 minutes at High pressure. Once cooking is complete, use a quick pressure release; carefully remove the lid.
Stir in the peanut butter and Swiss chard; seal the lid again and let it sit in the residual heat until your greens wilt. Serve warm.

64. French Onion-Bread Soup

(Ready in about 10 minutes)

Per serving: 330 Calories; 13.9g Fat; 31.7g Carbs; 19.2g Protein; 7.6g Sugars; 3.6g Fiber

INGREDIENTS

2 tablespoons butter, melted
1/2 pound onions, thinly sliced
Kosher salt and ground white pepper, to taste
1/2 teaspoon dried sage

2 cups chicken bone broth
1/2 loaf French bread, sliced
1/2 cup mozzarella cheese, shredded

DIRECTIONS

Press the "Sauté" button and melt the butter. Once hot, cook the onions until golden and caramelized.

Add the salt, pepper, sage, and chicken bone broth.

Secure the lid. Choose the "Manual" mode and cook for 2 minutes at High pressure. Once cooking is complete, use a quick pressure release; carefully remove the lid.

Divide the soup between four oven safe bowls; top with the bread and shredded cheese; now, place the bowls under the broiler for about 4 minutes or until the cheese has melted. Bon appétit!

65. Cheesy Broccoli Soup

(Ready in about 10 minutes)

Per serving: 398 Calories; 24.4g Fat; 32.3g Carbs; 17.1g Protein; 10.9g Sugars; 4.6g Fiber

INGREDIENTS

2 tablespoons butter
1 clove garlic, pressed
1/2 teaspoon shallot powder
2 cups cream of celery soup
1/2 pound small broccoli florets

Sea salt and ground black pepper, to taste
1/2 teaspoon chili powder
1 cup half and half
1 cup sharp cheddar cheese, freshly grated
1 scallion stalk, chopped

DIRECTIONS

Add the butter, garlic, shallot powder, cream of celery soup, broccoli, salt, black pepper, and chili powder to the inner pot.

Secure the lid. Choose the "Manual" mode and cook for 2 minutes at High pressure. Once cooking is complete, use a quick pressure release; carefully remove the lid.

Stir in the half and half and cheese. Let it simmer until everything is thoroughly heated.

Divide between serving bowls and serve garnished with chopped scallions. Bon appétit!

66. Ham Bone Soup with Vegetables

(Ready in about 30 minutes)

Per serving: 268 Calories; 12.2g Fat; 17.1g Carbs; 23.1g Protein; 6.7g Sugars; 4.65g Fiber

INGREDIENTS

1 tablespoon olive oil
1/2 cup onion, chopped
1 carrot, diced
1 rib celery, diced

1 parsnip, diced
1 ham bone
2 cups chicken stock
Sea salt and ground black pepper, to taste

DIRECTIONS

Press the "Sauté" button and heat the olive oil until sizzling. Then, sauté the onion, carrot, celery, and parsnip until tender.

Add the ham bone, chicken stock, salt, and black pepper to the inner pot.

Secure the lid. Choose the "Manual" mode and cook for 15 minutes at High pressure. Once cooking is complete, use a natural pressure release for 10 minutes; carefully remove the lid.

Remove the ham bone from the inner pot. Chop the meat from the bone; add back into the soup.

Serve in individual bowls and enjoy!

67. Lentil and Tomato Soup

(Ready in about 15 minutes)

Per serving: 305 Calories; 7.4g Fat; 45.9g Carbs; 17g Protein; 8.5g Sugars; 3.5g Fiber

INGREDIENTS

1 tablespoon butter
1/2 red onion, chopped
1/3 cup celery, chopped
1/2 teaspoon ground cumin

1/2 teaspoon ground coriander
1/2 teaspoon garlic powder
1/2 cup yellow lentils
1/2 teaspoon dried parsley flakes

1 cup roasted vegetable broth
1 cup tomato puree
1 green onion, sliced

DIRECTIONS

Press the "Sauté" button and melt the butter. Once hot, cook the onion and celery until just tender.
Stir in the remaining ingredients, except for the green onions.
Secure the lid. Choose the "Manual" mode and cook for 8 minutes at High pressure. Once cooking is complete, use a quick pressure release; carefully remove the lid.
Serve warm garnished with green onion. Enjoy!

68. Wild Rice Soup with Root Vegetable

(Ready in about 45 minutes)

Per serving: 240 Calories; 2g Fat; 44.6g Carbs; 12.8g Protein; 5.7g Sugars; 5g Fiber

INGREDIENTS

2 carrots, chopped
1 stalk celery, chopped
1/2 turnip, chopped
1/2 shallot, chopped
1/2 cups wild rice

4 ounces button mushrooms, sliced
2 cups vegetable broth
1/2 teaspoon granulated garlic
Sea salt and red pepper, to taste

DIRECTIONS

Place the ingredients in the inner pot; stir to combine.
Secure the lid. Choose the "Soup/Broth" mode and cook for 40 minutes at High pressure. Once cooking is complete, use a quick pressure release; carefully remove the lid.
Serve warm garnished with a few drizzles of olive oil if desired. Bon appétit!

69. Hearty Beef and Vegetable Soup

(Ready in about 40 minutes)

Per serving: 253 Calories; 11.6g Fat; 12.1g Carbs; 26g Protein; 5.6g Sugars; 3.1g Fiber

INGREDIENTS

1 tablespoon olive oil
1/2 pound beef stew meat, cubed
Sea salt and ground black pepper, to taste
1/2 onion, chopped
1 celery stalk, chopped
1 carrot, chopped
1 clove garlic, chopped

1 rosemary sprig
1 thyme sprig
2 tablespoons tamari sauce
1 bay leaf
2 cups beef bone broth
1/2 ripe tomato, pureed
2 ounces green beans, fresh or thawed

DIRECTIONS

Press the "Sauté" button and heat the oil until sizzling. Now, brown the beef meat for 3 to 4 minutes, stirring frequently to ensure even cooking.
Add the remaining ingredients, except for the green beans.
Secure the lid. Choose the "Manual" mode and cook for 13 minutes at High pressure. Once cooking is complete, use a natural pressure release for 15; carefully remove the lid.
Add the green beans.
Secure the lid. Choose the "Manual" mode and cook for 2 minutes at High pressure. Once cooking is complete, use a quick pressure release; carefully remove the lid. Bon appétit!

70. French Bouillabaisse with Pinot Grigio

(Ready in about 20 minutes)

Per serving: 320 Calories; 8.4g Fat; 27.1g Carbs; 31.6g Protein; 7.7g Sugars; 3.7g Fiber

INGREDIENTS

1 slice bacon, chopped
1 small leek, chopped
1/2 celery stalk, chopped
1 carrot, chopped
1 parsnip, chopped

1/4 cup Pinot Grigio
2 cups chicken broth
1/4 cup whole milk
1/4 pound frozen corn kernels, thawed
1 serrano pepper, minced

1 teaspoon granulated garlic
Seas salt and ground black pepper, to taste
1/2 pound shrimp, deveined

DIRECTIONS

Press the "Sauté" button and cook the bacon until it is crisp. Chop the bacon and set aside.

Then, sauté the leeks, celery, carrots, and parsnips in the bacon drippings. Cook for about 4 minutes or until they have softened. Add a splash of wine to deglaze the pot.

Press the "Cancel" button. Stir in the broth, milk, corn, pepper, granulated garlic, salt, and black pepper.

Secure the lid. Choose the "Manual" mode and cook for 2 minutes at High pressure. Once cooking is complete, use a quick pressure release; carefully remove the lid.

Stir in the shrimp and seal the lid again; allow it to stand in the residual heat for 5 to 10 minutes. Garnish with the reserved crumbled bacon. Bon appétit!

71. Creamed Clam Chowder

(Ready in about 15 minutes)

Per serving: 319 Calories; 18.4g Fat; 41.1g Carbs; 7.3g Protein; 8.4g Sugars; 3.4g Fiber

INGREDIENTS

1 tablespoon butter
1/2 onion, chopped
1 garlic clove, minced
1/2 stalk celery, diced
1/2 carrot, diced

1 cup water
1 cup fish stock
Sea salt and white pepper, to taste
1/2 pound Russet potatoes, peeled and diced

1 teaspoon cayenne pepper
6 ounces canned clams, chopped with juice
1/2 cup heavy cream

DIRECTIONS

Press the "Sauté" button and melt the butter; once hot, cook the onion, garlic, celery, and carrot for 3 minutes or until they have softened. Add the water, stock, salt, white pepper, potatoes, and cayenne pepper.

Secure the lid. Choose the "Manual" mode and cook for 2 minutes at High pressure. Once cooking is complete, use a quick pressure release; carefully remove the lid.

Press the "Sauté" button and use the lowest setting. Stir in the clams and heavy cream. Let it simmer for about 5 minutes or until everything is thoroughly heated. Bon appétit!

72. Classic New England Clam Chowder

(Ready in about 15 minutes)

Per serving: 264 Calories; 9.4g Fat; 26.2g Carbs; 20.8g Protein; 9.9g Sugars; 6g Fiber

INGREDIENTS

2 strips bacon, chopped
1/2 onion, chopped
1 carrot, diced
1 stalk celery, diced
1 clove garlic, minced

1/2 tablespoon Creole seasoning
Sea salt and ground black pepper, to taste
1 cup seafood stock
1 ripe tomato, pureed

1 tablespoon tomato paste
1 bay leaf
1/2 pound clams, chopped
1 tablespoon flaxseed meal

DIRECTIONS

Press the "Sauté" button to preheat your Instant Pot. Now, cook the bacon until it is crisp; crumble the bacon and set it aside.

Now, sauté the onion, carrot, celery, and garlic in bacon drippings.

Add the remaining ingredients, except for the chopped clams, to the inner pot.

Secure the lid. Choose the "Manual" mode and cook for 4 minutes at High pressure. Once cooking is complete, use a quick pressure release; carefully remove the lid.

Stir in the chopped clams and flaxseed meal.

Press the "Sauté" button and let it simmer for 2 to 3 minutes longer or until everything is heated through.

Serve in individual bowls topped with the reserved bacon. Bon appétit!

73. Country-Style Vegetable Chicken Soup

(Ready in about 20 minutes)

Per serving: 237 Calories; 10.8g Fat; 11.3g Carbs; 24.5g Protein; 5.1g Sugars; 3g Fiber

INGREDIENTS

1 tablespoon butter, melted
1/2 pound chicken legs, boneless and skinless
1/2 onion, diced
1/2 teaspoon garlic, minced

1/2 teaspoon ginger, peeled and grated
2 cups chicken stock
1/3 teaspoon dried sage
1/3 teaspoon dried thyme leaves
Sea salt and ground black pepper, to taste

1 tablespoon tamari sauce
1 carrot, diced
1 parsnip, diced
1 cup cauliflower florets

DIRECTIONS

Press the "Sauté" button and melt the butter. Once hot, sauté the chicken until golden brown; reserve.
Cook the onion, garlic, and ginger in pan drippings until just tender and aromatic.
Add the reserved chicken, stock, and spices.
Secure the lid. Choose the "Manual" mode and cook for 13 minutes at High pressure. Once cooking is complete, use a quick pressure release; carefully remove the lid.
Now, add the tamari sauce and vegetables to the inner pot.
Secure the lid. Choose the "Manual" mode and cook for 5 minutes at High pressure. Once cooking is complete, use a quick pressure release; carefully remove the lid. Serve immediately.

74. Vegetable Soup with Mediterranean Herbs

(Ready in about 15 minutes)

Per serving: 176 Calories; 9.2g Fat; 15.9g Carbs; 9.5g Protein; 6.1g Sugars; 4.5g Fiber

INGREDIENTS

1 tablespoon canola oil
1 shallot, chopped
1 garlic clove, minced
1/4 teaspoon dried oregano
1/3 teaspoon dried basil

1/3 teaspoon dried rosemary
1 ounce carrots, chopped
2 ounces frozen green peas
3 ounces frozen broccoli, chopped
2 ounces frozen green beans

1 ripe tomato, pureed
2 cups vegetable broth
Sea salt and ground black pepper, to taste
1/2 teaspoon red pepper flakes

DIRECTIONS

Press the "Sauté" button and heat the oil. Sauté the shallot until softened, approximately 4 minutes. Stir in the garlic and cook for 30 seconds more.
Add the dried herbs, frozen vegetables, tomatoes, vegetable broth, salt, and black pepper.
Secure the lid. Choose the "Manual" mode and cook for 4 minutes at High pressure. Once cooking is complete, use a quick pressure release; carefully remove the lid.
Divide between serving bowls and garnish with red pepper flakes. Bon appétit!

75. Creamy Asparagus Soup with Yogurt and Mint

(Ready in about 10 minutes)

Per serving: 146 Calories; 6.2g Fat; 14.4g Carbs; 11.3g Protein; 8g Sugars; 2.9g Fiber

INGREDIENTS

1/2 tablespoon butter
1/2 Asian shallot, chopped
1 garlic clove, minced
1/2 pound asparagus stalks, trimmed and chopped

Kosher salt and ground black pepper, to taste
2 cups chicken broth
1/2 cup yogurt
1 tablespoon fresh mint leaves, chopped

DIRECTIONS

Press the "Sauté" button and melt the butter. Once hot, cook the Asian shallots and garlic until just tender and fragrant.
Add the asparagus, salt, pepper, and broth.
Secure the lid. Choose the "Manual" mode and cook for 4 minutes at High pressure. Once cooking is complete, use a quick pressure release; carefully remove the lid.
Add the yogurt and blend the soup until it is completely smooth. Taste and season with more salt if desired.
Ladle into individual bowls; then, top each bowl with fresh mint leaves and serve.

76. Creamed Tomato Soup

(Ready in about 30 minutes)

Per serving: 245 Calories; 18g Fat; 12.6g Carbs; 7.3g Protein; 4.9g Sugars; 3.1g Fiber

INGREDIENTS

1/2 tablespoon olive oil
1/2 cup green onions, chopped
1 stalk green garlic, chopped
1/2 celery stalk, diced
1 carrot, diced

1 cup vegetable broth
Sea salt and ground black pepper, to your liking
1/2 teaspoon cayenne pepper
1/2 teaspoon fresh basil, chopped

1/2 teaspoon fresh rosemary, chopped
10 ounces cabbed tomatoes, crushed
1/4 cup double cream
2 ounces feta cheese, cubed
1/2 tablespoon olive oil

DIRECTIONS

Press the "Sauté" button and heat 1/2 tablespoon of olive oil. Sauté the green onions, garlic, celery, and carrots until softened.

Add the vegetable broth, salt, black pepper, cayenne pepper, basil, rosemary, and tomatoes to the inner pot.

Secure the lid. Choose the "Manual" mode and cook for 6 minutes at High pressure. Once cooking is complete, use a natural pressure release for 10 minutes; carefully remove the lid.

Stir in the double cream and seal the lid again; let it sit for 10 minutes more. Ladle into soup bowls; garnish with feta and 1/2 tablespoon of olive oil. Bon appétit!

77. Easy Ukrainian Borscht

(Ready in about 20 minutes)

Per serving: 266 Calories; 7.3g Fat; 42.3g Carbs; 4.6g Protein; 21g Sugars; 7.5g Fiber

INGREDIENTS

1 tablespoon safflower oil
1/2 red onion, chopped
1 clove garlic, minced
1/2 pound Yukon potatoes, peeled and diced

1 carrot, chopped
1 small red bell pepper, finely chopped
1/3 pound red bee roots, grated
1/2 tablespoon cider vinegar
1 tablespoon tomato paste

Sea salt and freshly ground black pepper, to taste
1 bay leaf
1/3 teaspoon ground cumin
2 cups chicken stock

DIRECTIONS

Press the "Sauté" button and heat the oil. Once hot, cook the onion for about 2 minutes or until softened.

Add the garlic, potatoes, carrots, bell pepper, and beets to the inner pot. Add the remaining ingredients to the inner pot and stir until everything is well combined.

Secure the lid. Choose the "Manual" mode and cook for 10 minutes at High pressure. Once cooking is complete, use a natural pressure release; carefully remove the lid.

To serve, add more salt and vinegar if desired. Bon appétit!

78. Ditalini Soup with Chicken

(Ready in about 25 minutes)

Per serving: 476 Calories; 20.4g Fat; 38.6g Carbs; 34.4g Protein; 6.6g Sugars; 5.3g Fiber

INGREDIENTS

1 tablespoon coconut oil, melted
1/2 pound chicken breast, skinless and boneless
1/2 white onion, chopped

1 clove garlic, pressed
1 serrano pepper, minced
2 tablespoons all-purpose flour
2 cups vegetable broth

1 cup cauliflower florets, frozen
1 cup Ditalini pasta
1/2 cup heavy cream
Sea salt and ground black pepper, to taste

DIRECTIONS

Press the "Sauté" button and heat the oil. Once hot, brown the chicken for 3 to 4 minutes per side; set aside.

Then, sauté the onion, garlic, and serrano pepper in pan drippings. Add the flour and continue to stir until your veggies are well coated.

Add the vegetable broth, cauliflower, and pasta to the inner pot; put the chicken back into the inner pot.

Secure the lid. Choose the "Manual" mode and cook for 6 minutes at High pressure. Once cooking is complete, use a quick pressure release; carefully remove the lid.

Stir in the cauliflower and Ditalini pasta. Secure the lid. Choose the "Manual" mode and cook for 5 minutes at High pressure. Once cooking is complete, use a quick pressure release; carefully remove the lid.

Shred the cooked chicken and add it back into the soup. Afterwards, add the heavy cream, salt, and black pepper. Seal the lid and let it sit in the residual heat for 5 minutes. Bon appétit!

79. Decadent Burger Soup

(Ready in about 30 minutes)

Per serving: 306 Calories; 16.2g Fat; 6.9g Carbs; 31.5g Protein; 0.9g Sugars; 1.1g Fiber

INGREDIENTS

1/2 tablespoon olive oil
1/2 pound ground beef
1/2 leek, diced
1 clove garlic, sliced
1 tablespoon cooking sherry
2 cups beef broth
4 ounces condensed tomato soup

1/2 teaspoon fish sauce
1/2 teaspoon basil
1/2 teaspoon oregano
1 bay leaf
1/4 teaspoon paprika
Sea salt and ground black pepper, to taste

DIRECTIONS

Press the "Sauté" button and heat the oil. Once hot, brown the ground beef for 2 to 3 minutes, stirring and crumbling with a wooden spoon.
Stir in the leeks and garlic; continue to sauté an additional 2 minutes, stirring continuously.
Add a splash of cooking sherry to deglaze the pot. Add the other ingredients to the inner pot.
Secure the lid. Choose the "Manual" mode and cook for 10 minutes at High pressure. Once cooking is complete, use a natural pressure release for 10 minutes; carefully remove the lid.
Serve warm with crusty bread, if desired. Bon appétit!

80. Italian-Style Sausage and Cabbage Soup

(Ready in about 20 minutes)

Per serving: 427 Calories; 33.4g Fat; 15.1g Carbs; 17.8g Protein; 5.8g Sugars; 6.8g Fiber

INGREDIENTS

1 tablespoon olive oil
1/2 pound beef sausage, thinly sliced
1/2 onion, chopped
1 clove garlic. minced
1/2 stalk celery, chopped
1/2 carrot, peeled and chopped
2 tablespoons Italian cooking wine

1/2 pound head cabbage, shredded into small pieces
2 cups beef bone broth
1/2 tablespoon Italia seasoning blend
1/2 teaspoon cayenne pepper
1 bay leaf
Salt and cracked black pepper, to taste

DIRECTIONS

Press the "Sauté" button and heat the oil. Once hot, cook the beef sausage until no longer pink. Now, stir in the onion and garlic; continue to sauté until they are fragrant.
Add a splash of cooking wine, scraping up any browned bits from the bottom of the inner pot. Add the remaining ingredients.
Secure the lid. Choose the "Manual" mode and cook for 6 minutes at High pressure. Once cooking is complete, use a quick pressure release; carefully remove the lid.
Divide between soup bowls and serve immediately.

SIDE DISHES

81. Couscous Florentine with Yogurt and Tahini

(Ready in about 10 minutes)

Per serving: 563 Calories; 9.2g Fat; 98g Carbs; 19.6g Protein; 7.3g Sugars; 6.7g Fiber

INGREDIENTS

1/2 tablespoon olive oil
1 bell peppers, diced
1/2 pound couscous
1 cup vegetable broth
1/2 cucumber, diced
1 tomato, sliced

1 tablespoon fresh mint, roughly chopped
A bunch of scallions, sliced
4 tablespoons yogurt
1 tablespoon sesame butter (tahini)
1/2 tablespoon honey

DIRECTIONS

Press the "Sauté" button and heat the oil; then, sauté the peppers until tender and aromatic. Stir in the couscous and vegetable broth.
Secure the lid. Choose the "Manual" mode and cook for 2 minutes at High pressure. Once cooking is complete, use a quick pressure release; carefully remove the lid.
Then, stir in the remaining ingredients; stir to combine well and enjoy!

82. Buttery Garlicky Mushrooms with Herbs

(Ready in about 20 minutes)

Per serving: 147 Calories; 12.2g Fat; 8.7g Carbs; 3.5g Protein; 3.6g Sugars; 2.5g Fiber

INGREDIENTS

2 tablespoons butter
1/2 pound white mushrooms
1 garlic clove, minced
1 thyme sprig, chopped

1 rosemary sprig, chopped
1/2 teaspoon cayenne pepper
Sea salt and ground black pepper, to taste

DIRECTIONS

Press the "Sauté" button and melt the butter. Once hot, cook your mushrooms for about 4 minutes, stirring occasionally to ensure even cooking.
Add the garlic and spices; toss to coat.
Secure the lid. Choose the "Manual" mode and cook for 12 minutes at High pressure. Once cooking is complete, use a natural pressure release for 5 minutes; carefully remove the lid. Serve warm.

83. French-Style Peppers

(Ready in about 10 minutes)

Per serving: 178 Calories; 13.7g Fat; 13.7g Carbs; 2.3g Protein; 8.4g Sugars; 1.7g Fiber

INGREDIENTS

2 tablespoons olive oil
4 bell peppers, seeded and sliced
Sea salt and ground black pepper, to taste

1/2 cup court bouillon
1/2 cup water
2 tablespoons balsamic vinegar

DIRECTIONS

Press the "Sauté" button and heat the oil. Once hot, cook the peppers until just tender and fragrant.
Add the salt and black pepper. Pour in the bouillon and water.
Secure the lid. Choose the "Manual" mode and cook for 3 minutes at High pressure. Once cooking is complete, use a quick pressure release.
Drizzle balsamic vinegar over your peppers and serve immediately.

84. Restaurant-Style Mexican Rice

(Ready in about 30 minutes)

Per serving: 376 Calories; 8.1g Fat; 61g Carbs; 6.9g Protein; 3.3g Sugars; 3.7g Fiber

INGREDIENTS

1 tablespoon canola oil
1 garlic clove, minced
1 small-sized leek, chopped
1 bell pepper, seeded and finely chopped
1 fresh serrano pepper, seeded and finely chopped
2 cups vegetable stock
1 tablespoon fresh parsley leaves, chopped

1/2 tablespoon cumin seeds
1/2 teaspoon mustard seeds
3/4 cup white rice
1/2 teaspoon salt
1/4 teaspoon cayenne pepper
1/4 teaspoon freshly ground black pepper

DIRECTIONS

Press the "Sauté" button and heat the oil. Once hot, cook the garlic, leek, and peppers until tender and aromatic.
Add the remaining ingredients and stir to combine.
Secure the lid. Choose the "Rice" mode and cook for 10 minutes. Once cooking is complete, use a natural pressure release for 15 minutes; carefully remove the lid.
Serve in individual bowls and enjoy!

85. Zingy Kamut with Spinach and Lime

(Ready in about 20 minutes)

Per serving: 314 Calories; 14.3g Fat; 43g Carbs; 7.2g Protein; 1.3g Sugars; 7.7g Fiber

INGREDIENTS

3/4 cup dried kamut
1 ½ cups water
1 cup baby spinach
1/2 carrot, cut into sticks
1 celery rib, sliced

1/2 shallot, finely chopped
2 tablespoons olive oil
Salt and freshly ground black pepper, to taste
1 tablespoon fresh lime juice

DIRECTIONS

Add the kamut and water to the inner pot.
Secure the lid. Choose the "Manual" mode and cook for 9 minutes at High pressure. Once cooking is complete, use a quick pressure release.
Add the vegetables, olive oil, salt, and black pepper.
Secure the lid. Choose the "Manual" mode and cook for 3 minutes at High pressure. Once cooking is complete, use a quick pressure release.
Drizzle fresh lime juice over each serving and enjoy!

86. Spicy Kashmiri Eggplant

(Ready in about 40 minutes)

Per serving: 105 Calories; 6.7g Fat; 11.2g Carbs; 2.1g Protein; 6.6g Sugars; 4.5g Fiber

INGREDIENTS

1/2 pound eggplant, sliced
1/2 tablespoon sea salt
1/2 tablespoon sesame oil
1/2 teaspoon cumin seeds
1 shallot, chopped

1/2 tablespoon butter
1/2 cup water
1/2 Kashmiri chili pepper, chopped
1 tomato, pureed
2 curry leaves

DIRECTIONS

Toss the eggplant with sea salt in a colander. Let it sit for 30 minutes; then squeeze out the excess liquid.
Press the "Sauté" button and heat the sesame oil; now sauté the cumin seeds for 30 seconds or until aromatic. Then, cook the shallots for 2 to 3 minutes more or until they have softened.
Then, melt the butter. Now, cook the eggplant until lightly charred. Add the water, chili pepper, tomatoes, and curry leaves to the inner pot.
Secure the lid. Choose the "Manual" mode and cook for 2 minutes at High pressure. Once cooking is complete, use a quick pressure release; carefully remove the lid.
Serve in individual bowls and enjoy!

87. Fettuccine Pasta alla Parmigiana

(Ready in about 20 minutes)

Per serving: 528 Calories; 15.2g Fat; 59g Carbs; 10g Protein; 0.1g Sugars; 12g Fiber

INGREDIENTS

1/2 pound fettuccine

2 cups water

2 tablespoons butter, cubed

Sea salt and ground black pepper, to season

2 tablespoons Parmesan cheese, grated

DIRECTIONS

Place the fettuccine and water in the inner pot of your Instant Pot.

Secure the lid. Choose the "Manual" mode and cook for 4 minutes at High pressure. Once cooking is complete, use a natural pressure release for 10 minutes; carefully remove the lid.

Toss the boiled fettuccine with the butter, salt, black pepper, and parmesan cheese; serve immediately. Bon appétit!

88. Sweet Potato Mash

(Ready in about 15 minutes)

Per serving: 303 Calories; 9g Fat; 43g Carbs; 9.3g Protein; 1.9g Sugars; 5.4g Fiber

INGREDIENTS

1 pound sweet potatoes, peeled and diced

1/2 cup water

1/2 teaspoon sea salt

2 scallion stalks, finely sliced

2 tablespoons fresh parsley leaves, roughly chopped

1 garlic clove, pressed

1/4 cup sour cream

1 tablespoon butter

A pinch of grated nutmeg

1/ teaspoon cayenne pepper

DIRECTIONS

Add the sweet potatoes and water to the Instant Pot.

Secure the lid. Choose the "Manual" mode and cook for 8 minutes at High pressure. Once cooking is complete, use a quick pressure release; carefully remove the lid.

Drain the potatoes. Mash the potatoes using a potato masher or your food processor.

Now, add the remaining ingredients and stir well to combine. Enjoy!

89. Black Eyed Peas with Spinach and Bacon

(Ready in about 40 minutes)

Per serving: 316 Calories; 11.1g Fat; 38.1g Carbs; 15.2g Protein; 0.4g Sugars; 7g Fiber

INGREDIENTS

2 strips bacon, cut into 1/2-inch pieces

1/2 pound dry black eyed peas

2 cups chicken stock

1/4 teaspoon cayenne pepper

1/4 teaspoon dried dill

1/4 teaspoon dried oregano

1/4 teaspoon dried sage

Kosher salt and freshly ground black pepper, to taste

1 cup spinach, torn into pieces

DIRECTIONS

Press the "Sauté" button to preheat your Instant Pot. Now, cook the bacon until it is crisp; reserve.

Add the black-eyed peas, chicken stock, and all the slices to the inner pot.

Secure the lid. Choose the "Manual" mode and cook for 18 minutes at High pressure. Once cooking is complete, use a natural pressure release for 10 minutes; carefully remove the lid.

Lastly, stir in the spinach leaves; seal the lid and let it sit in the residual heat for 5 to 10 minutes.

Ladle into serving bowls and garnish with the reserved bacon. Bon appétit!

90. Zingy Garlicky Kale with Lemon

(Ready in about 10 minutes)

Per serving: 146 Calories; 5.5g Fat; 20.9g Carbs; 9g Protein; 5.1g Sugars; 8g Fiber

INGREDIENTS

1/2 tablespoon olive oil

2 cloves garlic, slivered

1 pound kale, cleaned and trimmed

1 cup water

Kosher salt and ground black pepper, to taste

1/4 teaspoon cayenne pepper

Fresh juice squeezed from 1/2 a lemon

DIRECTIONS

Press the "Sauté" button and heat the oil until sizzling. Now, cook the garlic until just tender and aromatic.

Add the chopped kale and water to the inner pot. Sprinkle with salt, black pepper, and cayenne pepper.

Secure the lid. Choose the "Manual" mode and cook for 4 minutes at High pressure. Once cooking is complete, use a quick pressure release.

Scoop the kale out of the inner pot with a slotted spoon, leaving as much cooking liquid behind as possible. Drizzle fresh lemon juice over the kale and serve. Bon appétit!

91. Cauliflower Rice with Butter and Parsley

(Ready in about 10 minutes)

Per serving: 127 Calories; 8.3g Fat; 11.7g Carbs; 4.5g Protein; 4.4g Sugars; 4.8g Fiber

INGREDIENTS

1 pound cauliflower

Sea salt, to taste

1/2 teaspoon white pepper

1 tablespoon butter

1 tablespoon fresh parsley, roughly chopped

DIRECTIONS

Add the cauliflower florets and 1 cup of water to the inner pot.

Secure the lid. Choose the "Manual" mode and cook for 2 minutes at High pressure. Once cooking is complete, use a quick pressure release.

Stir the salt, pepper, and butter into warm cauliflower rice.

Serve garnished with fresh parsley and enjoy!

92. Hearty Cabbage Bowl

(Ready in about 10 minutes)

Per serving: 160 Calories; 8.4g Fat; 20g Carbs; 2.8g Protein; 10.1g Sugars; 5g Fiber

INGREDIENTS

1 tablespoon olive oil

2 cloves garlic, minced

1/3 cup green onions, sliced

3/4 pound purple cabbage, shredded

1 carrot, cut into sticks

Kosher salt and ground black pepper, to taste

1 tablespoon soy sauce

DIRECTIONS

Press the "Sauté" button and add the oil. Once hot, cook the garlic and green onions until softened.

Add the cabbage, carrots, salt, and black pepper.

Secure the lid. Choose the "Manual" mode and cook for 4 minutes at High pressure. Once cooking is complete, use a quick pressure release.

Lstly, add the soy sauce to the cabbage mixture and stir to combine well. Place in a serving bowl and serve immediately.

93. Mediterranean Saucy Eggplant

(Ready in about 10 minutes)

Per serving: 304 Calories; 29g Fat; 9.4g Carbs; 2.6g Protein; 6g Sugars; 3.6g Fiber

INGREDIENTS

1/2 pound eggplant, sliced
1/2 tablespoon sea salt
1 tablespoon olive oil
1/4 cup Greek yogurt
4 tablespoons mayonnaise

1 teaspoon balsamic vinegar
1 garlic clove, minced
1 tablespoon olives, pitted and minced
1 tablespoon fresh coriander, chopped

DIRECTIONS

Toss the eggplant with sea salt in a colander. Let it sit for 30 minutes; then squeeze out the excess liquid.

Press the "Sauté" button and heat the olive oil. Now, cook the eggplant until lightly charred. Add 1 cup of water to the inner pot.

Secure the lid. Choose the "Manual" mode and cook for 2 minutes at High pressure. Once cooking is complete, use a quick pressure release; carefully remove the lid.

Meanwhile, whisk the remaining ingredients until well combined. Drizzle this dressing over the eggplant and serve at once. Bon appétit!

94. Indian Rice with Yogurt

(Ready in about 25 minutes)

Per serving: 417 Calories; 11.7g Fat; 50.2g Carbs; 8.5g Protein; 4.9g Sugars; 2.4g Fiber

INGREDIENTS

2 tablespoons grapeseed oil
1/2 teaspoon fennel seeds
4 curry leaves
3/4 cup basmati rice, rinsed
1/2 chili pepper, minced

1/2 teaspoon fresh ginger, peeled and grated
1 cinnamon stick
Himalayan salt and ground black pepper, to taste
1/2 cup full-fat yogurt
1 tablespoon fresh dhania (coriander), chopped

DIRECTIONS

Press the "Sauté" button and heat the oil; now sauté the fennel seeds and curry leaves for 30 seconds or until aromatic.

Now, stir in the basmati rice, chili pepper, ginger, cinnamon, salt, and black pepper. Pour in 2 cups of water.

Secure the lid. Choose the "Manual" mode and cook for 4 minutes at High pressure. Once cooking is complete, use a natural pressure release for 15 minutes; carefully remove the lid.

Fluff your rice with a fork and stir in the yogurt. Stir until everything is well combined. Serve garnished with fresh dhania and enjoy!

95. Cholula Baked Beans

(Ready in about 1 hour 10 minutes)

Per serving: 605 Calories; 8.2g Fat; 109g Carbs; 25.2g Protein; 36.4g Sugars; 18.4g Fiber

INGREDIENTS

1/2 pounds pinto beans, rinsed and drained
4 cups water
1 tablespoon olive oil
1 onion, chopped
2 cloves garlic, minced

1/4 cup molasses
1/4 cup ketchup
1/2 teaspoon salt
1 tablespoon soy sauce
1/2 tablespoon Cholula hot sauce

DIRECTIONS

Place the beans and water in your Instant Pot.

Secure the lid. Choose the "Bean/Chili" mode and cook for 40 minutes at High pressure. Once cooking is complete, use a natural pressure release for 10 minutes; carefully remove the lid. Set aside.

Press the "Sauté" button and heat the oil until sizzling. Now, cook the onion and garlic until tender and fragrant. Add the reserved beans back to the inner pot. Stir in the remaining ingredients.

Secure the lid. Choose the "Manual" mode and cook for 10 minutes at High pressure. Once cooking is complete, use a quick pressure release. Bon appétit!

96. Tex-Mex Chili with Rice

(Ready in about 45 minutes)

Per serving: 328 Calories; 8.2g Fat; 52.3g Carbs; 15.3g Protein; 6.4g Sugars; 11.4g Fiber

INGREDIENTS

1 tablespoon canola oil
1 shallot, finely chopped
1/2 red chili pepper, seeded and minced
1 sweet pepper, seeded and finely chopped
1 tablespoon garlic, minced
1/2 cup tomato puree

1/2 cup brown rice
4 ounces black beans
1 cup chicken stock
Sea salt and ground black pepper, to taste
1 tablespoon fresh chives, chopped

DIRECTIONS

Press the "Sauté" button and heat the oil until sizzling. Now, cook the shallots, peppers, and garlic until tender and fragrant.
Add the tomato puree, rice, beans, stock, salt, and black pepper to the inner pot.
Secure the lid. Choose the "Manual" mode and cook for 25 minutes at High pressure. Once cooking is complete, use a natural pressure release for 15 minutes; carefully remove the lid.
Ladle into individual bowls and serve with fresh chives. Enjoy!

97. Crunchy Brussels Sprouts with Parmesan

(Ready in about 15 minutes)

Per serving: 184 Calories; 15.8g Fat; 10.1g Carbs; 3.9g Protein; 2.5g Sugars; 4.4g Fiber

INGREDIENTS

1/2 pound Brussels sprouts, trimmed and halved
1/4 stick butter
1/2 teaspoon basil
1/2 teaspoon rosemary

1/2 teaspoon garlic, minced
1/2 teaspoon shallot powder
Sea salt and red pepper, to taste

DIRECTIONS

Place 1 cup of water and a steamer basket in the inner pot of your Instant Pot. Place the Brussels sprouts in the steamer basket.
Secure the lid. Choose the "Steam" mode and cook for 3 minutes at High pressure. Once cooking is complete, use a quick pressure release; carefully remove the lid.
Press the "Sauté" button and melt the butter; once hot, cook the basil, rosemary, and garlic for 40 seconds or until aromatic.
Add in the Brussels sprouts, shallot powder, salt, and pepper. Press the "Cancel" button. Scatter the grated parmesan cheese over the Brussels sprouts and serve immediately. Bon appétit!

98. Steamed Sweet Potatoes with Butter

(Ready in about 30 minutes)

Per serving: 318 Calories; 23.3g Fat; 26.7g Carbs; 2.1g Protein; 8.7g Sugars; 3.8g Fiber

INGREDIENTS

2 medium sweet potatoes, scrubbed
1 cup water
1/4 cup butter

DIRECTIONS

Place 1 cup of water and a steamer basket in your Instant Pot. Place the sweet potatoes in the steamer basket.
Secure the lid. Choose the "Manual" mode and cook for 15 minutes at High pressure. Once cooking is complete, use a natural pressure release for 10 minutes; carefully remove the lid.
Garnish with butter and serve. Bon appétit!

99. Curried Chickpea with Avocado

(Ready in about 1 hour)

Per serving: 455 Calories; 30g Fat; 42g Carbs; 12.8g Protein; 13.1g Sugars; 11.3g Fiber

INGREDIENTS

1/2 cup chickpeas, rinsed
1/2 teaspoon sea salt
1/2 teaspoon baking soda
1/2 avocado, peeled, pitted, and sliced

1/4 cup scallions, sliced
1/2 cup cherry tomatoes, halved
1 bell pepper, sliced
3 tablespoons olive oil

1 tablespoon fresh lemon juice
1/4 teaspoon curry powder
Sea salt and ground black pepper, to taste

DIRECTIONS

Add the dry chickpeas to the inner pot; pour in 6 cups of water. Add the sea salt and baking soda.

Secure the lid. Choose the "Manual" mode and cook for 35 minutes at High pressure. Once cooking is complete, use a natural pressure release for 20 minutes; carefully remove the lid.

Drain and transfer to a nice serving bowl. Toss the cooked chickpeas with the other ingredients; toss to combine well. Bon appétit!

100. Sausage and Cheese Stuffed Mushrooms

(Ready in about 15 minutes)

Per serving: 268 Calories; 14.1g Fat; 17.2g Carbs; 16.2g Protein; 6.5g Sugars; 3.2g Fiber

INGREDIENTS

8 button mushrooms, stems removed
2 ounces smoked pork sausage, crumbled
1/2 shallot, finely chopped
1 clove garlic, minced
2 ounces cream cheese, softened

1/4 cup seasoned breadcrumbs
2 ounces cheddar cheese, shredded
1/3 cup vegetable broth
1 tablespoon fresh parsley leaves, roughly chopped

DIRECTIONS

Clean your mushrooms and set them aside.

Press the "Sauté" button to preheat your Instant Pot. Then, brown the sausage until it is fully cooked.

Stir in the shallot and garlic; cook for a further 4 minutes, or until they have softened. Scoop this mixture out of the inner pot into a mixing bowl. Stir in the cream cheese, breadcrumbs, and cheddar cheese.

Now, add a splash of the vegetable broth to deglaze the pan. Press the "Cancel" button.

Next, fill the mushroom caps with the stuffing mixture. Arrange the mushrooms in the bottom of the inner pot.

Secure the lid. Choose the "Manual" mode and cook for 5 minutes at High pressure. Once cooking is complete, use a quick pressure release; carefully remove the lid.

Sprinkle fresh parsley leaves on top before serving and enjoy!

101. Tangy Glazed Root Vegetables

(Ready in about 20 minutes)

Per serving: 181 Calories; 6.9g Fat; 31.5g Carbs; 3.4g Protein; 20g Sugars; 6.8g Fiber

INGREDIENTS

1/2 pound carrots
1/4 pound yellow beets
1/4 pound red beets
1 tablespoon cold butter

1 tablespoon orange juice
1/2 teaspoon orange peel, finely shredded
1 tablespoon maple syrup
Kosher salt and ground black pepper, to taste

DIRECTIONS

Place 1 cup of water and a steamer basket in your Instant Pot. Place the carrots and beets in the steamer basket.

Secure the lid. Choose the "Steam" mode and cook for 10 minutes at High pressure. Once cooking is complete, use a quick pressure release; carefully remove the lid.

Peel the carrots and beets and reserve; slice them into bite-sized pieces.

Press the "Sauté" button and choose the lowest setting. Cut in butter and add the remaining ingredients.

Drain the carrots and beets and add them back to the inner pot; let them cook until your vegetables are nicely coated with the glaze or about 5 minutes. Bon appétit!

102. Aromatic Baby Potatoes with Herbs

(Ready in about 15 minutes)

Per serving: 249 Calories; 7.1g Fat; 42.3g Carbs; 5.2g Protein; 3.1g Sugars; 5.8g Fiber

INGREDIENTS

1 pound baby potatoes, scrubbed
1 garlic clove, smashed
1/4 cup roasted vegetable broth
1/4 cup water
1 tablespoon olive oil
1/2 teaspoon paprika

1/2 teaspoon oregano
1/2 teaspoon basil
1/2 teaspoon rosemary
1/2 teaspoon sage
Sea salt and ground black pepper, to taste

DIRECTIONS

Pierce the baby potatoes with a fork; place them in the inner pot along with the garlic, broth, and water.
Secure the lid. Choose the "Manual" mode and cook for 10 minutes at High pressure. Once cooking is complete, use a quick pressure release; carefully remove the lid. Drain and reserve.
Press the "Sauté" button and heat the olive oil until sizzling. Now, sauté the seasonings for 30 seconds, stirring frequently. Throw the reserved potatoes into the inner pot.
Cook until they are browned and crisp on all sides. Serve warm.

103. Easy Okra with Tomato and Shallots

(Ready in about 25 minutes)

Per serving: 162 Calories; 4.5g Fat; 24.8g Carbs; 5.7g Protein; 8.4g Sugars; 7.8g Fiber

INGREDIENTS

1/2 tablespoon olive oil
1 shallot, chopped
1/2 cup tomato puree
2 tablespoons tomato ketchup
3/4 pound okra
1/2 cup chicken stock

1/2 teaspoon garlic powder
1/2 teaspoon turmeric powder
1/2 teaspoon porcini powder
1/2 teaspoon fish sauce
Sea salt and ground black pepper, to taste

DIRECTIONS

Press the "Sauté" button and heat the oil until sizzling. Now, sauté the shallot until tender and fragrant.
Add in the remaining ingredients and gently stir to combine well.
Secure the lid. Choose the "Manual" mode and cook for 5 minutes at High pressure. Once cooking is complete, use a natural pressure release for 15 minutes; carefully remove the lid.
Divide between serving bowls and serve warm. Bon appétit!

104. Decadent Balsamic Brussels Sprouts with Cranberries

(Ready in about 10 minutes)

Per serving: 185 Calories; 7.7g Fat; 26.3g Carbs; 8.2g Protein; 8.2g Sugars; 9.6g Fiber

INGREDIENTS

1 tablespoon sesame oil
2 cloves garlic, sliced
1 pound Brussels sprouts, halved
1/2 cup vegetable broth

4 tablespoons dried cranberries
2 tablespoons balsamic vinegar
1/4 teaspoon dried dill weed
Kosher salt and freshly ground black pepper, to taste

DIRECTIONS

Press the "Sauté" button and heat the oil; then, sauté the garlic until just tender and fragrant.
Stir in the Brussels sprouts and continue to sauté an additional 2 to 3 minutes.
Add the remaining ingredients to the inner pot.
Secure the lid. Choose the "Manual" mode and cook for 2 minutes at High pressure. Once cooking is complete, use a quick pressure release; carefully remove the lid. Bon appétit!

105. Steamed Spicy and Cheesy Potatoes

(Ready in about 30 minutes)

Per serving: 258 Calories; 5.9g Fat; 39.1g Carbs; 6g Protein; 3g Sugars; 5g Fiber

INGREDIENTS

2 medium potatoes, peeled
1/4 cup cream cheese
2 tablespoons salsa

DIRECTIONS

Place 1 cup of water and a metal trivet in the inner pot of your Instant Pot. Pierce your potatoes with a fork; place them on the trivet.
Secure the lid. Choose the "Steam" mode and cook for 15 minutes at High pressure. Once cooking is complete, use a natural pressure release for 10 minutes; carefully remove the lid.
Top the warm potatoes with the cream cheese and salsa and serve immediately. Bon appétit!

106. Sesame Crispy Asparagus

(Ready in about 10 minutes)

Per serving: 156 Calories; 11.9g Fat; 9.7g Carbs; 6.6g Protein; 4.3g Sugars; 6.3g Fiber

INGREDIENTS

1 pound fresh asparagus, trimmed
1 tablespoon sesame oil
2 tablespoons sesame seeds, toasted
1 teaspoon garlic powder
Kosher salt and red pepper, to taste

DIRECTIONS

Add 1 cup of water and a steamer basket to the inner pot. Place the asparagus in the steamer basket.
Secure the lid. Choose the "Steam" mode and cook for 3 minutes at High pressure. Once cooking is complete, use a quick pressure release; carefully remove the lid.
Toss the warm asparagus with the other ingredients. Enjoy!

107. Creamy Au Gratin Potatoes

(Ready in about 20 minutes)

Per serving: 440 Calories; 10.8g Fat; 60.1g Carbs; 16.5g Protein; 5.5g Sugars; 7.7g Fiber

INGREDIENTS

3 medium potatoes, peeled and thinly sliced
1/2 cup vegetable broth
1/2 shallot, chopped
1 garlic clove, sliced
1/2 teaspoon dried basil

Sea salt and ground black pepper, to taste
1/3 teaspoon paprika
1/4 cup heavy cream
1/2 cup Romano cheese, preferably freshly grated

DIRECTIONS

Arrange the sliced potatoes on the bottom of a lightly greased inner pot. Add the vegetable broth, shallot, garlic, basil, salt, black pepper and paprika to the inner pot.
Secure the lid. Choose the "Manual" mode and cook for 4 minutes at High pressure. Once cooking is complete, use a quick pressure release; carefully remove the lid.
Preheat your oven to broil. Transfer the potatoes to an oven-safe dish. Top with the heavy cream and Romano cheese.
Broil until the cheese is bubbling and golden brown. Let it sit on a cooling rack for 5 minutes before slicing and serving. Enjoy!

108. Spicy Corn on the Cob with Aioli

(Ready in about 10 minutes)

Per serving: 220 Calories; 10.2g Fat; 29.5g Carbs; 4.6g Protein; 0g Sugars; 3.8g Fiber

INGREDIENTS

2 ears corn on the cob, husked
Sriracha Aioli:
1/4 cup mayonnaise

1/2 tablespoon lemon juice
1 tablespoon Sriracha
1/4 teaspoon sea salt

DIRECTIONS

Add 1 cup of water and a metal trivet to the inner pot of your Instant Pot. Place your corn on the trivet.
Secure the lid. Choose the "Manual" mode and cook for 2 minutes at High pressure. Once cooking is complete, use a quick pressure release; carefully remove the lid.
Then, whisk the mayonnaise, lemon juice, Sriracha, and salt until well combined. Serve the warm corn on the cob with the Sriracha aioli on the side. Bon appétit!

109. Italian-Style Creamy Broccoli

(Ready in about 10 minutes)

Per serving: 246 Calories; 21g Fat; 12g Carbs; 4.2g Protein; 3.4g Sugars; 3.6g Fiber

INGREDIENTS

1/2 pound broccoli florets
2 garlic cloves, smashed
Kosher salt and ground black pepper, to taste

1/4 cup mayonnaise
1/2 tablespoon Italian seasoning mix

DIRECTIONS

Add 1 cup of water and steamer basket to the inner pot. Place the broccoli florets in the steamer basket.
Secure the lid. Choose the "Manual" mode and cook for 1 minute at High pressure. Once cooking is complete, use a quick pressure release; carefully remove the lid.
Sprinkle the garlic, salt, and black pepper over the cooked broccoli florets.
Mix the mayonnaise with the Italian seasoning mix; serve your broccoli with the Italian mayo on the side. Bon appétit!

110. Creamed Ranch Potatoes

(Ready in about 20 minutes)

Per serving: 379 Calories; 9.4g Fat; 66.7g Carbs; 8.5g Protein; 2.9g Sugars; 8.2g Fiber

INGREDIENTS

2 large Yukon gold potatoes
1/4 cup sour cream
2 tablespoons reduced-fat mayonnaise
1/2 teaspoon fresh parsley, chopped

1/2 teaspoon fresh chives, chopped
1 garlic clove, minced
Sea salt and ground black pepper, to taste

DIRECTIONS

Add 1 ½ cups of water and a steamer basket to the inner pot. Now, place the potatoes in the steamer basket.
Secure the lid. Choose the "Steam" mode and cook for 10 minutes at High pressure. Once cooking is complete, use a quick pressure release; carefully remove the lid.
Meanwhile, in a mixing bowl, whisk together the sour cream and mayonnaise. Stir in the fresh herbs, garlic, salt, and black pepper.
Drain your potatoes, peel and slice them; toss your potatoes with ranch dressing. Bon appétit!

111. Bucatini alla Puttanesca

(Ready in about 25 minutes)

Per serving: 490 Calories; 7.2g Fat; 77g Carbs; 19.3g Protein; 0.2g Sugars; 12g Fiber

INGREDIENTS

1/2 tablespoon olive oil
1 garlic clove, pressed
1/4 cup black olives, pitted, and thinly sliced
1 tablespoon capers, soaked and rinsed
4 vine-ripened tomato, pureed

1/2 tablespoon Italian seasoning blend
Coarse salt, to taste
1/2 pound bucatini pasta
1 cup water

DIRECTIONS

Press the "Sauté" button and add the oil. Once hot, cook the garlic until aromatic. Add the black olives, capers, tomatoes, Italian seasoning blend, and salt.
Bring to a boil and turn the Instant Pot to the lowest setting; let the sauce simmer for 10 to 13 minutes. Stir in the bucatini pasta and water.
Secure the lid. Choose the "Manual" mode and cook for 8 minutes at High pressure. Once cooking is complete, use a quick pressure release.
Serve warm and enjoy!

112. Green Beans with Garlic and Chives

(Ready in about 10 minutes)

Per serving: 117 Calories; 7.2g Fat; 12.6g Carbs; 3.3g Protein; 5.6g Sugars; 4.3g Fiber

INGREDIENTS

1 tablespoons olive oil
1 garlic clove, minced
1 pound green beans, trimmed

Salt and freshly ground black pepper, to taste
1/2 teaspoon cayenne pepper
1 tablespoon fresh chives, chopped

DIRECTIONS

Press the "Sauté" button and heat the oil until sizzling. Now, sauté the garlic until tender but not browned.
Add the green beans, salt, black pepper, and cayenne pepper to the inner pot. Pour in 1 cup of water.
Secure the lid. Choose the "Manual" mode and cook for 3 minutes at High pressure. Once cooking is complete, use a quick pressure release; carefully remove the lid.
Garnish with fresh chives and serve warm.

113. Warm Millet Salad with Roasted Tomatoes

(Ready in about 45 minutes)

Per serving: 278 Calories; 9.1g Fat; 42g Carbs; 6.5g Protein; 4.1g Sugars; 5.9g Fiber

INGREDIENTS

1/2 pound small-sized tomatoes, halved
1 tablespoon olive oil
Sea salt and ground black pepper, to taste
1/2 cup millet
1 cup water

DIRECTIONS

Preheat your oven to 350 degrees F. Place your tomatoes in a roasting pan. Drizzle olive oil over them; season with salt and pepper. Roast for about 35 minutes or until the tomatoes are soft.
Meanwhile, combine the millet with water in the inner pot of your Instant Pot.
Secure the lid. Choose the "Manual" mode and cook for 9 minutes at High pressure. Once cooking is complete, use a natural pressure release for 10 minutes; carefully remove the lid.
Add the roasted tomatoes to the warm millet and serve immediately.

114. Kidney Bean Curry

(Ready in about 35 minutes)

Per serving: 355 Calories; 18.2g Fat; 43.1g Carbs; 7.5g Protein; 2.4g Sugars; 8.6g Fiber

INGREDIENTS

1/2 pound red kidney beans
4 cups water
1 tablespoon canola oil
1/2 onion, finely sliced
1/2 teaspoon ginger garlic paste

1/4 teaspoon red curry paste
1 small-sized potato, peeled and diced
1/2 green chili pepper, finely chopped
Sea salt and freshly ground black
pepper, to taste

1/2 teaspoon turmeric powder
1/2 teaspoon avocado powder
1 tomato, pureed
1/2 tablespoon fenugreek, chopped

DIRECTIONS

Add the red kidney beans and water to the inner pot of your Instant Pot.

Secure the lid. Choose the "Bean/Chili" mode and cook for 25 minutes at High pressure. Once cooking is complete, use a quick pressure release; carefully remove the lid. Drain and reserve.

Press the "Sauté" button and heat the oil until sizzling. Now, sauté the onion until tender and translucent.

Add the remaining ingredients. Gently stir to combine.

Secure the lid. Choose the "Manual" mode and cook for 4 minutes at High pressure. Once cooking is complete, use a quick pressure release; carefully remove the lid.

Stir the reserved beans into the potato mixture and serve warm. Bon appétit!

115. Corn Chaat (Masala Corn)

(Ready in about 10 minutes)

Per serving: 124 Calories; 6.7g Fat; 16.1g Carbs; 2.8g Protein; 3.1g Sugars; 1.9g Fiber

INGREDIENTS

1 cup sweet corn kernels, frozen
1 tablespoon ghee
1/2 teaspoon turmeric powder

Himalayan salt and ground black pepper, to taste
1/3 teaspoon red chili powder
1/3 teaspoon chaat masala powder

DIRECTIONS

Place all ingredients in the inner pot of your Instant Pot.

Secure the lid. Choose the "Manual" mode and cook for 4 minutes at High pressure. Once cooking is complete, use a quick pressure release; carefully remove the lid.

Serve immediately.

116. Aromatic Cauliflower Kurma

(Ready in about 30 minutes)

Per serving: 262 Calories; 21.2g Fat; 18.1g Carbs; 4.1g Protein; 8.3g Sugars; 5.6g Fiber

INGREDIENTS

1 cup cauliflower florets
1 tablespoon grapeseed oil
1/2 teaspoon cumin seeds
1/2 teaspoon fennel seeds
1/2 dried red chili pepper, minced
1/2 onion, chopped

1/2 cup tomato puree
Kosher salt and ground black pepper,
to taste
1/2 teaspoon turmeric powder
1/2 cup fresh coconut, shredded
1 cup water

Tempering:
1 tablespoon peanut oil
1 teaspoon cumin seeds
4 curry leaves

DIRECTIONS

Add 1 cup of water and a steamer basket to the inner pot of your Instant Pot. Place the cauliflower florets in the steamer basket.

Secure the lid. Choose the "Steam" mode and cook for 3 minutes at High pressure. Once cooking is complete, use a quick pressure release; carefully remove the lid. Drain and reserve.

Press the "Sauté" button and heat the grapeseed oil until sizzling. Now, sauté the cumin seeds and fennel seeds for 30 seconds.

Stir in the chili pepper and onion and continue to sauté an additional 2 to 3 minutes. Add the tomato puree and let it cook on the lowest setting for 3 minutes longer.

Add the salt, black pepper, turmeric, coconut, and water.

Secure the lid. Choose the "Manual" mode and cook for 5 minutes at High pressure. Once cooking is complete, use a natural pressure release for 10 minutes; carefully remove the lid. Stir in the steamed cauliflower florets.

Meanwhile, heat the peanut oil in a cast-iron skillet over medium heat. Cook the cumin seeds and curry leaves until they are fragrant. Stir the tempering into the cauliflower mixture and serve warm.

117. Classic Italian Caponata

(Ready in about 15 minutes)

Per serving: 233 Calories; 17.1g Fat; 17.5g Carbs; 5.1g Protein; 7.7g Sugars; 2.9g Fiber

INGREDIENTS

2 tablespoons olive oil
1/2 onion, diced
1 garlic clove, minced
Sea salt and ground black pepper
1/2 cup butternut squash, cut into 1/2-inch chunks

2 bell peppers, cut into 1/2-inch chunks
1/2 cup vine-ripened tomatoes, pureed
1/2 tablespoon Italian seasoning mix
2 tablespoons Parmigiano-Reggiano cheese, grated

DIRECTIONS

Press the "Sauté" button and heat the olive oil until sizzling. Now, sauté the onion until tender and translucent.

Stir in the garlic and continue to sauté an additional 30 seconds, stirring frequently.

Stir in the salt, black pepper, butternut squash, peppers, tomatoes, and Italian seasoning mix.

Secure the lid. Choose the "Manual" mode and cook for 4 minutes at High pressure. Once cooking is complete, use a quick pressure release; carefully remove the lid.

Afterwards, scatter the grated cheese over the caponata and serve warm. Bon appétit!

118. Peppery Red Lentils

(Ready in about 10 minutes)

Per serving: 226 Calories; 1.3g Fat; 43g Carbs; 13.5g Protein; 2.6g Sugars; 7g Fiber

INGREDIENTS

1/2 cup red lentils
1 cup water
1 sweet pepper, seeded and chopped
1/2 habanero pepper, seeded and chopped

1/2 leek, sliced
1 teaspoon garlic, pressed
Kosher salt and ground black pepper, to taste
2 tablespoons fresh cilantro, roughly chopped

DIRECTIONS

Add all ingredients, except for the fresh cilantro, to the inner pot of your Instant Pot.

Secure the lid. Choose the "Manual" mode and cook for 2 minutes at High pressure. Once cooking is complete, use a quick pressure release; carefully remove the lid.

Spoon the lentil mixture into a nice serving bowl. Serve garnished with fresh cilantro and enjoy!

119. Sticky Cauliflower with Tahini

(Ready in about 15 minutes)

Per serving: 247 Calories; 19.2g Fat; 14.5g Carbs; 7.4g Protein; 3.9g Sugars; 5g Fiber

INGREDIENTS

1/2 pound cauliflower florets
1/2 tablespoon olive oil
1/4 cup tahini
1 tablespoon freshly squeezed lemon juice

1 clove garlic, grated
1 teaspoon agave syrup
Kosher salt and freshly ground black pepper, to taste
1 tablespoon fresh parsley, chopped

DIRECTIONS

Place 1 cup of water and a steamer basket in your Instant Pot. Place the cauliflower florets in the steamer basket.

Secure the lid. Choose the "Steam" mode and cook for 3 minutes at High pressure. Once cooking is complete, use a quick pressure release; carefully remove the lid.

Press the "Sauté" button and heat the oil. Roast the cauliflower florets for 2 to 3 minutes, stirring periodically to ensure even cooking.

Whisk the tahini, lemon juice, garlic agave syrup, salt, and black pepper until everything is well incorporated. Drizzle the tahini sauce over the roasted cauliflower and garnish with fresh parsley. Enjoy!

120. Fall Vegetable Mash

(Ready in about 10 minutes)

Per serving: 174 Calories; 6.3g Fat; 28g Carbs; 2.9g Protein; 10.2g Sugars; 6.4g Fiber

INGREDIENTS

1/3 pound carrots, quartered

1/3 pound parsnip, quartered

1/2 pound pumpkin, cut into small pieces

1 tablespoon butter

1 clove garlic, crushed

1/3 teaspoon basil

1/3 teaspoon thyme

1/3 teaspoon rosemary

DIRECTIONS

Add the carrots, parsnips, and pumpkin to the inner pot of your Instant Pot. Pour in 1 cup of water.

Secure the lid. Choose the "Manual" mode and cook for 6 minutes at High pressure. Once cooking is complete, use a quick pressure release; carefully remove the lid.

Drain your vegetables and mash them with a potato masher.

Press the "Sauté" button and melt the butter; the, sauté the aromatics for 1 minute or so. Add the vegetable mash and stir to combine well.

Transfer to a nice serving bowls and garnish with some extra herbs if desired. Bon appétit!

PASTA & GRAINS

121. Lasagna with Sausage and Italian Cheese

(Ready in about 50 minutes)

Per serving: 762 Calories; 43.1g Fat; 57.4g Carbs; 43g Protein; 20g Sugars; 10.5g Fiber

INGREDIENTS

1/2 tablespoon canola oil
1/2 pound Italian sausage, crumbled
1 small onion, chopped
1 garlic clove, minced
1 fresh bell pepper, seeded and chopped

Sea salt and ground black pepper, to taste
1/2 teaspoon dried oregano
1/2 teaspoon dried basil
1/2 teaspoon dried rosemary
1 teaspoon red pepper flakes, crushed

2 ounces cream cheese
1 egg
1/4 cup Romano cheese, grated
1 ½ cups pasta sauce
6 lasagna sheets
1/2 cup Asiago cheese, shredded

DIRECTIONS

Press the "Sauté" button and heat the oil. Once hot, cook the sausage for 3 to 4 minutes or until it starts to brown; crumble your sausage with a wooden spatula.

Now, stir in the onion, garlic, and bell pepper. Sauté for about 4 minutes or until the vegetables are fragrant. Season with salt, black pepper, oregano, basil, rosemary, and red pepper.

Add 1 ½ cups of water and a metal trivet in the inner pot of your Instant Pot. Spritz a casserole dish with cooking spray.

Then, thoroughly combine the cream cheese with an egg, and Romano cheese.

Place a thin layer of pasta sauce on the bottom of the prepared casserole dish.

Add 3 lasagna sheets and 1/2 of the cheese mixture. Top with 1/2 of the meat/vegetable mixture.

Repeat the layers one more time, ending with the marinara sauce. Top with Asiago cheese. Cover with a sheet of aluminum foil.

Secure the lid. Choose the "Manual" mode and cook for 23 minutes at High pressure. Once cooking is complete, use a natural pressure release for 10 minutes; carefully remove the lid.

Let your lasagna rest for 5 to 6 minutes before slicing and serving. Bon appétit!

122. Philadelphia Spaghetti Carbonara

(Ready in about 20 minutes)

Per serving: 560 Calories; 27.3g Fat; 32.6g Carbs; 46.6g Protein; 9.1g Sugars; 6.4g Fiber

INGREDIENTS

1 tablespoon olive oil
1/3 pound ground turkey
1/3 pound ground beef
1/2 onion, chopped
1 garlic clove, minced

1/2 tablespoon fish sauce
1 tablespoon tomato paste
Kosher salt and cracked black pepper, to taste
1 bay leaf

1 cup vegetable broth
1/3 cup tomato sauce
4 ounces spaghetti
1/2 cup Swiss cheese, shredded

DIRECTIONS

Press the "Sauté" button and heat the oil. Once hot, brown the ground meat for about 5 minutes until no longer pink, stirring and breaking the meat into smaller chunks.

Add the onion and garlic and cook for a further 2 minutes or until they are fragrant.

Stir in the fish sauce, tomato paste, salt, black pepper, bay leaf, vegetable broth, tomato sauce and spaghetti; do not stir, but make sure the spaghetti is covered.

Secure the lid. Choose the "Manual" mode and cook for 8 minutes at High pressure. Once cooking is complete, use a quick pressure release; carefully remove the lid.

Top with Swiss cheese and gently stir to combine; serve immediately!

123. Creamed Corn with Cottage Cheese

(Ready in about 15 minutes)

Per serving: 279 Calories; 19.3g Fat; 19.8g Carbs; 10g Protein; 5.6g Sugars; 2.2g Fiber

INGREDIENTS

1 cup corn kernels
1 tablespoon cold butter, cut into pieces
2 ounces Cottage cheese, at room temperature
1/3 cup double cream

1 cup water
Kosher salt and ground black pepper, to taste
1/4 teaspoon red pepper flakes
1/3 teaspoon dried parsley flakes

DIRECTIONS

Put all ingredients into the inner pot of your Instant Pot; stir to combine.

Secure the lid. Choose the "Manual" mode and cook for 4 minutes at High pressure. Once cooking is complete, use a quick pressure release; carefully remove the lid. Ladle into serving bowls and enjoy!

124. Za'atar Oatmeal with Eggs and Peppers

(Ready in about 35 minutes)

Per serving: 381 Calories; 17g Fat; 40.9g Carbs; 17.6g Protein; 8.4g Sugars; 5.2g Fiber

INGREDIENTS

1/2 cup steel cut oats
1 ½ cups vegetable broth
1 tomato, pureed
Kosher salt and freshly ground black pepper, to taste

2 teaspoons olive oil
1 onion, chopped
2 bell peppers, seeded and sliced
2 eggs, beaten

DIRECTIONS

Place the steel cut oats, vegetable broth, tomato, salt, and black pepper in the inner pot.

Secure the lid. Choose the "Manual" mode and cook for 3 minutes at High pressure. Once cooking is complete, use a natural pressure release for 20 minutes; carefully remove the lid.

Meanwhile, heat the olive oil in a skillet over medium-high heat. Now, sauté the onion and peppers until they have softened or 3 to 4 minutes.

Then, add the beaten eggs and continue to cook until they are no longer liquid. Serve over the warm oatmeal.

125. Bulgur Pilau with Shallots

(Ready in about 25 minutes)

Per serving: 200 Calories; 6.9g Fat; 29.4g Carbs; 7.1g Protein; 1.1g Sugars; 4.8g Fiber

INGREDIENTS

1 tablespoon butter
2 shallots, chopped
1 teaspoon fresh garlic, minced
1/2 cup bulgur wheat

1 cup vegetable broth
1/4 teaspoon ground black pepper
1/4 teaspoon fine sea salt

DIRECTIONS

Press the "Sauté" button and melt the butter. Now, cook the shallots until just tender and fragrant.

Then, stir in the garlic and continue to sauté an additional minute or so. Add the remaining ingredients to the inner pot.

Secure the lid. Choose the "Manual" mode and cook for 10 minutes at High pressure. Once cooking is complete, use a natural pressure release for 10 minutes; carefully remove the lid.

Fluff the bulgur wheat with a fork and serve immediately. Bon appétit!

126. Cheesy Farro with Mushrooms

(Ready in about 35 minutes)

Per serving: 394 Calories; 13.8g Fat; 60g Carbs; 14.8g Protein; 6.2g Sugars; 8.8g Fiber

INGREDIENTS

1 tablespoon olive oil
1 onion, chopped
1 cup mushrooms, sliced
1 sweet pepper, chopped
1 garlic clove, minced
1/2 cup white wine

3/4 cup farro
1 ½ cups vegetable broth
Sea salt and ground black pepper, to taste
1/3 cup Swiss cheese, grated
1 tablespoon fresh parsley, chopped

DIRECTIONS

Press the "Sauté" button and heat the oil; now, cook the onion until tender or 3 to 4 minutes. Stir in the mushrooms and peppers and cook an additional 3 minutes.

Stir in the garlic and continue to sauté for a minute or so.

Add the white wine to deglaze the pan. Now, add the farro, vegetable broth, salt, and black pepper to the inner pot.

Secure the lid. Choose the "Manual" mode and cook for 11 minutes at High pressure. Once cooking is complete, use a natural pressure release for 10 minutes; carefully remove the lid.

Top each serving with cheese and fresh parsley. Bon appétit!

127. Truffle and Parmesan Popcorn

(Ready in about 15 minutes)

Per serving: 413 Calories; 36.7g Fat; 15.5g Carbs; 11.1g Protein; 0g Sugars; 3g Fiber

INGREDIENTS

1/2 stick butter
1/2 cup popcorn kernels
1 tablespoon truffle oil
1/4 cup parmesan cheese, grated
Sea salt, to taste

DIRECTIONS

Press the "Sauté" button and melt the butter. Stir until it begins to simmer.
Stir in the popcorn kernels and cover. When the popping slows down, press the "Cancel" button.
Now, add the truffle oil, parmesan, and sea salt. Toss to combine and serve immediately.

128. Spicy Buckwheat with Manchego

(Ready in about 15 minutes)

Per serving: 413 Calories; 12.5g Fat; 64g Carbs; 17.1g Protein; 1.4g Sugars; 8.8g Fiber

INGREDIENTS

1 teaspoon olive oil
1/2 shallot, chopped
1 teaspoon garlic, minced
1 bell pepper, chopped
1 Chile de árbol, chopped

1 cup buckwheat
1 cup chicken broth
1 cup water
1/3 cup Manchego curado, grated

DIRECTIONS

Press the "Sauté" button and heat the oil until sizzling. Then, sauté the shallot until just tender or about 3 minutes.
Then, cook the garlic and peppers an additional 2 to 3 minutes or until they are fragrant.
Add the buckwheat, broth, and water to the inner pot.
Secure the lid. Choose the "Manual" mode and cook for 3 minutes at High pressure. Once cooking is complete, use a quick pressure release; carefully remove the lid.
Serve garnished with cheese. Enjoy!

129. Strawberries and Coconut Milk Bread Pudding

(Ready in about 55 minutes)

Per serving: 461 Calories; 25.3g Fat; 43.5g Carbs; 14.4g Protein; 25.1g Sugars; 2.8g Fiber

INGREDIENTS

2 cups croissants, cut into pieces
2 eggs
4 ounces coconut milk
2 ounces condensed milk
4 tablespoons sugar
1/2 teaspoon vanilla

A pinch of salt
1/4 teaspoon ground cloves
1/2 teaspoon ground cinnamon
1/2 cup strawberries
1 tablespoon cold butter, cut into pieces.

DIRECTIONS

Add 1 cup of water and a metal trivet to the Instant Pot. Spritz a 7-inch springform pan with butter spray. Throw the croissant pieces into the pan.
In a mixing bowl, thoroughly combine the eggs, milk, sugar, vanilla, salt, cloves, and cinnamon. Pour 1/2 of the mixture over the croissants and let them soak approximately 15 minutes, until they no longer look dry.
Scatter the strawberries on top. Pour the leftover custard on top. Afterwards, top with the butter pieces and lower the pan onto the trivet.
Secure the lid. Choose the "Manual" mode and cook for 25 minutes at High pressure. Once cooking is complete, use a natural pressure release for 10 minutes; carefully remove the lid. Bon appétit!

130. Hungarian Cornmeal Squares (Kukoricaprósza)

(Ready in about 1 hour)

Per serving: 607 Calories; 28g Fat; 77g Carbs; 14.3g Protein; 26.7g Sugars; 5.3g Fiber

INGREDIENTS

1 cup yellow cornmeal

1 cup yogurt

1/2 cups sour cream

1/4 cup water

2 tablespoons safflower oil

1 egg, beaten

1 teaspoon baking soda

1/4 teaspoon salt

4 tablespoons plum jam

DIRECTIONS

Add 1 cup of water and metal rack to the inner pot. Spritz a baking pan with cooking oil.

Thoroughly combine the cornmeal, yogurt, sour cream, water, oil, egg, baking soda, and salt.

Scrape the mixture into the prepared baking pan. Place the piles of plum jam all over the surface.

Cover with a sheet of greased aluminum foil. Lower the pan onto the rack.

Secure the lid. Choose the "Manual" mode and cook for 55 minutes at High pressure. Once cooking is complete, use a quick pressure release; carefully remove the lid.

Place the Kukoricaprósza on a cooling rack before slicing and serving. Bon appétit!

131. Squash and Quinoa Pilaf

(Ready in about 10 minutes)

Per serving: 468 Calories; 8.8g Fat; 85g Carbs; 14.4g Protein; 8.4g Sugars; 10.2g Fiber

INGREDIENTS

1/2 pound acorn squash, peeled and sliced

1/2 tablespoon coconut oil, melted

1 sweet onion, thinly sliced

1/2 teaspoon fresh ginger, chopped

2 cups vegetable stock

1 cup quinoa, rinsed

3 prunes, chopped

1 tablespoon fresh mint leaves, roughly chopped

DIRECTIONS

Add the acorn squash, coconut oil, sweet onions, ginger, and 1 cup of stock to the inner pot; stir to combine.

Secure the lid. Choose the "Manual" mode and cook for 3 minutes at High pressure. Once cooking is complete, use a quick pressure release; carefully remove the lid.

Add the remaining stock, quinoa, and prunes to the inner pot.

Secure the lid. Choose the "Manual" mode and cook for 1 minute at High pressure. Once cooking is complete, use a quick pressure release; carefully remove the lid.

Serve garnished with fresh mint leaves. Bon appétit!

132. Cheese Pie with Pancetta and Scallions

(Ready in about 35 minutes)

Per serving: 573 Calories; 40.4g Fat; 28.5g Carbs; 23.1g Protein; 3.7g Sugars; 1.2g Fiber

INGREDIENTS

1/2 refrigerated pie crust

2 eggs

1/4 cup milk

1/4 cup sour cream

Sea salt and ground black pepper, to taste

2 ounces pancetta, chopped

1/2 cup Swiss cheese, shredded

2 tablespoons scallions, chopped

DIRECTIONS

Press the pie crust into a baking pan, crimping the top edges. In a mixing bowl, combine the eggs, milk, sour cream, salt, and pepper.

Place the pancetta on the pie crust; pour the egg/milk mixture over the top. Top with Swiss cheese.

Add 1 cup of water and a metal trivet to the Instant Pot. Lower the baking pan onto the trivet; cover with a sheet of greased aluminum foil.

Secure the lid. Choose the "Manual" mode and cook for 25 minutes at High pressure. Once cooking is complete, use a quick pressure release; carefully remove the lid.

Garnish with scallions and serve warm.

133. Buckwheat Porridge with Blueberries

(Ready in about 10 minutes)

Per serving: 328 Calories; 4.4g Fat; 66g Carbs; 11.4g Protein; 15.8g Sugars; 8.5g Fiber

INGREDIENTS

3/4 cup buckwheat grouts
3/4 cup water
3/4 cup orange juice
1/2 cup coconut milk

2 tablespoons agave nectar
1 teaspoon carob powder
1/2 teaspoon ground cardamom
1/2 teaspoon ground cinnamon

A pinch of kosher salt
A pinch of grated nutmeg
1/2 cup fresh blueberries

DIRECTIONS

Add the buckwheat, water, orange juice, coconut milk, agave nectar, carob powder, and spices to the inner pot.
Secure the lid. Choose the "Manual" mode and cook for 3 minutes at High pressure. Once cooking is complete, use a quick pressure release; carefully remove the lid.
Serve in individual bowls garnished with fresh blueberries. Bon appétit!

134. Three-Grain Porridge

(Ready in about 30 minutes)

Per serving: 284 Calories; 9.6g Fat; 38.1g Carbs; 11.1g Protein; 1.6g Sugars; 5.4g Fiber

INGREDIENTS

1 tablespoon olive oil
1/2 leek, chopped
1 garlic clove, pressed
1 sweet pepper, deveined and sliced
Sea salt and freshly ground black pepper, to taste

1/3 cup pearl barley
1/4 cup sorghum
1/4 cup congee
3 cups chicken bone broth

DIRECTIONS

Press the "Sauté" button and heat the oil until sizzling. Once hot, sauté the leeks, garlic and peppers for 3 to 4 minutes or until just tender and fragrant.
Add a splash of broth to deglaze the pot. Next, stir in the remaining ingredients.
Secure the lid. Choose the "Multigrain" mode and cook for 20 minutes at High pressure. Once cooking is complete, use a quick pressure release; carefully remove the lid.
Ladle into individual bowls and serve immediately.

135. Hearty Chicken Soup with Couscous

(Ready in about 20 minutes)

Per serving: 343 Calories; 7.2g Fat; 44.7g Carbs; 23.3g Protein; 3.6g Sugars; 4.9g Fiber

INGREDIENTS

1/2 tablespoon chicken schmaltz
1/3 pound chicken breasts, cubed
1/2 onion, chopped
1 carrot, sliced
1 celery rib, sliced
1 parsnip, sliced

1 tablespoon lemongrass, minced
1 teaspoon garlic paste
1/4 teaspoon turmeric powder
1/4 teaspoon mustard powder
2 cups chicken bone broth
1/2 cup couscous

Sea salt and ground black pepper, to taste
1/2 tablespoon fresh parsley, chopped
1 tablespoon fresh chives, chopped

DIRECTIONS

Press the "Sauté" button and melt the chicken schmaltz. Once hot, sauté the chicken until golden brown; reserve.
Cook the onion, carrot, celery, and parsnip in pan drippings until just tender and aromatic.
Add the reserved chicken, lemongrass, garlic paste, turmeric, mustard powder, and broth.
Secure the lid. Choose the "Manual" mode and cook for 11 minutes at High pressure. Once cooking is complete, use a quick pressure release; carefully remove the lid.
Now, stir in the couscous; season with salt and pepper.
Secure the lid. Choose the "Manual" mode and cook for 2 minutes at High pressure. Once cooking is complete, use a quick pressure release; carefully remove the lid.
Serve garnished with fresh parsley and chives. Bon appétit!

136. Chicken and Kamut Soup Provençale

(Ready in about 20 minutes)

Per serving: 462 Calories; 26.1g Fat; 33.1g Carbs; 24.8g Protein; 8.1g Sugars; 6g Fiber

INGREDIENTS

1 tablespoon olive oil
1/2 pound chicken thighs, boneless
1/2 onion, chopped
1/3 cup kamut
1/2 celery stalk, chopped

1 parsnip, chopped
1 carrot, chopped
Sea salt and freshly ground black
pepper, to taste

1/2 tablespoon Herbes de Provence
2 cups chicken broth
1/2 cup tomato puree

DIRECTIONS

Press the "Sauté" button and heat the oil; now, cook chicken thighs for 3 to 4 minutes.

Add the onion and continue to sauté until tender and translucent. Add the remaining ingredients and stir to combine.

Secure the lid. Choose the "Manual" mode and cook for 12 minutes at High pressure. Once cooking is complete, use a quick pressure release; carefully remove the lid.

Ladle your soup into individual bowls. Bon appétit!

137. Pasta al' Arrabbiata

(Ready in about 40 minutes)

Per serving: 560 Calories; 35.1g Fat; 45.2g Carbs; 19.4g Protein; 11.8g Sugars; 8.5g Fiber

INGREDIENTS

Arrabbiata Sauce:
1 tablespoon olive oil
10 ounces canned tomatoes, with juice
2 garlic cloves, minced
1 tablespoon brown sugar
1/2 teaspoon dried oregano

1/2 teaspoon dried basil
Sea salt and ground black pepper, to
your liking
1/2 teaspoon cayenne pepper
1/4 cup cooking wine

Pasta:
8 ounces spaghetti
4 cup vegetable stock
4 ounces cream cheese
2 ounces Parmesan cheese, grated

DIRECTIONS

Put all ingredients for the sauce in the inner pot.

Secure the lid. Choose the "Manual" mode and cook for 10 minutes at High pressure. Once cooking is complete, use a natural pressure release for 10 minutes; carefully remove the lid.

Stir in the spaghetti and vegetable stock.

Secure the lid. Choose the "Manual" mode and cook for 5 minutes at High pressure. Once cooking is complete, use a natural pressure release for 10 minutes; carefully remove the lid.

Divide your pasta between serving bowls. Top with cheese and serve. Bon appétit!

138. Macaroni and Cheese Pot Pie

(Ready in about 20 minutes)

Per serving: 575 Calories; 38.8g Fat; 30.3g Carbs; 27.8g Protein; 5.6g Sugars; 5.3g Fiber

INGREDIENTS

1 tablespoon olive oil
1/2 pound chicken drumsticks, boneless and cut into small cubes
1/2 shallot, chopped
1 garlic clove, minced
1 bell pepper, seeded and chopped

1 habanero pepper, seeded and
chopped
Kosher salt and ground black pepper,
to taste
1/2 teaspoon cayenne pepper

1 cup chicken bone broth, preferably
homemade
1 cup dried elbow pasta
1/2 cup cream cheese
1/2 tablespoon flaxseed meal

DIRECTIONS

Press the "Sauté" button and heat the olive oil. Once hot, brown the chicken drumsticks for 3 to 4 minutes, stirring frequently to ensure even cooking.

Add the shallot, garlic, and peppers; continue to cook an additional 3 minute or until they have softened.

Add the salt, black pepper, cayenne pepper, broth, and pasta to the inner pot.

Secure the lid. Choose the "Manual" mode and cook for 6 minutes at High pressure. Once cooking is complete, use a quick pressure release; carefully remove the lid.

Add the cream cheese and flaxseed meal; stir to combine and press the "Sauté" button; let it cook for a few minutes longer or until your sauce has reduced slightly and the flavors have concentrated. Bon appétit!

139. Basic Breakfast Oatmeal

(Ready in about 25 minutes)

Per serving: 228 Calories; 4.1g Fat; 60.6g Carbs; 9.6g Protein; 0g Sugars; 7.2g Fiber

INGREDIENTS

1 cup steel cut oats
3 ½ cups water
A pinch of kosher salt
A pinch of grated nutmeg

DIRECTIONS

Place all ingredients in the inner pot.
Secure the lid. Choose the "Manual" mode and cook for 3 minutes at High pressure. Once cooking is complete, use a natural pressure release for 20 minutes; carefully remove the lid.
Serve warm with a splash of milk and fruits of choice. Enjoy!

140. Creamy and Cheesy Baked Ziti

(Ready in about 20 minutes)

Per serving: 551 Calories; 7.2g Fat; 84.9g Carbs; 23.8g Protein; 14g Sugars; 11.2g Fiber

INGREDIENTS

1 cup vegetable broth
1/4 cup double cream
1 garlic clove, minced
Sea salt and ground black pepper, to taste

6 ounces dry ziti pasta
1 cup tomato sauce
1/2 cup Mozzarella cheese, shredded

DIRECTIONS

Add the broth, double cream, garlic, salt, black pepper, ziti pasta, and tomato sauce to the inner pot.
Secure the lid. Choose the "Manual" mode and cook for 8 minutes at High pressure. Once cooking is complete, use a quick pressure release; carefully remove the lid.
Stir in the Mozzarella cheese and seal the lid; let it sit in the residual heat until the cheese melts. The sauce will thicken as it cools. Bon appétit!

141. Breakfast Millet Porridge with Nuts

(Ready in about 25 minutes)

Per serving: 428 Calories; 10.1g Fat; 66.8g Carbs; 11.8g Protein; 13.4g Sugars; 8.2g Fiber

INGREDIENTS

3/4 cup millet
2 cups water
1/4 cup golden raisins

1/4 cup almonds, roughly chopped
1 tablespoon orange juice
A pinch of sea salt

DIRECTIONS

Place all ingredients in the inner pot of your Instant Pot and close the lid.
Secure the lid. Choose the "Manual" mode and cook for 12 minutes at High pressure. Once cooking is complete, use a natural pressure release for 10 minutes; carefully remove the lid.
Taste and adjust the seasonings. Bon appétit!

142. Sweet Buttermilk Cornbread

(Ready in about 1 hour)

Per serving: 402 Calories; 21.8g Fat; 43.3g Carbs; 5.6g Protein; 15.3g Sugars; 2.2g Fiber

INGREDIENTS

1/3 cup yellow cornmeal
1/3 cup all-purpose flour
1/2 teaspoon baking powder

1/4 cup granulated sugar
A pinch of salt
A pinch of grated nutmeg

1/2 cup buttermilk
3 tablespoons safflower oil

DIRECTIONS

Add 1 cup of water and metal rack to the inner pot. Spritz a baking pan with cooking oil.

Thoroughly combine the cornmeal, flour, baking powder, sugar, salt, and grated nutmeg. In another mixing bowl, whisk buttermilk with safflower oil.

Add the wet mixture to the cornmeal mixture. Scrape the mixture into the prepared baking pan. Cover with a sheet of greased aluminum foil.

Lower the pan onto the rack.

Secure the lid. Choose the "Manual" mode and cook for 55 minutes at High pressure. Once cooking is complete, use a quick pressure release; carefully remove the lid.

Place the cornbread on a cooling rack before slicing and serving. Bon appétit!

143. Quinoa and Chickpea Salad

(Ready in about 15 minutes + chilling time)

Per serving: 447 Calories; 24.8g Fat; 47.5g Carbs; 1.2g Protein; 3.4g Sugars; 7.5g Fiber

INGREDIENTS

1/2 cup quinoa, rinsed
1 cup water
1/2 cup boiled chickpeas
1 sweet pepper, seeded and chopped
1 serrano pepper, seeded and chopped

1/2 onion, thinly sliced
3 tablespoons extra-virgin olive oil
1 tablespoon fresh lime juice
Sea salt and ground black pepper, to taste
1/4 teaspoon red pepper flakes

DIRECTIONS

Spritz the inner pot with cooking oil and stir in the rinsed quinoa and water.

Secure the lid. Choose the "Manual" mode and cook for 1 minute at High pressure. Once cooking is complete, use a natural pressure release for 10 minutes; carefully remove the lid.

Fluff the quinoa with a fork and allow it to cool. Toss the cooled quinoa with the remaining ingredients; toss to combine well and serve. Bon appétit!

144. Cheesy Chicken Bake

(Ready in about 20 minutes)

Per serving: 499 Calories; 19.5g Fat; 43.1g Carbs; 39.4g Protein; 7.1g Sugars; 7.4g Fiber

INGREDIENTS

1/2 cup kamut
1/2 cup vegetable broth
1/2 cup tomato puree
Sea salt and freshly ground black
pepper, to taste

1/2 teaspoon basil
1/2 teaspoon thyme
1/2 pound chicken, boneless, skinless
and chopped
1/2 shallot, chopped

1 teaspoon fresh garlic, pressed
1 sweet pepper, chopped
1 serrano pepper, chopped
1 tablespoon butter, melted
2 ounces Colby cheese, shredded

DIRECTIONS

Add the kamut to the bottom of a lightly greased inner pot. Now, pour in the broth and tomato puree; add the spices.

Add the chicken, shallot, garlic, and peppers; drizzle melted butter over everything.

Secure the lid. Choose the "Manual" mode and cook for 12 minutes at High pressure. Once cooking is complete, use a quick pressure release; carefully remove the lid.

Top with shredded cheese and seal the lid again. Let it sit in the residual heat until the cheese melts. Enjoy!

145. Breakfast Amaranth Porridge

(Ready in about 15 minutes)

Per serving: 185 Calories; 4.5g Fat; 34.8g Carbs; 4.8g Protein; 28.1g Sugars; 4.8g Fiber

INGREDIENTS

1 cup amaranth
1 cup coconut milk
1 cup water
1 apple, cored and sliced
1 pear, cored and sliced

1/4 teaspoon ground cardamom
1/4 teaspoon ground cloves
1/2 teaspoon ground cinnamon
1 tablespoon honey

DIRECTIONS

Thoroughly combine all ingredients in the inner pot.
Secure the lid. Choose the "Manual" mode and cook for 4 minutes at High pressure. Once cooking is complete, use a quick pressure release; carefully remove the lid.
Ladle into individual bowls and enjoy!

146. Traditional Moroccan Couscous

(Ready in about 15 minutes)

Per serving: 454 Calories; 7.1g Fat; 84.2g Carbs; 14.1g Protein; 7.7g Sugars; 8g Fiber

INGREDIENTS

1 tablespoon butter, softened
1/2 onion, chopped
1 teaspoon garlic, pressed
1 (1-inch) piece ginger, peeled and grated
1 carrot, trimmed and chopped
1/2 stalk celery, peeled and chopped
1 cup couscous
2 cups water

1/2 tablespoon chicken bouillon granules
Sea salt and ground white pepper, to taste
1 teaspoon dried parsley flakes
1 teaspoon cayenne pepper
1/2 teaspoon ground cumin
1/4 teaspoon ground cinnamon
1 Peppadew pepper, chopped
1/2 cup tomato puree

DIRECTIONS

Press the "Sauté" button and melt the butter. Once hot, cook the onion, garlic, ginger, carrots, and celery until tender or about 4 minutes.
Add the other ingredients; stir to combine well.
Secure the lid. Choose the "Manual" mode and cook for 3 minutes at High pressure. Once cooking is complete, use a quick pressure release; carefully remove the lid. Ladle into serving bowls and enjoy!

147. Wheat Berry Salad

(Ready in about 40 minutes + chilling time)

Per serving: 246 Calories; 16.5g Fat; 23.3g Carbs; 4.4g Protein; 0.4g Sugars; 4g Fiber

INGREDIENTS

1/2 cup wheat berries
2 cups water
1 tomato, sliced
1/2 cucumber, sliced
1/2 red onion, sliced

2 tablespoons good olive oil
2 tablespoons red wine vinegar
1/2 teaspoon oregano
1/2 teaspoon basil
1/4 cup Kalamata olives

DIRECTIONS

Add the wheat berries and water to the inner pot.
Secure the lid. Choose the "Manual" mode and cook for 35 minutes at High pressure. Once cooking is complete, use a quick pressure release; carefully remove the lid.
Now, toss the cooked wheat berries with the remaining ingredients. Cover and refrigerate; the longer your salad sits, the more intense the flavor becomes. Enjoy!

148. Korean Sorghum Pudding

(Ready in about 25 minutes)

Per serving: 496 Calories; 20.7g Fat; 66g Carbs; 13.8g Protein; 30g Sugars; 3.4g Fiber

INGREDIENTS

3/4 cup dried sorghum
2 cups soy milk
1 tablespoon ghee

1/3 cup brown sugar
1/4 cup cashews, roughly chopped

DIRECTIONS

Place the dries sorghum, milk, ghee, and brown sugar in the inner pot.

Secure the lid. Choose the "Porridge" mode and cook for 20 minutes at High pressure. Once cooking is complete, use a quick pressure release; carefully remove the lid.

Serve in individual bowls garnished with chopped cashews. Enjoy!

149. Old-Fashioned Spaghetti with Ground Meat Sauce

(Ready in about 20 minutes)

Per serving: 570 Calories; 21.9g Fat; 49.9g Carbs; 35.1g Protein; 6.1g Sugars; 3.5g Fiber

INGREDIENTS

1 teaspoon olive oil
1/4 pound ground pork
1/4 pound ground beef chuck
1/4 cup red wine
1/2 teaspoon cayenne pepper
Kosher salt and ground black pepper, to taste

1/2 teaspoon garlic powder
1/3 teaspoon shallot powder
1/2 cup marinara sauce
1 cup water
4 ounces dry spaghetti
1/3 cup Romano cheese, preferably freshly grated

DIRECTIONS

Press the "Sauté" button and heat the oil. Once hot, brown the ground meat for about 5 minutes until no longer pink, stirring and breaking the meat into smaller chunks.

Scrape the bottom of the pot with red wine. Add the cayenne pepper, salt, black pepper, garlic powder, shallot powder, and marinara sauce; stir to combine.

Pour in the water and gently stir to combine. Add the dry spaghetti.

Secure the lid. Choose the "Manual" mode and cook for 8 minutes at High pressure. Once cooking is complete, use a quick pressure release; carefully remove the lid.

Serve warm with Romano cheese. Bon appétit!

150. Peppery Pearl Barley with Chives

(Ready in about 30 minutes)

Per serving: 339 Calories; 8.8g Fat; 60.3g Carbs; 7.6g Protein; 5.2g Sugars; 12.5g Fiber

INGREDIENTS

1 tablespoon sesame oil
1/2 yellow onion, chopped
1 garlic clove, minced
1 bell pepper, seeded and chopped

1 jalapeno pepper, seeded and chopped
3/4 cup pearl barley, rinsed
1 ½ cups roasted vegetable broth
2 tablepsoons chives, chopped

DIRECTIONS

Press the "Sauté" button and heat the oil. Once hot, cook the onion until just tender and fragrant or about 3 minutes.

Stir in the garlic and peppers; continue cooking for 2 minutes more or until they are aromatic. Add the barley and vegetable broth to the inner pot.

Secure the lid. Choose the "Multigrain" mode and cook for 20 minutes at High pressure. Once cooking is complete, use a quick pressure release; carefully remove the lid.

Fluff the barley with a fork; garnish with chopped chives and serve with your favorite main dish. Bon appétit!

151. Paprika Creamed Grits

(Ready in about 25 minutes)

Per serving: 412 Calories; 25.7g Fat; 36.7g Carbs; 10.4g Protein; 5.1g Sugars; 3.7g Fiber

INGREDIENTS

1 ½ cups of water
3/4 cup stone ground grits
1/2 teaspoon sea salt
1/2 cup cream cheese, room temperature

1/2 teaspoon paprika
1/4 teaspoon porcini powder
1/2 teaspoon garlic powder
1/4 cup milk

DIRECTIONS

Place the water, grits, and salt in the inner pot of your Instant Pot.

Secure the lid. Choose the "Manual" mode and cook for 10 minutes at High pressure. Once cooking is complete, use a natural pressure release for 10 minutes; carefully remove the lid.

Now, stir the cheese, paprika, porcini powder, garlic powder and milk into warm grits; stir to combine well and serve immediately.

152. Corn with Cilantro Butter

(Ready in about 15 minutes)

Per serving: 225 Calories; 13.4g Fat; 26.7g Carbs; 4.8g Protein; 8.9g Sugars; 3.9g Fiber

INGREDIENTS

2 large ears corn, husked and halved
2 tablespoons butter, softened
1 tablespoon cilantro, chopped

1/2 teaspoon paprika
Sea salt and ground black pepper, to taste

DIRECTIONS

Place 1 cup of water and a metal trivet in your Instant Pot. Now, lower the corn onto the trivet.

Secure the lid. Choose the "Manual" mode and cook for 6 minutes at High pressure. Once cooking is complete, use a quick pressure release; carefully remove the lid.

Press the "Sauté" button and melt the butter; add the cilantro, paprika, salt, and black pepper to the melted butter.

Pour the cilantro butter over the steamed corn and enjoy!

153. Chocolate Croissant Breakfast Bake

(Ready in about 20 minutes)

Per serving: 524 Calories; 9g Fat; 54g Carbs; 12.3g Protein; 55.4g Sugars; 4.8g Fiber

INGREDIENTS

4 slices of French bread, broken into pieces
1 egg, whisked
1/4 cup milk
1/4 cup sour cream
2 tablespoons honey

1/2 teaspoon vanilla paste
1/4 teaspoon nutmeg, preferably freshly grated
1/4 teaspoon ground cardamom
1/2 teaspoon ground cinnamon
1/2 cup chocolate chips

DIRECTIONS

Place 1 cup of water and metal rack in your Instant Pot. Now, spritz a round cake pan with cooking oil. Throw the bread pieces in the pan. In a mixing bowl, thoroughly combine the eggs, milk, sour cream, honey, and spices. Pour the mixture over the bread pieces and press with a wide spatula.

Cover the pan with a sheet of aluminum foil. Lower the pan onto the rack.

Secure the lid. Choose the "Manual" mode and cook for 13 minutes at High pressure. Once cooking is complete, use a quick pressure release; carefully remove the lid.

Sprinkle with chocolate chips and serve. Bon appétit!

154. Indian Spicy Bulgur with Chicken

(Ready in about 30 minutes)

Per serving: 416 Calories; 16.6g Fat; 37.1g Carbs; 31.4g Protein; 6.4g Sugars; 5.7g Fiber

INGREDIENTS

1/2 tablespoon sesame oil

1/2 pound chicken breasts, boneless and skinless, cut into bite-sized pieces

1/2 onion, chopped

1 teaspoon fresh garlic, minced

1-inch galangal piece, peeled and sliced

1 Bird's eye chili pepper, seeded and minced

1/2 teaspoon ground cumin

1/2 teaspoon turmeric powder

1 teaspoon garam masala

1/2 cup bulgur

1/2 cup coconut milk

1 cup chicken stock

Sea salt and ground black pepper, to taste

1 tablespoon fresh coriander, chopped

DIRECTIONS

Press the "Sauté" button and heat the sesame oil. Now, brown the chicken breast for 3 to 4 minutes; reserve.

Then, add the onion and cook until just tender and fragrant. Stir in the garlic and continue to sauté an additional minute or so.

Stir in the galangal, chili pepper, cumin, turmeric powder, garam masala, bulgur, coconut milk, chicken stock, salt, and black pepper; add the reserved chicken to the inner pot.

Secure the lid. Choose the "Manual" mode and cook for 10 minutes at High pressure. Once cooking is complete, use a natural pressure release for 10 minutes; carefully remove the lid. Serve garnished with fresh coriander and enjoy!

155. Cheesy Porridge with Kale

(Ready in about 20 minutes)

Per serving: 319 Calories; 15.5g Fat; 34.4g Carbs; 10.3g Protein; 2.4g Sugars; 4.1g Fiber

INGREDIENTS

1/2 cup teff grains

2 cups water

1/2 teaspoon sea salt

1 tablespoon olive oil

1 cup kale, torn into pieces

1/3 cup goat cheese, crumbled

1 tomato, sliced

DIRECTIONS

Place the teff grains, water, salt, and olive oil in the inner pot of your Instant Pot.

Secure the lid. Choose the "Manual" mode and cook for 3 minutes at High pressure. Once cooking is complete, use a quick pressure release; carefully remove the lid.

Add the kale and seal the lid again; let it soak for 5 to 10 minutes. Serve garnished with goat cheese and fresh tomatoes. Bon appétit!

156. Amaranth Pilaf with Eggs and Cheese

(Ready in about 15 minutes)

Per serving: 536 Calories; 28.6g Fat; 46.5g Carbs; 24.5g Protein; 8.8g Sugars; 5.3g Fiber

INGREDIENTS

3/4 cup amaranth

2 cups water

1/2 cup milk

Sea salt and freshly cracked black pepper, to taste

1 tablespoon olive oil

2 eggs

1/2 cup cheddar cheese, shredded

2 tablespoons fresh chives, roughly chopped

DIRECTIONS

Place the amaranth, water, and milk in the inner pot of your Instant Pot.

Secure the lid. Choose the "Manual" mode and cook for 4 minutes at High pressure. Once cooking is complete, use a quick pressure release; carefully remove the lid. Season with salt and black pepper.

Meanwhile, heat the oil in a skillet over medium-high heat. Then, fry the egg until crispy on the edges.

Divide the cooked amaranth between serving bowls; top with the fried eggs and cheese. Garnish with fresh chives. Bon appétit!

157. Spelt Grains with Spinach and Mushrooms

(Ready in about 35 minutes)

Per serving: 238 Calories; 8g Fat; 37.4g Carbs; 7.7g Protein; 5.1g Sugars; 5.8g Fiber

INGREDIENTS

1 tablespoon olive oil
1/2 leek, chopped
1 teaspoon garlic, minced
1 cup cremini mushrooms, sliced
1/2 cup spelt grains

1 cup water
Sea salt and white pepper, to taste
1/2 tablespoon oyster sauce
1 cup spinach leaves

DIRECTIONS

Press the "Sauté" button and heat the oil until sizzling. Then, sauté the leek for 3 to 4 minutes or until tender.

Add the garlic and mushrooms and cook an additional 2 minutes or until they are fragrant. Reserve the sautéed mixture.

Add the spelt grains, water, salt, pepper, and oyster sauce to the inner pot.

Secure the lid. Choose the "Porridge" mode and cook for 30 minutes at High pressure. Once cooking is complete, use a quick pressure release; carefully remove the lid.

Afterwards, stir in the spinach leaves and seal the lid; let it sit until the leaves wilt. Serve topped with the sautéed mushroom mixture. Bon appétit!

158. Polenta with Feta Cheese and Herbs

(Ready in about 15 minutes)

Per serving: 309 Calories; 23.9g Fat; 14.7g Carbs; 9.4g Protein; 2.7g Sugars; 0.8g Fiber

INGREDIENTS

1/2 cup polenta
2 cups water
A pinch of sea salt
1/2 teaspoon red pepper flakes, crushed
1/2 teaspoon dried parsley flakes

1/2 teaspoon oregano
1 teaspoon dried onion flakes
2 tablespoons butter
4 ounces Feta cheese, crumbled

DIRECTIONS

Add the polenta, water, and salt to the inner pot of your Instant Pot. Press the "Sauté" button and bring the mixture to a simmer. Press the "Cancel" button.

Add the spices to your polenta. Secure the lid. Choose the "Manual" mode and cook for 8 minutes at High pressure. Once cooking is complete, use a quick pressure release; carefully remove the lid.

Stir the butter into the polenta, whisking until it has melted. Add more salt, if needed.

Top with Feta cheese and serve warm.

BEANS, LEGUMES & LENTILS

159. Kidney Bean and Vegetable Soup

(Ready in about 25 minutes)

Per serving: 487 Calories; 15.2g Fat; 72.5g Carbs; 31.4g Protein; 5.9g Sugars; 16g Fiber

INGREDIENTS

2 ounces bacon, cut into small pieces
1/2 leek, chopped
1 garlic clove, sliced
1/2 parsnip, coarsely chopped
1 carrot, coarsely chopped
Sea salt and freshly cracked black pepper, to taste

1 canned chipotle chilis in adobo, chopped
1 teaspoon basil
1/2 teaspoon rosemary
1 cup dried red kidney beans, soaked and rinsed
2 cups chicken broth
A small handful cilantro leaves, roughly chopped

DIRECTIONS

Press the "Sauté" button to preheat your Instant Pot. Now, cook the bacon until crisp; reserve.

Add the leek and garlic; continue to sauté an additional 3 minute or until they are fragrant.

Stir in the other ingredients, except for the fresh cilantro.

Secure the lid. Choose the "Manual" mode and cook for 8 minutes at High pressure. Once cooking is complete, use a natural pressure release for 10 minutes; carefully remove the lid.

Afterwards, purée your soup using a food processor or an immersion blender. Serve garnished with fresh cilantro and the reserved bacon. Bon appétit!

160. Indian Aromatic Chili

(Ready in about 35 minutes)

Per serving: 304 Calories; 5.6g Fat; 50.1g Carbs; 16.5g Protein; 4.6g Sugars; 8.4g Fiber

INGREDIENTS

1 tablespoon butter, at room temperature
1/2 teaspoon cumin seeds
1 onion, chopped
1 clove garlic, pressed
1 ghost jolokia chili pepper, chopped
1/2 teaspoon red pepper flakes, crushed

1/2 teaspoon coriander
1 ripe tomato, pureed
1/2 cup dried adzuki beans
Kosher salt and ground black pepper, to taste
1/2 teaspoon garam masala

2 cups vegetable broth, preferably homemade
1 bay leaf
1-inch cinnamon stick
1 green cardamom

DIRECTIONS

Press the "Sauté" button and melt the butter. Once hot, cook the cumin seeds for 30 seconds to 1 minute or until the seeds begin to sizzle.

Now, stir in the onion, garlic, and chili pepper; continue to sauté an additional 3 minutes or until they have softened.

Stir in the remaining ingredients.

Secure the lid. Choose the "Bean/Chili" mode and cook for 25 minutes at High pressure. Once cooking is complete, use a quick pressure release; carefully remove the lid.

Serve with hot steamed rice if desired. Enjoy!

161. The Best Minestrone Soup Ever

(Ready in about 35 minutes)

Per serving: 420 Calories; 7.6g Fat; 73.4g Carbs; 15.6g Protein; 5.7g Sugars; 16.1g Fiber

INGREDIENTS

1 tablespoon olive oil
1/2 onion, chopped
1 teaspoon garlic, minced
1 carrot, sliced
1 celery stalk, diced

1/2 cup yellow squash, diced
1/2 cup dried Great Northern beans
2 medium-sized potatoes, peeled and diced
3 cups water

1 tomato, pureed
1/2 tablespoon Italian seasoning blend
Sea salt and ground black pepper, to taste
1 cup Swiss chard, torn into pieces

DIRECTIONS

Press the "Sauté" button and heat the olive oil until sizzling. Then, sauté the onion and garlic until just tender and fragrant.

Now, add the remaining ingredients, except for the Swiss chard.

Secure the lid. Choose the "Bean/Chili" mode and cook for 30 minutes at High pressure. Once cooking is complete, use a quick pressure release; carefully remove the lid.

Stir in the Swiss chard. Seal the lid and let it sit in the residual heat until it wilts. Serve warm.

162. Spicy and Herby Chickpea Stew

(Ready in about 55 minutes)

Per serving: 443 Calories; 13.8g Fat; 62.4g Carbs; 17.5g Protein; 14.1g Sugars; 13.5g Fiber

INGREDIENTS

1 tablespoon olive oil
1/2 large yellow onion, chopped
3/4 cup chickpeas
2 cups water
1/2 cup tomato sauce

1/2 teaspoon salt
1/2 teaspoon baking soda
1 rosemary sprig
1 thyme sprig
1 teaspoon mixed peppercorns

1 bay leaf
1/2 whole capsicum, deseeded and chopped
Sea salt, to taste

DIRECTIONS

Press the "Sauté" button and heat the olive oil; now, sauté the onion until tender and translucent. Then, add the remaining ingredients and stir to combine.

Secure the lid. Choose the "Bean/Chili" mode and cook for 40 minutes at High pressure. Once cooking is complete, use a natural pressure release for 10 minutes; carefully remove the lid.

Ladle into serving bowls and garnish with fresh chives if desired. Bon appétit!

163. Tangy Lentil Curry

(Ready in about 30 minutes)

Per serving: 319 Calories; 5.6g Fat; 52.1g Carbs; 7.5g Protein; 6.1g Sugars; 3.5g Fiber

INGREDIENTS

1/2 tablespoon sesame oil
1/2 onion, chopped
1/2 tablespoon fresh ginger, peeled and grated
1 garlic clove, minced

1 teaspoon coconut sugar
Sea salt and white pepper, to taste
1/2 teaspoon ground turmeric
4 curry leaves
3/4 cup brown lentils, rinsed

1 teaspoon cayenne pepper
8 ounces canned coconut milk
1 tablespoon freshly squeezed lime juice

DIRECTIONS

Press the "Sauté" button and heat the sesame oil. Once hot, cook the onion until tender and translucent.

Now, add the ginger and garlic and continue to sauté an additional minute or so.

Stir in the coconut sugar, salt, white pepper, ground turmeric, curry leaves, brown lentils, and cayenne pepper. Pour in 2 cups of water.

Secure the lid. Choose the "Manual" mode and cook for 14 minutes at High pressure. Once cooking is complete, use a natural pressure release for 10 minutes; carefully remove the lid.

Now, pour in the coconut milk and press the "Sauté" button. Let it simmer on the lowest setting until thoroughly warmed.

Taste and adjust the seasoning. Serve with a few drizzles of lime juice. Enjoy!

164. Indian Tarka Dal

(Ready in about 20 minutes)

Per serving: 235 Calories; 6.3g Fat; 33.8g Carbs; 12.3g Protein; 2.2g Sugars; 2.6g Fiber

INGREDIENTS

Moong Dal:
1/2 cup moong dal, soaked 2 hours and drained
2 cups water
1 teaspoon curry paste
Kosher salt and red pepper, to taste
1 teaspoon Garam masala

Tarka:
2 tablespoons butter
1/2 teaspoon cumin seeds
2 garlic cloves, pressed
1/2 white onion, chopped
1 bird eye chili, sliced

DIRECTIONS

Add the moong dal, water, curry paste, salt, pepper, and Garam masala to the inner pot.

Secure the lid. Choose the "Manual" mode and cook for 2 minutes at High pressure. Once cooking is complete, use a natural pressure release for 10 minutes; carefully remove the lid.

Melt the butter in a nonstick skillet over medium-high heat. Then, sauté the cumin seeds for 30 seconds or until fragrant.

After that, sauté the garlic, onion, and chili pepper for 4 to 5 minutes or until they have softened. Stir the contents of the skillet into the warm dal. Bon appétit!

165. Authentic Greek Fasolakia

(Ready in about 15 minutes)

Per serving: 274 Calories; 17.5g Fat; 20.1g Carbs; 12.7g Protein; 3.9g Sugars; 6.8g Fiber

INGREDIENTS

1 tablespoon olive oil
2 garlic cloves, chopped
1 pound fresh green beans
4 vine-ripened tomato, pureed
Sea salt and freshly ground black pepper, to season
1/2 cup bone broth, preferably homemade

1/2 teaspoon paprika
1/2 teaspoon dried oregano
1/2 teaspoon dried basil
1/2 dried dill
3 ounces Feta cheese, crumbled

DIRECTIONS

Press the "Sauté" button and heat the oil. Now, sauté the garlic until it is fragrant but not browned.

Add the other ingredients, except for the feta cheese, to the inner pot; and stir to combine.

Secure the lid. Choose the "Manual" mode and cook for 5 minutes at High pressure. Once cooking is complete, use a quick pressure release; carefully remove the lid.

Ladle into individual bowls and serve with Feta cheese on the side. Enjoy!

166. Lebanese Lentils with Rice (Mujadara)

(Ready in about 35 minutes)

Per serving: 403 Calories; 17.8g Fat; 26.7g Carbs; 36.7g Protein; 13g Sugars; 9.8g Fiber

INGREDIENTS

1 tablespoon grapeseed oil
1 small onion, thinly sliced
2 cloves garlic, rough chopped
1/2 teaspoon cumin
1 cinnamon stick
1 teaspoon turmeric powder

1/2 teaspoon ground ginger
Kosher salt and red pepper, to season
1/4 cup red cooking wine
1/2 cup brown lentils, sorted and rinsed
1 ½ cups water

1 tablespoon fresh parsley
1 tablespoon fresh lemon juice
1/2 cup basmati rice, rinsed
2 cups mustard greens

DIRECTIONS

Press the "Sauté" button and heat the oil until sizzling. Once hot, cook the onion and garlic until just tender and fragrant.

Stir in the remaining ingredients, except for the mustard greens. Give it a good stir.

Secure the lid. Choose the "Manual" mode and cook for 10 minutes at High pressure. Once cooking is complete, use a natural pressure release for 10 minutes; carefully remove the lid.

Add the mustard greens to the inner pot. Seal the lid and let it sit in the residual heat for 10 minutes. Serve warm.

167. Mexican Vegetarian Tacos

(Ready in about 35 minutes)

Per serving: 487 Calories; 11.5g Fat; 75.5g Carbs; 23.8g Protein; 8.1g Sugars; 18.2g Fiber

INGREDIENTS

1 tablespoon sesame oil
1/2 onion, chopped
1 teaspoon garlic, minced
1 sweet pepper, seeded and sliced
1 jalapeno pepper, seeded and minced
1 teaspoon ground cumin

1/2 teaspoon ground coriander
8 ounces black beans, rinsed
2 (8-inches) whole wheat tortillas, warmed
1/2 cup cherry tomatoes, halved
1/3 cup sour cream

DIRECTIONS

Press the "Sauté" button and heat the oil. Now, cook the onion, garlic, and peppers until tender and fragrant.

Add the ground cumin, coriander, and beans to the inner pot.

Secure the lid. Choose the "Manual" mode and cook for 20 minutes at High pressure. Once cooking is complete, use a natural pressure release for 10 minutes; carefully remove the lid.

Serve the bean mixture in the tortillas; garnish with the cherry tomatoes and sour cream. Enjoy!

168. Split Pea Soup with Ham

(Ready in about 35 minutes)

Per serving: 463 Calories; 17.8g Fat; 26.7g Carbs; 36.7g Protein; 13g Sugars; 5.2g Fiber

INGREDIENTS

1 tablespoon butter
1/2 leek, diced
1/2 celery stalk, diced
1 carrot, diced
1/2 turnip, diced
1 jalapeno pepper, seeded and minced

2 ounces ham, diced
1 cup split peas, rinsed
2 cups chicken stock, veggie stock, water, or a mixture
1/2 teaspoon dried thyme
1/2 teaspoon garlic powder
Kosher salt and ground black pepper, to taste

DIRECTIONS

Press the "Sauté" button and melt the butter. Once hot, sauté the leek, celery, carrot, turnip, and jalapeno until they have softened.
Add the remaining ingredients to the inner pot.
Secure the lid. Choose the "Manual" mode and cook for 15 minutes at High pressure. Once cooking is complete, use a natural pressure release for 15 minutes; carefully remove the lid.
Taste and adjust seasonings. Serve warm.

169. Creole Boiled Peanuts

(Ready in about 1 hour 5 minutes)

Per serving: 372 Calories; 28.5g Fat; 20.2g Carbs; 14.9g Protein; 5.3g Sugars; 7.2g Fiber

INGREDIENTS

1/4 pound raw peanuts in the shell
4 tablespoons salt
1 tablespoon Creole seasoning

1/2 tablespoon garlic powder
1/2 tablespoon cayenne pepper
1 jalapeno, sliced

DIRECTIONS

Add all ingredients to the inner pot of your Instant Pot. Pour in enough water to cover the peanuts.
Use a steamer to gently press down your peanuts.
Secure the lid. Choose the "Manual" mode and cook for 45 minutes at High pressure. Once cooking is complete, use a natural pressure release for 15 minutes; carefully remove the lid.
Place in a container with a bunch of the liquid; refrigerate for 3 hours. Bon appétit!

170. Green Pea and Mushroom Soup

(Ready in about 20 minutes)

Per serving: 311 Calories; 9.6g Fat; 44.6g Carbs; 8.3g Protein; 17g Sugars; 11.7g Fiber

INGREDIENTS

1 teaspoon avocado oil
1/2 shallot, chopped
1 garlic clove, minced
1 cup cream of mushroom soup
1 cup water

1 cup tomato sauce
1/2 teaspoon dried tarragon
1/2 teaspoon dried dill
Kosher salt and freshly ground black pepper, to taste
4 ounces frozen green peas

DIRECTIONS

Press the "Sauté" button and heat the oil. Once hot, cook the shallot until tender and translucent; add the garlic to the inner pot and continue sautéing an additional 30 seconds.
Now, stir in the remaining ingredients.
Secure the lid. Choose the "Manual" mode and cook for 12 minutes at High pressure. Once cooking is complete, use a quick pressure release; carefully remove the lid.
Ladle into soup bowls. Bon appétit!

171. Mom's Lentil Salad

(Ready in about 30 minutes)

Per serving: 492 Calories; 14.9g Fat; 68.6g Carbs; 25.6g Protein; 6.1g Sugars; 11.9g Fiber

INGREDIENTS

1 cup green lentils, rinsed
2 cups water
1/3 cup scallions, chopped
1 bell pepper, seeded and sliced
1/2 carrot, julienned
1 cucumber, sliced

1/2 cup grape tomatoes, halved
4 tablespoons extra-virgin olive oil
1/2 fresh lemon, juiced
1/2 teaspoon red pepper flakes
Sea salt and ground white pepper, to taste

DIRECTIONS

Add the lentils and water to the inner pot.

Secure the lid. Choose the "Manual" mode and cook for 8 minutes at High pressure. Once cooking is complete, use a natural pressure release for 15 minutes; carefully remove the lid.

In a salad bowl, combine the lentils with the remaining ingredients. Toss to combine well. Serve well chilled. Bon appétit!

172. Classic Spicy Hummus

(Ready in about 1 hour)

Per serving: 478 Calories; 34.1g Fat; 34.3g Carbs; 11.6g Protein; 5.2g Sugars; 7g Fiber

INGREDIENTS

1/2 cup dry chickpeas, rinsed
1/2 teaspoon sea salt
1/2 teaspoon baking soda
1 tablespoon fresh lemon juice
1 garlic clove

4 tablespoons olive oil
1/2 teaspoon cayenne pepper
2 dashes hot pepper sauce
1 tablespoon tahini (sesame butter)

DIRECTIONS

Add the dry chickpeas to the inner pot; pour in 6 cups of water. Add the sea salt and baking soda.

Secure the lid. Choose the "Manual" mode and cook for 35 minutes at High pressure. Once cooking is complete, use a natural pressure release for 20 minutes; carefully remove the lid. Reserve the cooking liquid.

Transfer the warm, drained chickpeas to your food processor; add the remaining ingredients. While the food processor is running, pour in the cooking liquid to achieve the desired consistency.

To serve, drizzle olive oil on top of the hummus if desired. Bon appétit!

173. Scarlet Runner with Turkey and Herbs

(Ready in about 45 minutes)

Per serving: 350 Calories; 24.1g Fat; 9.7g Carbs; 23.2g Protein; 2.7g Sugars; 2.8g Fiber

INGREDIENTS

1 tablespoon olive oil
1/2 onion, chopped
1 garlic clove, minced
1 bell pepper, sliced
1/4 pound Scarlet Runner beans
2 ounces smoked turkey, boneless and shredded

1 tablespoon sherry wine
1 cup turkey broth
1 bay leaf
1 sprig thyme
1 sprig rosemary
Kosher salt and ground black pepper, to taste

DIRECTIONS

Press the "Sauté" button and heat the oil. Now, sauté the onion until tender and translucent. Then, stir in the garlic and bell pepper and continue to sauté until they are aromatic but not browned.

Add the other ingredients to the inner pot; stir to combine well.

Secure the lid. Choose the "Bean/Chili" mode and cook for 25 minutes at High pressure. Once cooking is complete, use a natural pressure release for 10 minutes; carefully remove the lid.

Taste, adjust the seasonings and serve warm. Bon appétit!

174. Mediterranean Lima Beans with Ham

(Ready in about 45 minutes)

Per serving: 490 Calories; 4.4g Fat; 75g Carbs; 38.2g Protein; 10.6g Sugars; 22g Fiber

INGREDIENTS

1/2 pound dry baby lima beans, rinsed
4 ounces cooked ham, chopped
1/2 onion, chopped
1 clove garlic, minced
2 cups beef bone broth

1 thyme sprig
1 rosemary sprig
1 teaspoon dried parsley flakes
Sea salt and freshly ground black pepper, to taste
1 bay leaf

DIRECTIONS

Place all ingredients in the inner pot of your Instant Pot.
Secure the lid. Choose the "Bean/Chili" mode and cook for 25 minutes at High pressure. Once cooking is complete, use a natural pressure release for 10 minutes; carefully remove the lid.
Ladle into individual bowls and enjoy!

175. Oriental Bean and Cheese Dip

(Ready in about 55 minutes)

Per serving: 316 Calories; 16.7g Fat; 31.7g Carbs; 12.1g Protein; 5.8g Sugars; 6.3g Fiber

INGREDIENTS

3 ounces garbanzo beans, rinsed
1 ½ cups of water
1/4 cup cream cheese
1 teaspoon hot sauce
1/2 teaspoon dried thyme
1/2 teaspoon cumin

1/2 teaspoon garlic powder
1/2 teaspoon onion powder
1 tablespoon lime juice
1 tablespoon tahini (sesame butter)
1 tablespoon cilantro, chopped

DIRECTIONS

Add the garbanzo beans and water to the inner pot.
Secure the lid. Choose the "Bean/Chili" mode and cook for 40 minutes at High pressure. Once cooking is complete, use a natural pressure release for 10 minutes; carefully remove the lid. Reserve the cooking liquid.
Transfer the boiled garbanzo beans to your blender or food processor; add the other ingredients and blend until smooth and creamy. Add the reserved liquid as needed for desired consistency.
Place in your refrigerator until ready to use. Enjoy!

176. Country-Style Anasazi Bean Soup

(Ready in about 40 minutes)

Per serving: 494 Calories; 17.3g Fat; 63.2g Carbs; 23.8g Protein; 4.5g Sugars; 12.7g Fiber

INGREDIENTS

3 ounces smoked bacon, chopped
6 ounces Anasazi beans, rinsed
2 cloves garlic, pressed
2 cups vegetable broth
1/2 cup tomato puree

1 bay leaf
1/2 teaspoon dried sage
1/2 teaspoon dried oregano
1/2 onion, chopped
Kosher salt and ground black pepper, to taste

DIRECTIONS

Press the "Sauté" button to preheat the Instant Pot. Cook the bacon for 2 to 3 minutes or until it is crisp.
Place the other ingredients in the inner pot of your Instant Pot.
Secure the lid. Choose the "Bean/Chili" mode and cook for 25 minutes at High pressure. Once cooking is complete, use a natural pressure release for 10 minutes; carefully remove the lid.
Ladle into soup bowls and serve garnished with the reserved bacon. Serve with salsa if desired. Bon appétit!

177. Green Lentil Stew

(Ready in about 20 minutes)

Per serving: 353 Calories; 8.1g Fat; 55.5g Carbs; 15.8g Protein; 12.3g Sugars; 13g Fiber

INGREDIENTS

1 tablespoon peanut oil
1/2 cup scallions, chopped onion
1 clove garlic, minced
1 bell pepper, chopped
1 carrot, chopped
1/2 celery rib, chopped

1/2 teaspoon oregano
1/2 teaspoon basil
1/2 teaspoon red pepper flakes, crushed
1/2 cup green lentils
2 cups vegetable broth

1/2 cup tomato sauce
1 cup green beans, trimmed
Sea salt and ground black pepper, to season

DIRECTIONS

Press the "Sauté" button and heat the oil until sizzling; once hot, cook the scallions, garlic, bell peppers, carrots, and celery until they have softened.

Add the spices, lentils, broth, and tomato sauce; gently stir to combine.

Secure the lid. Choose the "Manual" mode and cook for 8 minutes at High pressure. Once cooking is complete, use a natural pressure release for 5 minutes; carefully remove the lid.

Afterwards, add the green beans, salt, and black pepper to the inner pot; gently stir to combine.

Secure the lid. Choose the "Manual" mode and cook for 3 minutes at High pressure. Once cooking is complete, use a quick pressure release; carefully remove the lid. Serve warm.

178. Traditional Japanese Kuromame

(Ready in about 30 minutes)

Per serving: 302 Calories; 1.5g Fat; 61.2g Carbs; 12.5g Protein; 26.4g Sugars; 3.1g Fiber

INGREDIENTS

1/3 pound black soybeans, rinsed
2 cups water
1/2 cup sugar

1 tablespoon soy sauce
A pinch of kosher salt
2-inch square of kombu

DIRECTIONS

Add all ingredients to the inner pot of your Instant Pot.

Secure the lid. Choose the "Manual" mode and cook for 15 minutes at High pressure. Once cooking is complete, use a natural pressure release for 10 minutes; carefully remove the lid.

Let the beans soak in the sauce for 24 hours. The black soybeans should be soft and glossy. Cover and refrigerate. Enjoy!

179. Traditional Indian Matar

(Ready in about 20 minutes)

Per serving: 182 Calories; 7.9g Fat; 21.5g Carbs; 7.6g Protein; 10.9g Sugars; 5g Fiber

INGREDIENTS

1/2 tablespoon ghee, melted
1/4 teaspoon cumin seeds
1/2 yellow onion, chopped
1 cup green peas
1 tomato, pureed

1/2 teaspoon garam masala
1/2 tablespoon coriander
1/2 teaspoon chili powder
Sea salt and ground black pepper, to taste

2 curry leaves
1 ½ cups vegetable broth
1 tablespoon chickpea flour
1/2 cup yogurt

DIRECTIONS

Press the "Sauté" button and melt the ghee. Once hot, cook the cumin seeds for about 1 minute or until fragrant.

Add the onion and continue sautéing an additional 3 minutes.

Now, stir in the green peas, tomatoes, garam masala, coriander, chili powder, salt, black pepper, curry leaves, and broth.

Secure the lid. Choose the "Manual" mode and cook for 12 minutes at High pressure. Once cooking is complete, use a quick pressure release; carefully remove the lid.

Now, stir in the chickpea flour and let it simmer on the "Sauté" button until the cooking liquid has thickened. Serve in soup bowls with yogurt on the side. Bon appétit!

180. Thanksgiving Beans with Turkey

(Ready in about 40 minutes)

Per serving: 543 Calories; 13.4g Fat; 47.1g Carbs; 58.4g Protein; 4.1g Sugars; 10.6g Fiber

INGREDIENTS

1 tablespoon grapeseed oil
1/2 onion, chopped
1 teaspoon garlic, minced
1 sweet pepper, seeded and chopped
1/2 poblano pepper, seeded and minced
4 ounces dry kidney beans, rinsed

1/2 smoked turkey drumsticks
1 bay leaf
1/2 teaspoon dried oregano
1/2 teaspoon dried basil
Sea salt and ground black pepper, to taste
2 cups chicken broth, low sodium

DIRECTIONS

Press the "Sauté" button and heat the oil until sizzling. Once hot, cook the onion for 3 to 4 minutes or until tender.

Now, stir in garlic and peppers; continue to cook until tender and aromatic. Str in the remaining ingredients.

Secure the lid. Choose the "Bean/Chili" mode and cook for 25 minutes at High pressure. Once cooking is complete, use a natural pressure release for 10 minutes; carefully remove the lid. Bon appétit!

181. Indian Sorakkai Sambar

(Ready in about 35 minutes)

Per serving: 218 Calories; 5.9g Fat; 33.8g Carbs; 6.9g Protein; 11.2g Sugars; 8.2g Fiber

INGREDIENTS

3/4 cup Pigeon pea lentils
1 teaspoon sesame oil
1/2 yellow onion, chopped
2 curry leaves
1/2 Indian ghost jolokia chili pepper, chopped
1/2 tablespoon tamarind

1/2 teaspoon Urad Dal
1/2 tablespoon sambar powder
1/2 teaspoon turmeric powder
Sea salt and ground black pepper, to taste
1/2 teaspoon cayenne pepper
1/2 cup tomato sauce

DIRECTIONS

Add the lentils and 4 cups of water to the inner pot.

Secure the lid. Choose the "Manual" mode and cook for 10 minutes at High pressure. Once cooking is complete, use a natural pressure release for 10 minutes; carefully remove the lid.

Meanwhile, heat a saucepan over medium-high heat. Cook the onion for about 3 minutes or until translucent. Now, add the curry leaves and chili pepper to the skillet. Let it cook for a further minute or until they are aromatic.

Add the other ingredients, cover, and reduce the heat to medium-low; let it simmer for about 13 minutes or until everything is thoroughly cooked.

Transfer the onion/tomato mixture to the inner pot of your Instant Pot. Stir to combine and serve immediately. Bon appétit!

182. Pinto Beans with Turkey Sausage and Tomato

(Ready in about 45 minutes)

Per serving: 439 Calories; 13.6g Fat; 57.6g Carbs; 28.8g Protein; 4.9g Sugars; 13.1g Fiber

INGREDIENTS

1 tablespoon canola oil
3 ounces turkey sausage sliced
1/2 onion, chopped
1 clove garlic, minced
1 bell pepper, sliced

3/4 cup dry pinto beans
1 bay leaf
1/2 teaspoon dried sage
Sea salt and ground black pepper, to taste

1/2 teaspoon cayenne pepper
2 cups chicken broth
1/2 tomato, crushed

DIRECTIONS

Press the "Sauté" button and heat the oil. Sauté the sausage until it becomes slightly crispy.

Now, add the onion, garlic, and pepper; continue to cook until they are tender. Add the remaining ingredients to the inner pot.

Secure the lid. Choose the "Bean/Chili" mode and cook for 30 minutes at High pressure. Once cooking is complete, use a natural pressure release for 10 minutes; carefully remove the lid.

Press the "Sauté" button and let it simmer until the cooking liquid has thickened. Serve with your favorite toppings. Bon appétit!

183. Italian-Style Heirloom Beans

(Ready in about 45 minutes)

Per serving: 409 Calories; 1.3g Fat; 76.2g Carbs; 25.7g Protein; 5g Sugars; 23.1g Fiber

INGREDIENTS

2 cups water

1/2 pound heirloom beans

1/2 tablespoon Italian Seasoning blend

1 bell pepper, seeded and chopped

1 jalapeño pepper, seeded and chopped

1/2 teaspoon liquid smoke

1/2 teaspoon onion powder

1 teaspoon granulated garlic

DIRECTIONS

Add all ingredients to the inner pot of your Instant Pot.

Secure the lid. Choose the "Bean/Chili" mode and cook for 30 minutes at High pressure. Once cooking is complete, use a natural pressure release for 10 minutes; carefully remove the lid.

Ladle into serving bowls and garnish with fresh scallions if desired. Bon appétit!

184. Spicy Pea Dip with Herbs

(Ready in about 45 minutes)

Per serving: 42 Calories; 0.1g Fat; 7.8g Carbs; 2.7g Protein; 2.9g Sugars; 2.1g Fiber

INGREDIENTS

4 ounces frozen peas

1 cup water

2 tablespoons basil leaves, roughly chopped

1 tablespoon fresh parsley, chopped

1/2 tablespoon fresh cilantro, chopped

1 tablespoon fresh chives, chopped

1/4 fresh lemon, zested and juiced

1/2 teaspoon cayenne pepper

1/4 teaspoon hot sauce

Kosher salt and freshly ground black pepper, to taste

DIRECTIONS

Add the frozen peas and water to the inner pot of your Instant Pot.

Secure the lid. Choose the "Manual" mode and cook for 10 minutes at High pressure. Once cooking is complete, use a natural pressure release for 15 minutes; carefully remove the lid.

Transfer the boiled green peas to a bowl of your food processor; add the remaining ingredients and process until creamy and smooth, gradually adding the cooking liquid.

Serve with pita bread, tortilla chips or bread sticks if desired. Bon appétit!

185. Vegetarian Chili with Sour Cream

(Ready in about 40 minutes)

Per serving: 448 Calories; 12.5g Fat; 65.7g Carbs; 23g Protein; 11.4g Sugars; 6.5g Fiber

INGREDIENTS

1 tablespoon olive oil

1/2 onion, chopped

1 clove garlic, minced

1 sweet pepper, chopped

1 red chili pepper, chopped

1/2 carrot, chopped

1/2 celery stalk, chopped

Sea salt and ground black pepper, to taste

1/2 teaspoon red pepper

1/2 teaspoon ground cumin

1/2 teaspoon Mexican oregano

10 ounces canned tomatoes, diced with their juices

4 ounces dried navy beans

1 cup vegetable broth

1 bay leaf

1 thyme sprig

1/3 cup sour cream

DIRECTIONS

Press the "Sauté" button and heat the oil. Now, cook the onion until it is softened. Stir in the garlic and peppers; continue sautéing an additional 2 minutes or until fragrant.

Add the carrot, celery, salt, black pepper, red pepper, cumin, oregano, tomatoes, beans, broth, bay leaf, and thyme sprig to the inner pot.

Secure the lid. Choose the "Bean/Chili" mode and cook for 25 minutes at High pressure. Once cooking is complete, use a natural pressure release for 10 minutes; carefully remove the lid.

Serve with a dollop of sour cream. Enjoy!

186. Bean Soup with Potatoes and Parmesan

(Ready in about 50 minutes)

Per serving: 453 Calories; 11.6g Fat; 65.3g Carbs; 24.5g Protein; 6.1g Sugars; 10.2g Fiber

INGREDIENTS

1 tablespoon grapeseed oil
1/2 onion, chopped
1 garlic clove, minced
1/2 carrot, chopped
1/2 celery rib, sliced
1 cup water

1 cup cream of mushroom soup
1 potato, peeled and grated
1 bay leaf
1/2 teaspoon marjoram
Sea salt and ground black pepper, to taste

4 ounces dry white kidney beans, rinsed
1 cup fresh spinach, torn into pieces
2 tablespoons Parmigiano-Reggiano cheese, grated

DIRECTIONS

Press the "Sauté" button and heat the oil. Now, cook the onion, garlic, carrot, and celery until they have softened.

Now, add the water, cream of mushrooms soup, potatoes, spices, and beans to the inner pot.

Secure the lid. Choose the "Bean/Chili" mode and cook for 30 minutes at High pressure. Once cooking is complete, use a natural pressure release for 15 minutes; carefully remove the lid.

Mash the soup with a potato masher or use an immersion blender. Add the spinach and press the "Sauté" button again. Let it simmer on the lowest setting until the leaves wilt.

Ladle the soup into four serving bowls. Top each serving with 1 tablespoon of the Parmigiano Reggiano cheese. Bon appétit!

187. Wax Bean Salad with Peanut Butter

(Ready in about 10 minutes + chilling time)

Per serving: 316 Calories; 25.4g Fat; 12.2g Carbs; 2.8g Protein; 5.9g Sugars; 2.3g Fiber

INGREDIENTS

6 ounces yellow wax beans, trimmed and halved crosswise
1/2 red onion, sliced
1 bell pepper, deveined and sliced
4 tablespoons extra-virgin olive oil
1/2 tablespoon fresh lemon juice
1/2 tablespoon balsamic vinegar

1 tablespoon peanut butter
1/2 teaspoon Dijon mustard
1/2 teaspoon garlic powder
Salt and white pepper, to taste
1/4 teaspoon red pepper flakes
1 tablespoon fresh Italian parsley, roughly chopped

DIRECTIONS

Place 1 cup of water and a steamer basket in the inner pan of your Instant Pot. Place the wax beans in the steamer basket.

Secure the lid. Choose the "Manual" mode and cook for 3 minutes at High pressure. Once cooking is complete, use a quick pressure release; carefully remove the lid.

Toss the chilled wax beans with the other ingredients; toss to combine well. Serve well chilled.

188. Summer Bean Salad

(Ready in about 35 minutes)

Per serving: 557 Calories; 14.1g Fat; 76g Carbs; 34.1g Protein; 2.7g Sugars; 23g Fiber

INGREDIENTS

1/2 pound cannellini beans, rinsed
1/2 cup fresh tomatoes, sliced
1/2 cucumber, sliced
1/2 onion, thinly sliced
1/2 teaspoon garlic, minced

1/3 cup Kalamata olives, pitted and halved
1 sweet pepper, seeded and diced
1/2 pepperoncini, seeded and diced
1/4 cup Halloumi cheese, crumbled
3 basil leaves, roughly chopped

2 tablespoons extra virgin olive oil
2 tablespoons balsamic vinegar, or more to taste
Sea salt and freshly cracked black pepper, to taste

DIRECTIONS

Add the cannellini beans to the inner pot of your Instant Pot. Pour in 8 cups of water.

Secure the lid. Choose the "Bean/Chili" mode and cook for 30 minutes at High pressure. Once cooking is complete, use a quick pressure release; carefully remove the lid.

Transfer your beans to a salad bowl. Add the remaining ingredients and toss to combine well.

Serve well chilled.

189. Snap Pea and Chicken Medley

(Ready in about 50 minutes)

Per serving: 471 Calories; 21.3g Fat; 14.5g Carbs; 52.1g Protein; 2.2g Sugars; 3.3g Fiber

INGREDIENTS

1/2 pound chicken breast, cut into small chunks
1 tablespoon arrowroot powder
1/2 tablespoon teriyaki sauce
1 clove garlic, minced
1/2 teaspoon cayenne pepper
1 teaspoon sesame oil, toasted

1 cup chicken broth
1 cup sugar snap peas
1 carrot, sliced
1 small onion, chopped
3 tablespoons peanuts, dry-roasted and roughly chopped

DIRECTIONS

Combine the chicken breasts, arrowroot powder, teriyaki sauce, garlic, and cayenne pepper in a mixing bowl.
Press the "Sauté" button. Preheat the oil and cook the seasoned chicken for 5 to 6 minutes or until no longer pink.
Pour in a splash of the broth, scraping the pot to loosen the browned bits. Stir in the remaining broth, sugar snap peas, carrots, and onions.
Secure the lid. Choose the "Slow Cook" button and "More" mode; cook for 30 minutes. When time is up, carefully remove the lid.
Garnish with the dry-roasted peanuts and serve warm. Enjoy!

190. Dad's Lima Beans with Bacon

(Ready in about 20 minutes)

Per serving: 461 Calories; 25.7g Fat; 39.6g Carbs; 16.8g Protein; 10.3g Sugars; 10g Fiber

INGREDIENTS

4 ounces bacon
1/2 yellow onion, chopped
1 garlic clove, pressed
1/2 pound dry lima beans
2 cups chicken broth

1 cup water
1/2 cup tomato sauce
1 bay leaf
1 sprig rosemary
1 sprig thyme

DIRECTIONS

Press the "Sauté" button to preheat your Instant Pot. Cook the bacon until crisp; crumble with a fork and reserve.
Add the onion and garlic and continue to cook them in pan drippings until tender and fragrant.
Now, stir in the remaining ingredients.
Secure the lid. Choose the "Manual" mode and cook for 12 minutes at High pressure. Once cooking is complete, use a quick pressure release; carefully remove the lid.
Discard the bay leaf and garnish with the reserved bacon; serve warm. Bon appétit!

191. Balsamic Lentils with Brown Rice

(Ready in about 35 minutes)

Per serving: 434 Calories; 6g Fat; 85g Carbs; 10.7g Protein; 3.4g Sugars; 5g Fiber

INGREDIENTS

1 cup brown rice, rinsed
1/2 cups du Puy lentils
1 cup cream of celery soup
1/2 cup water
1/2 cup shallots, chopped
1/2 teaspoon garlic, chopped

1 teaspoon cayenne pepper
1 teaspoon fennel seeds
Kosher salt and black pepper, to season
1 bay leaf
1 tablespoon balsamic vinegar

DIRECTIONS

Place all ingredient, except for the vinegar, in the inner pot of your Instant Pot.
Secure the lid. Choose the "Manual" mode and cook for 15 minutes at High pressure. Once cooking is complete, use a natural pressure release for 15 minutes; carefully remove the lid.
Afterward, stir in the vinegar and serve immediately. Enjoy!

192. Mom's Black-Eyed Peas

(Ready in about 50 minutes)

Per serving: 317 Calories; 20.7g Fat; 22.7g Carbs; 12.9g Protein; 3.7g Sugars; 7.3g Fiber

INGREDIENTS

3 ounces pancetta
3/4 cup black eyed peas, rinsed
1 cup cream of celery soup
1 cup water

Sea salt and ground black pepper, to taste
1 teaspoon paprika
1 tablespoon fresh parsley, chopped

DIRECTIONS

Press the "Sauté" button to preheat your Instant Pot; now, cook the pancetta until browned and reserve.

Add the black eyed peas, cream of celery soup, water, salt, pepper, and paprika to the inner pot.

Secure the lid. Choose the "Bean/Chili" mode and cook for 30 minutes at High pressure. Once cooking is complete, use a natural pressure release for 15 minutes; carefully remove the lid.

Ladle into serving bowls and garnish with fresh parsley and the reserved pancetta. Bon appétit!

193. Baked Beans with Colby Cheese

(Ready in about 1 hour 5 minutes)

Per serving: 348 Calories; 14.7g Fat; 36.6g Carbs; 19.6g Protein; 4.6g Sugars; 8.2g Fiber

INGREDIENTS

1/2 tablespoon olive oil
1/2 onion, chopped
1 clove garlic, pressed
1 chili pepper, seeded and chopped
2 cups roasted vegetable broth

1/2 cups white kidney beans, rinsed
1 bay leaf
Kosher salt and ground black pepper, to taste
1/2 teaspoon ground cumin
1/2 cup Colby cheese, shredded

DIRECTIONS

Press the "Sauté" button and heat the olive oil until sizzling. Then, sauté the onion for about 3 minutes or until tender.

Now, stir in the garlic and chili pepper; continue to cook for 1 minute more or until fragrant. Add a splash of broth to deglaze the pan.

Add the remaining broth, beans, bay leaves, salt, black pepper, and cumin to the inner pot of your Instant Pot.

Secure the lid. Choose the "Bean/Chili" mode and cook for 40 minutes at High pressure. Once cooking is complete, use a natural pressure release for 20 minutes; carefully remove the lid. Reserve 1 cup of the cooking liquid.

Then, puree the beans with an immersion blender until they reach your desired consistency. Sprinkle with the shredded Colby cheese and serve warm.

CHICKEN

194. Mexican-Style Chicken Sandwiches

(Ready in about 25 minutes)

Per serving: 449 Calories; 14.1g Fat; 46.3g Carbs; 32.9g Protein; 7.5g Sugars; 2.8g Fiber

INGREDIENTS

1/2 pound chicken breasts, boneless and skinless
Kosher salt and freshly ground black pepper, to taste
1/2 cup chicken broth

1/2 cup red enchilada sauce
1/2 cup spring onions, sliced
4 slider buns

DIRECTIONS

Place the chicken breasts in the inner pot. Season with salt and pepper; pour in the chicken broth and enchilada sauce.
Secure the lid. Choose the "Manual" mode and cook for 9 minutes at High pressure. Once cooking is complete, use a quick pressure release; carefully remove the lid.
Place the bottom half of the slider buns on a baking sheet. Top with layers of the chicken mixture and spring onions. Put on the top buns and spritz with cooking spray.
Bake about 10 minutes in the preheated oven until buns are golden. Enjoy!

195. Roast Chicken with Garlic and Herbs

(Ready in about 35 minutes)

Per serving: 493 Calories; 20.9g Fat; 3g Carbs; 69.9g Protein; 1.3g Sugars; 0.9g Fiber

INGREDIENTS

2 tablespoons butter, softened
1/2 head of garlic, crushed
Salt and ground black pepper, to taste
1/2 tablespoon paprika

1 rosemary sprig, crushed
1 thyme sprig, crushed
2 cups water
1 ½ pounds whole chicken

DIRECTIONS

In a small mixing dish, thoroughly combine the butter, garlic, salt, black pepper, paprika, rosemary, and thyme.
Pour the water into the inner pot.
Pat the chicken dry. Then, rub the butter mixture all over the chicken to season well. Place the chicken in the inner pot.
Secure the lid. Choose "Manual" mode. Cook for 20 minutes at High pressure. Once cooking is complete, use a natural pressure release; carefully remove the lid.
Afterwards, place the chicken under the broiler for 10 minutes until the skin is lightly crisped. Bon appétit!

196. Classic Chicken Gumbo

(Ready in about 25 minutes)

Per serving: 551 Calories; 29.2g Fat; 35.2g Carbs; 52.1g Protein; 6.2g Sugars; 7.2g Fiber

INGREDIENTS

2 tablespoons olive oil
1/2 onion, chopped
1 sweet pepper, deseeded and chopped
1/2 pounds chicken breasts, boneless, skinless, and cubed
2 ounces Andouille sausage, sliced
1/2 red chili pepper, deseeded and chopped

1 celery stalk, trimmed and diced
1 carrot, trimmed and diced
1 clove garlic, sliced
1 ripe tomatoes, pureed
1/2 teaspoon basil, dried
1/2 teaspoon paprika
Kosher salt and ground black pepper, to taste

1 bay leaf, dried
1/2 tablespoon gumbo file
1/2 tablespoon chicken bouillon granules
4 cups water
1/4 cup all-purpose flour
1/3 pound okra, cut into bite-sized pieces

DIRECTIONS

Press the "Sauté" button and heat 1 tablespoon of oil until sizzling. Now, sweat the onion and peppers until tender and aromatic or about 3 minutes; reserve.
Then, heat the remaining tablespoon of olive oil and cook the chicken and sausage until no longer pink, about 4 minutes. Make sure to stir periodically to ensure even cooking.
Stir the chili pepper, celery, carrot, garlic, tomatoes, basil, paprika, salt, black pepper, bay leaves, gumbo file, and chicken bouillon granules into the inner pot. Add the reserved onion/pepper mixture. Pour in 6 cups of water.
Secure the lid. Choose the "Manual" mode. Cook for 7 minutes at High pressure. Once cooking is complete, use a quick pressure release; carefully remove the lid.
Mix the flour with 1 cup of cooking liquid and reserve. Afterwards, stir in the okra and flour mixture into the inner pot.
Secure the lid. Choose "Manual" mode. Cook for 3 minutes at High pressure. Once cooking is complete, use a natural pressure release; carefully remove the lid.
Serve in individual bowls, garnished with garlic croutons if desired. Bon appétit!

197. Spicy Chicken Bake with Beans

(Ready in about 25 minutes)

Per serving: 358 Calories; 11.7g Fat; 28.2g Carbs; 38.7g Protein; 3g Sugars; 7.2g Fiber

INGREDIENTS

1 tablespoon olive oil
1/2 pound chicken drumettes, cut into bite-sized pieces
1/2 onion, chopped

1 cup chicken bone broth
1/2 teaspoon granulated garlic
1/2 teaspoon cayenne pepper
Salt and ground black pepper, to taste

1/2 teaspoon Sriracha sauce
8 ounces canned kidney beans, drained
1/2 tablespoon fresh cilantro, chopped

DIRECTIONS

Press the "Sauté" button and heat the olive oil.
Now, cook the chicken drumettes until no longer pink or about 4 minutes.
Add the onion, chicken broth, garlic, cayenne pepper, salt, black pepper, and Sriracha sauce to the inner pot; gently stir to combine.
Secure the lid and choose the "Poultry" mode. Cook for 15 minutes at High pressure. Once cooking is complete, use a quick pressure release; carefully remove the lid.
Stir in the kidney beans; secure the lid and let it sit in the residual heat until thoroughly heated. Serve garnished with fresh cilantro. Enjoy!

198. Traditional Locrio de Pollo

(Ready in about 20 minutes)

Per serving: 528 Calories; 19.1g Fat; 54.4g Carbs; 34.9g Protein; 6.1g Sugars; 4.5g Fiber

INGREDIENTS

1/2 tablespoon olive oil
1/2 cup brown onion, chopped
1/2 pound chicken breasts, trimmed and cut into bite-sized pieces
1 tablespoon Rueda
1/2 cup short-grain white rice

1 cup chicken broth
1/2 cup tomato puree
1/2 teaspoon dried oregano
Sea salt and ground black pepper, to taste
1/2 teaspoon saffron threads

2 ounces seafood mix
2 ounces chorizo sausage, casings removed and crumbled
1 lemon, juiced and zested
1 tablespoon fresh parsley, roughly chopped

DIRECTIONS

Press the "Sauté" button and heat the olive oil.
Now, cook the brown onion and chicken until the onion is translucent and the chicken is no longer pink or about 4 minutes. Deglaze the pot with the Rueda wine.
Stir in the rice, broth, tomato puree, oregano, salt, black pepper, and saffron.
Secure the lid and choose the "Manual" mode. Cook for 5 minutes at High pressure. Afterwards, use a quick release and carefully remove the lid.
Add the seafood mix and sausage. Secure the lid and choose the "Manual" mode. Cook for 4 to 5 minutes at High pressure; use a quick release and carefully remove the lid.
Add the lemon and parsley and serve immediately. Bon appétit!

199. Chicken Medley with Garden Vegetables

(Ready in about 20 minutes)

Per serving: 377 Calories; 17.5g Fat; 30g Carbs; 28.1g Protein; 12.4g Sugars; 9.2g Fiber

INGREDIENTS

1 tablespoon lard, at room temperature
1/2 pound chicken breasts, sliced into serving-size pieces
1/2 teaspoon dried marjoram

1/2 teaspoon dried sage
1/2 teaspoon ground black pepper
Sea salt, to taste
1/3 cup leeks, sliced
1 garlic clove, sliced

1 cup chicken bone broth
1 cup butternut squash, diced
1/2 eggplant, diced
1/2 head cabbage, diced
2 tablespoons fresh chives, chopped

DIRECTIONS

Press the "Sauté" button and melt the lard until sizzling.
Then, sear the chicken breasts until it is lightly browned or about 5 minutes. Add the spices and stir to combine.
Add the leeks and garlic. Pour in the chicken bone broth. Afterwards, add the vegetables and secure the lid.
Choose the "Manual" mode. Cook for 8 minutes at High pressure. Once cooking is complete, use a quick pressure release; carefully remove the lid.
Using a slotted spoon, remove the chicken and vegetables to a serving platter.
Press the "Sauté" button and simmer the cooking liquid for about 3 minutes until slightly thickened. Serve garnished with fresh chives. Bon appétit!

200. Spicy Chicken and Root Vegetable Mélange

(Ready in about 20 minutes)

Per serving: 331 Calories; 9.3g Fat; 24g Carbs; 38.2g Protein; 6.3g Sugars; 5.2g Fiber

INGREDIENTS

3/4 pound whole chicken, boneless, skinless, and cubed
1/2 celery stalk, trimmed and sliced
1 carrot, trimmed and sliced
1 parsnip, trimmed and sliced

1 bell pepper, seeded and thinly sliced
1 habanero pepper, seeded and thinly sliced
1 cup vegetable broth
1 garlic clove, smashed

1/2 teaspoon ginger, grated
1/2 teaspoon smoked paprika
1 tablespoon sesame seed oil
1 tablespoon arrowroot powder
1 tablespoon toasted sesame seeds

DIRECTIONS

Place the chicken pieces in the inner pot. Place the vegetables on the top. Pour in the vegetable broth.

Add the remaining ingredients, except for the toasted sesame seeds.

Secure the lid. Choose the "Poultry" mode and High pressure; cook for 15 minutes. Once cooking is complete, use a quick release.

Transfer the chicken and veggies to serving plates using a slotted spoon. Press the "Sauté" button to preheat the Instant Pot. Stir the arrowroot powder into the cooking liquid to thicken the sauce.

Spoon the sauce over the warm chicken and vegetables. Garnish with the toasted sesame seeds. Bon appétit!

201. Chicken Drumsticks with Millet and Green Beans

(Ready in about 25 minutes)

Per serving: 521 Calories; 21.2g Fat; 50g Carbs; 32.1g Protein; 7.1g Sugars; 7.7g Fiber

INGREDIENTS

2 chicken drumsticks, skinless and boneless
Sea salt and ground black pepper, to taste
1/2 teaspoon red pepper flakes, crushed

1/3 teaspoon dried basil
1/3 teaspoon dried oregano
1/3 teaspoon ground cumin
1 tablespoon olive oil
1/4 cup shallots, chopped
1 garlic clove, finely chopped

1 bell pepper, deseeded and chopped
1/2 cup millet
1 cup vegetable broth
1/2 cup tomato puree
1 bay leaf
1 cup green beans

DIRECTIONS

Season the chicken drumsticks with salt, black pepper, red pepper, basil, oregano, and cumin.

Press the "Sauté" button and heat the olive oil. Sear the chicken drumsticks for 5 minutes, turning them to ensure even cooking.

Add the shallots, garlic, pepper, millet, broth, tomato puree, and bay leaf to the Instant Pot.

Secure the lid and choose the "Poultry" mode. Cook for 15 minutes at High pressure. Once cooking is complete, use a quick pressure release; carefully remove the lid.

Add the green beans and secure the lid again; let it sit in the residual heat until wilts. Enjoy!

202. Chicken and Pasta Bake with Ricotta Cheese

(Ready in about 20 minutes)

Per serving: 626 Calories; 25.5g Fat; 55.1g Carbs; 38.7g Protein; 3g Sugars; 2.7g Fiber

INGREDIENTS

1 tablespoon olive oil
1 garlic clove, minced
1 strip bacon, diced
1/2 pound chicken legs, boneless skinless, cubed

1 ounce vermouth
4 ounces Ricotta cheese, crumbled, at room temperature
1 cup water
1 cup elbow pasta

1/2 onion, sliced
1 sweet pepper, seeded and thinly sliced
1 cup chicken broth

DIRECTIONS

Press the "Sauté" button to preheat your Instant Pot.

Once hot, heat the olive oil. Now, cook the garlic and bacon until they are fragrant.

Stir in the cubed chicken and cook for 3 minutes more or until it is no longer pink. Use vermouth to scrape the remaining bits of meat off the bottom of the inner pot.

Add the softened Ricotta cheese and water. Secure the lid. Choose the "Poultry" mode and High pressure; cook for 5 minutes. Once cooking is complete, use a quick release.

Add the elbow pasta, onion, and peppers. Pour in the chicken broth; gently stir to combine.

Secure the lid and choose the "Manual" mode. Cook for 4 minutes longer. Afterwards, use a quick release and carefully remove the lid. Bon appétit!

203. Saucy Chicken Fillets with Olives

(Ready in about 20 minutes)

Per serving: 328 Calories; 13.1g Fat; 13.3g Carbs; 37.5g Protein; 8.1g Sugars; 2.4g Fiber

INGREDIENTS

3/4 pound chicken fillets
1 garlic clove, halved
1 tablespoon olive oil
1/4 cup tamari sauce
1/2 cup tomato puree

1/2 cup chicken broth
1/2 tablespoon molasses
Sea salt and freshly ground black pepper, to taste
1/2 teaspoon red pepper flakes

1 bay leaf
1 rosemary sprig
1/4 cup Kalamata olives, pitted and halved

DIRECTIONS

Rub the chicken fillets with the garlic halves on all sides. Press the "Sauté" button to preheat your Instant Pot.

Heat the olive oil and sear the chicken fillets for 2 minutes per side.

Add the tamari sauce, tomato puree, broth, molasses, salt, black pepper, red pepper, bay leaf and rosemary sprig.

Secure the lid. Choose the "Manual" mode and High pressure; cook for 9 minutes. Once cooking is complete, use a quick release; remove the lid.

Serve garnished with Kalamata olives. Enjoy!

204. Hot Chicken Tacos

(Ready in about 20 minutes)

Per serving: 545 Calories; 18.5g Fat; 64g Carbs; 29.8g Protein; 13.2g Sugars; 7.4g Fiber

INGREDIENTS

1 tablespoon olive oil
1/4 pound ground chicken
1/4 pound ground turkey
1 clove garlic, minced
1/2 onion, chopped
1 sweet pepper, deseeded and chopped
1 serrano pepper, deseeded and chopped

1/4 cup hoisin sauce
1 cup water
1/2 tablespoon tamari sauce
Salt, to taste
1/2 teaspoon freshly ground black pepper
1/2 teaspoon Mexican oregano

2 (approx. 6-inch diameter) tortillas
1/2 cup sweet corn kernels, cooked
1/2 cup canned black beans, drained
1/2 tablespoon Dijon mustard
1/2 teaspoon jalapeno pepper, minced
1 tomato, sliced
1 head butter lettuce

DIRECTIONS

Press the "Sauté" button. Once hot, heat the olive oil until sizzling. Now, brown the ground meat for 2 to 3 minutes, stirring continuously.

Add the garlic, onion, peppers, hoisin sauce, water, tamari sauce, salt, black pepper, and Mexican oregano.

Secure the lid. Choose the "Manual" mode and High pressure; cook for 6 minutes. Once cooking is complete, use a quick pressure release; carefully remove the lid.

Assemble the tortillas with the ground chicken filling, corn, beans, mustard, jalapeno pepper, tomatoes, and lettuce. Enjoy!

205. Cholula Chicken Wings

(Ready in about 40 minutes)

Per serving: 418 Calories; 22.1g Fat; 8.8g Carbs; 41.6g Protein; 2.8g Sugars; 0.5g Fiber

INGREDIENTS

1 pound chicken wings
1 garlic clove, halved
1/2 teaspoon sea salt
1/4 teaspoon ground black pepper

1/2 teaspoon cayenne pepper flakes
2 tablespoons butter, melted
1/2 cup roasted vegetable broth
1/4 cup Cholula hot sauce

1/2 tablespoon brown sugar
1/2 teaspoon barbecue sauce
1 teaspoon corn starch, dissolved in 1 tablespoon of water

DIRECTIONS

Rub the chicken legs with the garlic halves; then, season with salt, black pepper, and cayenne pepper. Press the "Sauté" button.

Once hot, melt 2 tablespoons of the melted butter and sear the chicken wings approximately 4 minutes, turning them once during the cooking time. Add a splash of vegetable broth to deglaze the bottom of the pan.

Now, add the remaining broth and secure the lid. Choose the "Manual" mode and High pressure; cook for 12 minutes. Once the cooking is complete, use a quick pressure release; carefully remove the lid.

Remove the chicken wings from the Instant Pot, reserving the cooking liquid. Place the chicken wings on a lightly greased baking sheet.

Turn your oven on to High Broil. Broil the chicken wings approximately 15 minutes until it is crisp and golden brown; make sure to turn them over halfway through the cooking time.

Press the "Sauté" button and add the remaining 2 tablespoons of butter. Once hot, add the hot sauce, sugar, and barbecue sauce; pour in the reserved cooking liquid.

Let it simmer for 4 minutes; add the corn starch slurry and continue to simmer until the cooking liquid has reduced and concentrated.

Pour the prepared sauce over the reserved chicken and serve warm. Bon appétit!

206. Meatloaf with Parmesan and Peppers

(Ready in about 45 minutes)

Per serving: 521 Calories; 28.3g Fat; 23.7g Carbs; 44.1g Protein; 9g Sugars; 3.4g Fiber

INGREDIENTS

1 tablespoons olive oil
1 tablespoon Worcestershire sauce
1/2 pound ground chicken
1/4 pound ground beef
1/4 cup crackers, crushed
1/4 cup Parmesan cheese, grated

1 medium carrot, grated
1 sweet pepper, deseeded and chopped
1 chili pepper, deseeded and finely chopped
1/2 onion, finely chopped
1 garlic clove, minced

1 egg, beaten
1/4 cup BBQ sauce
Smoked salt flakes and freshly ground black pepper, to taste

DIRECTIONS

Place a steamer rack inside the inner pot; add 1/2 cup water. Cut 1 sheet of heavy-duty foil and brush with cooking spray.

In large mixing dish, thoroughly combine all ingredients until mixed well.

Shape the meat mixture into a loaf; place the meatloaf in the center of the foil. Wrap your meatloaf in the foil and lower onto the steamer rack.

Secure the lid. Choose the "Poultry" mode and cook for 30 minutes at High pressure. Once cooking is complete, use a quick pressure release; carefully remove the lid.

Then, transfer your meatloaf to a cutting board. Let it stand for 10 minutes before cutting and serving. To serve, brush with some extra BBQ sauce, if desired. Bon appétit!

207. Classic Teriyaki Chicken with Broccoli

(Ready in about 30 minutes)

Per serving: 294 Calories; 13.3g Fat; 15.1g Carbs; 27g Protein; 9.8g Sugars; 5.1g Fiber

INGREDIENTS

1 tablespoon sesame oil
1/2 pound chicken drumettes, skinless, boneless, cut into bite-sized chunks
1 garlic clove, minced

2 tablespoons soy sauce
3/4 cup water
2 tablespoons rice vinegar
2 tablespoons brown sugar

1 teaspoon ground ginger
2 tablespoons Mirin
3/4 pound broccoli florets
1 teaspoon arrowroot powder

DIRECTIONS

Press the "Sauté" button to preheat your Instant Pot. Heat the sesame oil and cook the chicken drumettes for 3 to 4 minutes.

Then, add the garlic and cook for 30 seconds more or until fragrant. Add the soy sauce, water, vinegar, sugar, ginger, rice wine, and Mirin. Secure the lid.

Choose the "Manual" mode and cook for 10 minutes at High pressure. Once cooking is complete, use a quick pressure release; carefully remove the lid.

Add the broccoli florets and secure the lid. Choose the "Manual" mode and cook for 2 minutes at High pressure. Once cooking is complete, use a quick pressure release; carefully remove the lid.

Transfer the chicken and broccoli to a nice serving platter.

Press the "Sauté" button to preheat your Instant Pot again. Add the arrowroot powder and stir until it is completely dissolved. Cook for 5 to 6 minutes or until the sauce thickens slightly. Spoon over the chicken and serve.

208. Cheesy Chicken Tenders

(Ready in about 25 minutes)

Per serving: 358 Calories; 14.1g Fat; 2.6g Carbs; 52.1g Protein; 1.5g Sugars; 0.2g Fiber

INGREDIENTS

1 tablespoon butter, softened
1 pound chicken tenders
1/2 cup vegetable broth
1/2 teaspoon shallot powder

1/2 teaspoon garlic powder
1/4 teaspoon smoked paprika
Sea salt and freshly ground black pepper, to taste

1/2 cup Cottage cheese, crumbled
1 heaping tablespoon fresh chives, roughly chopped

DIRECTIONS

Press the "Sauté" button and melt the butter. Sear the chicken tenders for 2 to 3 minutes.

Add the vegetable broth, shallot powder, garlic powder, paprika, salt, and black pepper.

Secure the lid. Choose "Manual" mode and cook for 8 minutes at High pressure. Once cooking is complete, use a natural pressure release; carefully remove the lid.

Stir in the cheese; cover with the lid and let it sit in the residual heat for 5 minutes. Garnish with fresh chives and serve immediately.

209. Creamy Dijon Chicken

(Ready in about 20 minutes)

Per serving: 419 Calories; 27.2g Fat; 4.3g Carbs; 37.8g Protein; 1.7g Sugars; 1g Fiber

INGREDIENTS

1 tablespoon olive oil, divided
1/2 pound chicken breasts, boneless
1/2 teaspoon dried basil
1/2 teaspoon dried oregano
1/2 teaspoon dried sage
1/2 teaspoon paprika

1/2 teaspoon garlic powder
Sea salt and ground black pepper, to taste
1/2 tablespoon Dijon mustard
1/2 cup chicken bone broth
1/4 cup heavy cream

DIRECTIONS

Press the "Sauté" button and heat the olive oil. Sear the chicken breasts until they are no longer pink.

Add the seasonings, mustard, and chicken bone broth.

Secure the lid. Choose "Manual" mode and cook for 8 minutes at High pressure. Once cooking is complete, use a natural pressure release; carefully remove the lid.

Lastly, add the heavy cream, cover with the lid, and let it sit in the residual heat for 6 to 8 minutes. Serve in individual bowls. Enjoy!

210. Asian Glazed Chicken Drumsticks

(Ready in about 25 minutes)

Per serving: 367 Calories; 14.6g Fat; 32.1g Carbs; 28g Protein; 27.4g Sugars; 1.8g Fiber

INGREDIENTS

1 tablespoon sesame seed oil
2 chicken drumsticks
1/4 teaspoon fresh ground pepper, or more to taste
Sea salt, to taste
1/2 tablespoon Chinese rice vinegar
3 tablespoons honey
1 tablespoon sweet chili sauce

1 clove garlic, minced
1/4 cup low-sodium soy sauce
1/4 cup no salt ketchup
1/2 cup water
1 tablespoon fresh cilantro, chopped
Small bunch scallions, chopped

DIRECTIONS

Press the "Sauté" button to preheat your Instant Pot.

Heat the sesame seed oil and sear the chicken for 5 minutes, stirring periodically. Season with black pepper and salt.

After that, stir in the vinegar, honey, chili sauce, garlic, soy sauce, ketchup, water, and cilantro; stir well to combine.

Secure the lid and choose the "Poultry" mode. Cook for 15 minutes. Afterwards, use a natural release and carefully remove the lid.

Garnish with chopped scallions. Bon appétit!

211. Creamed Chicken Salad

(Ready in about 10 minutes + chilling time)

Per serving: 356 Calories; 24.6g Fat; 4.5g Carbs; 27.3g Protein; 0.9g Sugars; 1.2g Fiber

INGREDIENTS

1/2 pound chicken breasts, skinless and boneless
1 cup chicken stock
1 garlic clove, crushed
1 tablespoon fresh basil leaves, roughly chopped
2 tablespoons sour cream
1/3 cup mayonnaise

1 tablespoon yellow mustard
1/2 tablespoon fresh lime juice
1/2 Lebanese cucumber, sliced
1/3 cup scallions, chopped
Coarse sea salt and ground black pepper, to taste

DIRECTIONS

Place the chicken breasts, stock, and garlic in the Instant Pot.

Secure the lid. Choose the "Manual" mode and High pressure; cook for 8 minutes. Once cooking is complete, use a quick release.

Shred the chicken breasts with 1/2 cup of cooking liquid and transfer to a salad bowl; add the remaining ingredients and gently stir to combine.

Place in your refrigerator until ready to serve. Bon appétit!

212. Zingy Ranch Chicken with Butter

(Ready in about 25 minutes)

Per serving: 356 Calories; 13.1g Fat; 2.1g Carbs; 53.1g Protein; 0.5g Sugars; 0.4g Fiber

INGREDIENTS

1 tablespoon butter, melted
1 pound chicken thighs, bone-in, skin-on
1 garlic clove, minced
1/2 yellow onion, sliced

1 tablespoon dry ranch salad dressing mix
1/2 teaspoon paprika
1/2 teaspoon ground bay leaf
1/4 teaspoon ground black pepper

Sea salt, to taste
1 tablespoon champagne vinegar
1 cup chicken bone broth

DIRECTIONS

Press the "Sauté" button and melt the butter.

Now, sear the chicken thighs for 4 to 5 minutes or until browned on all sides.

Add the remaining ingredients in the order listed above.

Secure the lid. Choose the "Poultry" setting and cook for 15 minutes at High pressure. Once cooking is complete, use a natural release and carefully remove the lid.

You can thicken the sauce on the "Sauté" mode. Serve over hot cooked rice if desired. Enjoy!

213. Chicken Drumsticks with Lemon Sauce

(Ready in about 25 minutes)

Per serving: 418 Calories; 24.2g Fat; 5.9g Carbs; 41.1g Protein; 1.5g Sugars; 1g Fiber

INGREDIENTS

1 tablespoon sesame oil
2 chicken drumsticks, boneless and skinless
2/3 cup chicken broth
1 teaspoon garlic powder

1/2 teaspoon cayenne pepper
1/4 teaspoon ground black pepper, or more to taste
1/2 teaspoon oregano
1/2 teaspoon basil

1/2 teaspoon thyme
1/2 onion, chopped
1/2 lemon, juiced and zested
1/4 heavy cream

DIRECTIONS

Press the "Sauté" button and heat the oil until sizzling. Sear the chicken drumsticks, stirring occasionally, for about 4 minutes.

Add a few tablespoons of broth to deglaze the bottom of the pan. Stir in the spices, onion, and chicken broth; stir to combine well.

Secure the lid. Choose the "Poultry" mode. Cook for 15 minutes at High pressure. Once cooking is complete, use a quick pressure release; carefully remove the lid.

Remove the chicken from the Instant Pot using a slotted spoon.

Add the lemon and heavy cream to the cooking liquid; stir to combine. Press the "Sauté" button and let it simmer until the sauce has thickened slightly.

Spoon the sauce over the reserved chicken and serve warm. Enjoy!

214. Greek-Style Chicken with Haloumi and Couscous

(Ready in about 20 minutes)

Per serving: 457 Calories; 15.2g Fat; 47.4g Carbs; 32.4g Protein; 3.8g Sugars; 4.2g Fiber

INGREDIENTS

1 teaspoons butter, at room temperature
1/2 pound chicken fillets, diced
1/2 onion, diced
1 sweet pepper, deseeded and sliced

1/2 red chili pepper, deseeded and sliced
2 cloves garlic, minced
1/2 teaspoon dried rosemary
1/2 teaspoon dried oregano

Kosher salt and ground black pepper, to taste
1 cup vegetable broth
1/2 cup dry couscous
2 ounces halloumi cheese, crumbled

DIRECTIONS

Press the "Sauté" button to preheat your Instant Pot. Melt 1 teaspoon of the butter. Cook the chicken fillets until golden brown. Set aside.

Then, melt the remaining 1 teaspoon of butter. Now, sauté the onion, peppers, and garlic until tender and aromatic.

Add the rosemary, oregano, salt, pepper, and vegetable broth.

Secure the lid. Choose the "Poultry" mode and cook for 5 minutes at High pressure. Once cooking is complete, use a quick pressure release; carefully remove the lid.

Add the couscous and stir to combine. Secure the lid. Choose the "Manual" mode and cook for 2 minutes at High pressure. Once cooking is complete, use a quick pressure release; carefully remove the lid.

Divide between serving plates; garnish each serving with halloumi cheese and enjoy!

215. Summer Chicken Sandwiches

(Ready in about 25 minutes)

Per serving: 452 Calories; 27.1g Fat; 25.2g Carbs; 26.1g Protein; 4.5g Sugars; 1.3g Fiber

INGREDIENTS

1 tablespoon butter, at room temperature
1/2 pound whole chicken, skinless and boneless
1 garlic clove, crushed
1/2 yellow onion, chopped
Sea salt and ground black pepper, to your liking
1 teaspoon cayenne pepper

2 hamburger buns
1/2 tablespoons mustard
1 small tomato, sliced
1/2 Lebanese cucumber, sliced
1 tablespoon fresh cilantro, chopped
1 tablespoon fresh green onion, chopped

DIRECTIONS

Press the "Sauté" button to preheat your Instant Pot. Melt the butter and cook the chicken for 3 to 4 minutes or until slightly brown. Add the garlic, onion, salt, black pepper, and cayenne pepper.

Secure the lid. Choose the "Poultry" mode and cook for 15 minutes at High pressure. Once cooking is complete, use a quick pressure release; carefully remove the lid.

Shred the chicken with two forks.

Spread the mustard on the bottom half of each hamburger bun. Top with the tomato, cumber, chicken, cilantro, and green onions; top with the remaining bun halves. Serve immediately.

216. Spicy Chicken Meatballs

(Ready in about 15 minutes)

Per serving: 548 Calories; 34.7g Fat; 14g Carbs; 45.1g Protein; 4g Sugars; 1.3g Fiber

INGREDIENTS

2 tablespoons olive oil
1/2 carrot, finely chopped
1/2 celery stalk, finely chopped
1 shallot, minced
1 garlic clove, minced
1 pounds ground chicken

1 egg, beaten
1/4 cup buttermilk
1/2 teaspoon celery seeds
1/3 teaspoon mustard seeds
Sea salt and ground black pepper, to taste

1/2 cup fine panko crumbs
1 cup chicken broth
1/4 cup Cholula's hot sauce
1 tablespoon arrowroot powder

DIRECTIONS

Press the "Sauté" button and heat 1 tablespoon of olive oil. Cook the carrot, celery, shallot, and garlic until tender and fragrant.

Stir in the ground chicken, egg, buttermilk, celery seeds, mustard seeds, salt, pepper, and panko crumbs. Mix to combine well and shape the chicken/vegetable mixture into 1-inch balls.

Heat 1 tablespoon of olive oil and sear the meatballs until golden brown on all sides.

Add 2 tablespoons of olive oil, chicken broth, Cholula's hot sauce, and arrowroot to the inner pot; stir to combine. Fold in the prepared meatballs.

Secure the lid. Choose the "Poultry" mode and cook for 5 minutes at High pressure. Once cooking is complete, use a quick pressure release; carefully remove the lid. Serve warm.

217. Chicken Tenders with Cheese and Potatoes

(Ready in about 25 minutes)

Per serving: 486 Calories; 15.6g Fat; 41.1g Carbs; 44.1g Protein; 1.9g Sugars; 5.2g Fiber

INGREDIENTS

1 tablespoon olive oil
3/4 pound chicken tenders
1 pound Yukon Gold potatoes, peeled and diced
1 clove garlic, smashed

1/4 teaspoon ground black pepper
1/2 teaspoon red pepper flakes
Pink Himalayan salt, to taste
1/2 teaspoon shallot powder
1/2 teaspoon dried basil

1/2 teaspoon dried rosemary
1 cup chicken stock
3 tablespoons Romano cheese, grated

DIRECTIONS

Press the "Sauté" button to preheat your Instant Pot. Now, heat the olive oil and sear the chicken tenders for 3 to 4 minutes.

Add the potatoes and garlic; sprinkle with black pepper, red pepper, salt, shallot powder, basil, and rosemary.

Pour in the chicken stock and secure the lid. Choose the "Poultry" mode and High pressure; cook for 15 minutes. Once cooking is complete, use a quick pressure release; carefully remove the lid.

Top with the grated Romano cheese and serve warm. Enjoy!

218. Chicken and Bacon in Orange Sauce

(Ready in about 15 minutes)

Per serving: 434 Calories; 32.3g Fat; 11.8g Carbs; 25.2g Protein; 2.9g Sugars; 2.1g Fiber

INGREDIENTS

1 tablespoon olive oil
1/2 pound ground chicken
2 ounces bacon, chopped
1 tablespoon sherry wine

1 small red onion, chopped
1 garlic clove, minced
1/2 jalapeno pepper, chopped
Sea salt and ground black pepper, to taste

1/2 teaspoon paprika
Fresh juice and zest of 1/2 orange
1 tablespoon arrowroot powder

DIRECTIONS

Press the "Sauté" button and heat the oil until sizzling. Sear the chicken and bacon until they are slightly brown.

Add the sherry wine and stir with a wooden spoon, scraping up the browned bits on the bottom of the pan. Add the red onion, garlic, and jalapeno pepper; stir to combine.

Season with salt, black pepper, and paprika. Pour in 1 cup of water.

Secure the lid. Choose "Poultry" mode. Cook for 5 minutes at High pressure. Once cooking is complete, use a quick pressure release; carefully remove the lid.

Add the orange juice and zest; stir in the arrowroot powder. Press the "Sauté" button and simmer, stirring occasionally, until it thickens. Bon appétit!

219. Marsala Chicken Wings with Cream Cheese

(Ready in about 25 minutes)

Per serving: 448 Calories; 27.7g Fat; 21.1g Carbs; 28.5g Protein; 4.2g Sugars; 1.9g Fiber

INGREDIENTS

1 tablespoon butter, room temperature
2 chicken drumsticks, boneless
4 tablespoons all-purpose flour
1/2 teaspoon Italian seasoning mix

Sea salt and ground black pepper, to taste
1 bell pepper, deseeded and sliced
1/2 cup scallions, chopped

2 cloves garlic, smashed
1/4 cup Marsala wine
3/4 cup chicken broth
2 ounces cream cheese

DIRECTIONS

Press the "Sauté" button to preheat your Instant Pot. Melt 1/2 tablespoon of the butter.

Dredge your chicken in the flour; season with spices and cook until slightly brown; reserve.

Melt the remaining 1/2 tablespoon of butter and sauté the peppers, scallions, and garlic. Pour in the wine, scraping up any browned bits from the bottom of the pan. Add the chicken broth and secure the lid.

Choose the "Manual" mode and cook for 10 minutes at High pressure. Once cooking is complete, use a natural pressure release; carefully remove the lid.

Press the "Sauté" button to preheat your Instant Pot one more time. Add the cream cheese and cook for a further 4 to 5 minutes or until everything is thoroughly heated.

To serve, spoon the sauce over the chicken drumsticks. Bon appétit!

220. Mexican Chicken Casserole

(Ready in about 20 minutes)

Per serving: 591 Calories; 31.9g Fat; 33.1g Carbs; 45.6g Protein; 3.7g Sugars; 4.9g Fiber

INGREDIENTS

1 tablespoon olive oil
1/2 pound chicken breast, boneless, cut into chunks

1 cup cream of celery soup
1 cup spiral pasta
1/2 cup Cotija cheese, crumbled

1/2 cup queso fresco, crumbled
1/2 cup salsa
1/2 cup fresh breadcrumbs

DIRECTIONS

Press the "Sauté" button and heat the olive oil. Now, brown the chicken breasts for 3 to 4 minutes.

Add the remaining ingredients in the order listed above.

Secure the lid. Choose "Manual" mode and cook for 6 minutes at High pressure. Once cooking is complete, use a natural pressure release; carefully remove the lid.

Serve warm.

221. Chicken Cutlets in Herb Sauce

(Ready in about 25 minutes)

Per serving: 544 Calories; 15.9g Fat; 47g Carbs; 54.2g Protein; 2.3g Sugars; 7.3g Fiber

INGREDIENTS

1 pound chicken cutlets
Kosher salt and ground black pepper,
to taste
1/2 teaspoon dried oregano
1/2 teaspoon dried basil

1/2 teaspoon dried rosemary
1/2 teaspoon dried parsley flakes
1/4 cup dry white wine
1 cup vegetable broth
1 garlic clove, minced

1/4 cup double cream
1 tablespoons cornstarch
2 cups pasta, cooked

DIRECTIONS

Season the chicken cutlets with salt, black pepper, oregano, basil, rosemary, and parsley. Press the "Sauté" button to preheat your Instant Pot.

Once hot, cook the seasoned chicken cutlets for 5 minutes, turning once during cooking. Add the white wine and scrape the bottom of the pan to deglaze.

Pour in the vegetable broth. Add the garlic and secure the lid.

Choose the "Manual" mode and High pressure; cook for 8 minutes. Once cooking is complete, use a quick release and remove the lid. Reserve the chicken cutlets, keeping them warm.

Stir the double cream and cornstarch into the cooking liquid.

Press the "Sauté" button and simmer for 6 minutes or until the cooking liquid has reduced by half. Serve with warm pasta. Bon appétit!

222. Mexican Taco Meat

(Ready in about 35 minutes)

Per serving: 295 Calories; 9.8g Fat; 2.4g Carbs; 46.6g Protein; 1.1g Sugars; 0.4g Fiber

INGREDIENTS

1 pound whole chicken, meat and skin
1 teaspoon Old El Paso Taco spice mix
1/2 tablespoon canola oil
1/2 fresh jalapeño chili, seeded and finely chopped

Kosher salt and ground black pepper, to taste
Fresh juice of 1/2 orange
1 cup chicken broth
A small handful of coriander, roughly chopped

DIRECTIONS

Toss the chicken in the Taco spice mix to coat. Press the "Sauté" button to preheat your Instant Pot.

Heat the canola oil and sear the chicken, stirring periodically, for 3 to 4 minutes or until golden brown.

Add the jalapeño chili, salt, black pepper, fresh orange juice, and chicken broth; stir to combine. Secure the lid.

Choose the "Poultry" mode and High pressure; cook for 30 minutes. Once cooking is complete, use a quick release.

Shred the chicken and garnish with fresh coriander leaves. Enjoy!

223. Easy Chicken Congee

(Ready in about 20 minutes)

Per serving: 558 Calories; 20.8g Fat; 41.1g Carbs; 28.2g Protein; 14.7g Sugars; 3.3g Fiber

INGREDIENTS

1 tablespoons sesame oil
2 chicken drumsticks
2 garlic cloves, minced
1 tablespoons Worcestershire sauce

1 tablespoon champagne vinegar
1 cup vegetable broth
1 cup water
2 tablespoons honey

Salt and ground black pepper, to taste
1 teaspoon Wuxiang powder
1/2 cup rice
1 tablespoons flaxseed meal

DIRECTIONS

Press the "Sauté" button and heat 2 tablespoons of the sesame oil. Sear the chicken drumsticks until slightly brown on all sides. Add the garlic and cook for 1 minute or so, until aromatic.

Add the remaining ingredients, except for the flaxseed meal.

Secure the lid. Choose "Poultry" mode. Cook for 15 minutes at High pressure. Once cooking is complete, use a quick pressure release; carefully remove the lid.

Afterwards, stir in the flaxseed meal; stir until everything is well combined. Press the "Sauté" button and cook until the cooking liquid is reduced by about half. Bon appétit!

DUCK

224. Indian Duck Masala

(Ready in about 35 minutes)

Per serving: 411 Calories; 20.2g Fat; 12.2g Carbs; 45.1g Protein; 5g Sugars; 2.5g Fiber

INGREDIENTS

1 tablespoon butter, melted at room temperature
1 pound duck thighs
Sea salt, to taste
1/4 teaspoon crushed black peppercorns, or more to taste
1 teaspoon ginger powder
1/2 teaspoon chili powder
1/2 tablespoon rosemary

1/2 tablespoon sage
1/2 teaspoon allspice berries, lightly crushed
1 garlic clove, sliced
1/3 cup tomato paste
1/2 cup bone broth
1/2 tablespoon Garam masala
1 small bunch of fresh coriander, roughly chopped

DIRECTIONS

Press the "Sauté" button and melt the butter. Now, cook the duck thighs until golden brown on both sides. Add all seasonings.

Next, stir in the garlic, tomato paste, broth, and Garam masala.

Secure the lid. Choose the "Manual" mode and cook for 25 minutes at High pressure. Once cooking is complete, use a quick pressure release; carefully remove the lid.

Serve with fresh coriander. Enjoy!

225. Duck with Curried Cherry Sauce

(Ready in about 30 minutes)

Per serving: 529 Calories; 34.2g Fat; 11.6g Carbs; 41.1g Protein; 7.5g Sugars; 1.7g Fiber

INGREDIENTS

1 pound whole duck
1/2 teaspoon curry paste
Salt and ground black pepper, to taste
1/2 onion, finely chopped

1 garlic clove, minced
2 ounces canned red tart cherries
1/2 tablespoon lemon rind, grated
1 tablespoon dry white wine

4 tablespoon balsamic vinegar
1 cup vegetable broth

DIRECTIONS

Place all ingredients in the inner pot.

Secure the lid. Choose the "Manual" mode and cook for 20 minutes at High pressure. Once cooking is complete, use a quick pressure release; carefully remove the lid.

Remove the duck from the inner pot.

Press the "Sauté" button and cook the cooking liquid until it is reduced by about half. Bon appétit!

226. Thai Duck Breasts

(Ready in about 50 minutes)

Per serving: 622 Calories; 39.2g Fat; 11.1g Carbs; 56g Protein; 2.5g Sugars; 3.4g Fiber

INGREDIENTS

1 tablespoon Thai red curry paste
Zest and juice of 1 fresh lime
1 pound duck breast
1 tablespoon olive oil
1/4 teaspoon black peppercorns, crushed

1/2 teaspoon cayenne pepper
1/2 teaspoon sea salt
2 garlic cloves, minced
1 thyme sprig, chopped
1 rosemary sprig, chopped
1/2 cup light coconut milk

1/2 cup chicken broth, preferably homemade
2 tablespoons pack coriander, roughly chopped

DIRECTIONS

Combine the red curry paste with the lime zest and juice; rub the mixture all over the duck breast and leave it to marinate for 30 minutes.

Press the "Sauté" button and heat the oil until sizzling. Cook the duck breast until slightly brown on both sides.

Then, season the duck breasts with the peppercorns, cayenne pepper, and salt. Add the garlic, thyme, rosemary, coconut milk, and chicken broth.

Secure the lid. Choose the "Poultry" mode and cook for 15 minutes at High pressure. Once cooking is complete, use a quick pressure release; carefully remove the lid.

Garnish with chopped coriander and serve warm. Bon appétit!

227. Spicy Glazed Duck Breast

(Ready in about 25 minutes)

Per serving: 491 Calories; 14.5g Fat; 22.1g Carbs; 47.6g Protein; 18.5g Sugars; 1.7g Fiber

INGREDIENTS

1 teaspoon sesame oil
1 pound duck breasts
1/2 teaspoon red pepper flakes
Sea salt and freshly ground black pepper, to taste
1 teaspoon dry mustard
1/2 tablespoon paprika

1/2 teaspoon ground star anise
1/2 teaspoon ground ginger
Kosher salt and ground black pepper, to taste
1 cup chicken broth
Ginger Glaze:
1 tablespoon peanut oil

1-inch piece ginger, finely chopped
1 clove garlic, finely chopped
1/2 tablespoon Sriracha sauce
2 tablespoons soy sauce
2 tablespoons honey

DIRECTIONS

Press the "Sauté" button to preheat your Instant Pot.

Heat the sesame seed oil and sear the duck breasts for 5 minutes, stirring periodically. Sprinkle your spices all over the duck breasts. Add the chicken broth.

Secure the lid and choose the "Poultry" mode. Cook for 15 minutes. Afterwards, use a quick release and carefully remove the lid. Remove the duck breasts from the inner pot.

After that, stir in the other ingredients for the ginger glaze; stir well to combine.

Press the "Sauté" button to preheat your Instant Pot. Cook until thoroughly heated. Place the duck breasts in the serving plates and brush with the ginger glaze. Serve warm and enjoy!

228. Japanese Duck with Rice and Eggs

(Ready in about 20 minutes + marinating time)

Per serving: 731 Calories; 40g Fat; 36.8g Carbs; 52.6g Protein; 4.6g Sugars; 1.8g Fiber

INGREDIENTS

1 pound duck breasts, skinless and boneless
1 tablespoon orange juice
1 tablespoon Mirin
1 tablespoon tamari
1 tablespoon sesame oil
1 cup vegetable broth
1 garlic clove, grated

1 teaspoon honey
Sea salt and freshly ground pepper, to taste
1 shallot, chopped
1/4 cup loosely packed fresh parsley leaves, roughly chopped
1 fresh lemon, juiced
1 tablespoon extra-virgin oil

1 cup Chinese cabbage, shredded
1 tablespoon sesame seeds, toasted
1/2 red chili, finely chopped
1 cup cooked rice
1 tablespoon olive oil
2 eggs

DIRECTIONS

Place the duck breasts, orange juice, Mirin, and tamari sauce in a ceramic dish. Let it marinate for 1 hour in your refrigerator.

Press the "Sauté" button and heat the oil until sizzling. Cook the duck for about 5 minutes or until it is no longer pink.

Add the vegetable broth and secure the lid.

Choose the "Manual" mode and cook for 10 minutes at High pressure. Once cooking is complete, use a quick pressure release; carefully remove the lid.

Slice the duck and transfer to a nice serving bowl. Add the garlic, honey, salt, black pepper, shallot, fresh parsley, lemon, oil, cabbage, sesame seeds, chili pepper, and cooked rice.

Heat the olive oil in a skillet over medium-high flame. Fry the eggs until the whites are completely set. Place the fried eggs on the top and serve immediately.

229. The Best Duck Ragù

(Ready in about 30 minutes)

Per serving: 678 Calories; 19g Fat; 85g Carbs; 35.1g Protein; 4.7g Sugars; 4.3g Fiber

INGREDIENTS

1/2 pound fettuccine
1/2 pound duck legs
1 clove garlic, crushed
1/2 onion, chopped

1/2 red chili pepper, minced
1 sweet pepper, deseeded and finely chopped
Sea salt and freshly ground black

pepper, to taste
1/4 cup tomato purée
1/4 cup chicken bone broth
1 tablespoon dry cooking wine

DIRECTIONS

Bring a pot of salted water to a boil. Cook the fettuccine, stirring occasionally, until al dente. Drain, reserving 1 cup of the pasta water; set aside.

Add the reserved pasta water along with the duck legs to the Instant Pot.

Secure the lid. Choose the "Manual" mode and cook for 20 minutes at High pressure. Once cooking is complete, use a quick pressure release; carefully remove the lid.

Shred the meat with two forks. Add the meat back to the Instant Pot. Add the remaining ingredients and press the "Sauté" button.

Let it cook for 5 to 7 minutes more or until everything is heated through. Serve with the reserved pasta and enjoy!

230. Chinese-Style Duck Salad

(Ready in about 25 minutes)

Per serving: 430 Calories; 16.1g Fat; 24.9g Carbs; 47.4g Protein; 11.5g Sugars; 8.7g Fiber

INGREDIENTS

1 pound duck breasts
1 cup water
Salt and black pepper, to taste
1 head romaine lettuce, torn into small pieces

1 tomato, diced
1 small red onion, sliced diagonally
1 tablespoon balsamic vinegar
1 garlic clove, minced
1 teaspoon fresh ginger, grated

1 tablespoons tamari sauce
1 tablespoons peanut butter

DIRECTIONS

Put the duck breasts and water into the inner pot.

Secure the lid and choose the "Poultry" mode. Cook for 15 minutes at High pressure. Afterwards, use a quick release and carefully remove the lid.

Now, slice the meat into strips and place in a salad bowl. Season with salt and pepper. Add the romaine lettuce, tomatoes, and onion.

In a small mixing dish, whisk the balsamic vinegar, garlic, ginger, tamari sauce, and peanut butter. Dress the salad and serve well chilled. Bon appétit!

231. Duck with Apricot and Orange Sauce

(Ready in about 35 minutes)

Per serving: 488 Calories; 14.2g Fat; 42.8g Carbs; 42.4g Protein; 9.7g Sugars; 4.7g Fiber

INGREDIENTS

1/2 tablespoon olive oil
1 pound duck breast
1 blood orange, juiced
Sea salt and ground black pepper, to taste

1/3 teaspoon cayenne pepper
1/2 teaspoon dried dill weed
1/2 cup chicken bone broth
1/2 cup dry white wine

1 tablespoon apricot jam
1 tablespoon potato starch

DIRECTIONS

Press the "Sauté" button and heat the oil until sizzling. Then, cook the duck breasts for 4 minutes per side.

Add the oranges, salt, black pepper, cayenne pepper, dill, and broth.

Secure the lid. Choose the "Poultry" mode and cook for 15 minutes at High pressure. Once cooking is complete, use a quick pressure release; carefully remove the lid.

Remove the duck from the cooking liquid using a slotted spoon. Add the remaining ingredients to the cooking liquid and press the "Sauté" button again.

Let it simmer for 5 to 7 minutes or until slightly thickened. Spoon the sauce onto the duck and serve immediately. Bon appétit!

232. Chinese-Style Saucy Duck

(Ready in about 40 minutes)

Per serving: 444 Calories; 15.2g Fat; 30.5g Carbs; 44.1g Protein; 15.1g Sugars; 3.4g Fiber

INGREDIENTS

1 pound whole duck
Salt and ground black pepper, to your liking
1 cup roasted vegetable broth
1 carrot, chopped

1 cup broccoli, chopped into florets
1/2 leek, white part only, chopped
2 tablespoons fresh coriander stalks, roughly chopped
1 clove garlic, sliced

1 bay leaf
1/3 cup Hoisin sauce
1/2 lemon, cut into wedges

DIRECTIONS

Press the "Sauté" button to preheat your Instant Pot.

Now, cook the duck for 4 to 5 minutes or until the skin turns golden brown. Pour in the roasted vegetable broth.

Secure the lid and choose the "Manual" mode. Cook for 25 minutes at High pressure. Afterwards, use a quick release and carefully remove the lid.

Add the vegetables, coriander, garlic, and bay leaf.

Secure the lid. Choose the "Manual" mode and cook for 3 minutes at High pressure. Once cooking is complete, use a quick pressure release; carefully remove the lid.

Remove the duck to a chopping board and rest for 5 minutes before cutting and serving.

Lastly, slice the duck and serve with the braised vegetables, Hoisin sauce, and lemon wedges. Bon appétit!

233. Balsamic Duck with Mixed Vegetables

(Ready in about 30 minutes)

Per serving: 391 Calories; 16.7g Fat; 15.3g Carbs; 43.3g Protein; 3.5g Sugars; 1.8g Fiber

INGREDIENTS

1 pound whole duck
1/2 cup chicken stock
Kosher salt and ground black pepper, to taste
1/2 teaspoon smoked paprika
1 bay leaf

1/2 tablespoon butter, melted
1/2 onion, quartered
1 bell pepper, deseeded and sliced
1 carrot, sliced
1 celery stalk, sliced
2 cloves garlic, sliced

1 rosemary sprig
1 thyme sprig
1 tablespoon balsamic vinegar
1 tablespoon Worcestershire sauce

DIRECTIONS

Press the "Sauté" button to preheat your Instant Pot. Now, place the duck skin-side down in the inner pot and sear until the skin is crisp and brown. Turn and cook the other side for 4 to 5 minutes.

Add the chicken stock, salt, black pepper, smoked paprika, and bay leaf to the inner pot.

Secure the lid and choose the "Manual" mode. Cook for 20 minutes at High pressure. Afterwards, use a quick release and carefully remove the lid.

Add the remaining ingredients in the order listed above.

Secure the lid. Choose the "Manual" mode and cook for 3 minutes at High pressure. Once cooking is complete, use a quick pressure release; carefully remove the lid. Serve immediately.

234. Traditional Szechuan Duck

(Ready in about 35 minutes)

Per serving: 575 Calories; 40.2g Fat; 9.5g Carbs; 41.5g Protein; 3.9g Sugars; 2.2g Fiber

INGREDIENTS

1/2 tablespoon Szechuan peppercorns
1/2 teaspoon Chinese 5-spice powder
1/2 tablespoon salt
1 pound whole duck

1 clove garlic, sliced
1 star anise
2 tablespoons soy sauce
2 tablespoons Shaoxing rice wine

1/2 red chili pepper, chopped
1/2 tablespoon dark brown sugar
1 cup water

DIRECTIONS

Press the "Sauté" button to preheat your Instant Pot. Then, add the Szechuan peppercorn to the inner pot and roast until really fragrant. Remove it to a spice grinder and ground into a powder.

Add the Chinese 5-spice powder and salt. Rub the duck with the spice mixture. Leave it to marinate overnight.

Press the "Sauté" button to preheat your Instant Pot. Now, place the duck skin-side down in the inner pot and sear until the skin is crisp and brown. Turn and cook the other side for 4 to 5 minutes.

Stir in the other ingredients.

Secure the lid and choose the "Manual" mode. Cook for 25 minutes at High pressure. Afterwards, use a quick release and carefully remove the lid. Serve warm.

235. Decadent Duck in Cranberry Sauce

(Ready in about 35 minutes)

Per serving: 393 Calories; 19.7g Fat; 9.9g Carbs; 41.6g Protein; 5.7g Sugars; 0.3g Fiber

INGREDIENTS

1 pound whole duck
Kosher salt, to taste
1/4 teaspoon freshly ground black pepper
1/3 teaspoon red pepper flakes

1/4 teaspoon smoked paprika
1/2 teaspoon onion powder
1 clove garlic, minced
1 cup chicken stock
1 tablespoon butter

1/4 cup cranberries, halved
1/2 tablespoon brown sugar
3 tablespoons raspberry vinegar
1 teaspoon wholegrain mustard

DIRECTIONS

Press the "Sauté" button and melt the butter; place the duck skin-side down in the inner pot and sear until the skin is crisp and brown. Turn and cook the other side for about 4 minutes.

Pour away all but a tablespoon of the fat. Add the salt, black pepper, red pepper, paprika, onion powder, garlic, and chicken stock to the inner pot.

Secure the lid. Choose the "Manual" mode and cook for 25 minutes at High pressure. Once cooking is complete, use a natural pressure release; carefully remove the lid.

Now, remove the duck from the inner pot.

Press the "Sauté" button and add the remaining ingredients to the cooking liquid.

Continue to cook for 5 to 6 minutes, until the cranberries start to slightly break down and soften. Spoon over the reserved duck and serve immediately. Bon appétit!

TURKEY

236. Holiday Turkey Breasts with Herbs

(Ready in about 45 minutes)

Per serving: 449 Calories; 24.4g Fat; 5.3g Carbs; 50.6g Protein; 1.6g Sugars; 0.9g Fiber

INGREDIENTS

1 tablespoon olive oil
1/2 teaspoon sage, chopped
1 teaspoon basil, chopped
1 teaspoon rosemary, chopped
Sea salt and freshly cracked black pepper, to taste
1/2 teaspoon paprika

1 pound turkey breasts, boneless
1 splash dry white wine
1 cup chicken bone broth
1/2 tablespoon mustard
1 tablespoons half-and-half
1/2 tablespoon cornstarch, dissolved in 1 tablespoon of water

DIRECTIONS

Mix the olive oil with the spices; brush the mixture all over the turkey breasts. Press the "Sauté" button to preheat your Instant Pot.
Add the turkey breasts, skin side down and cook until slightly brown on all sides. Add a splash of wine to deglaze the pot.
Pour the chicken bone broth into the inner pot. Add the mustard and half-and-half.
Secure the lid. Choose the "Poultry" mode and cook for 30 minutes at High pressure. Once cooking is complete, use a natural pressure release; carefully remove the lid.
Afterwards, place the turkey breast under the broiler until the outside is crisp.
Meanwhile, press the "Sauté" button to preheat your Instant Pot again; add the cornstarch slurry and whisk to combine well. Let it cook until the sauce is slightly thickened. Slice the turkey breasts and serve with the pan juices. Enjoy!

237. Turkey Sandwich with Mustard and Cheese

(Ready in about 35 minutes)

Per serving: 645 Calories; 32.1g Fat; 23.5g Carbs; 60g Protein; 3.5g Sugars; 1.8g Fiber

INGREDIENTS

1 pound turkey breast
1 clove garlic
Salt and ground black pepper, to taste
1/2 teaspoon thyme
1/2 teaspoon marjoram

1 teaspoon basil
1 tablespoon butter, at room temperature
1 cup vegetable broth
4 slices bread

1 tablespoon Dijon mustard
4 lettuce leaves
2 (1-ounce) slices white cheddar cheese

DIRECTIONS

Place the turkey breasts, garlic, salt, black pepper, thyme, marjoram, basil, and butter in the inner pot; pour in the vegetable broth.
Secure the lid. Choose the "Manual" mode and cook for 25 minutes at High pressure. Once cooking is complete, use a natural pressure release; carefully remove the lid.
Spread the mustard on 4 slices of bread. Layer the slices of bread with the turkey, lettuce, and cheese.
Place remaining 4 slices of bread on top of the sandwiches and serve immediately.

238. Caribbean-Style Turkey with Beer

(Ready in about 30 minutes)

Per serving: 394 Calories; 17.3g Fat; 3.7g Carbs; 50.1g Protein; 0.7g Sugars; 0.9g Fiber

INGREDIENTS

1 pound turkey drumsticks, boneless
6 ounces bottle beer
1 carrot, sliced
1 small leek, sliced
1 garlic clove, sliced

1/4 teaspoon ground allspice
1 sprig rosemary, chopped
1 bay leaf
Sea salt and freshly ground black pepper, to taste

DIRECTIONS

Add all ingredients to the inner pot.
Secure the lid. Choose the "Manual" mode and cook for 20 minutes at High pressure. Once cooking is complete, use a natural pressure release; carefully remove the lid.
You can thicken the pan juices if desired. Enjoy!

239. Creamed Turkey Salad with Apples

(Ready in about 20 minutes + chilling)

Per serving: 621 Calories; 45g Fat; 10.2g Carbs; 40.9g Protein; 7g Sugars; 2.1g Fiber

INGREDIENTS

3/4 pound turkey breasts, boneless and skinless

1 cup water

1 celery stalk, diced

1/2 apple, cored and diced

1/3 cup spring onions, chopped

1/2 head butterhead lettuce, shredded

1/3 cup cream cheese

1/4 cup mayonnaise

1/2 tablespoon fresh lemon juice

1 teaspoon sage

Kosher salt and white pepper, to taste

DIRECTIONS

Place the turkey breasts and water in the inner pot.

Secure the lid. Choose the "Manual" mode and cook for 9 minutes at High pressure. Once cooking is complete, use a natural pressure release; carefully remove the lid.

Add the remaining ingredients; gently stir to combine. Serve well chilled and enjoy!

240. Herby Turkey with Gravy

(Ready in about 35 minutes)

Per serving: 458 Calories; 26.1g Fat; 4.1g Carbs; 49g Protein; 1.3g Sugars; 1.6g Fiber

INGREDIENTS

1 pound turkey breasts

1 bell pepper, deseeded and chopped

1 serrano pepper, deseeded and chopped

1 garlic clove, minced

1 cup turkey stock

1 tablespoon olive oil

1 thyme sprig

1 teaspoon dried sage

1/2 teaspoon dried dill

Sea salt and ground black pepper, to taste

1 tablespoon butter

1 tablespoon flour

4 tablespoons dry white wine

Sea salt and ground black pepper, to taste

DIRECTIONS

Add the turkey, peppers, garlic, turkey stock, olive oil, thyme, sage, dried dill, salt, and black pepper to the inner pot.

Secure the lid. Choose the "Manual" mode and cook for 25 minutes at High pressure. Once cooking is complete, use a natural pressure release; carefully remove the lid.

Press the "Sauté" button again and melt the butter. Now, add the flour, wine, salt, and pepper; let it cook until the sauce has thickened.

Spoon the gravy over the turkey breasts and serve warm. Bon appétit!

241. Spicy Turkey Meatballs

(Ready in about 15 minutes)

Per serving: 391 Calories; 16.8g Fat; 23.9g Carbs; 33.3g Protein; 7.1g Sugars; 5.2g Fiber

INGREDIENTS

Meatballs:

1/2 pound ground turkey

1/3 cup seasoned breadcrumbs

1 tablespoon fresh cilantro, chopped

1 egg, whisked

1 clove garlic, minced

Sea salt, to taste

1/4 teaspoon freshly cracked black pepper

Sauce:

1 tablespoon butter, at room temperature

1 clove garlic, minced

1/2 cup tomatoes puree

1/2 onion, minced

2 tablespoons fresh basil, chopped

Salt, to taste

1 teaspoon hot sauce

Meatball Sliders:

1/3 cup mozzarella, shredded

4 honey wheat slider buns, toasted

DIRECTIONS

Mix all ingredients for the meatballs until everything is well incorporated; form the mixture into small balls.

Spritz the sides and bottom of the inner pot with cooking spray. Press the "Sauté" button and cook your meatball until they are golden brown on all sides.

Add all ingredients for the sauce to the inner pot. Fold in the meatballs.

Secure the lid. Choose the "Poultry" mode and cook for 5 minutes at High pressure. Once cooking is complete, use a quick pressure release; carefully remove the lid. Serve warm.

Preheat your oven to broil.

To assemble the slider, place 1 meatball and a spoonful of sauce on the bottom of each bun. Top with mozzarella. Place under the broiler and bake until the cheese has melted about 2 minutes.

Top with another bun half and serve immediately. Bon appétit!

242. Festive Roast Turkey

(Ready in about 35 minutes)

Per serving: 686 Calories; 51.3g Fat; 2.5g Carbs; 52.1g Protein; 0.8g Sugars; 0.1g Fiber

INGREDIENTS

1 pound turkey breasts
2 garlic cloves, smashed
1 thyme sprig
1 rosemary sprig

1/2 cup mayonnaise
1 teaspoon coarse salt
1/2 teaspoon mixed peppercorns, crushed

1 tablespoon ghee, softened
1/2 lemon, sliced

DIRECTIONS

Pat the turkey dry. In a mixing dish, thoroughly combine the garlic, thyme, rosemary, mayonnaise, salt, peppercorns, and ghee. Rub the mayonnaise mixture all over the turkey breasts.

Add a steamer rack and 1/2 cup of water to the bottom of your Instant Pot. Throw in the lemon slices.

Secure the lid. Choose the "Manual" mode and cook for 20 minutes at High pressure. Once cooking is complete, use a natural pressure release; carefully remove the lid.

Let your turkey stand for 5 to 10 minutes before slicing and serving. Bon appétit!

243. Italian Turkey with Garden Vegetables

(Ready in about 30 minutes)

Per serving: 422 Calories; 6.5g Fat; 17.2g Carbs; 70.6g Protein; 5.2g Sugars; 2.8g Fiber

INGREDIENTS

1 pound whole turkey breasts
1/2 cup cream of celery soup
1/2 celery stalk, cut into bite-sized chunks

1 carrot, cut into bite-sized chunks
1 bell pepper, cut into bite-sized chunks
1/2 onion, quartered

2 cloves garlic, halved
2 tablespoons tomato paste
1/2 tablespoon Italian spice blend
1 tablespoon arrowroot powder

DIRECTIONS

Place the turkey breasts and cream of celery soup in the inner pot.

Secure the lid. Choose the "Manual" mode and cook for 20 minutes at High pressure. Once cooking is complete, use a natural pressure release; carefully remove the lid.

Add the vegetables and tomato paste; sprinkle with the Italian spice blend.

Secure the lid. Choose the "Manual" mode and cook for 3 minutes at High pressure. Once cooking is complete, use a quick pressure release; carefully remove the lid.

Transfer the turkey and vegetables to a serving bowl.

Press the "Sauté" button; add the arrowroot powder and cook until the cooking liquid is reduced by about half. Bon appétit!

244. The Best Thanksgiving Meatloaf Ever

(Ready in about 40 minutes)

Per serving: 570 Calories; 31.5g Fat; 20.6g Carbs; 53.3g Protein; 13.1g Sugars; 1g Fiber

INGREDIENTS

1 tablespoon olive oil
1/2 shallot, minced
1 pound ground turkey
1/4 cup Romano cheese, grated
1/4 cup fine breadcrumbs

1 egg, whisked
Sea salt and ground black pepper, to taste
1/2 tablespoon garlic and herb seasoning blend

1/3 cup ketchup
1 teaspoon molasses
1/2 teaspoon Dijon mustard
1 tablespoon soy sauce

DIRECTIONS

Press the "Sauté" button to preheat your Instant Pot. Heat the oil and sauté the shallot until tender and aromatic.

Add the ground turkey, cheese, breadcrumbs, egg, salt, pepper, and herb seasoning blend. Shape the mixture into a meatloaf and wrap it into a piece of foil.

Mix the ketchup, molasses, mustard and soy sauce in a small bowl. Pour the mixture on top of the meatloaf, spreading it into an even layer.

Place a steamer rack and 1 cup of water inside the inner pot. Lower your meatloaf onto the steamer rack.

Secure the lid. Choose the "Poultry" mode and cook for 30 minutes at High pressure. Once cooking is complete, use a quick pressure release; carefully remove the lid.

Let your meatloaf stand for 10 minutes before cutting and serving. Bon appétit!

245. Turkey and Barley Bowl

(Ready in about 20 minutes)

Per serving: 426 Calories; 14.5g Fat; 43.6g Carbs; 30.1g Protein; 2.4g Sugars; 8.5g Fiber

INGREDIENTS

1/2 pound turkey breast fillet, slice into bite-sized pieces
1/2 cup pearl barley
1 bay leaf
1 carrot, trimmed and thinly sliced
1 ½ cups vegetable broth

2 stalks spring onions, thinly sliced
1 medium cucumber, sliced
1 medium vine-ripened tomatoes, sliced
1 garlic clove, crushed
1/2 tablespoon harissa paste

1 lime, freshly squeezed
2 tablespoons extra-virgin olive oil
1/4 teaspoon freshly ground black pepper
Pink salt, to taste

DIRECTIONS

Add the turkey breast fillets, barley, bay leaf, carrots, and vegetable broth to the inner pot.
Secure the lid. Choose the "Manual" mode and cook for 9 minutes at High pressure. Once cooking is complete, use a quick pressure release; carefully remove the lid.
Drain, chill and transfer to a serving bowl. Add the spring onions, cucumber, tomatoes, and garlic to the bowl.
In a small mixing dish, thoroughly combine the remaining ingredients. Drizzle this dressing over your salad and serve immediately. Bon appétit!

246. Fontina Meatballs with Herbed Sauce

(Ready in about 15 minutes)

Per serving: 567 Calories; 31.9g Fat; 24.4g Carbs; 47.1g Protein; 7.1g Sugars; 2.6g Fiber

INGREDIENTS

1 slice bacon, chopped
1/2 pound ground turkey
1/4 pound ground beef
1 shallot, finely minced
1 bell pepper, deseeded and finely minced

1 garlic clove, minced
1/2 cup crushed saltines
Sea salt and freshly cracked black pepper, to taste
1/2 teaspoon dried basil
1/2 teaspoon dried rosemary

1 teaspoon dried parsley flakes
1/4 cup buttermilk
2 ounces Fontina cheese, cut into 8 pieces
1 teaspoon mustard
1/2 cup marinara sauce

DIRECTIONS

Press the "Sauté" button to preheat your Instant Pot. Cook the chopped bacon until crisp; reserve. Cook the ground turkey, beef, shallot, pepper, and garlic until the meat is no longer pink.
Add the crushed saltines, salt, black pepper, basil, rosemary, parsley, and buttermilk. Stir in the reserved bacon. Shape the meat mixture into 8 meatballs. Insert 1 cube of Fontina cheese into the center of each meatball.
Add the mustard and marinara sauce to the inner pot; stir to combine and fold in the meatballs.
Secure the lid. Choose the "Poultry" mode and cook for 5 minutes at High pressure. Once cooking is complete, use a quick pressure release; carefully remove the lid. Serve warm.

247. Sticky Orange Turkey Thighs

(Ready in about 25 minutes)

Per serving: 429 Calories; 19g Fat; 25.5g Carbs; 36.7g Protein; 24.2g Sugars; 0.2g Fiber

INGREDIENTS

1 pound turkey thighs
Sea salt and freshly ground black pepper, to taste
1/2 teaspoon red pepper flakes

1 teaspoon dried parsley flakes
2 tablespoons olive oil
1/2 orange, sliced
1/2 cup water

1/2 cup turkey stock
2 tablespoons honey
1 tablespoon all-purpose flour

DIRECTIONS

Rub the salt, black pepper, red pepper, and parsley flakes all over the turkey thighs.
Press the "Sauté" button and heat the olive oil. Sear the turkey thighs for 3 minutes per side. Then, add the orange, water, stock, and honey.
Secure the lid. Choose the "Manual" mode and cook for 15 minutes at High pressure. Once cooking is complete, use a quick pressure release; carefully remove the lid.
Then, add the flour to thicken the cooking liquid. Spoon the sauce over the turkey thighs and serve warm. Bon appétit!

248. Country-Style Turkey and Cabbage Bake

(Ready in about 20 minutes)

Per serving: 590 Calories; 29.1g Fat; 48g Carbs; 54.1g Protein; 23g Sugars; 17g Fiber

INGREDIENTS

1/2 tablespoon lard
1 pound ground turkey
1 (1/2-pound) head of cabbage, shredded
1 ripe tomato, pureed
1 sweet pepper, sliced
1/2 red chili pepper, minced

1/2 yellow onion, chopped
2 garlic cloves, smashed
1 tablespoon fresh parsley, roughly chopped
1 bay leaf
Salt and ground black pepper, to taste

DIRECTIONS

Press the "Sauté" button and melt the lard. Now, brown the ground turkey until no longer pink, about 3 minutes.
Add the remaining ingredients and secure the lid.
Secure the lid. Choose the "Manual" mode and cook for 10 minutes at High pressure. Once cooking is complete, use a natural pressure release; carefully remove the lid.
Divide between individual bowls and serve warm. Enjoy!

249. Mediterranean Turkey Salad with Cheese

(Ready in about 25 minutes + chilling time)

Per serving: 413 Calories; 32.2g Fat; 15.2g Carbs; 33.1g Protein; 4.4g Sugars; 3g Fiber

INGREDIENTS

1/2 pound turkey breast, skinless and boneless, slice into bite-sized pieces
1 cup chicken bone broth
1 small red onion
1 sweet pepper, deseeded and thinly sliced
1 serrano pepper, deseeded and thinly sliced
1/2 tablespoon mustard
1 tablespoon fresh lime juice

1/2 tablespoon champagne vinegar
2 tablespoons extra-virgin olive oil
1/2 teaspoon dried dill
1/2 teaspoon dried oregano
Sea salt and ground black pepper, to taste
1/2 cup feta cheese, cubed
1/3 cup Kalamata olives, pitted and sliced

DIRECTIONS

Place the turkey breasts in the inner pot; pour in the chicken bone broth.
Secure the lid. Choose the "Manual" mode and cook for 12 minutes at High pressure. Once cooking is complete, use a quick pressure release; carefully remove the lid. Transfer to a big tray and allow it to cool.
Place the chilled turkey breast in a serving bowl. Add the red onion and peppers. In a small dish, whisk the mustard, lime juice, vinegar, olive oil, dill, oregano, salt, and black pepper.
Dress the salad and serve topped with feta cheese and Kalamata olives. Serve well chilled and enjoy!

250. Turkey with Bacon and Sherry Gravy

(Ready in about 35 minutes)

Per serving: 543 Calories; 30.3g Fat; 11.3g Carbs; 53.9g Protein; 0.3g Sugars; 1.2g Fiber

INGREDIENTS

1/2 tablespoon butter, melted
1 pound turkey breasts, boneless and skinless
2 rashers smoked bacon
1 garlic clove, minced

1 teaspoon onion powder
Salt, to taste
1/4 teaspoon mixed peppercorns, crushed
1 sweet pepper, sliced

1/2 cup cherry wine
1/2 cup chicken stock
1 tablespoon arrowroot powder

DIRECTIONS

Press the "Sauté" button to preheat your Instant Pot. Melt the butter and cook the turkey breasts for 4 to 6 minutes until golden brown on both sides.
Top with the bacon; add the garlic, onion powder, salt, and crushed peppercorns. Add the sweet peppers.
Pour in the wine and chicken stock and secure the lid.
Choose the "Manual" mode and cook for 25 minutes at High pressure. Once cooking is complete, use a quick pressure release; carefully remove the lid.
Press the "Sauté" button again and thicken the pan juices with the arrowroot powder. Spoon the gravy over the turkey breasts and serve immediately. Bon appétit!

FISH & SEAFOOD

251. Tangy Haddock with Green Beans

(Ready in about 15 minutes)

Per serving: 288 Calories; 13.1g Fat; 9.1g Carbs; 33.7g Protein; 1.9g Sugars; 3.4g Fiber

INGREDIENTS

1/2 lime, cut into wedges
1 cup water
2 haddock fillets
1 rosemary sprig

1 thyme sprig
1 tablespoon fresh parsley
2 teaspoons ghee
Sea salt and ground black pepper, to taste

1 clove garlic, minced
2 cups green beans

DIRECTIONS

Place the lime wedges and water in the inner pot. Add a steamer rack.

Lower the haddock fillets onto the rack; place the rosemary, thyme, parsley, and ghee on the haddock fillets. Season with salt and pepper.

Secure the lid. Choose the "Steam" mode and cook for 3 minutes at Low pressure. Once cooking is complete, use a quick pressure release; carefully remove the lid. Reserve.

Then, add the garlic and green beans to the inner pot.

Secure the lid. Choose the "Steam" mode and cook for 3 minutes at Low pressure. Once cooking is complete, use a quick pressure release; carefully remove the lid.

Serve the haddock fillets with green beans on the side. Bon appétit!

252. South Indian Fish Curry (Meen Kulambu)

(Ready in about 10 minutes)

Per serving: 363 Calories; 18.8g Fat; 10.5g Carbs; 35.1g Protein; 5.3g Sugars; 2.3g Fiber

INGREDIENTS

1 tablespoon butter
3 curry leaves
1/2 onion, chopped
1 clove garlic, crushed
1 (1-inch) piece fresh ginger, grated

1/2 dried Kashmiri chili, minced
1/2 cup canned tomatoes, crushed
1/2 teaspoon turmeric powder
1/2 teaspoon ground coriander
1/2 teaspoon ground cumin

Kosher salt and ground black pepper, to taste
5 ounces can coconut milk
3/4 pound salmon fillets
1 tablespoon lemon juice

DIRECTIONS

Press the "Sauté" button and melt the butter. Once hot, cook the curry leaves for about 30 seconds.

Stir in the onions, garlic, ginger and Kashmiri chili and cook for 2 minutes more or until they are fragrant.

Add the tomatoes, turmeric, coriander, cumin, salt, and black pepper. Continue to sauté for 30 seconds more.

Add the coconut milk and salmon.

Secure the lid. Choose the "Manual" mode and cook for 2 minutes at Low pressure. Once cooking is complete, use a quick pressure release; carefully remove the lid.

Spoon the fish curry into individual bowls. Drizzle lemon juice over the fish curry and serve. Enjoy!

253. Mexican-Style Haddock Tacos

(Ready in about 13 minutes)

Per serving: 408 Calories; 22.4g Fat; 28.3g Carbs; 24.2g Protein; 2.2g Sugars; 2.3g Fiber

INGREDIENTS

1/2 lemon, sliced
1tablespoon olive oil
1/2 pound haddock fillets
1/2 teaspoon ground cumin
1/2 teaspoon onion powder

1/2 teaspoon garlic powder
1/4 teaspoon paprika
Sea salt and freshly ground black pepper, to taste
1/2 teaspoon dried basil

1/2 tablespoon ancho chili powder
2 (6-inch) flour tortillas
2 tablespoons mayonnaise
2 tablespoons sour cream
1 tablespoon fresh cilantro, chopped

DIRECTIONS

Add 1/2 cup of water, 1/2 of lemon slices, and a steamer rack to the bottom of the inner pot.

Press the "Sauté" button and heat the olive oil until sizzling. Now, sauté the haddock fillets for 1 to 2 minutes per side.

Season the fish fillets with all the spices and lower them onto the rack.

Secure the lid. Choose the "Steam" mode and cook for 3 minutes at Low pressure. Once cooking is complete, use a quick pressure release; carefully remove the lid.

Break the fish fillets into large bite-sized pieces and divide them between the tortillas.

Add the mayonnaise, sour cream and cilantro to each tortilla. Garnish with the remaining lemon slices and enjoy!

254. Sea Bass in Orange Sauce

(Ready in about 15 minutes)

Per serving: 254 Calories; 9.4g Fat; 7.8g Carbs; 26.4g Protein; 6.5g Sugars; 0.3g Fiber

INGREDIENTS

1 tablespoon safflower oil

1/2 pound sea bass

Sea salt, to taste

1/4 teaspoon white pepper

1 tablespoon tamari sauce

1 clove garlic, minced

1/2 teaspoon dried dill weed

1/2 orange, juiced

1 tablespoon honey

DIRECTIONS

Press the "Sauté" button and heat the oil. Now, cook the sea bass for 1 to 2 minutes per side. Season your fish with salt and pepper.

Add 1 cup of water and a steamer rack to the bottom of your Instant Pot. Lower the fish onto the rack.

Secure the lid. Choose the "Steam" mode and cook for 10 minutes at Low pressure. Once cooking is complete, use a quick pressure release; carefully remove the lid. Reserve.

Add the remaining ingredients to the cooking liquid and stir to combine well. Press the "Sauté" button again and let it simmer until the sauce thickens.

Spoon the sauce over the reserved fish. Bon appétit!

255. Cheesy Tuna and Asparagus Bake

(Ready in about 15 minutes)

Per serving: 386 Calories; 12.3g Fat; 14.1g Carbs; 53.4g Protein; 5g Sugars; 3.8g Fiber

INGREDIENTS

3/4 pound tuna fillets

1/2 pound asparagus, trimmed

1 ripe tomato, pureed

Sea salt and ground black pepper, to taste

1/2 teaspoon paprika

A pinch of fresh thyme

1 tablespoon dry white wine

1/2 cup Cheddar cheese, grated

DIRECTIONS

Place the tuna fillets in a lightly greased baking dish. Add the asparagus, tomatoes, salt, black pepper, paprika, thyme, and wine.

Place a steamer rack inside the inner pot; add 1/2 cup water. Cut 1 sheet of heavy-duty foil and brush with cooking spray.

Top with the cheese. Cover with foil and lower the baking dish onto the rack.

Secure the lid. Choose the "Manual" mode and cook for 9 minutes at Low pressure. Once cooking is complete, use a quick pressure release; carefully remove the lid.

Place the baking dish on a cooling rack for a couple of minutes before slicing and serving. Bon appétit!

256. Buttery Codfish with Scallions

(Ready in about 10 minutes)

Per serving: 237 Calories; 5.4g Fat; 3.4g Carbs; 41.3g Protein; 1.5g Sugars; 0.5g Fiber

INGREDIENTS

1/2 lemon, sliced

1/2 cup water

2 fillets smoked codfish

2 teaspoons butter

2 tablespoons scallions, chopped

Sea salt and ground black pepper, to taste

DIRECTIONS

Place the lemon and water in the bottom of the Instant Pot. Place the steamer rack on top.

Place the cod fish fillets on the steamer rack. Add the butter, scallions, salt, and black pepper.

Secure the lid. Choose the "Steam" mode and cook for 3 minutes at Low pressure. Once cooking is complete, use a quick pressure release; carefully remove the lid.

Serve warm and enjoy!

257. Southern California Fish Stew

(Ready in about 50 minutes)

Per serving: 454 Calories; 19.3g Fat; 25.2g Carbs; 46g Protein; 9.1g Sugars; 6.2g Fiber

INGREDIENTS

1 tablespoon coconut oil
1/2 onion, diced
2 garlic cloves, minced
1 celery stalk, diced
1 carrot, diced
1 sweet pepper, diced
12 ounces canned tomatoes, crushed
1/2 cup clam juice

1 teaspoon oyster sauce
1/2 teaspoon dried parsley flakes
1/2 teaspoon dried rosemary
1/2 teaspoon dried basil
1/2 teaspoon paprika
1 bay leaf
Sea salt and freshly ground black pepper, to taste

1/4 pound halibut steaks, cubed
1/4 pound sea scallops, rinsed and drained
1/4 pound shrimp, peeled and deveined
1/4 pound crab legs
3 tablespoons dry white wine

DIRECTIONS

Press the "Sauté" button to heat the coconut oil. Once hot, sauté the onion, garlic, celery, carrots, and pepper for about 3 minutes or until they are just tender.

Add the canned tomatoes, clam juice, oyster sauce, parsley, rosemary, basil, paprika, bay leaf, salt, and black pepper to the inner pot.

Secure the lid. Choose the "Soup/Broth" mode and cook for 30 minutes at High pressure. Once cooking is complete, use a natural pressure release for 10 minutes; carefully remove the lid.

Add the seafood and wine.

Secure the lid. Choose the "Steam" mode and cook for 3 minutes at Low pressure. Once cooking is complete, use a quick pressure release; carefully remove the lid. Serve in individual bowls and enjoy!

258. Exotic and Saucy Thai Prawns

(Ready in about 10 minutes)

Per serving: 356 Calories; 11.9g Fat; 18.2g Carbs; 43.1g Protein; 10.4g Sugars; 1.3g Fiber

INGREDIENTS

1 tablespoon coconut oil
1/2 white onion, chopped
1 clove garlic, minced
1 pound prawns, deveined
1/2 teaspoon red chili flakes
1 bell pepper, seeded and sliced

1/2 cup coconut milk
1 tablespoon fish sauce
1 tablespoon lime juice
1 tablespoon sugar
Kosher salt and white pepper, to your liking

1/2 teaspoon cayenne pepper
1/2 teaspoon fresh ginger, ground
1 tablespoon fresh cilantro, roughly chopped

DIRECTIONS

Press the "Sauté" button and heat the coconut oil; once hot, sauté the onion and garlic until aromatic.

Add the prawns, red chili flakes, bell pepper, coconut milk, fish sauce, lime juice, sugar, salt, white pepper, cayenne pepper, and ginger.

Secure the lid. Choose the "Manual" mode and cook for 3 minutes at Low pressure. Once cooking is complete, use a quick pressure release; carefully remove the lid.

Divide between serving bowls and serve garnished with fresh cilantro. Enjoy!

259. Rich and Easy Creole Gumbo

(Ready in about 15 minutes)

Per serving: 339 Calories; 8.7g Fat; 18g Carbs; 47.3g Protein; 9.5g Sugars; 2g Fiber

INGREDIENTS

1 tablespoon butter, melted
1/2 shallot, diced
1/2 sweet pepper, sliced
1 jalapeno pepper, sliced
1/2 pound tuna, cut into 2-inch chunks

1/2 tablespoon Creole seasoning
1 carrot, sliced
1 celery stalk, diced
1 ripe tomato, pureed
1/4 cup ketchup
1 bay leaf

1/2 cup beef broth
1 tablespoon Worcestershire sauce
1/2 pound raw shrimp, deveined
1/2 teaspoon filé powder
Sea salt and freshly ground black pepper, to taste

DIRECTIONS

Press the "Sauté" button and melt the butter. Once hot, cook the shallot and peppers for about 3 minutes until just tender and fragrant.

Add the remaining ingredients; gently stir to combine.

Secure the lid. Choose the "Manual" mode and cook for 5 minutes at High pressure. Once cooking is complete, use a quick pressure release; carefully remove the lid. Serve in individual bowls and enjoy!

260. Seafood Hot Pot with Jasmine Rice

(Ready in about 25 minutes)

Per serving: 520 Calories; 16.2g Fat; 56.1g Carbs; 39.5g Protein; 3.6g Sugars; 4.1g Fiber

INGREDIENTS

1/2 cup jasmine rice
1/2 tablespoon butter
1/2 tablespoon olive oil
1/4 pound chicken breasts, cubed
1/2 pound shrimp
1 sweet pepper, deveined and sliced

1 habanero pepper, deveined and sliced
1/2 onion, chopped
2 cloves garlic, minced
1 cup chicken bone broth
1 bay leaf
1 teaspoon oregano

1 teaspoon sage
1/2 teaspoon basil
1 teaspoon paprika
1 tablespoon fish sauce
Sea salt and ground black pepper, to taste
1 tablespoon cornstarch

DIRECTIONS

Combine the rice, butter and 1 ½ cups of water in a pot and bring to a rapid boil. Cover and let it simmer on low for 15 minutes. Fluff with a fork and reserve.

Press the "Sauté" button and heat the oil. Once hot, cook the chicken breasts for 3 to 4 minutes, stirring periodically.

Add the remaining ingredients, except for the cornstarch.

Secure the lid. Choose the "Manual" mode and cook for 3 minutes at Low pressure. Once cooking is complete, use a quick pressure release; carefully remove the lid.

Mix the cornstarch with 2 tablespoons of cold water. Add the cornstarch slurry to the cooking liquid and stir on the "Sauté" mode until the sauce thickens.

Serve over hot jasmine rice. Bon appétit!

261. Fish en Papillote

(Ready in about 15 minutes)

Per serving: 244 Calories; 16.4g Fat; 9.5g Carbs; 13.5g Protein; 6.5g Sugars; 1.8g Fiber

INGREDIENTS

6 ounces halibut steaks, cut into four pieces
1 red bell pepper, sliced
1/2 onion, sliced
1 garlic clove, minced

1/2 cup cherry tomatoes, halved
Sea salt and ground black pepper, to taste
1/2 teaspoon dried rosemary
1 teaspoon basil

1/2 teaspoon oregano
1/2 teaspoon paprika
2 teaspoons olive oil

DIRECTIONS

Place 1 cup of water and a metal trivet in the bottom of the inner pot.

Place 4 large sheets of heavy-duty foil on a flat surface. Divide the ingredients between sheets of foil. Add a splash of water.

Bring the ends of the foil together; fold in the sides to seal. Place the fish packets on the trivet.

Secure the lid. Choose the "Steam" mode and cook for 10 minutes at Low pressure. Once cooking is complete, use a quick pressure release; carefully remove the lid. Bon appétit!

262. Lemony Sole with Fennel

(Ready in about 20 minutes)

Per serving: 401 Calories; 23.3g Fat; 14.6g Carbs; 34.2g Protein; 7.5g Sugars; 4.8g Fiber

INGREDIENTS

1 tablespoon coconut oil
1 small shallot, quartered
2 cloves garlic, sliced
1/2 cup beef stock

1 ripe tomato, puréed
Salt and ground black pepper, to taste
1/2 pound fennel, quartered
3/4 pound sole fillets

1/2 lemon, cut into wedges
1 tablespoon fresh Italian parsley

DIRECTIONS

Press the "Sauté" button and melt the coconut oil. Once hot, sauté the shallot and garlic until tender and aromatic.

Add the beef stock, tomato, salt, pepper, and fennel.

Secure the lid. Choose the "Manual" mode and cook for 10 minutes at High pressure. Once cooking is complete, use a quick pressure release; carefully remove the lid.

Then, remove all the vegetables with a slotted spoon and reserve, keeping them warm.

Add the sole fillets to the inner pot. Secure the lid. Choose the "Steam" mode and cook for 3 minutes at Low pressure. Once cooking is complete, use a quick pressure release; carefully remove the lid.

Garnish the fish fillets with lemon and parsley; serve with the reserved vegetables. Enjoy!

263. Blue Crab with Lemon and Herbs

(Ready in about 15 minutes)

Per serving: 363 Calories; 17.1g Fat; 4.1g Carbs; 46.3g Protein; 1.4g Sugars; 0.4g Fiber

INGREDIENTS

1 pound frozen blue crab
1/2 cup water
1/3 cup dry white wine
Sea salt and ground black pepper, to taste

1 sprig rosemary
1 sprig thyme
1/2 lemon, cut into wedges

DIRECTIONS

Add the frozen crab legs, water, wine, salt, black pepper, rosemary, and thyme to the inner pot.

Secure the lid. Choose the "Manual" mode and cook for 3 minutes at High pressure. Once cooking is complete, use a quick pressure release; carefully remove the lid.

Serve warm, garnished with fresh lemon wedges. Bon appétit!

264. Salmon Salad Sandwich

(Ready in about 10 minutes + chilling time)

Per serving: 496 Calories; 20.7g Fat; 24.8g Carbs; 50.6g Protein; 11.5g Sugars; 3.1g Fiber

INGREDIENTS

1 pound salmon fillets
1/2 red onion, thinly sliced
2 tablespoons prepared horseradish, drained
2 tablespoons mayonnaise
2 tablespoons sour cream
Salt and white pepper, to taste

1/2 teaspoon red pepper flakes, crushed
1/2 teaspoon dried rosemary, only leaves crushed
1/4 teaspoon dried oregano
1/2 cup cherry tomatoes, halved
1 cup Iceberg lettuce leaves, torn into pieces
2 croissants, split

DIRECTIONS

Add 1 cup of water and metal trivet to your Instant Pot. Lower the salmon fillets onto the trivet.

Secure the lid. Choose the "Steam" mode and cook for 3 minutes at Low pressure. Once cooking is complete, use a quick pressure release; carefully remove the lid.

Add the remaining ingredients and stir to combine well. Place in your refrigerator until ready to serve.

Serve on croissants and enjoy!

265. Glazed Sea Bass Fillets

(Ready in about 10 minutes)

Per serving: 443 Calories; 19.1g Fat; 14.3g Carbs; 51.2g Protein; 11g Sugars; 0.6g Fiber

INGREDIENTS

1 tablespoon coconut oil, melted
2 tablespoons brown sugar
1 tablespoon fish sauce
1 tablespoon soy sauce
1 (1-inch) ginger root, grated

Juice of 1/2 lime
Sea salt and white pepper, to taste
1 cup chicken broth
2 (7-ounce) sea bass fillets
1 tablespoon fresh chives, chopped

DIRECTIONS

Press the "Sauté" button and heat the coconut oil. Once hot, cook the brown sugar, fish sauce, soy sauce, ginger, lime, salt, white pepper, and broth. Bring to a simmer and press the "Cancel" button.

Add sea bass. Secure the lid. Choose the "Manual" mode and cook for 4 minutes at High pressure. Once cooking is complete, use a quick pressure release; carefully remove the lid.

Remove the sea bass fillets from the cooking liquid. Press the "Sauté" button one more time. Reduce the sauce until it is thick and syrupy.

Spoon the sauce over the reserved sea bass fillets. Garnish with fresh chives. Bon appétit!

266. Mussels with Butter-Scallion Sauce

(Ready in about 10 minutes)

Per serving: 254 Calories; 9.6g Fat; 7.8g Carbs; 20.4g Protein; 0.4g Sugars; 0.2g Fiber

INGREDIENTS

1/2 cup water

1/2 cup cooking wine

1 garlic clove, sliced

1 pound frozen mussels, cleaned and debearded

1 tablespoon butter

2 tablespoons fresh scallion, chopped

DIRECTIONS

Add the water, wine, and garlic to the inner pot. Add a metal rack to the inner pot.

Put the mussels into the steamer basket; lower the steamer basket onto the rack.

Secure the lid. Choose the "Steam" mode and cook for 3 minutes at Low pressure. Once cooking is complete, use a quick pressure release; carefully remove the lid.

Press the "Sauté" button and add butter and scallions; let it cook until the sauce is thoroughly heated and slightly thickened. Press the "Cancel" button and add the mussels. Serve warm. Bon appétit!

267. Greek-Style Seafood Tart

(Ready in about 20 minutes)

Per serving: 419 Calories; 22.8g Fat; 5.5g Carbs; 47g Protein; 3.1g Sugars; 0.6g Fiber

INGREDIENTS

2 eggs

1/4 cup cream cheese

1/4 cup Greek-style yogurt

Himalayan salt and ground black pepper, to taste

1/2 teaspoon cayenne pepper

1/2 teaspoon dried basil

1/2 teaspoon dried oregano

1/2 pound crab meat, chopped

1/4 pound raw shrimp, chopped

1/3 cup Colby cheese, shredded

DIRECTIONS

In a mixing bowl, whisk the eggs with the cream cheese and yogurt. Season with salt, black pepper, cayenne pepper, basil, and oregano.

Stir in the seafood; stir to combine and spoon the mixture into a lightly greased baking pan. Lastly, top with the shredded cheese.

Cover with a piece of aluminum foil.

Secure the lid. Choose the "Steam" mode and cook for 10 minutes at Low pressure. Once cooking is complete, use a quick pressure release; carefully remove the lid. Bon appétit!

268. Traditional Japanese Yosenabe

(Ready in about 15 minutes)

Per serving: 407 Calories; 25.6g Fat; 7.3g Carbs; 38.1g Protein; 3.2g Sugars; 1.9g Fiber

INGREDIENTS

1 tablespoon butter, softened

1/2 onion, chopped

1 clove garlic, minced

1 (1-inch) pieces fresh ginger, ground

1/2 red chili, deseeded and minced

1/2 pound pollack, cut into large chunks

1/3 pound shrimps, deveined

1 tablespoon sesame oil

1/2 tablespoon garam masala

1 teaspoon curry paste

1 (3-inch) kombu (dried kelp)

1/2 package Japanese curry roux

1 tablespoon Shoyu sauce

1 ripe tomato, pureed

DIRECTIONS

Press the "Sauté" button and melt the butter; cook the onion, garlic, ginger, and red chili until just tender and fragrant.

Add the pollack and shrimp and continue to sauté for a couple of minutes more. Add the remaining ingredients.

Secure the lid. Choose the "Manual" mode and cook for 5 minutes at Low pressure. Once cooking is complete, use a quick pressure release; carefully remove the lid.

Serve your curry over hot steamed rice. Enjoy!

269. Shrimp with Feta Cheese and Mint

(Ready in about 15 minutes)

Per serving: 253 Calories; 13g Fat; 9.5g Carbs; 27.4g Protein; 5.2g Sugars; 4.2g Fiber

INGREDIENTS

1/2 pound frozen shrimp
1 tablespoon extra-virgin olive oil
1 glove garlic, minced
1/2 teaspoon basil
1/2 teaspoon dry dill weed
1/2 teaspoon oregano

12 ounces canned diced tomatoes
1/4 cup Kalamata olives
1 ounce feta cheese, crumbled
1/2 lemon, sliced
Chopped fresh mint leaves, for garnish

DIRECTIONS

Add the shrimp, olive oil, garlic, basil, dill, oregano, and tomatoes to the inner pot.

Secure the lid. Choose the "Manual" mode and cook for 2 minutes at Low pressure. Once cooking is complete, use a quick pressure release; carefully remove the lid.

Top with Kalamata olives and feta cheese. Serve garnished with lemon and mint leaves. Enjoy!

270. Tangy Cheese and Crab Dip

(Ready in about 10 minutes)

Per serving: 242 Calories; 14.1g Fat; 6g Carbs; 21.3g Protein; 1.9g Sugars; 0.7g Fiber

INGREDIENTS

1/4 pound lump crab meat
1 ounce Cottage cheese, at room temperature
1/4 cup Romano cheese, shredded
1/4 cup sour cream
Kosher salt and ground black pepper, to taste

1/2 teaspoon smoked paprika
1/4 cup Cheddar cheese, shredded
2 tablespoons fresh chives, chopped
1 tablespoon fresh lime juice

DIRECTIONS

Place 1 cup of water and a metal trivet in the inner pot.

Spritz a casserole dish with nonstick cooking spray. Place the crab meat, Cottage cheese, Romano cheese and sour cream in the casserole dish.

Season with salt, black pepper, and smoked paprika. Top with the Cheddar cheese. Lower the dish onto the trivet.

Secure the lid. Choose the "Manual" mode and cook for 3 minutes at Low pressure. Once cooking is complete, use a quick pressure release; carefully remove the lid.

Scatter the chopped chives over the top and add a few drizzles of lime juice. Serve warm or at room temperature. Enjoy!

271. Fish Masala Curry

(Ready in about 10 minutes)

Per serving: 460 Calories; 36.1g Fat; 18g Carbs; 21.9g Protein; 7.3g Sugars; 8.5g Fiber

INGREDIENTS

1 tablespoon peanut oil
1/2 onion, chopped
1 garlic clove, minced
1 (1-inch) piece fresh root ginger, peeled and grated
1 long red chilis, deseeded and minced
1 tablespoons tamarind paste
1/2 teaspoon mustard seeds

1/2 teaspoon turmeric powder
1/2 teaspoon ground cumin
Sea salt and freshly ground black pepper
6 ounces coconut milk
1/2 cup chicken stock
1/2 pound haddock

DIRECTIONS

Press the "Sauté" button and heat the peanut oil; once hot, sauté the onion, garlic, ginger, and chilis until aromatic.

Add the remaining ingredients and gently stir to combine.

Secure the lid. Choose the "Manual" mode and cook for 4 minutes at Low pressure. Once cooking is complete, use a quick pressure release; carefully remove the lid.

Divide between serving bowls and serve warm. Enjoy!

272. Parmesan and Prawn Dip

(Ready in about 10 minutes)

Per serving: 427 Calories; 34.7g Fat; 19.4g Carbs; 10.2g Protein; 7.1g Sugars; 2.2g Fiber

INGREDIENTS

1 cup crabmeat, flaked

1/2 onion, chopped

1 clove garlic, smashed

4 tablespoons cream cheese, softened

4 tablespoons mayonnaise

1/4 cup Parmesan cheese, grated

1 tablespoon cornichon, finely chopped

1/4 cup tomato paste

2 or so dashes of Tabasco

2 tablespoons fresh breadcrumbs

DIRECTIONS

Place all ingredients, except for the breadcrumbs, in a baking dish. Stir until everything is well incorporated. Top with breadcrumbs.

Secure the lid. Choose the "Steam" mode and cook for 3 minutes at Low pressure. Once cooking is complete, use a quick pressure release; carefully remove the lid.

Serve with raw vegetable sticks if desired. Bon appétit!

273. Spanish Paella with White Wine

(Ready in about 15 minutes)

Per serving: 597 Calories; 28.1g Fat; 48.2g Carbs; 37g Protein; 3.7g Sugars; 4.6g Fiber

INGREDIENTS

1 tablespoon olive oil

1 link (6-ounce) Spanish chorizo sausage, cut into slices

1/2 yellow onion, chopped

1 clove garlic, minced

1 sweet pepper, sliced

1/2 Chiles de Árbol, minced

1/2 cup Arborio rice, rinsed

1 pound shrimp, deveined

1/2 cup chicken broth

1/2 cup water

1/4 cup white wine

1/2 teaspoon curry paste

Sea salt and white pepper, to taste

1/2 cup green peas, fresh or thawed

2 tablespoons fresh parsley leaves, roughly chopped

DIRECTIONS

Press the "Sauté" button and heat the oil until sizzling. Cook the sausage for 2 minutes, stirring continuously to ensure even cooking.

Stir in the onions and garlic; cook for about a minute longer, stirring frequently.

Add the peppers, rice, shrimp, broth, water, wine, curry paste, salt, and white pepper.

Secure the lid. Choose the "Manual" mode and cook for 3 minutes at High pressure. Once cooking is complete, use a quick pressure release; carefully remove the lid.

Add the green peas and seal the lid one more time; let it sit in the residual heat until warmed through.

Serve garnished with fresh parsley and enjoy!

274. Buttery Lobster Tails

(Ready in about 10 minutes)

Per serving: 233 Calories; 12.7g Fat; 0g Carbs; 28.2g Protein; 0.1g Sugars; 0g Fiber

INGREDIENTS

3/4 pound lobster tails, halved

1/4 stick butter, at room temperature

Sea salt and freshly ground black pepper, to taste

1/2 teaspoon red pepper flakes

DIRECTIONS

Add a metal trivet, steamer basket, and 1 cup of water in your Instant Pot.

Place the lobster tails, shell side down, in the prepared steamer basket.

Secure the lid. Choose the "Steam" mode and cook for 3 minutes at Low pressure. Once cooking is complete, use a quick pressure release; carefully remove the lid.

Drizzle with butter. Season with salt, black pepper, and red pepper and serve immediately. Enjoy!

275. Spicy Shrimp Salad

(Ready in about 15 minutes + chilling time)

Per serving: 207 Calories; 7.3g Fat; 12.1g Carbs; 26g Protein; 3.6g Sugars; 4.5g Fiber

INGREDIENTS

1/2 pound shrimp, deveined
Kosher salt and white pepper, to taste
1/2 onion, thinly sliced
1/2 sweet pepper, thinly sliced
1 jalapeno pepper, deseeded and minced

1 heaping tablespoon fresh parsley, chopped
1/2 head romaine lettuce, torn into pieces
2 tablespoons extra-virgin olive oil
1/2 lime, juiced and zested
1/2 tablespoon Dijon mustard

DIRECTIONS

Add a metal trivet and 1 cup of water to your Instant Pot.
Put the shrimp into the steamer basket. Lower the steamer basket onto the trivet.
Secure the lid. Choose the "Steam" mode and cook for 3 minutes at Low pressure. Once cooking is complete, use a quick pressure release; carefully remove the lid.
Transfer steamed shrimp to a salad bowl; toss your shrimp with the remaining ingredients and serve well chilled. Bon appétit!

276. French-Style Fish Packets

(Ready in about 10 minutes)

Per serving: 291 Calories; 12.5g Fat; 8g Carbs; 34.6g Protein; 4.1g Sugars; 2.3g Fiber

Ingredients
1 tablespoon olive oil
2 (7-ounces) rainbow trout fillets
1 tablespoon fresh chives, chopped
1 tablespoon fresh parsley, chopped

Sea salt and white pepper, to taste
1/4 pound sugar snap peas, trimmed
1 tomatillo, sliced
1 garlic clove, minced

DIRECTIONS

Place 1 cup of water and a metal rack in your Instant Pot.
Place all ingredients in a large sheet of foil. Fold up the sides of the foil to make a bowl-like shape. Lower the fish packet onto the rack.
Secure the lid. Choose the "Steam" mode and cook for 3 minutes at Low pressure. Once cooking is complete, use a quick pressure release; carefully remove the lid. Bon appétit!

277. Tilapia with Lemon and Peppers

(Ready in about 10 minutes)

Per serving: 239 Calories; 7.6g Fat; 8.5g Carbs; 35.6g Protein; 1.3g Sugars; 1.6g Fiber

INGREDIENTS

1/2 lemon, sliced
2 (6-ounce) tilapia fillets, skin on
2 teaspoons olive oil
Sea salt and white pepper, to taste
1 tablespoon fresh parsley, chopped

1 tablespoon fresh tarragon, chopped
1/2 red onion, sliced into rings
1 sweet pepper, julienned
2 tablespoons dry white wine

DIRECTIONS

Place the lemon slices, 1 cup of water, and a metal trivet in the bottom of the inner pot.
Place 4 large sheets of heavy-duty foil on a flat surface. Divide the ingredients between the sheets of foil.
Bring the ends of the foil together; fold in the sides to seal. Place the fish packets on the trivet.
Secure the lid. Choose the "Steam" mode and cook for 3 minutes at Low pressure. Once cooking is complete, use a quick pressure release; carefully remove the lid. Bon appétit!

278. Indian Biryani with Halibut

(Ready in about 10 minutes)

Per serving: 456 Calories; 27g Fat; 29.1g Carbs; 24.7g Protein; 7.1g Sugars; 3.5g Fiber

INGREDIENTS

1 tablespoon butter
1/2 yellow onion, chopped
1 cup couscous
1/2 cups water
1/2 cup vegetable broth
1/2 cup coconut milk

Sea salt and ground black pepper, to taste
1 teaspoon cayenne pepper
1 teaspoon dried basil
1 ripe tomato, pureed
1/2 pound halibut, cut into chunks
1/2 teaspoon coriander

1/2 teaspoon curry paste
1/2 teaspoon ancho chili powder
1 bay leaf
2cardamom pods
1 teaspoon garam masala
1 tablespoon almonds, slivered

DIRECTIONS

Press the "Sauté" button and melt the butter. Once hot, cook the onions until tender and translucent.

Add the remaining ingredients, except for the slivered almonds, to the inner pot; stir to combine.

Secure the lid. Choose the "Manual" mode and cook for 4 minutes at High pressure. Once cooking is complete, use a quick pressure release; carefully remove the lid.

Serve garnished with almonds. Bon appétit!

279. Old Bay Crab Salad Rolls

(Ready in about 10 minutes)

Per serving: 506 Calories; 25g Fat; 44.5g Carbs; 24.5g Protein; 6.5g Sugars; 2.6g Fiber

INGREDIENTS

6 ounces crabmeat
2 heaping tablespoons fresh chives, chopped
1 garlic clove, minced
1/4 cup mayonnaise
1/3 teaspoon hot sauce

1/2 teaspoon Old Bay seasoning
1/4 cup celery stalk, chopped
1/2 tablespoon fresh lime juice
4 mini slider rolls
1 cup Iceberg lettuce, torn into pieces

DIRECTIONS

Add 1 cup of water, metal trivet, and a steamer basket to your Instant Pot.

Place the crabmeat in the prepared steamer basket.

Secure the lid. Choose the "Steam" mode and cook for 3 minutes at Low pressure. Once cooking is complete, use a quick pressure release; carefully remove the lid.

Add the chives, garlic, mayo, hot sauce, Old Bay seasoning, celery, and lime juice; stir to combine well.

Divide the mixture between slider rolls and garnish with lettuce. Serve and enjoy!

280. Spicy Red Snapper

(Ready in about 10 minutes)

Per serving: 353 Calories; 19.4g Fat; 11.2g Carbs; 33.3g Protein; 4.6g Sugars; 2g Fiber

INGREDIENTS

1/2 tablespoon ghee, at room temperature
1/2 leek, chopped
2 cloves garlic, minced
1/2 tablespoon capers
1 medium ripe tomato, chopped
1 cup chicken broth
1/2 red chili pepper, seeded and chopped

1/2 teaspoon basil
1/2 teaspoon oregano
1/2 teaspoon rosemary
2 (6-ounce) red snapper fillets
Coarse sea salt and ground black pepper, to taste
1/2 teaspoon Fish taco seasoning mix
1/2 lemon, cut into wedges

DIRECTIONS

Press the "Sauté" button and melt the ghee. Once hot, sauté the leek and garlic until tender.

Add the remaining ingredients, except for the lemon wedges, to the inner pot.

Secure the lid. Choose the "Manual" mode and cook for 4 minutes at High pressure. Once cooking is complete, use a quick pressure release; carefully remove the lid.

Serve in individual bowls, garnished with lemon wedges. Enjoy!

281. Crabs with Garlic Sauce

(Ready in about 15 minutes)

Per serving: 356 Calories; 24.8g Fat; 1.5g Carbs; 31.1g Protein; 0.3g Sugars; 0.1g Fiber

INGREDIENTS

3/4 pounds crabs
1/2 stick butter
1 clove garlic, minced

1/2 teaspoon Old Bay seasoning
1/2 lemon, sliced

DIRECTIONS

Place 1 cup water and a metal trivet in the bottom of your Instant Pot.
Lower the crabs onto the trivet.
Secure the lid. Choose the "Steam" mode and cook for 3 minutes at Low pressure. Once cooking is complete, use a quick pressure release; carefully remove the lid. Reserve.
Press the "Sauté" button and melt butter. Once hot, sauté the garlic and Old Bay seasoning for 2 to 3 minutes or until fragrant and thoroughly heated.
Add the cooked crabs and gently stir to combine. Serve with lemon slices. Bon appétit!

282. Tuna Fillets with Tarragon and Onion

(Ready in about 10 minutes)

Per serving: 281 Calories; 8g Fat; 8.6g Carbs; 45g Protein; 3.7g Sugars; 1.3g Fiber

INGREDIENTS

1 cup water
A few sprigs of tarragon
1 lemon, sliced
1 pound tuna filets

1 tablespoon butter, melted
Sea salt and freshly ground black pepper, to taste
1 large onion, sliced into rings

DIRECTIONS

Put the water, herbs and lemon slices in the inner pot; now, place the steamer rack in the inner pot.
Lower the tuna fillets onto the rack. Add butter, salt, and pepper; top with onion slices.
Secure the lid. Choose the "Steam" mode and cook for 3 minutes at Low pressure. Once cooking is complete, use a quick pressure release; carefully remove the lid. Serve immediately.

283. Cheesy Cod Fish with Potatoes

(Ready in about 10 minutes)

Per serving: 431 Calories; 17.9g Fat; 21g Carbs; 45.5g Protein; 1.1g Sugars; 2.8g Fiber

INGREDIENTS

1/2 pound baby potatoes
1 tablespoon coconut oil, at room temperature
Sea salt and freshly ground pepper, to taste
1 pound cod fish fillets
1/2 teaspoon smoked paprika

1 tablespoon fresh Italian parsley, chopped
1/2 teaspoon fresh ginger, grated
1 clove garlic, minced
1/2 cup goat cheese, crumbled

DIRECTIONS

Place the potatoes in the bottom of the inner pot. Add 1 cup of water; then, add coconut oil, salt and pepper. Place the rack over the potatoes.
Place the cod fish fillets on the rack. Season the fillets with paprika and parsley.
Secure the lid. Choose the "Steam" mode and cook for 3 minutes at Low pressure. Once cooking is complete, use a quick pressure release; carefully remove the lid.
Remove the salmon and the rack from the inner pot. Continue to cook the potatoes until fork tender; add the ginger and garlic and cook for 2 minutes more.
Top with goat cheese and serve. Bon appétit!

284. Seafood Stew with Sausage

(Ready in about 15 minutes)

Per serving: 444 Calories; 21.2g Fat; 34.2g Carbs; 32g Protein; 3.1g Sugars; 4.2g Fiber

INGREDIENTS

2 ounces beef sausage, sliced
2 baby potatoes
1 cup fume (fish stock)
2 tablespoons butter

1 clove garlic, minced
1/2 teaspoon Old Bay seasoning
1/4 teaspoon Tabasco sauce
Sea salt and white pepper, to taste

1/2 pound prawns
1 fresh lemon, juiced

DIRECTIONS

Place the sausage and potatoes in the inner pot; cover with the fish stock.

Secure the lid. Choose the "Manual" mode and cook for 5 minutes at High pressure. Once cooking is complete, use a quick pressure release; carefully remove the lid. Reserve. Clean the inner pot.

Press the "Sauté" button and melt the butter. Once hot, sauté the minced garlic until aromatic or about 1 minute. Stir in the Old Bay seasoning, Tabasco, salt, and white pepper. Lastly, stir in the prawns.

Continue to simmer for 1 to 2 minutes or until the shrimp turn pink. Press the "Cancel" button. Add the sausages and potatoes, drizzle lemon juice over the top and serve warm.

285. Cheese and Spinach-Stuffed Salmon Fillets

(Ready in about 10 minutes)

Per serving: 442 Calories; 23.5g Fat; 8.1g Carbs; 44g Protein; 1.1g Sugars; 2.8g Fiber

INGREDIENTS

2 (6-ounce) salmon fillets
Kosher salt and freshly ground black
pepper, to taste
1/4 teaspoon cayenne pepper
1/3 teaspoon celery seed, crushed

1/3 teaspoon dried basil
1/3 teaspoon dried marjoram
1/3 cup sour cream
1/4 cup mozzarella, shredded
1 cup frozen spinach, defrosted

1 clove garlic, minced
1 tablespoon olive oil
1/2 lemon, cut into wedges

DIRECTIONS

Add 1 cup of water and a steamer rack to the bottom of your Instant Pot.

Sprinkle your salmon with all spices. In a mixing bowl, thoroughly combine sour cream, mozzarella, spinach, and garlic.

Cut a pocket in each fillet to within 1/2-inch of the opposite side. Stuff the pockets with the spinach/cheese mixture. Drizzle with olive oil. Wrap the salmon fillets in foil and lower onto the rack.

Secure the lid. Choose the "Manual" mode and cook for 4 minutes at Low pressure. Once cooking is complete, use a quick pressure release; carefully remove the lid.

Garnish with lemon wedges and serve warm.

286. Tilapia with Spinach

(Ready in about 15 minutes)

Per serving: 303 Calories; 10.4g Fat; 3.6g Carbs; 49g Protein; 1.3g Sugars; 0.7g Fiber

INGREDIENTS

1 cup chicken broth
1 clove garlic, sliced
1 pound tilapia, cut into 2 pieces

1/2 tablepsoon Worcestershire sauce
Salt and ground black pepper, to taste
1 tablepsoon butter, melted

1 cup fresh spinach

DIRECTIONS

Place the chicken broth and garlic in the inner pot. Place the trivet on top.

Place the tilapia fillets on a sheet of foil; add Worcestershire sauce, salt, pepper, and butter. Bring up all sides of the foil to create a packet around your fish.

Secure the lid. Choose the "Steam" mode and cook for 10 minutes at Low pressure. Once cooking is complete, use a quick pressure release; carefully remove the lid.

Add the spinach leaves to the cooking liquid. Press the "Sauté" function and let it simmer for 1 to 2 minutes or until wilted.

Place the fish fillets on top of the wilted spinach, adjust the seasonings, and serve immediately. Bon appétit!

287. Easy Teriyaki Salmon

(Ready in about 15 minutes)

Per serving: 393 Calories; 19.1g Fat; 16.1g Carbs; 37.3g Protein; 10g Sugars; 0.7g Fiber

INGREDIENTS

1 tablespoon butter, melted
2 (6-ounce) salmon steaks
1 clove garlic, smashed
1 (1-inch) piece fresh ginger, peeled and grated
1/4 cup soy sauce

1/2 cup water
1 tablespoon brown sugar
1 teaspoon wine vinegar
1 tablespoon cornstarch

DIRECTIONS

Press the "Sauté" button and melt the butter. Once hot, cook the salmon steaks for 2 minutes per side.

Add the garlic, ginger, soy sauce, water, sugar, and vinegar.

Secure the lid. Choose the "Manual" mode and cook for 5 minutes at Low pressure. Once cooking is complete, use a quick pressure release; carefully remove the lid. Reserve the fish steaks.

Mix the cornstarch with 1 tablespoon of cold water. Add the slurry to the cooking liquid. Let it simmer until the sauce thickens. Spoon the sauce over the fish steaks. Bon appétit!

288. Halibut with Mayo Sauce

(Ready in about 1 hour)

Per serving: 568 Calories; 30.5g Fat; 33.5g Carbs; 39.3g Protein; 2.8g Sugars; 3g Fiber

INGREDIENTS

1/2 cup wild rice, rinsed and drained
1 tablespoon butter
1/3 teaspoon salt flakes
1/3 teaspoon red pepper flakes, crushed

3/4 pound halibut steaks
1 tablespoon olive oil
Sea salt and ground pepper, to your liking
2 tablespoons cream cheese

2 tablespoons mayonnaise
1 teaspoon stone-ground mustard
1 clove garlic, minced

DIRECTIONS

In a saucepan, bring 3 cups of water and rice to a boil. Reduce the heat to simmer; cover and let it simmer for 45 to 55 minutes. Add the butter, salt, and red pepper; fluff with a fork. Cover and reserve, keeping your rice warm.

Cut 2 sheets of aluminum foil. Place the halibut steak in each sheet of foil. Add the olive oil, salt, and black pepper to the top of the fish; close each packet and seal the edges.

Add 1 cup of water and a steamer rack to the bottom of your Instant Pot. Lower the packets onto the rack.

Secure the lid. Choose the "Steam" mode and cook for 3 minutes at Low pressure. Once cooking is complete, use a natural pressure release; carefully remove the lid.

Meanwhile, mix the cream cheese, mayonnaise, stone-ground mustard, and garlic until well combined. Serve the steamed fish with the mayo sauce and wild rice on the side. Bon appétit!

289. Greek-Style Cod with Olives

(Ready in about 10 minutes)

Per serving: 280 Calories; 9.8g Fat; 8.4g Carbs; 41.5g Protein; 4.1g Sugars; 2.4g Fiber

INGREDIENTS

1 tablespoon olive oil
1 pound cod fillets
1/2 pound tomatoes, chopped

Sea salt and ground black pepper, to taste
1 sprig rosemary, chopped
1 sprig thyme, chopped

1 bay leaf
1 clove garlic, smashed
1/3 cup Greek olives, pitted and sliced

DIRECTIONS

Place 1 cup of water and a metal trivet in the bottom of the inner pot. Brush the sides and bottom of a casserole dish with olive oil.

Place the cod fillets in the greased casserole dish. Add the tomatoes, salt, pepper, rosemary, thyme, bay leaf, and garlic. Lower the dish onto the trivet.

Secure the lid. Choose the "Steam" mode and cook for 3 minutes at Low pressure. Once cooking is complete, use a quick pressure release; carefully remove the lid.

Serve garnished with Greek olives and enjoy!

290. Saucy Shrimp Scampi with Wine

(Ready in about 10 minutes | Servings 4)

Per serving: 417 Calories; 10.4g Fat; 12.1g Carbs; 70g Protein; 4.3g Sugars; 3g Fiber

INGREDIENTS

1 tablespoon olive oil

2 garlic cloves, sliced

1 bunch scallions, chopped

2 carrots, grated

1 ½ pounds shrimp, deveined and rinsed

1/2 cup dry white wine

1/2 cup cream of celery soup

Sea salt and freshly cracked black pepper, to taste

1 teaspoon cayenne pepper

1/2 teaspoon dried basil

1 teaspoon dried rosemary

1/2 teaspoon dried oregano

DIRECTIONS

Press the "Sauté" button and heat the oil. Once hot, cook the garlic, scallions, and carrots for 2 to 3 minutes or until fragrant; add a splash of wine to deglaze the inner pot.

Add the remaining ingredients.

Secure the lid. Choose the "Manual" mode and cook for 3 minutes at Low pressure. Once cooking is complete, use a quick pressure release; carefully remove the lid.

Divide between serving bowls and enjoy!

PORK

291. Saucy Pork Loin Roast

(Ready in about 45 minutes)

Per serving: 406 Calories; 18.8g Fat; 4.3g Carbs; 52.2g Protein; 3.4g Sugars; 0.4g Fiber

INGREDIENTS

1 tablespoon sesame oil
1 pound pork loin roast, boneless
Sea salt and freshly ground black pepper, to taste
1/2 teaspoon dried basil
1/2 teaspoon dried oregano

1/2 teaspoon paprika
1/2 lemon, juiced and zested
1/2 cup vegetable broth
1/2 cup milk

DIRECTIONS

Press the "Sauté" button and heat the oil until sizzling; once hot, sear the pork for 4 to 5 minutes or until browned on all sides. Work in batches.
Add the remaining ingredients.
Secure the lid. Choose the "Meat/Stew" mode and cook for 35 minutes at High pressure. Once cooking is complete, use a quick pressure release; carefully remove the lid.
Turn on your broiler. Roast the pork under the broiler for about 3 minutes or until the skin is crisp.
To carve the pork, remove the cracklings and cut the crisp pork skin into strips. Carve the pork roast across the grain into thin slices and serve.

292. Barbecued Pork with Ketchup

(Ready in about 45 minutes)

Per serving: 387 Calories; 15.6g Fat; 9g Carbs; 48.2g Protein; 6.1g Sugars; 1.4g Fiber

INGREDIENTS

1 pound pork spare ribs, cut into 4 equal portions
1/2 tablespoon sea salt
1/4 teaspoon black pepper
1/3 teaspoon chili flakes
1/2 teaspoon cayenne pepper
1/2 teaspoon shallot powder

1/2 teaspoon garlic powder
1/2 teaspoon fennel seeds
1/2 tablespoon sugar
1/2 cup chicken stock
1/2 cup tomato ketchup
2 tablespoons dark soy sauce

DIRECTIONS

Generously sprinkle the pork spare ribs with all spices and sugar. Add the chicken stock and secure the lid.
Choose the "Meat/Stew" mode and cook for 35 minutes at High pressure. Once cooking is complete, use a quick pressure release; carefully remove the lid.
Transfer the pork ribs to a baking pan. Mix the tomato ketchup and soy sauce; pour the mixture over the pork ribs and roast in the preheated oven at 425 degrees F for 6 to 8 minutes. Bon appétit!

293. Pork Medallions with Lemon-Butter Sauce

(Ready in about 30 minutes)

Per serving: 356 Calories; 15g Fat; 1.4g Carbs; 51g Protein; 0.3g Sugars; 0.1g Fiber

INGREDIENTS

1 tablespoon butter, melted
1 pound pork medallions
Kosher salt and freshly ground black pepper, to taste
1/2 teaspoon garlic powder

1/2 teaspoon shallot powder
1 cup vegetable broth
1 sprig fresh rosemary
1/2 lemon, juice and zest

DIRECTIONS

Press the "Sauté" button and melt the butter. Sear the pork medallions until no longer pink.
Add the salt, black pepper, garlic powder, shallot powder, and vegetable broth.
Secure the lid. Choose the "Manual" mode and cook for 20 minutes at High pressure. Once cooking is complete, use a quick pressure release; carefully remove the lid.
Remove the pork medallions to a serving platter. Now, add the fresh rosemary, lemon juice and zest to the cooking liquid. Let it simmer for 2 to 3 minutes.
Spoon the sauce over the pork medallions and serve immediately. Enjoy!

294. Pork Chops with Tomato and Parmesan

(Ready in about 20 minutes)

Per serving: 575 Calories; 26g Fat; 7.6g Carbs; 73g Protein; 1.5g Sugars; 0.6g Fiber

INGREDIENTS

1/2 tablespoon lard, at room temperature
2 pork chops, bone-in
Sea salt and freshly ground black pepper, to taste

4 tablespoons tomato puree
1 cup chicken bone broth
2 ounces parmesan cheese, preferably freshly grated

DIRECTIONS

Press the "Sauté" button and melt the lard. Sear the pork chops for 3 to 4 minutes per side. Season with salt and pepper.
Place the tomato puree and chicken broth in the inner pot.
Secure the lid. Choose the "Manual" mode and cook for 10 minutes at High pressure. Once cooking is complete, use a natural pressure release; carefully remove the lid.
Top with parmesan cheese and serve warm. Bon appétit!

295. Orange and Bourbon Glazed Ham

(Ready in about 20 minutes)

Per serving: 437 Calories; 19.5g Fat; 20g Carbs; 37.8g Protein; 14.1g Sugars; 3g Fiber

INGREDIENTS

1 pound spiral sliced ham
1/4 cup orange juice
1 tablespoon bourbon

2 tablespoons maple syrup
Sea salt and ground black pepper, to taste

DIRECTIONS

Place 1 cup of water and a metal trivet in the inner pot.
Then, thoroughly combine the orange juice, bourbon, maple syrup, salt and pepper.
Place the ham on foil. Fold up the sides of the foil to make a bowl-like shape. Pour the orange glaze all over the ham; wrap the foil around the ham. Lower the ham onto the trivet.
Secure the lid. Choose the "Manual" mode and cook for 10 minutes at High pressure. Once cooking is complete, use a quick pressure release; carefully remove the lid.
Transfer to a cooling rack before serving. Bon appétit!

296. Ground Pork Goulash with Sweet Corn

(Ready in about 25 minutes)

Per serving: 575 Calories; 37.4g Fat; 20.4g Carbs; 38.2g Protein; 7g Sugars; 5.1g Fiber

INGREDIENTS

1/2 tablespoon olive oil
1/2 pound ground pork
1/4 pound ground turkey
1/2 onion, chopped
1 clove garlic, minced
1 bay leaf

1 thyme sprig
1 rosemary sprig
1 teaspoon paprika
Sea salt and ground black pepper, to taste
1/2 cup beef bone broth

1/2 cup rice wine
1 ripe tomato, pureed
1/2 cup sweet corn kernels
1/2 cup green peas
1/4 cup Colby cheese, shredded

DIRECTIONS

Press the "Sauté" button to preheat your Instant Pot. Heat the oil and sear the meat until no longer pink, stirring continuously with a spatula. Use a splash of wine to deglaze the pan.
Add the onion and garlic to the meat mixture and cook an additional 3 minutes or until tender and fragrant.
Next, stir in the spices, broth, wine, and tomatoes.
Secure the lid. Choose the "Manual" mode and cook for 10 minutes at High pressure. Once cooking is complete, use a quick pressure release; carefully remove the lid.
Press the "Sauté" button and add the corn and green peas. Cook an additional 3 minutes or until everything is heated through.
Top with cheese and allow it to stand until the cheese has melted. Bon appétit!

297. Spicy Ground Pork Omelet

(Ready in about 25 minutes)

Per serving: 449 Calories; 33.6g Fat; 4.3g Carbs; 32.2g Protein; 1.6g Sugars; 1g Fiber

INGREDIENTS

1 tablespoon canola oil
1/2 pound ground pork
1 yellow onion, thinly sliced
1 red chili pepper, minced

4 eggs, whisked
1/2 teaspoon garlic powder
1/3 teaspoon cumin powder
1 teaspoon oyster sauce

Kosher salt and ground black pepper, to taste
1/2 teaspoon paprika

DIRECTIONS

Press the "Sauté" button and heat the oil until sizzling; once hot, cook the ground pork until no longer pink, crumbling with a spatula. Add the onion and pepper; cook an additional 2 minutes. Whisk the eggs with the remaining ingredients. Pour the egg mixture over the meat mixture in the inner pot.

Secure the lid. Choose the "Manual" mode and cook for 8 minutes at High pressure. Once cooking is complete, use a natural pressure release for 10 minutes; carefully remove the lid. Bon appétit!

298. Asian-Style Pork

(Ready in about 30 minutes)

Per serving: 387 Calories; 12.1g Fat; 12.1g Carbs; 53.2g Protein; 5.7g Sugars; 1.5g Fiber

INGREDIENTS

1/2 tablespoon sesame oil
1 pound pork medallions
1/4 cup tamari sauce
1/2 cup chicken stock
2 tablespoons rice vinegar

1/2 teaspoon cayenne pepper
1/4 teaspoon salt
1/2 tablespoon maple syrup
1/2 tablespoon Sriracha sauce
1 clove garlic, minced

4 ounces mushrooms, chopped
1 tablespoon arrowroot powder, dissolved in 2 tablespoons of water

DIRECTIONS

Press the "Sauté" button and heat the oil; once hot, cook the pork medallions for 3 minutes per side.

Add the tamari sauce, chicken stock, vinegar, cayenne pepper, salt, maple syrup, Sriracha, garlic, and mushrooms to the inner pot.

Secure the lid. Choose the "Meat/Stew" mode and cook for 20 minutes at High pressure. Once cooking is complete, use a quick pressure release; carefully remove the lid. Remove the pork from the inner pot.

Add the thickener to the cooking liquid. Press the "Sauté" button again and let it boil until the sauce has reduced slightly and the flavors have concentrated.

Serve over hot steamed rice if desired. Enjoy!

299. Authentic Pork Carnitas

(Ready in about 50 minutes)

Per serving: 606 Calories; 23.2g Fat; 46g Carbs; 51g Protein; 21.7g Sugars; 2g Fiber

INGREDIENTS

1 pound pork butt roast
1/2 cup Mexican coke
1/2 cup beef bone broth
1/4 cup tomato ketchup
2 tablespoons honey

1 teaspoon liquid smoke
1 tablespoon balsamic vinegar
1/2 jalapeno, deveined and chopped
1/4 teaspoon cumin powder
1/2 teaspoon shallot powder

1/2 teaspoon garlic powder
1/4 teaspoon Mexican oregano
Sea salt and ground black pepper, to taste
2 warm tortillas

DIRECTIONS

Place all ingredients, except for the tortillas, in the inner pot.

Secure the lid. Choose the "Meat/Stew" mode and cook for 35 minutes at High pressure. Once cooking is complete, use a quick pressure release; carefully remove the lid.

Remove the pork from the inner pot and shred with two forks.

Transfer the pork to a baking sheet lightly greased with cooking spray. Pour 1 ladle of the cooking liquid over the pork. Broil for 7 to 10 minutes until the meat becomes crispy on the edges.

Spoon the pulled pork into the warm tortillas and serve with your favorite toppings. Bon appétit!

300. Spicy Roasted Pork Sandwich

(Ready in about 40 minutes)

Per serving: 520 Calories; 14.4g Fat; 37.1g Carbs; 56.7g Protein; 15.2g Sugars; 3.3g Fiber

INGREDIENTS

1/2 tablespoon olive oil
1 pound pork shoulder roast
1/4 cup tomato paste
1/2 cup beef bone broth
2 tablespoons balsamic vinegar
2 tablespoons brown sugar

1/2 tablespoon mustard
1/2 teaspoon Cholula hot sauce
1 clove garlic, minced
1 teaspoon dried marjoram
2 hamburger buns

DIRECTIONS

Add all ingredients, except for the hamburger buns, to the inner pot.

Secure the lid. Choose the "Meat/Stew" mode and cook for 35 minutes at High pressure. Once cooking is complete, use a quick pressure release; carefully remove the lid.

Remove the pork from the inner pot and shred with two forks. Spoon the pulled pork into the hamburger buns and serve with your favorite toppings. Bon appétit!

301. Saucy Boston-Style Butt

(Ready in about 20 minutes)

Per serving: 407 Calories; 18.4g Fat; 11.7g Carbs; 46.4g Protein; 4.9g Sugars; 1g Fiber

INGREDIENTS

1 tablespoon olive oil
3/4 pound Boston-style butt, sliced into four pieces
Coarse sea salt and freshly ground black pepper, to taste
1/2 shallot, sliced
1 clove garlic, sliced
1/2 stalk celery, chopped
1 bell pepper, deveined and sliced

1/4 cup apple juice
1/2 cup chicken broth
1 tablespoon stone ground mustard
1/2 teaspoon basil
1/2 teaspoon thyme
1 tablespoon plain flour, mixed with 1 tablespoon of cold water

DIRECTIONS

Press the "Sauté" button and heat the oil. Then, sear the Boston butt until it is golden brown on all sides.

Add the salt, pepper, shallot, garlic, celery, bell pepper, apple juice, chicken broth, mustard, basil, and thyme to the inner pot.

Secure the lid. Choose the "Manual" mode and cook for 15 minutes at High pressure. Once cooking is complete, use a quick pressure release; carefully remove the lid. Remove the meat from the cooking liquid.

Add the slurry and press the "Sauté" button one more time. Let it simmer until your sauce has thickened. Spoon the gravy over the pork and serve. Bon appétit!

302. Winter Pork Burgers

(Ready in about 20 minutes)

Per serving: 551 Calories; 33.7g Fat; 29.2g Carbs; 31.5g Protein; 5.5g Sugars; 3.5g Fiber

INGREDIENTS

1/2 pound ground pork
1 large sweet pepper, minced
1/2 chipotle pepper, minced
1 clove garlic, minced

Sea salt and ground black pepper, to taste
1/2 teaspoon red pepper flakes, crushed
2 burger buns
2 (1-ounce) slices Swiss cheese, sliced

DIRECTIONS

Mix the ground pork, peppers, garlic, salt, black pepper, and red pepper flakes until well combined.

Form the meat mixture into 3 patties. Place your patties on squares of aluminum foil and wrap them loosely.

Add 1 cup water and a metal trivet to the Instant Pot; lower the foil packs onto the top of the metal trivet.

Secure the lid. Choose the "Meat/Stew" mode and cook for 10 minutes at High pressure. Once cooking is complete, use a natural pressure release; carefully remove the lid.

Place your patties on a baking sheet and broil for 5 to 6 minutes. Serve on buns topped with Swiss cheese. Enjoy!

303. Pineapple Glazed Pork

(Ready in about 35 minutes)

Per serving: 362 Calories; 12g Fat; 13.5g Carbs; 48g Protein; 11.5g Sugars; 0.8g Fiber

INGREDIENTS

1 tablespoon canola oil

1 pound pork tenderloin, slice into 4 pieces

Kosher salt and freshly ground black pepper, to taste

1/2 shallot, chopped

1 garlic clove, chopped

1/2 teaspoon ground ginger

1 thyme sprig

1 rosemary sprig

1/4 cup unsweetened pineapple juice

1/2 cup vegetable broth

2 pineapple rings

DIRECTIONS

Press the "Sauté" button to preheat your Instant Pot. Heat the canola oil.

Season the pork tenderloin on both sides with salt and black pepper. Cook the pork chops with shallot and garlic for 3 minutes or until the pork chops are no longer pink.

Add the ginger, thyme, rosemary, pineapple juice, and vegetable broth.

Secure the lid. Choose the "Manual" mode and cook for 10 minutes at High pressure. Once cooking is complete, use a natural pressure release for 10 minutes; carefully remove the lid.

Preheat the broiler. Place the pork chops on a broil pan. Brush with the pan juices and place one pineapple ring on top of each pork piece. Broil for 5 minutes. Serve warm.

304. Indian-Style Pork Curry

(Ready in about 30 minutes)

Per serving: 408 Calories; 19.8g Fat; 18.3g Carbs; 43.7g Protein; 6g Sugars; 1.6g Fiber

INGREDIENTS

3/4 pound pork stew meat, cubed

1/4 cup all-purpose flour

1 tablespoon ghee

1 onion, sliced

1 (1-inch) piece ginger

1 clove garlic, sliced

1 green cardamom

1/4 teaspoon ground allspice

1/2 tablespoon garam masala

1/2 tablespoon cider vinegar

Salt and black pepper, to taste

1/2 teaspoon curry powder

1/2 teaspoon coriander seeds

1/3 teaspoon Fenugreek seeds

1 dried chili de árbol, chopped

3/4 cup yogurt

DIRECTIONS

Toss the pork stew meat with the flour until well coated.

Press the "Sauté" button and melt the ghee. Once hot, cook the pork for 3 to 4 minutes, stirring frequently to ensure even cooking.

Add the remaining ingredients, except for the yogurt.

Secure the lid. Choose the "Manual" mode and cook for 15 minutes at High pressure. Once cooking is complete, use a natural pressure release for 10 minutes; carefully remove the lid.

Add the yogurt and press the "Sauté" button; let it cook for a few minutes more or until everything is thoroughly heated. Bon appétit!

305. Traditional Arepas with Pork Roast

(Ready in about 40 minutes)

Per serving: 512 Calories; 22g Fat; 22.2g Carbs; 54.2g Protein; 4.4g Sugars; 1.8g Fiber

INGREDIENTS

1 tablespoon butter

1 pound boneless pork butt roast

1 cup cream of mushroom soup

1 tablespoon Worcestershire sauce

2 cloves garlic, finely chopped

Sea salt and ground black pepper, to taste

1/2 teaspoon cayenne pepper

1/2 teaspoon garlic powder

1/2 teaspoon onion powder

1/4 teaspoon ground cumin

2 Venezuelan-style arepas (corn cakes)

DIRECTIONS

Place all ingredients, except for the arepas, in the inner pot.

Secure the lid. Choose the "Meat/Stew" mode and cook for 35 minutes at High pressure. Once cooking is complete, use a quick pressure release; carefully remove the lid.

Remove the pork from the inner pot and shred with two forks.

Fill each arepa with the pork mixture and serve with your favorite toppings. Enjoy!

306. Picnic Ham with Peppers

(Ready in about 30 minutes + marinating time)

Per serving: 439 Calories; 28.1g Fat; 9.5g Carbs; 32.9g Protein; 3.1g Sugars; 1.4g Fiber

INGREDIENTS

1 tablespoon olive oil

1/2 teaspoon cayenne pepper

1/4 cup red wine

1/2 cup fresh orange juice

1 clove garlic, minced

1/2 tablespoon mustard

1 pound picnic ham

1 tablespoon parsley, chopped

1/2 shallot, sliced

1 sweet pepper, julienned

DIRECTIONS

Mix the olive oil, cayenne pepper, red wine, orange juice, garlic, and mustard in a glass bowl. Add the pork and let it marinate for 2 hours. Transfer the pork along with its marinade to the inner pot. Add the parsley, shallot, and peppers.

Secure the lid. Choose the "Meat/Stew" mode and cook for 20 minutes at High pressure. Once cooking is complete, use a quick pressure release; carefully remove the lid.

Spoon over hot steamed rice. Bon appétit!

307. Pork Cutlets with Ricotta Sauce

(Ready in about 30 minutes)

Per serving: 466 Calories; 23.3g Fat; 3.1g Carbs; 57.1g Protein; 0.5g Sugars; 0g Fiber

INGREDIENTS

1 tablespoon olive oil

2 pork cutlets

Sea salt and freshly ground black pepper, to taste

1/2 onion, thinly sliced

1 chicken bouillon cube

1 cup water

4 ounces Ricotta cheese

DIRECTIONS

Press the "Sauté" button and heat the oil until sizzling. Sear the pork cutlets for 3 minutes per side.

Add the salt, black pepper, onion, chicken bouillon cubes, water to the Instant Pot.

Secure the lid. Choose the "Manual" mode and cook for 10 minutes at High pressure. Once cooking is complete, use a natural pressure release for 10 minutes; carefully remove the lid.

Top with Ricotta cheese; seal the lid and let it stand for 5 to 10 minutes or until thoroughly heated. Bon appétit!

308. Country-Style Huevos Rancheros

(Ready in about 35 minutes)

Per serving: 529 Calories; 21.3g Fat; 29.4g Carbs; 53.2g Protein; 8.7g Sugars; 5.3g Fiber

INGREDIENTS

1/2 tablespoon coarse sea salt

1/4 teaspoon ground black pepper

1/2 teaspoon paprika

1/2 teaspoon onion powder

1/2 teaspoon garlic powder

1/2 teaspoon ancho chili powder

1/2 tablespoon dark brown sugar

1 pound Boston butt, cut into bite-sized pieces

1/2 tablespoon olive oil

1/2 cup tomato paste

1/4 cup roasted vegetable broth

1/2 tablespoon fish sauce

2 eggs

1 tablespoon corn salsa

2 warm corn tortillas

DIRECTIONS

In a resealable bag, mix the all spices and sugar. Add the pork chunks and shake to coat well.

Press the "Sauté" button and heat the oil until sizzling. Now, sear and brown the Boston butt on all sides until you have a crispy crust.

Add the tomato paste, broth, and fish sauce.

Secure the lid. Choose the "Manual" mode and cook for 30 minutes at High pressure. Once cooking is complete, use a quick pressure release; carefully remove the lid.

Meanwhile, crack the eggs into a lightly greased pan; fry your eggs until the whites are set.

Stack the tortilla, pork mixture, and corn salsa on a plate. Place the fried egg onto the stack using a spatula. Make four servings and enjoy!

309. Mexican Chile Verde

(Ready in about 40 minutes)

Per serving: 455 Calories; 13.1g Fat; 29g Carbs; 55.4g Protein; 9g Sugars; 5.3g Fiber

INGREDIENTS

1 pound pork shoulder, cut into bite-sized pieces
2 tablespoons flour
Kosher salt and ground black pepper, to your liking
1/2 tablespoon canola oil
1/2 onion, chopped

1 clove garlic, sliced
1/2 teaspoon Mexican oregano
1/4 teaspoon coriander seeds
1/2 teaspoon ground cumin
1/2 teaspoon turmeric powder
1 cup beef broth
1 sweet pepper, seeded and sliced

2 fresh chili pepper, seeded and sliced
1/2 pound fresh tomatillos, husked and sliced into 1/2-inch wedges
2 tablespoons fresh cilantro leaves, roughly chopped

DIRECTIONS

Toss the pork pieces with the flour until everything is well coated. Generously season the pork with salt and pepper.

Press the "Sauté" button and heat the oil. Once hot, sear the pork, stirring periodically to ensure even cooking.

Now, add the remaining ingredients, except for the cilantro leaves.

Secure the lid. Choose the "Meat/Stew" mode and cook for 35 minutes at High pressure. Once cooking is complete, use a quick pressure release; carefully remove the lid.

Serve in individual bowls, garnished with fresh cilantro. Enjoy!

310. Sicily Pork and Vegetable Bake

(Ready in about 25 minutes)

Per serving: 596 Calories; 39g Fat; 28.1g Carbs; 32.2g Protein; 5.7g Sugars; 5.4g Fiber

INGREDIENTS

1 teaspoon olive oil
3/4 pound ground pork
1 carrot, sliced
1/2 parsnip, sliced
1 stalk celery, sliced

1 sweet pepper, sliced
1/2 onion, sliced
2 cloves garlic, sliced
1 cup whole kernel corn, frozen
4 tablespoons Marsala wine

1 fresh tomato, pureed
1/2 cup water
Kosher salt and ground black pepper, to taste

DIRECTIONS

Press the "Sauté" button and heat the oil. Once hot, cook the ground pork for 2 to 3 minutes, stirring frequently.

Add a splash of wine to deglaze the pot. Add the remaining ingredients.

Secure the lid. Choose the "Manual" mode and cook for 18 minutes at High pressure. Once cooking is complete, use a quick pressure release; carefully remove the lid.

Taste and adjust the seasonings. Bon appétit!

311. Family Roast Pork

(Ready in about 1 hour 10 minutes)

Per serving: 445 Calories; 19.4g Fat; 9.2g Carbs; 44.2g Protein; 4.2g Sugars; 1.8g Fiber

INGREDIENTS

1 garlic clove, minced
1 teaspoon stone-ground mustard
Sea salt and ground black pepper, to taste

1 teaspoon freshly grated lemon zest
1 pound pork butt
1 tablespoon lard, at room temperature

1/2 cup red wine
1/2 leek, sliced into long pieces
1 carrot, halved lengthwise

DIRECTIONS

Combine the garlic, mustard, salt, pepper and lemon zest in a mixing bowl. Using your hands, spread the rub evenly onto the pork butt.

Press the "Sauté" button to preheat your Instant Pot. Melt the lard and sear the meat for 3 minutes per side.

Pour a splash of wine into the inner pot, scraping any bits from the bottom with a wooden spoon.

Place a trivet and 1 cup of water in the bottom of the inner pot. Lower the pork butt onto the trivet; scatter the leeks and carrots around.

Secure the lid. Choose the "Manual" mode and cook for 50 minutes at High pressure. Once cooking is complete, use a natural pressure release for 10 minutes; carefully remove the lid.

Transfer the pork butt to a cutting board and let it sit for 5 minutes before carving and serving. Enjoy!

312. Pork with Italian Mushroom Sauce

(Ready in about 30 minutes)

Per serving: 507 Calories; 30g Fat; 12.3g Carbs; 44.5g Protein; 4g Sugars; 3.2g Fiber

INGREDIENTS

1 tablespoon butter
2 pork chops
1/2 tablespoon Italian seasoning blend
1/2 teaspoon coarse sea salt

1/4 teaspoon cracked black pepper
1/2 pound white mushrooms, sliced
1/2 tablespoon fresh coriander, chopped

1/2 teaspoon dill weed, minced
1 clove garlic crushed
1/4 cup double cream
1/2 cup cream of onion soup

DIRECTIONS

Press the "Sauté" button and melt the butter. Once hot, sear the pork chops until golden browned, about 4 minutes per side.
Add the remaining ingredients and gently stir to combine.
Secure the lid. Choose the "Meat/Stew" mode and cook for 20 minutes at High pressure. Once cooking is complete, use a quick pressure release; carefully remove the lid.
Serve over mashed potatoes. Bon appétit!

313. Classic Pork with Garlic Mayo

(Ready in about 25 minutes)

Per serving: 553 Calories; 36.3g Fat; 3.3g Carbs; 50.1g Protein; 1.4g Sugars; 0.7g Fiber

INGREDIENTS

1 pound center-cut loin chops
Kosher salt and ground black pepper, to taste
1/2 teaspoon paprika

1/2 teaspoon mustard powder
1/2 teaspoon celery seeds
1 tablespoon canola oil
1 cup beef bone broth

1/4 cup mayonnaise
1 clove garlic, crushed

DIRECTIONS

Press the "Sauté" button and heat the oil. Sear the pork until it is golden brown on both sides.
Add the salt, black pepper, mustard powder, celery seeds oil, and broth.
Secure the lid. Choose the "Manual" mode and cook for 10 minutes at High pressure. Once cooking is complete, use a natural pressure release for 10 minutes; carefully remove the lid.
Meanwhile, whisk the mayonnaise with the garlic; serve the warm loin chops with the garlic mayo on the side. Bon appétit!

314. Pork Meatballs with Marinara Sauce

(Ready in about 20 minutes)

Per serving: 720 Calories; 53.1g Fat; 21.7g Carbs; 38.4g Protein; 7.7g Sugars; 3g Fiber

INGREDIENTS

1 tablespoon vegetable oil
Meatballs:
3/4 pound ground pork
Kosher salt and ground black pepper, to your liking
1/2 teaspoon chili flakes
1 teaspoon mustard powder
1 egg
1/4 cup Parmesan, grated
1 bread slice, soaked in 2 tablespoons of milk

Marinara Sauce:
1 tablespoon olive oil
1/2 onion, chopped
2 cloves garlic, minced
1/2 tablespoon cayenne pepper
1 teaspoon maple syrup
1 large ripe tomato, crushed
1/2 teaspoon dried parsley flakes
1 cup water

DIRECTIONS

Mix all ingredients for the meatballs until everything is well incorporated. Shape the mixture into small meatballs.
Press the "Sauté" button and heat 2 tablespoons of vegetable oil. Sear your meatballs until golden brown on all sides. Work in batches as needed. Reserve.
Press the "Sauté" button one more time; heat 2 tablespoons of olive oil. Cook the onion and garlic until tender and fragrant.
Now, add the remaining ingredients for the marinara sauce. Gently fold in the meatballs and secure the lid.
Choose the "Poultry" mode and cook for 5 minutes at High pressure. Once cooking is complete, use a quick pressure release; carefully remove the lid. Serve warm.

315. Winter Pork and Sauerkraut

(Ready in about 40 minutes)

Per serving: 517 Calories; 35.6g Fat; 6.3g Carbs; 41.1g Protein; 2.2g Sugars; 3.1g Fiber

INGREDIENTS

1 tablespoon oil
3/4 pound pork shoulder, cubed
2 ounces pork sausage, sliced
Sea salt and, to taste
1/2 teaspoon black peppercorns
6 ounces sauerkraut, drained

1 cup beef broth
1/2 onion, sliced
1 garlic clove, minced
1 bay leaf
1/2 teaspoon smoked paprika
1/2 dried chili pepper, minced

DIRECTIONS

Press the "Sauté" button and heat the oil. Once hot, cook the pork and sausage until they are no longer pink.
Add the remaining ingredients; gently stir to combine.
Secure the lid. Choose the "Meat/Stew" mode and cook for 35 minutes at High pressure. Once cooking is complete, use a quick pressure release; carefully remove the lid. Enjoy!

316. Pork Steak and Pepper Bake

(Ready in about 40 minutes)

Per serving: 504 Calories; 25.5g Fat; 12g Carbs; 53.5g Protein; 5.5g Sugars; 2g Fiber

INGREDIENTS

1/2 tablespoon lard, melted
1 pound pork steaks, cut into large pieces
1/2 onion, thinly
1 clove garlic, sliced
2 colored peppers, deveined and chopped
1 serrano pepper, deveined and chopped
Sea salt and ground black pepper, to taste

1/2 tablespoon Cajun seasonings
2 sage leaves
1 teaspoon mustard
1 tablespoon red wine
1 cup chicken broth
1/2 cup goat cheese, crumbled

DIRECTIONS

Press the "Sauté" button and melt the lard; once hot, sear the pork in batches until golden brown all over.
Add the onions, garlic, and peppers. Season with salt, black pepper, and Cajun seasonings. Add the sage leaves, mustard, wine, and broth.
Secure the lid. Choose the "Manual" mode and cook for 30 minutes at High pressure. Once cooking is complete, use a quick pressure release; carefully remove the lid.
Add the goat cheese on top, seal the lid again, and let it sit in the residual heat until the cheese melts.
Let it rest for 5 to 10 minutes before slicing and serving. Bon appétit!

317. Japanese Buta Niku No Mushimono

(Ready in about 15 minutes)

Per serving: 488 Calories; 37.3g Fat; 4.9g Carbs; 29.7g Protein; 1.9g Sugars; 1g Fiber

INGREDIENTS

1/2 teaspoon sesame oil
3/4 pound ground pork
2 fresh shiitake, sliced
1 cup chicken broth
1 tablespoon tamari sauce

1 clove garlic, minced
1 tablespoon sake
1/2 teaspoon fresh ginger, grated
Sea salt and ground black pepper, to taste

DIRECTIONS

Press the "Sauté" button and heat the oil. Once hot, cook the ground pork until no longer pink.
Add the fresh shiitake, chicken broth, tamari sauce, garlic, sake, ginger, salt, and black pepper.
Secure the lid. Choose the "Poultry" mode and High pressure; cook for 5 minutes. Once cooking is complete, use a quick release.
Spoon into individual bowls. Enjoy!

318. Pork Stew with Polenta

(Ready in about 30 minutes)

Per serving: 494 Calories; 21.6g Fat; 18g Carbs; 45.9g Protein; 2.9g Sugars; 1.7g Fiber

INGREDIENTS

1 tablespoon olive oil
1/2 pound boneless pork top loin roast, cut into cubes
1 spicy pork sausage, sliced
1 bell pepper, sliced

1 jalapeno pepper, sliced
1 garlic clove, chopped
1 cup chicken bone broth
Salt and ground black pepper, to taste
1/2 cup polenta

2 cups water
1 teaspoon salt
1/2 teaspoon paprika

DIRECTIONS

Press the "Sauté" button and heat the oil. Once hot, cook the pork until no longer pink; add the sausage and cook for 2 to 3 minutes more. Add the peppers, garlic, broth, salt, and black pepper.

Secure the lid. Choose the "Manual" mode and cook for 15 minutes at High pressure. Once cooking is complete, use a quick pressure release; carefully remove the lid.

Clean the inner pot. Add the polenta, water and 1 teaspoon of salt and mix to combine.

Secure the lid. Choose the "Manual" mode and cook for 9 minutes at High pressure. Once cooking is complete, use a quick pressure release; carefully remove the lid.

Divide your polenta between serving bowls; top with the pork mélange and paprika. Serve warm.

319. Sausage Bake with Bacon and Herbs

(Ready in about 20 minutes)

Per serving: 611 Calories; 51.8g Fat; 10.2g Carbs; 21.6g Protein; 5.5g Sugars; 1.6g Fiber

INGREDIENTS

1 tablespoon canola oil
1/2 pound pork sausages, sliced
2 ounces streaky bacon
1/2 onion, sliced
2 garlic cloves, minced

1 bell pepper, sliced
1 red chili pepper, sliced
1/2 teaspoon brown sugar
1/2 teaspoon dried rosemary
1/2 teaspoon dried basil

Sea salt and freshly ground black pepper, to taste
1 tomato, pureed
1/2 cup chicken stock
1/2 cup white wine

DIRECTIONS

Press the "Sauté" button and heat the oil. Sear the pork sausage until no longer pink. Add the bacon and cook until it is crisp.

Add a layer of onions and garlic; then, add the peppers. Sprinkle with sugar, rosemary, basil, salt and black pepper.

Add the tomatoes, chicken stock, and wine to the inner pot.

Secure the lid. Choose the "Manual" mode and cook for 10 minutes at High pressure. Once cooking is complete, use a natural pressure release; carefully remove the lid. Bon appétit!

320. Pork with Port and Root Vegetables

(Ready in about 30 minutes)

Per serving: 547 Calories; 30.6g Fat; 17.4g Carbs; 49g Protein; 5.1g Sugars; 3.5g Fiber

INGREDIENTS

3/4 pound Boston butt, cut into small chunks
1/2 teaspoon garlic powder
1/2 teaspoon shallot powder
Sea salt and ground black pepper
1/2 teaspoon dried marjoram

1/2 teaspoon mustard powder
1/2 teaspoon smoked paprika
1 tablespoon olive oil
1/4 cup port
1/2 cup roasted vegetable broth
1 large carrot, cut into 1.5-inch chunks

1 large celery stalk, cut into 1.5-inch chunks
1/2 parsnip, cut into 1.5-inch chunks
1 mild green chilies, roasted, seeded and diced
1 tablespoon arrowroot powder

DIRECTIONS

In a resealable bag, mix the garlic powder, shallot powder, salt, black pepper, marjoram, mustard powder, and paprika.

Add the pork cubes and shake to coat well. Press the "Sauté" button and heat the oil until sizzling.

Cook the Boston butt for 2 to 4 minutes, stirring periodically to ensure even cooking. Add the remaining ingredients, except for the arrowroot powder.

Secure the lid. Choose the "Meat/Stew" mode and cook for 20 minutes at High pressure. Once cooking is complete, use a quick pressure release; carefully remove the lid.

Stir in the arrowroot powder and let it simmer until the sauce thickens. Serve in individual bowls and enjoy!

321. Pork Loin with Garlic Sauce

(Ready in about 30 minutes)

Per serving: 516 Calories; 32.1g Fat; 11.3g Carbs; 42.4g Protein; 8.4g Sugars; 1.6g Fiber

INGREDIENTS

1/2 tablespoon lard, at room temperature
3/4 pound pork loin roast, cut into three pieces
Sauce:
1 garlic clove, chopped
1 tablespoon maple syrup
4 tablespoons rice vinegar

1/2 cup water
1/3 cup dry white wine
1 tablespoon tamari sauce
1 tablespoon flaxseed meal
1/2 cup cream cheese

DIRECTIONS

Press the "Sauté" button and melt the lard. Once hot, cook the pork loin until no longer pink.

Add the garlic, maple syrup, vinegar, water, wine and tamari sauce.

Secure the lid. Choose the "Manual" mode and cook for 10 minutes at High pressure. Once cooking is complete, use a natural pressure release for 10 minutes; carefully remove the lid. Reserve the meat.

Meanwhile, make the slurry by whisking the flaxseed meal with 2 tablespoons of cold water.

Stir in the slurry and press the "Sauté" button again. Cook the sauce until it has thickened; fold in the cheese and stir until heated through. Bon appétit!

322. Italian-Style Meatloaf with Bacon

(Ready in about 35 minutes)

Per serving: 511 Calories; 37.6g Fat; 12.7g Carbs; 29.4g Protein; 5.1g Sugars; 3.4g Fiber

INGREDIENTS

2 ounces bacon, chopped
1/2 onion, chopped
2 cloves garlic, minced
1/2 pound ground pork
1 egg, beaten
1/2 tablespoon fish sauce
1/4 cup breadcrumbs

1/4 cup Romano cheese, grated
1/4 cup tomato sauce
1/2 tablespoon mustard
1/2 teaspoon dried basil
1/2 teaspoon dried sage
1/2 teaspoon dried oregano
1/2 teaspoon chili flakes

DIRECTIONS

Place a steamer rack inside the inner pot; add 1/2 cup of water. Cut 1 sheet of heavy-duty foil and brush with cooking spray.

In mixing dish, thoroughly combine all ingredients.

Shape the meat mixture into a loaf; place the meatloaf in the center of the foil. Wrap your meatloaf in foil and lower onto the steamer rack.

Secure the lid. Choose the "Meat/Stew" mode and cook for 20 minutes at High pressure. Once cooking is complete, use a quick pressure release; carefully remove the lid. Let it stand for 10 minutes before cutting and serving. Bon appétit!

323. Pork Chops and Potatoes and Onion

(Ready in about 20 minutes)

Per serving: 372 Calories; 13.1g Fat; 20g Carbs; 41.4g Protein; 0.9g Sugars; 2.4g Fiber

INGREDIENTS

1 tablespoon lard, at room temperature
2 pork chops
1 cup chicken broth

1/2 onion, sliced
1/2 pound potatoes, quartered
Sea salt and ground black pepper, to taste

DIRECTIONS

Press the "Sauté" button and melt the lard. Once hot, brown the pork chops for 3 minutes per side.

Add the remaining ingredients.

Secure the lid. Choose the "Manual" mode and cook for 10 minutes at High pressure. Once cooking is complete, use a natural pressure release; carefully remove the lid.

Serve warm.

324. Spicy Cheesy Pork Frittata

(Ready in about 50 minutes)

Per serving: 544 Calories; 37g Fat; 5.2g Carbs; 45.3g Protein; 2.8g Sugars; 0.6g Fiber

INGREDIENTS

1 tablespoon butter, at room temperature
3/4 pound pork shoulder
1 cup chicken broth

Sea salt and ground black pepper, to taste
1 clove garlic, minced
1 shallot, thinly sliced

4 eggs, beaten
1/3 cup cream cheese
1/2 teaspoon paprika
1/2 teaspoon hot sauce

DIRECTIONS

Press the "Sauté" button to preheat your Instant Pot. Melt the butter and brown the pork for 4 minutes per side.

Add the chicken broth, salt, and black pepper.

Secure the lid. Choose the "Manual" mode and cook for 15 minutes at High pressure. Once cooking is complete, use a natural pressure release for 5 minutes; carefully remove the lid.

Shred the meat with two forks.; add the remaining ingredients and stir to combine well.

Lightly spritz a baking pan with cooking oil. Spoon the meat/egg mixture into the baking pan.

Cover with foil. Add 1 cup of water and a metal trivet to the Instant Pot. Lower the baking pan onto the trivet.

Secure the lid. Choose the "Manual" mode and cook for 15 minutes at High pressure. Once cooking is complete, use a natural pressure release for 10 minutes; carefully remove the lid. Bon appétit!

325. Grandma's Stuffed Peppers

(Ready in about 30 minutes)

Per serving: 593 Calories; 40.3g Fat; 27.5g Carbs; 30.1g Protein; 4.5g Sugars; 3.3g Fiber

INGREDIENTS

1 tablespoon olive oil
1/2 onion, chopped
1 clove garlic, minced
1/2 pound ground pork
1/4 pound brown mushrooms, sliced

1 cup cooked rice
Sea salt and white pepper, to taste
1/2 teaspoon cayenne pepper
1/2 teaspoon celery seeds
1/2 teaspoon ground cumin

2 bell peppers, deveined and halved
6 ounces canned tomatoes, crushed
2 ounces Colby cheese, shredded

DIRECTIONS

Press the "Sauté" button and heat the oil. Cook the onion, garlic, and pork until the onion is translucent and the pork is no longer pink. Add the mushrooms and sauté until fragrant or about 2 minutes.

Add the rice, salt, white pepper, cayenne pepper, celery seeds, and ground cumin.

Add 1 cup of water and a metal trivet to the bottom. Fill the pepper halves with the meat/mushroom mixture. Place the peppers in a casserole dish; stir in the canned tomatoes.

Lower the casserole dish onto the trivet in the Instant Pot.

Secure the lid. Choose the "Manual" mode and cook for 9 minutes at High pressure. Once cooking is complete, use a natural pressure release for 5 minutes; carefully remove the lid.

Top with the cheese and secure the lid again; let it sit in the residual heat until the cheese melts approximately 10 minutes. Serve and enjoy!

326. Pork Liver Mousse

(Ready in about 20 minutes)

Per serving: 277 Calories; 16.6g Fat; 9.1g Carbs; 22.4g Protein; 2.7g Sugars; 0.8g Fiber

INGREDIENTS

1 tablespoon butter
1/2 onion, chopped
1 clove garlic, minced
1/2 pound pork livers

1 cup water
1 sprig thyme
1 sprig rosemary

Himalayan pink salt and ground black pepper, to taste
3 tablespoons brandy
1/4 cup heavy cream

DIRECTIONS

Press the "Sauté" button and melt the butter. Then, sauté the onion and garlic until just tender and aromatic.

Add the pork livers and cook for 3 minutes on both sides or until the juices run clear. Deglaze the pan with a splash of brandy.

Add the water, thyme, rosemary, salt, and ground black pepper.

Secure the lid. Choose the "Manual" mode and cook for 5 minutes at High pressure. Once cooking is complete, use a quick pressure release; carefully remove the lid.

Add the brandy and heavy cream. Press the "Sauté" button and cook for 2 to 3 minutes more.

Transfer to your food processor and blend the mixture to a fine mousse. Bon appétit!

327. Easy Dad's Pork Chops

(Ready in about 30 minutes)

Per serving: 370 Calories; 18.8g Fat; 6.4g Carbs; 42.7g Protein; 3.1g Sugars; 1.2g Fiber

INGREDIENTS

1 tablespoon ghee, at room temperature
2 pork chops
3/4 cup beef broth
1 teaspoon garlic powder
1/2 teaspoon onion powder

1/2 tablespoon paprika
Sea salt and ground black pepper, to taste
1/3 cup double cream
1/2 teaspoon xanthan gum

DIRECTIONS

Press the "Sauté" button and melt the ghee. Once hot, sear the pork chops until golden browned, about 4 minutes per side.

Add the beef broth, garlic powder, onion powder, paprika, salt, and black pepper to the inner pot.

Secure the lid. Choose the "Manual" mode and cook for 10 minutes at High pressure. Once cooking is complete, use a natural pressure release; carefully remove the lid.

Transfer just the pork chops to a serving plate and cover to keep them warm. Press the "Sauté" button again.

Whisk in the cream and xanthan gum. Let it simmer approximately 4 minutes or until the sauce has thickened. Spoon the sauce over the pork chops and enjoy!

328. Barbecued Pork Ribs

(Ready in about 45 minutes)

Per serving: 386 Calories; 14.9g Fat; 4.9g Carbs; 54.7g Protein; 2.9g Sugars; 1.2g Fiber

INGREDIENTS

1 pound country style pork ribs
Coarse sea salt and freshly ground black pepper, to taste
1/2 teaspoon red pepper flakes

1/4 cup Marsala wine
1/4 cup chicken broth
1/2 cup BBQ sauce

DIRECTIONS

Place the pork ribs, salt, black pepper, red pepper, wine, and chicken broth in the inner pot.

Choose the "Meat/Stew" mode and cook for 35 minutes at High pressure. Once cooking is complete, use a quick pressure release; carefully remove the lid.

Transfer the pork ribs to a baking pan. Pour the BBQ sauce over the pork ribs and roast in the preheated oven at 425 degrees F for 6 to 8 minutes. Bon appétit!

329. Oaxacan Pork Fajitas

(Ready in about 50 minutes)

Per serving: 584 Calories; 21.9g Fat; 43.5g Carbs; 51.1g Protein; 11.7g Sugars; 2.2g Fiber

INGREDIENTS

1/2 teaspoon paprika
1/2 tablespoon brown sugar
1/2 teaspoon dried sage
1/2 teaspoon ground cumin
Coarse sea salt and freshly ground pepper, to taste
3/4 pound pork tenderloins, halved crosswise
1 tablespoon grapeseed oil

3 tablespoons balsamic vinegar
3 tablespoons tomato puree
1/2 cup beef broth
8 small flour tortillas
A bunch of scallions, chopped
1/2 cup sour cream
1/2 cup Pico de Gallo

DIRECTIONS

Mix the paprika, sugar, sage, cumin, salt, and black pepper. Rub the spice mixture all over the pork tenderloins.

Press the "Sauté" button to preheat your Instant Pot. Heat the oil and sear the pork until browned, about 4 minutes per side.

Add the balsamic vinegar, tomato puree, and beef broth.

Secure the lid. Choose the "Manual" mode and cook for 40 minutes at High pressure. Once cooking is complete, use a quick pressure release; carefully remove the lid.

Warm the tortillas until soft; serve with the pork mixture, scallions, sour cream, and Pico de Gallo. Enjoy!

330. Broiled St. Louis-Style Ribs

(Ready in about 45 minutes)

Per serving: 432 Calories; 14.4g Fat; 20.4g Carbs; 49.5g Protein; 12g Sugars; 4.2g Fiber

INGREDIENTS

1 pound St. Louis-style pork ribs
1/2 cup tomato sauce
1/2 cup water
1 tablespoon brown sugar
1 clove garlic, minced

1/2 tablespoon oyster sauce
1 tablespoon soy sauce
1/2 tablespoon paprika
Pink salt and ground black pepper, to taste

DIRECTIONS

Place all ingredients in the inner pot.

Choose the "Meat/Stew" mode and cook for 35 minutes at High pressure. Once cooking is complete, use a quick pressure release; carefully remove the lid.

Turn your broiler to low. Coat the ribs with the pan juices and cook under the broiler for about 2 minutes.

Turn them over, coat with another layer of sauce and cook for 2 to 3 minutes more. Taste, adjust the seasonings and serve. Enjoy!

BEEF

331. Cheesy Beef Enchilada Pasta

(Ready in about 15 minutes)

Per serving: 570 Calories; 21.1g Fat; 57.1g Carbs; 36.6g Protein; 5.1g Sugars; 3.9g Fiber

INGREDIENTS

1 tablespoon olive oil
1/2 pound ground chuck
1/3 pound elbow macaroni
4 ounces canned enchilada sauce
1/2 cup beef bone broth

1/2 cup water
Sea salt and ground black pepper, to taste
1 bay leaf
1 teaspoon paprika
1/3 cup Cotija cheese, crumbled

DIRECTIONS

Press the "Sauté" button to preheat your Instant Pot. Heat the oil and brown the ground chuck for 2 to 3 minutes.
Add the other ingredients, except for the cheese, to the Instant Pot.
Secure the lid. Choose the "Manual" mode and cook for 5 minutes at High pressure. Once cooking is complete, use a natural pressure release; carefully remove the lid.
Serve in individual bowls topped with the crumbled cheese. Enjoy!

332. Japanese-Style Beef Shanks

(Ready in about 45 minutes)

Per serving: 378 Calories; 16.4g Fat; 3.6g Carbs; 50.1g Protein; 1.9g Sugars; 0.3g Fiber

INGREDIENTS

1 pound beef shank
1/2 teaspoon garlic, minced
1 tablespoon sesame oil
1/4 cup rice wine
1 tablespoon soy sauce

1/2 teaspoon Five spice powder
1/2 dried red chili, sliced
1 clove star anise
1 teaspoon instant dashi granules
3/4 cup water

DIRECTIONS

Add all ingredients to the inner pot.
Secure the lid. Choose the "Manual" mode and cook for 30 minutes at High pressure. Once cooking is complete, use a natural pressure release for 10 minutes; carefully remove the lid.
Slice across the grain and serve over hot cooked rice if desired. Enjoy!

333. New York Strip with Sauce

(Ready in about 30 minutes)

Per serving: 445 Calories; 21.9g Fat; 11.1g Carbs; 50g Protein; 2.9g Sugars; 1.3g Fiber

INGREDIENTS

1 tablespoon sesame oil
1 pound New York strip, sliced into thin strips
Kosher salt and ground black pepper, to taste
1/3 cup dry red wine
1/2 cup cream of mushroom soup

1/2 leek, sliced
1 clove garlic, sliced
1 carrot, sliced
1/2 tablespoon tamari sauce
1/4 cup heavy cream

DIRECTIONS

Press the "Sauté" button to preheat your Instant Pot. Heat the sesame oil until sizzling. Once hot, brown the beef strips in batches.
Add wine to deglaze the pan. Stir in the remaining ingredients, except for the heavy cream.
Secure the lid. Choose the "Manual" mode and cook for 20 minutes at High pressure. Once cooking is complete, use a quick pressure release; carefully remove the lid.
Remove the beef from the cooking liquid. Mash the vegetables using a potato masher.
Press the "Sauté" button one more time. Now, bring the liquid to a boil. Heat off and stir in the heavy cream.
Spoon the sauce over the New York strip and serve immediately. Enjoy!

334. Mustard and Parmesan Meatballs

(Ready in about 40 minutes)

Per serving: 624 Calories; 45.2g Fat; 15.6g Carbs; 39g Protein; 4.3g Sugars; 2g Fiber

INGREDIENTS

1/2 pound ground beef
1/4 pound beef sausage, crumbled
1 shallot, minced
1 clove garlic, smashed
1 egg, beaten

1 slices bread (soaked in 2 tablespoons of milk)
1/4 cup parmesan cheese
Kosher salt and ground black pepper, to taste

1/2 teaspoon cayenne pepper
1 tablespoon canola oil
1/2 cup tomato puree
1/2 cup chicken bone broth
1 teaspoon Dijon mustard

DIRECTIONS

In a mixing dish, thoroughly combine the beef, sausage, shallot, garlic, egg, soaked bread, parmesan, salt, black pepper, and cayenne pepper Mix to combine well and shape the mixture into 12 meatballs. Set aside.

Press the "Sauté" button and heat the oil. Once hot, brown the meatballs for 7 to 8 minutes, rolling them around so that they will brown evenly all around.

Mix the tomato puree, broth and mustard in the inner pot. Gently fold in the meatballs.

Secure the lid. Choose the "Meat/Stew" mode and cook for 20 minutes at High pressure. Once cooking is complete, use a natural pressure release for 10 minutes; carefully remove the lid. Bon appétit!

335. Steak Salad with Peppers and Olives

(Ready in about 40 minutes)

Per serving: 482 Calories; 28.8g Fat; 4.6g Carbs; 50.6g Protein; 2.3g Sugars; 1g Fiber

INGREDIENTS

3/4 pound steak
1/4 cup red wine
Sea salt and ground black pepper, to taste
1/2 teaspoon red pepper flakes
3/4 cup water
2 tablespoons extra-virgin olive oil

1 tablespoon wine vinegar
1/2 red onion, thinly sliced
1 sweet pepper, cut into strips
1 butterhead lettuce, separate into leaves
1/4 cup feta cheese, crumbled
1/4 cup black olives, pitted and sliced

DIRECTIONS

Add the steak, red wine, salt, black pepper, red pepper, and water to the inner pot.

Secure the lid. Choose the "Manual" mode and cook for 25 minutes at High pressure. Once cooking is complete, use a natural pressure release for 10 minutes; carefully remove the lid.

Thinly slice the steak against the grain and transfer to a salad bowl. Toss with the olive oil and vinegar.

Add the red onion, peppers, and lettuce; toss to combine well. Top with cheese and olives and serve. Bon appétit!

336. BBQ Back Ribs with Beer

(Ready in about 1 hour)

Per serving: 552 Calories; 35g Fat; 36.3g Carbs; 19.7g Protein; 21g Sugars; 1.6g Fiber

INGREDIENTS

1/2 pound back ribs
4 ounces beers
1/2 cup Asian BBQ sauce
1/2 onion, chopped

1 garlic clove, minced
1/2 red Fresno chili, sliced
1-inch piece fresh ginger, minced
2 tablespoons tamari sauce

1 tablespoon agave nectar
Sea salt and ground black pepper, to taste
1 teaspoon toasted sesame seeds

DIRECTIONS

Place the back ribs, beers, BBQ sauce, onion, garlic, Fresno chili, and ginger in the inner pot.

Secure the lid. Choose the "Manual" mode and cook for 40 minutes at High pressure. Once cooking is complete, use a natural pressure release for 10 minutes; carefully remove the lid.

Add the tamari sauce, agave, salt and pepper and place the beef ribs under the broiler.

Broil ribs for 10 minutes or until they are evenly browned. Serve garnished with sesame seeds. Bon appétit!

337. Beef Stroganoff with a Twist

(Ready in about 50 minutes)

Per serving: 503 Calories; 31.1g Fat; 15.5g Carbs; 39.1g Protein; 6.4g Sugars; 2.9g Fiber

INGREDIENTS

1 tablespoon cornstarch

Coarse sea salt, to taste

1/4 teaspoon ground black pepper

1/2 teaspoon cayenne pepper

1/2 teaspoon smoked paprika

3/4 pound beef sirloin, cut into bite-sized chunks

1/2 tablespoon lard, melted

1/2 teaspoon dried basil

1/3 teaspoon dried marjoram

1 clove garlic, peeled and halved

1 cup beef broth

1/2 pound button mushrooms, quartered

1/2 red onion, quartered

2 tablespoons tomato paste

1/4 cup double cream

DIRECTIONS

In a shallow dish, combine the cornstarch with the salt, black pepper, cayenne pepper, and smoked paprika.

Dredge the beef pieces in the seasoned mixture to coat on all sides.

Press the "Sauté" button to preheat your Instant Pot. Melt the lard and brown the beef until no longer pink.

Add the basil, marjoram, garlic, and beef broth.

Secure the lid. Choose the "Meat/Stew" mode and cook for 35 minutes at High pressure. Once cooking is complete, use a quick pressure release; carefully remove the lid.

Add the button mushrooms, onions and tomato paste.

Secure the lid. Choose the "Manual" mode and cook for 3 minutes at High pressure. Once cooking is complete, use a quick pressure release; carefully remove the lid.

Stir in the double cream; seal the lid and let it sit in the residual heat for 5 to 7 minutes. Serve warm.

338. Short Ribs with Leek and Herbs

(Ready in about 1 hour 45 minutes)

Per serving: 450 Calories; 27.8g Fat; 5.3g Carbs; 45.7g Protein; 2g Sugars; 0.8g Fiber

INGREDIENTS

1 pound beef short ribs, bone-in

Sea salt and ground black pepper, to taste

1 tablespoon olive oil

1/2 medium leek, sliced

1 clove garlic, sliced

1 cup water

1 packet of onion soup mix

1 sprig thyme

1 sprig rosemary

1/2 teaspoon celery seeds

DIRECTIONS

Place all ingredients in the inner pot.

Secure the lid. Choose the "Manual" mode and cook for 90 minutes at High pressure. Once cooking is complete, use a natural pressure release; carefully remove the lid.

Afterwards, place the short ribs under the broiler until the outside is crisp or about 10 minutes.

Transfer the ribs to a serving platter and enjoy!

339. Beef Round Roast with veggies

(Ready in about 50 minutes)

Per serving: 583 Calories; 21.1g Fat; 43g Carbs; 52g Protein; 5.1g Sugars; 6.1g Fiber

INGREDIENTS

1 tablespoon olive oil, divided

1 pound beef round roast, cut into bite-sized pieces

1/2 white onion, chopped

1 garlic clove, sliced

1 bell pepper, sliced

2 tablespoons tomato puree

1/4 cup dry red wine

3/4 cup beef broth

1 pound whole small potatoes

DIRECTIONS '

Press the "Sauté" button to preheat your Instant Pot. Heat the oil and brown the beef round roast for 3 to 4 minutes, working in batches.

Add the white onion, garlic, pepper, tomato puree, red wine, and broth.

Secure the lid. Choose the "Meat/Stew" mode and cook for 35 minutes at High pressure. Once cooking is complete, use a quick pressure release; carefully remove the lid.

Add the potatoes. Secure the lid. Choose the "Manual" mode and cook for 10 minutes at High pressure. Once cooking is complete, use a quick pressure release; carefully remove the lid.

Serve in individual bowls and enjoy!

340. Sticky Beef with Syrah Reduction

(Ready in about 40 minutes)

Per serving: 469 Calories; 18.7g Fat; 22.5g Carbs; 51.3g Protein; 15.7g Sugars; 0.9g Fiber

INGREDIENTS

1 tablespoon olive oil
1 pound beef stew meat, cubed
1/4 cup Syrah wine
3 tablespoons dark brown sugar
2 cloves garlic, sliced
1/2 cup beef bone broth

2 tablespoons soy sauce
1/2 teaspoon red pepper flakes
1 bay leaf
1 tablespoon arrowroot powder
1/4 cup scallions, roughly chopped

DIRECTIONS

Press the "Sauté" button and heat the oil until sizzling. Then, brown the beef in batches.

Add a splash of red wine to deglaze the pot. Add the remaining wine, sugar, garlic, broth, soy sauce, red pepper, and bay leaf.

Secure the lid. Choose the "Meat/Stew" mode and cook for 35 minutes at High pressure. Once cooking is complete, use a quick pressure release; carefully remove the lid.

Press the "Sauté" button again and add the arrowroot powder. Let it cook until the sauce has reduced slightly and the flavors have concentrated. Serve garnished with fresh scallions and enjoy!

341. Boozy Tequila Ribs

(Ready in about 40 minutes + marinating time)

Per serving: 441 Calories; 29.2g Fat; 17g Carbs; 20.7g Protein; 13g Sugars; 2g Fiber

INGREDIENTS

1 pound chuck short ribs
1 shot tequila
Kosher salt and cracked black pepper, to taste
1 tablespoon honey

1/2 teaspoon garlic powder
1/2 teaspoon shallot powder
1/2 teaspoon marjoram
1/2 tablespoon Sriracha sauce
1/2 teaspoon paprika

1/2 cup apple cider
1 tablespoon tomato paste
1/2 tablespoon stone ground mustard
3/4 cup beef bone broth

DIRECTIONS

Place all ingredients, except for beef broth, in a ceramic dish. Cover with a foil and let it marinate for 3 hours in your refrigerator.

Place the beef along with its marinade in the inner pot. Pour in the beef bone broth.

Secure the lid. Choose the "Meat/Stew" mode and cook for 35 minutes at High pressure. Once cooking is complete, use a natural pressure release; carefully remove the lid.

Bon appétit!

342. Bœuf à la Bourguignonne

(Ready in about 55 minutes)

Per serving: 499 Calories; 28.2g Fat; 8.3g Carbs; 44.1g Protein; 2.5g Sugars; 1.1g Fiber

INGREDIENTS

3/4 pound boneless beef steak, cut into bite-sized pieces
1 tablespoon cornstarch
Coarse sea salt and ground black pepper, to taste
1/2 teaspoon red pepper flakes
1 tablespoon olive oil

1/2 shallot, chopped
1 clove garlic, sliced
4 ounces mushrooms, sliced
1/4 cup Burgundy wine
3/4 cup beef bone broth

DIRECTIONS

Toss the beef steak with the cornstarch, salt, black pepper, and red pepper flakes.

Press the "Sauté" button to preheat your Instant Pot. Heat the oil until sizzling. Now, cook the beef until well browned.

Add the remaining ingredients; gently stir to combine.

Secure the lid. Choose the "Manual" mode and cook for 40 minutes at High pressure. Once cooking is complete, use a natural pressure release for 10 minutes; carefully remove the lid.

Divide between individual bowls and serve warm with garlic croutons if desired. Enjoy!

343. Delmonico Steak with Gorgonzola Cheese

(Ready in about 20 minutes)

Per serving: 584 Calories; 36.9g Fat; 6.1g Carbs; 55.3g Protein; 2.2g Sugars; 0.6g Fiber

INGREDIENTS

1 tablespoon butter
1 pound Delmonico steak, cubed
1 clove garlic, minced
1/2 cup beef broth
1/2 cup double cream

1/4 cup sour cream
1 teaspoon cayenne pepper
Sea salt and ground black pepper, to taste
1/4 cup gorgonzola cheese, shredded

DIRECTIONS

Press the "Sauté" button to preheat your Instant Pot. Melt the butter and brown the beef cubes in batches for about 4 minutes per batch.
Add the garlic, broth, double cream, and sour cream to the inner pot; season with cayenne pepper, salt, and black pepper.
Secure the lid. Choose the "Manual" mode and cook for 10 minutes at High pressure. Once cooking is complete, use a quick pressure release; carefully remove the lid.
Top with gorgonzola cheese and serve. Bon appétit!

344. Châteaubriand with Red Wine Reduction

(Ready in about 25 minutes)

Per serving: 559 Calories; 33.3g Fat; 19.6g Carbs; 47.1g Protein; 5.3g Sugars; 1g Fiber

INGREDIENTS

1 pound center-cut beef tenderloin
1 cup cream of onion soup
1 tablespoon butter
1 shallot, sliced

2 cloves garlic, finely minced
1/2 cup red wine
Kosher salt and ground black pepper, to taste
1 tablespoon fresh tarragon

DIRECTIONS

Add the beef and cream of onion soup to a lightly greased inner pot.
Secure the lid. Choose the "Manual" mode and cook for 13 minutes at High pressure. Once cooking is complete, use a quick pressure release; carefully remove the lid.
Press the "Sauté" button to preheat your Instant Pot. Melt the butter and cook the shallots until tender or about 3 minutes.
Then, stir in the garlic; cook an additional 30 seconds or so.
Pour the wine into the inner pot, scraping up all the browned bits on the bottom of the pan. Add the salt, pepper, and tarragon.
Continue boiling the sauce until it reduces by half. Serve the sliced chateaubriand with the wine sauce and enjoy!

345. Hearty Ground Beef Chili

(Ready in about 25 minutes)

Per serving: 586 Calories; 17.5g Fat; 66g Carbs; 44g Protein; 7.1g Sugars; 12g Fiber

INGREDIENTS

1 tablespoon olive oil
1/2 pound ground chuck
1/4 cup leeks, chopped
1 clove garlic, minced
1/2 teaspoon dried oregano
1/2 teaspoon dried basil
1/2 teaspoon cumin powder

1/2 teaspoon ancho chili powder
Kosher salt and ground black pepper, to taste
1/2 cup beef stock
1/2 red chili pepper, minced
1 (15-ounces) can black beans, drained and rinsed
8 ounces canned tomatoes, diced
2 tablespoon tomato ketchup

DIRECTIONS

Press the "Sauté" button and heat the oil. Once hot, cook the ground chuck, leeks, and garlic until the meat is no longer pink.
Add the remaining ingredients; gently stir to combine.
Secure the lid. Choose the "Manual" mode and cook for 15 minutes at High pressure. Once cooking is complete, use a quick pressure release; carefully remove the lid.
Serve in individual bowls garnished with green onions if desired. Bon appétit!

346. Rump Steak in Tomato Sauce

(Ready in about 1 hour)

Per serving: 420 Calories; 19.2g Fat; 12g Carbs; 48.5g Protein; 1.8g Sugars; 1.2g Fiber

INGREDIENTS

Sea salt, to taste

1/2 teaspoon mixed peppercorns, crushed

1/2 teaspoon marjoram

1/2 teaspoon ginger powder

3 tablespoons flour

1 tablespoon olive oil

1 pound rump steak, trimmed and sliced into small pieces

2 garlic cloves, halved

1 carrot, sliced

1/2 cup vegetable broth

1 ripe tomato, pureed

1/2 teaspoon hot sauce

DIRECTIONS

In a shallow dish, combine the salt, black peppercorns, marjoram, ginger powder, and flour. Dredge the beef pieces in the seasoned mixture to coat on all sides.

Press the "Sauté" button to preheat your Instant Pot. Heat the oil and brown beef until no longer pink.

Add the remaining ingredients.

Secure the lid. Choose the "Manual" mode and cook for 60 minutes at High pressure. Once cooking is complete, use a quick pressure release; carefully remove the lid. Bon appétit!

347. Chunky Beef Frittata

(Ready in about 25 minutes)

Per serving: 368 Calories; 24.1g Fat; 3.7g Carbs; 33.9g Protein; 2.4g Sugars; 0.8g Fiber

INGREDIENTS

1 tablespoon olive oil

1/2 pound ground chuck

4 eggs, whisked

A small bunch of green onions, chopped

1 small tomato, chopped

Sea salt and freshly ground black pepper, to your liking

1/2 teaspoon paprika

1/2 teaspoon garlic powder

DIRECTIONS

Press the "Sauté" button to preheat your Instant Pot. Heat the oil and brown the beef for 2 to 3 minutes, stirring continuously.

Lightly spritz a baking pan with cooking oil. Add all ingredients, including the browned beef to the baking pan.

Cover with foil. Add 1 cup of water and a metal trivet to the Instant Pot. Lower the baking pan onto the trivet.

Secure the lid. Choose the "Manual" mode and cook for 6 minutes at High pressure. Once cooking is complete, use a natural pressure release for 10 minutes; carefully remove the lid.

Slice in half and serve. Bon appétit!

348. Boozy Glazed Roast Beef

(Ready in about 1 hour)

Per serving: 521 Calories; 19.1g Fat; 14.3g Carbs; 67g Protein; 8.8g Sugars; 0.8g Fiber

INGREDIENTS

3/4 pound chuck roast

3/4 cup beef broth

2 tablespoons soy sauce

2 tablespoons champagne vinegar

Sea salt and ground black pepper, to taste

1/2 teaspoon red pepper flakes

1 clove garlic, sliced

Margarita Glaze:

1/4 cup tequila

3 tablespoons orange juice

1 tablespoon lime juice

1 tablespoon dark brown sugar

DIRECTIONS

Add the chuck roast, beef broth, soy sauce, champagne vinegar, salt, black pepper, red pepper flakes, and garlic to the inner pot.

Secure the lid. Choose the "Manual" mode and cook for 40 minutes at High pressure. Once cooking is complete, use a natural pressure release for 10 minutes; carefully remove the lid.

Meanwhile, whisk all ingredients for the margarita glaze. Now, glaze the ribs and place under the broiler for 5 minutes; then, turn them over and glaze on the other side. Broil an additional 5 minutes.

Cut the chuck roast into slices and serve the remaining glaze on the side as a sauce. Bon appétit!

349. Classic Homemade Cheeseburgers

(Ready in about 45 minutes)

Per serving: 444 Calories; 25.4g Fat; 2.9g Carbs; 47.5g Protein; 1.7g Sugars; 1g Fiber

INGREDIENTS

3/4 pound ground chuck
1 tablespoon tomato puree
Sea salt and freshly ground black pepper, to taste
1/2 teaspoon cayenne pepper

1/2 onion, finely chopped
1 garlic clove, minced
3 ounces Monterey-Jack cheese, sliced

DIRECTIONS

Mix the ground chuck, tomato puree, salt, black pepper, cayenne pepper, onion, and garlic until well combined.

Form the meat mixture into patties. Place your patties on squares of aluminum foil and wrap them loosely.

Add 1 cup water and a metal trivet to the Instant Pot; lower the foil packs onto the top of the metal trivet.

Secure the lid. Choose the "Meat/Stew" mode and cook for 35 minutes at High pressure. Once cooking is complete, use a natural pressure release; carefully remove the lid.

Place your patties on a baking sheet and broil for 5 to 6 minutes. Serve on buns topped with cheese. Enjoy!

350. Korean Beef Bulgogi

(Ready in about 50 minutes + marinating time)

Per serving: 518 Calories; 29.5g Fat; 19g Carbs; 50.6g Protein; 13.6g Sugars; 2.3g Fiber

INGREDIENTS

3 tablespoons tamari sauce
1 tablespoon Korean rice wine
1 tablespoon agave syrup
Salt and black pepper, to taste

1 pound rib-eye steak, cut into strips
1 tablespoon sesame oil
1/2 onion, sliced
1 clove garlic, minced

1 tablespoon pickled red ginger
1/2 Asian pear, cored and sliced
1 tablespoon sesame seeds, toasted

DIRECTIONS

Mix the tamari sauce, rice, wine, agave syrup, salt, and black pepper in a ceramic bowl; add the beef, cover, and let it marinate for 1 hour.

Press the "Sauté" button and heat the sesame oil. Once hot, brown the beef strips in batches. Add the onion, garlic, pickled ginger, and Asian pear.

Secure the lid. Choose the "Meat/Stew" mode and cook for 35 minutes at High pressure. Once cooking is complete, use a natural pressure release for 10 minutes; carefully remove the lid.

Serve garnished with toasted sesame seeds. Enjoy!

351. Crustless Beef Mince Pie

(Ready in about 45 minutes)

Per serving: 455 Calories; 28.2g Fat; 8.4g Carbs; 38.5g Protein; 4.7g Sugars; 1.1g Fiber

INGREDIENTS

1 tablespoon olive oil
1/2 pound ground beef
1/2 onion, chopped
2 cloves garlic, minced
Sea salt and ground black pepper, to taste

1/2 teaspoon basil
1/4 teaspoon thyme
1/2 teaspoon oregano
2 eggs
1/4 cup milk

1 ounce cream cheese, at room temperature
1/2 cup cheddar cheese, shredded
1 tomato, sliced

DIRECTIONS

Press the "Sauté" button and heat the olive oil until sizzling. Now, cook the ground beef until no longer pink.

Transfer the browned beef to a lightly greased soufflé dish. Add the onion, garlic, and seasonings.

In a mixing dish, whisk the eggs, milk, and cream cheese. Top with the cheddar cheese. Cover with a foil.

Place the rack and 1 ½ cups of water inside the Instant Pot. Lower the soufflé dish onto the rack.

Secure the lid. Choose the "Manual" mode and cook for 30 minutes at High pressure. Once cooking is complete, use a quick pressure release; carefully remove the lid.

Let it rest for 10 minutes before slicing and serving. Garnish with tomatoes and serve. Enjoy!

352. Rosemary and Cheeseburger Dip

(Ready in about 25 minutes)

Per serving: 300 Calories; 13.7g Fat; 3.6g Carbs; 38.9g Protein; 1.8g Sugars; 0.7g Fiber

INGREDIENTS

1/2 pound ground chuck roast
1 clove garlic, minced
1/2 teaspoon shallot powder
1/2 teaspoon mustard powder

1 teaspoon dried rosemary
1 bay leaf
1 tablespoon Worcestershire sauce
1 cup water

1 ounce cream cheese, room temperature
2 ounces mozzarella, shredded

DIRECTIONS

Add all ingredients, except for the cheese, to your Instant Pot.

Secure the lid. Choose the "Manual" mode and cook for 20 minutes at High pressure. Once cooking is complete, use a quick pressure release; carefully remove the lid.

Top with the cheese and allow it to stand until the cheese has melted

Serve with assorted vegetables or breadsticks if desired. Bon appétit!

353. Homemade Philly Cheese Steaks

(Ready in about 35 minutes)

Per serving: 549 Calories; 30.6g Fat; 25.1g Carbs; 35.9g Protein; 4.1g Sugars; 2.7g Fiber

INGREDIENTS

1 tablespoon lard, melted
3/4 pound top sirloin steak, sliced into thin strips
1 onion, sliced
1 sweet pepper, deseeded and sliced
1 red chili pepper, minced
Kosher salt and freshly ground pepper, to taste
1 teaspoon paprika

4 tablespoons dry red wine
1/2 cup beef broth
2 Hoagie rolls
1/2 tablespoon Dijon mustard
2 ounces yellow American cheese, sliced
1 ounce mild Provolone cheese, sliced

DIRECTIONS

Press the "Sauté" button to preheat your Instant Pot. Melt the lard and cook your steak for about 4 minutes.

Add the onions, peppers, salt, black pepper, paprika, wine, and broth.

Secure the lid. Choose the "Manual" mode and cook for 25 minutes at High pressure. Once cooking is complete, use a quick pressure release; carefully remove the lid.

Serve the meat mixture in rolls topped with mustard and cheese. Bon appétit!

354. Festive Beef with Gravy

(Ready in about 1 hour 15 minutes)

Per serving: 606 Calories; 13.3g Fat; 70g Carbs; 48.5g Protein; 4.5g Sugars; 9.7g Fiber

INGREDIENTS

1 pound top round roast
Sea salt and ground black pepper, to taste
1/2 teaspoon paprika

1/2 teaspoon dried rosemary
1 tablespoon lard, melted
1 pound fingerling potatoes
1/2 onion, thinly sliced

1 clove garlic, smashed
1 bell pepper, deseeded and sliced
1 cup beef bone broth
1 tablespoon potato starch

DIRECTIONS

Toss the beef with the salt, black pepper, paprika, and rosemary until well coated on all sides.

Press the "Sauté" button to preheat your Instant Pot and melt the lard. Sear the beef for about 4 minutes per side until it is browned.

Scatter the potatoes, onion, garlic, peppers around the top round roast. Add the beef bone broth.

Secure the lid. Choose the "Manual" mode and cook for 60 minutes at High pressure. Once cooking is complete, use a natural pressure release for 10 minutes; carefully remove the lid.

Transfer the roast and vegetables to a serving platter; shred the roast with 2 forks.

Mix the potato starch with 4 tablespoons of water. Press the "Sauté" button to preheat your Instant Pot again. Once the liquid is boiling, add the slurry and let it cook until the gravy thickens.

Taste and adjust the seasonings. Serve warm.

355. Moussaka with Ground Beef and Potatoes

(Ready in about 40 minutes)

Per serving: 553 Calories; 28.3g Fat; 41g Carbs; 34.4g Protein; 3.8g Sugars; 3g Fiber

INGREDIENTS

1/2 tablespoon olive oil
1/2 pounds ground beef
3/4 pound Russet potatoes, peeled and thinly sliced

1/2 shallot, thinly sliced
1 garlic clove, sliced
1 cup cream of celery soup
1 egg

1/4 cup half-and-half
Kosher salt and ground pepper, to taste
1/4 cup Colby cheese, shredded

DIRECTIONS

Press the "Sauté" button to preheat your Instant Pot. Heat the olive oil and cook the ground beef until no longer pink.

Now, add the layer of potatoes; top with the layer of shallots and garlic. Pour in the soup.

Whisk the egg with half-and-half until well combined; season with salt and pepper. Pour the egg mixture over the top of the meat and vegetable layers.

Smooth the sauce on top with a spatula.

Secure the lid. Choose the "Meat/Stew" mode and cook for 35 minutes at High pressure. Once cooking is complete, use a quick pressure release; carefully remove the lid.

Add the shredded cheese and seal the lid again. Let it sit in the residual heat until the cheese melts. Bon appétit!

356. Japanese-Style Beef Bowl

(Ready in about 40 minutes + marinating time)

Per serving: 565 Calories; 17.7g Fat; 54.5g Carbs; 43.2g Protein; 10.4g Sugars; 2.3g Fiber

INGREDIENTS

1 pound beef stew meat, cut into 1-inch cubes
2 tablespoons Shoyu sauce
2 tablespoons brown sugar
1 clove garlic, minced
1 tablespoon cider vinegar

1 tablespoon sake
1 tablespoon pickled red ginger
1 teaspoon hot sauce
1 tablespoon cornstarch
1 tablespoon olive oil
1/2 teaspoon onion powder

1 bay leaf
1 rosemary sprig
Salt and black pepper, to taste
1/2 cup beef broth
1 egg, whisked
1/2 cup steamed rice

DIRECTIONS

In a ceramic bowl, place the meat, Shoyu sauce, brown sugar, garlic, cider vinegar, sake, ginger, and hot sauce. Let it marinate for 2 hours.

Discard the marinade and toss the beef cubes with the cornstarch.

Press the "Sauté" button and heat the oil until sizzling. Brown the beef cubes for 3 to 4 minutes, stirring periodically.

Add the onion powder, bay leaves, rosemary sprig, salt, black pepper, and beef broth.

Secure the lid. Choose the "Meat/Stew" mode and cook for 35 minutes at High pressure. Once cooking is complete, use a quick pressure release; carefully remove the lid.

Slowly stir in the whisked eggs and press the "Sauté" button. Continue to cook until the eggs are done.

Serve over steamed rice.

357. Sticky Sloppy Joes

(Ready in about 20 minutes)

Per serving: 429 Calories; 19.1g Fat; 37.3g Carbs; 28.6g Protein; 10.2g Sugars; 3.4g Fiber

INGREDIENTS

1 teaspoon lard
1/2 pound ground beef
1/2 onion, chopped
1 teaspoon fresh garlic, minced
1/2 sweet pepper, chopped
1 serrano pepper, chopped

Salt and ground black pepper, to taste
1/2 teaspoon red pepper flakes
1/2 tablespoon stone ground mustard
1/2 teaspoon celery seeds
1/2 teaspoon dried rosemary
1/2 cup beef stock

1/3 cup tomato puree
1 tablespoon ketchup
1 teaspoon brown sugar
2 soft hamburger buns

DIRECTIONS

Press the "Sauté" button and melt the lard. Once hot, cook the ground beef until it is brown.

Add the onion, garlic, and peppers; continue to cook for 1 to 2 minutes more.

Add the salt, black pepper, red pepper flakes, mustard, celery seeds, rosemary, stock, tomato puree, ketchup, and brown sugar. Mix to combine.

Secure the lid. Choose the "Manual" mode and cook for 5 minutes at High pressure. Once cooking is complete, use a natural pressure release for 10 minutes; carefully remove the lid.

Serve on hamburger buns and enjoy!

358. Decadent Filet Mignon

(Ready in about 30 minutes)

Per serving: 346 Calories; 13.6g Fat; 14.1g Carbs; 41.8g Protein; 0.8g Sugars; 1g Fiber

INGREDIENTS

3/4 pound filet mignon, about 1 ½-inch thick
1/2 teaspoon sea salt
1/3 teaspoon red pepper flakes, crushed
1/3 teaspoon ground black pepper
4 tablespoons flour
1 tablespoon butter
1 cup wild mushrooms, sliced
1/2 onion, thinly sliced
1 garlic clove, sliced
1 cup chicken broth

DIRECTIONS

Toss the filet mignon with salt, red pepper, black pepper, and flour.

Press the "Sauté" button and melt the butter. Once hot, sear the filet mignon for 2 minutes. Turn it over and cook for 2 minutes more on the other side.

Add the remaining ingredients and secure the lid.

Choose the "Meat/Stew" mode and cook for 20 minutes at High pressure. Once cooking is complete, use a quick pressure release; carefully remove the lid.

You can thicken the sauce on the "Sauté" mode if desired. Serve warm.

359. Classic Corned Beef Brisket

(Ready in about 1 hour 25 minutes)

Per serving: 632 Calories; 37g Fat; 31g Carbs; 42.3g Protein; 10.5g Sugars; 7.4g Fiber

INGREDIENTS

3/4 pound corned beef brisket
4 clove peeled garlic
1 sprig thyme
1 sprig rosemary
1 tablespoon olive oil
1/2 cup chicken broth
1/4 cup tomato puree
1/2 leek, sliced
1/4 pound rutabaga, peeled and cut into 1-inch chunks
1/4 pound turnips, peeled and cut into 1-inch chunks
1 parsnip, cut into 1-inch chunks
1 bell pepper, halved

DIRECTIONS

Place the beef brisket, garlic, thyme, rosemary, olive oil, chicken broth, and tomato puree in the inner pot.

Secure the lid. Choose the "Manual" mode and cook for 80 minutes at High pressure. Once cooking is complete, use a quick pressure release; carefully remove the lid.

Add the other ingredients. Gently stir to combine.

Secure the lid. Choose the "Manual" mode and cook for 4 minutes at High pressure. Once cooking is complete, use a quick pressure release; carefully remove the lid. Bon appétit!

360. Mexican Beef Tacos

(Ready in about 30 minutes)

Per serving: 628 Calories; 38.1g Fat; 31g Carbs; 39.1g Protein; 5.5g Sugars; 5.4g Fiber

INGREDIENTS

1 tablespoon canola oil
3/4 pounds ground beef
1/2 onion, chopped
1 sweet pepper, deseeded and sliced
1/2 chili pepper, minced
2 garlic cloves, minced
1/2 teaspoon marjoram
1/2 teaspoon Mexican oregano
Kosher salt and ground black pepper, to taste
1/2 teaspoon cumin powder
1/2 teaspoon red pepper flakes
1/2 teaspoon mustard seeds
4 small taco shells
1 head lettuce
1/4 cup chunky salsa
1/4 cup sour cream

DIRECTION

Press the "Sauté" button to preheat your Instant Pot. Heat the oil and sear the ground chuck for 2 to 3 minutes or until mostly brown.

Add the onion, peppers, garlic, and spices to the inner pot.

Secure the lid. Choose the "Manual" mode and cook for 10 minutes at High pressure. Once cooking is complete, use a natural pressure release; carefully remove the lid.

Press the "Sauté" button and cook, stirring continuously, until the liquid has almost evaporated or about 10 minutes.

To assemble your tacos, layer the beef mixture and lettuce in each taco shell. Serve with the salsa and sour cream. Enjoy!

361. Ground Beef and Cheese Bowl

(Ready in about 20 minutes)

Per serving: 532 Calories; 22g Fat; 41g Carbs; 40.1g Protein; 6.4g Sugars; 11.4g Fiber

INGREDIENTS

1 teaspoon olive oil

1/2 pound lean ground chuck

1 (1-ounce) packet taco seasoning mix

1/2 cup vegetable broth

1/2 onion, chopped

1 garlic clove, minced

1 red bell pepper, deseeded and sliced

1/2 cup tomato puree

1 tablespoon chipotle paste

8 ounces canned black beans, drained and rinsed

1/2 cup Monterey-Jack cheese, shredded

1 tablespoon fresh cilantro leaves, chopped

DIRECTIONS

Press the "Sauté" button to preheat your Instant Pot. Heat the oil and cook the ground chuck for 2 to 3 minutes or until mostly brown. Next, add the taco seasoning mix, broth, onion, garlic, and peppers.

Secure the lid. Choose the "Manual" mode and cook for 10 minutes at High pressure. Once cooking is complete, use a natural pressure release; carefully remove the lid.

Divide the meat mixture between four serving bowls. Add the tomato puree, chipotle paste, and black beans; gently stir to combine.

Top with the cheese and serve garnished with fresh cilantro leaves. Enjoy!

362. Beer Braised Chuck Roast

(Ready in about 45 minutes)

Per serving: 403 Calories; 22.3g Fat; 4g Carbs; 47.1g Protein; 2g Sugars; 0.8g Fiber

INGREDIENTS

1 tablespoon sesame oil

1 pound chuck roast, slice into pieces

1/2 cup beef bone broth

1/2 cup beer

1/2 tablespoon mustard

1/2 tablespoon granulated sugar

Kosher salt and freshly ground black pepper, to taste

1/2 teaspoon onion powder

1/2 teaspoon garlic powder

1/2 teaspoon ginger powder

1/4 teaspoon ground allspice

1 tablespoon sesame seeds, toasted

DIRECTIONS

Press the "Sauté" button to preheat your Instant Pot. Heat the oil and brown the beef in batches; cook for about 3 minutes per batch.

Add the broth, beer, mustard, sugar, salt, black pepper, onion powder, garlic powder, ginger, and ground allspice.

Secure the lid. Choose the "Manual" mode and cook for 40 minutes at High pressure. Once cooking is complete, use a quick pressure release; carefully remove the lid.

Serve garnished with toasted sesame seeds. Enjoy!

363. Italian Spaghetti Bolognese

(Ready in about 15 minutes)

Per serving: 690 Calories; 27.6g Fat; 73g Carbs; 39g Protein; 7.9g Sugars; 6g Fiber

INGREDIENTS

1 tablespoon olive oil

1/2 onion, chopped

1 clove garlic, chopped

1/2 pound ground beef

3 tablespoons rose wine

1 carrot, thinly sliced

8 ounces canned tomatoes

1/3 cup beef bone broth

1/2 teaspoon dried basil

1/2 teaspoon dried oregano

1/2 teaspoon dried rosemary

Sea salt and ground black pepper, to taste

6 ounces spaghetti

1/4 cup Romano cheese, preferably freshly grated

DIRECTIONS

Press the "Sauté" button to preheat your Instant Pot.

Once hot, heat the olive oil and cook the onion, garlic and beef until the beef is no longer pink.

Use rose wine to scrape the remaining bits of meat off the bottom of the inner pot.

Add the carrots, tomatoes, beef bone broth, basil, oregano, rosemary, salt, and black pepper. Secure the lid. Choose the "Poultry" mode and High pressure; cook for 5 minutes. Once cooking is complete, use a quick release.

Add the spaghetti and gently stir to combine.

Secure the lid and choose the "Manual" mode. Cook for 4 minutes longer. Afterwards, use a quick release and carefully remove the lid. Bon appétit!

364. Paprika Pot Roast with Vegetables

(Ready in about 55 minutes)

Per serving: 393 Calories; 17g Fat; 11.6g Carbs; 48.5g Protein; 1.9g Sugars; 1.7g Fiber

INGREDIENTS

3/4 pound pot roast, cut into bite-sized chunks
4 tablespoons all-purpose flour
1 tablespoon butter, melted
1/2 habanero pepper, minced

1 garlic clove, chopped
1/2 teaspoon smoked Spanish paprika
1/2 teaspoon achiote seasoning
1 tablespoon bouillon granules
1 cup water

1/4 cup shallots, chopped
1 carrot, cut into bite-sized chunks
1 celery rib, cut into bite-sized chunks
Sea salt and ground black pepper, to taste

DIRECTIONS

Toss the beef with flour.

Press the "Sauté" button to preheat your Instant Pot. Melt the butter and cook the beef chunks for 4 to 5 minutes, stirring frequently.

Add the habanero pepper, garlic, Spanish paprika, achiote seasoning, bouillon granules, and water.

Secure the lid. Choose the "Meat/Stew" mode and cook for 35 minutes at High pressure. Once cooking is complete, use a natural pressure release; carefully remove the lid.

Add the vegetables, salt, and black pepper.

Secure the lid. Choose the "Manual" mode and cook for 7 minutes at High pressure. Once cooking is complete, use a quick pressure release; carefully remove the lid. Serve the beef and vegetables in individual bowls and enjoy!

365. Traditional Beef Peperonata

(Ready in about 30 minutes + marinating time)

Per serving: 388 Calories; 15.9g Fat; 22.2g Carbs; 40.1g Protein; 6.9g Sugars; 2.8g Fiber

INGREDIENTS

1 tablespoon soy sauce
1 tablespoon tomato paste
3 tablespoons rice vinegar
1/2 tablespoon brown sugar
1 clove garlic, minced

3/4 pound blade roast, sliced into 1/2-inch pieces
1/2 tablespoon canola oil
Salt and ground black pepper, to taste
1/2 teaspoon cayenne pepper

1 cup broth
1/2 onion, thinly sliced
2 sweet peppers, cut Julienne
1 serrano pepper, minced
1 tablespoon capers with juices

DIRECTIONS

In a ceramic or glass dish, mix the soy sauce, tomato paste, vinegar, sugar, and garlic. Place the blade roast in the dish, cover with plastic wrap and let it marinate at least 3 hours in the refrigerator.

Press the "Sauté" button to preheat your Instant Pot. Heat the oil and brown the beef for 4 to 5 minutes, brushing occasionally with the marinade.

Add the other ingredients. Secure the lid. Choose the "Meat/Stew" mode and cook for 20 minutes at High pressure.

Once cooking is complete, use a quick pressure release; carefully remove the lid. Serve warm.

366. Fall-Apart Beef Brisket with Broccoli

(Ready in about 30 minutes)

Per serving: 357 Calories; 24.2g Fat; 15.1g Carbs; 20.9g Protein; 4.5g Sugars; 4.4g Fiber

INGREDIENTS

1 tablespoon sesame oil
1/2 pound beef brisket, thinly sliced against the grain
1/4 cup rice wine
1/2 cup beef bone broth

2 tablespoons tamari sauce
1/2 tablespoon yellow mustard
1/2 teaspoon fresh ginger, grated
1 clove garlic, minced
Pink salt and ground black pepper, to taste

1/2 teaspoon paprika
1/2 pound broccoli, broken into florets
1/2 tablespoon arrowroot flour
1/4 cup spring onions, sliced

DIRECTIONS

Press the "Sauté" button to preheat your Instant Pot. Heat the sesame oil and brown the beef in batches; cook for about 3 minutes per batch.

Add the wine to deglaze the pot. Once your beef is browned, add the beef broth, tamari sauce, mustard, ginger, garlic, salt, pepper, and paprika.

Secure the lid. Choose the "Manual" mode and cook for 15 minutes at High pressure. Once cooking is complete, use a quick pressure release; carefully remove the lid.

Add the broccoli and arrowroot flour and press the "Sauté" button again. Cook until the broccoli florets are tender, but still slightly crisp and not mushy, about 4 minutes.

Garnish with spring onions and serve immediately. Bon appétit!

367. Cheesy Beef Stuffed Peppers

(Ready in about 25 minutes)

Per serving: 457 Calories; 22.5g Fat; 29.5g Carbs; 37.1g Protein; 11.2g Sugars; 4.5g Fiber

INGREDIENTS

1/3 cup parboiled rice
3/4 pound ground beef
1/2 onion, chopped
1 garlic clove, minced
1/2 carrot, grated

Sea salt and ground black pepper, to taste
1/2 teaspoon cayenne pepper
1/3 teaspoon celery seeds
1/4 teaspoon mustard seeds
1/2 teaspoon basil

2 large bell peppers, deseeded, cored and halved
3/4 cup tomato puree
1 tablespoon ketchup
1/2 cup cheddar cheese, grated

DIRECTIONS

In a mixing bowl, thoroughly combine the rice, ground beef, onion, garlic, carrot, salt, black pepper, cayenne pepper, celery seeds, mustard seeds, and basil.

Add 1 cup of water and a metal trivet to the bottom. Fill the pepper halves with the rice/meat mixture. Place the peppers in a casserole dish; add the tomato puree and ketchup.

Lower the casserole dish onto the trivet in the Instant Pot.

Secure the lid. Choose the "Manual" mode and cook for 9 minutes at High pressure. Once cooking is complete, use a natural pressure release for 5 minutes; carefully remove the lid.

Afterwards, broil your peppers until the cheese melts approximately 5 minutes. Serve and enjoy!

368. Mexican-Style Meatloaf

(Ready in about 35 minutes)

Per serving: 557 Calories; 30.7g Fat; 32g Carbs; 39.6g Protein; 14.1g Sugars; 3.7g Fiber

INGREDIENTS

1 egg, beaten
1/4 cup milk
1/2 cup tortilla chips, crushed
1/2 onion, finely chopped
1 sweet pepper, finely chopped

1 clove garlic, minced
Sea salt and ground black pepper, to taste
1/2 teaspoon rosemary
1/2 pound ground beef

1/4 pound ground pork
1/2 cup tomato puree
1/2 teaspoon mustard
1 tablespoon brown sugar
1 tablespoon tamari sauce

DIRECTIONS

Place a steamer rack inside the inner pot; add 1/2 cup of water. Cut 1 sheet of heavy-duty foil and brush with cooking spray.

In mixing dish, combine the egg, milk, tortilla chips, onion, sweet pepper, garlic, salt, black pepper, rosemary, and ground meat.

Shape the meat mixture into a loaf; place the meatloaf in the center of foil. Wrap your meatloaf in foil and lower onto the steamer rack.

Secure the lid. Choose the "Meat/Stew" mode and cook for 20 minutes at High pressure. Once cooking is complete, use a quick pressure release; carefully remove the lid.

Then, transfer your meatloaf to a cutting board. Let it stand for 10 minutes before cutting and serving. Bon appétit!

369. Pot Roast with Harvest Vegetables

(Ready in about 50 minutes)

Per serving: 454 Calories; 20.2g Fat; 19.1g Carbs; 49g Protein; 6.5g Sugars; 3.7g Fiber

INGREDIENTS

1/2 tablespoon lard, melted
1 pound pot roast
Pink salt and ground black pepper, to taste
1/4 teaspoon ground cumin

1/2 teaspoon onion powder
1/2 teaspoon garlic powder
1 cup cream of celery soup
1 celery stalk
2 carrots

1 onion, halved
1 tablespoon fresh parsley leaves, roughly chopped

DIRECTIONS

Press the "Sauté" button to preheat your Instant Pot. Melt the lard and cook your pot roast until slightly brown on all sides.

Season with salt, black pepper, cumin, onion powder, and garlic powder. Pour in the cream of celery soup.

Secure the lid. Choose the "Meat/Stew" mode and cook for 35 minutes at High pressure. Once cooking is complete, use a natural pressure release; carefully remove the lid.

After that, stir in the celery, carrots, and onion.

Secure the lid. Choose the "Manual" mode and cook for 8 minutes at High pressure. Once cooking is complete, use a quick pressure release; carefully remove the lid.

Garnish with fresh parsley and serve immediately. Bon appétit!

370. Breakfast Cheeseburger Cups

(Ready in about 30 minutes)

Per serving: 522 Calories; 33.1g Fat; 14.3g Carbs; 43.1g Protein; 8.5g Sugars; 2.2g Fiber

INGREDIENTS

3/4 pound ground beef
Sea salt and ground black pepper, to taste
1/2 teaspoon onion powder
1/3 teaspoon garlic powder
1/2 tablespoon Italian seasoning blend

1/4 cup tomato paste
1/2 tablespoon maple syrup
1 teaspoon Dijon mustard
1/2 cup Cheddar cheese, shredded

DIRECTIONS

Spritz a silicone muffin pan with non-stick cooking oil.

In a large bowl, thoroughly combine the ground beef, salt, black pepper, onion powder, garlic powder, Italian seasoning blend, tomato paste, and Dijon mustard with your hands.

Scrape the beef mixture into the silicone muffin pan.

Place a steamer rack inside the inner pot; add 1/2 cup of water. Lower the muffin pan onto the rack.

Secure the lid. Choose the "Manual" mode and cook for 20 minutes at High pressure. Once cooking is complete, use a quick pressure release; carefully remove the lid.

Top with cheese; allow the cheese to melt and serve warm.

STEWS

371. Bean and Beef Steak Chili

(Ready in about 25 minutes)

Per serving: 501 Calories; 15.6g Fat; 53.5g Carbs; 35.2g Protein; 12.2g Sugars; 11.6g Fiber

INGREDIENTS

1/2 pound beef steak, cut into bite-sized cubes
2 tablespoons all-purpose flour
1 tablespoon vegetable oil
1/2 onion, chopped
1 clove garlic, minced
1/2 jalapeño pepper, seeded and minced

1 cup beef broth
Sea salt and ground black pepper, to taste
1/2 teaspoon paprika
1/2 teaspoon celery seeds
1/2 teaspoon mustard seeds
1 tablespoon ground cumin

1/2 tablespoon brown sugar
1 cup red kidney beans, soaked overnight and rinsed
1/2 cup tomato sauce
1 tablespoon cornstarch, mixed with 2 tablespoons of water

DIRECTIONS

Toss the beef steak with the the flour. Press the "Sauté" button and heat the oil until sizzling. Now, cook the beef steak in batches until browned on all side. Reserve.

Then, cook the onion, garlic, and jalapeño until they soften. Scrape the bottom of the pot with a splash of beef broth. Add the beef broth, spices, sugar, beans, and tomato sauce to the inner pot; stir to combine well.

Secure the lid. Choose the "Manual" mode. Cook for 18 minutes at High pressure. Once cooking is complete, use a natural pressure release; carefully remove the lid.

Press the "Sauté" button. Stir in the cornstarch slurry; stir for a few minutes to thicken the cooking liquid. Bon appétit!

372. French Beef Bourguignon

(Ready in about 30 minutes)

Per serving: 455 Calories; 23.3g Fat; 8.6g Carbs; 51.2g Protein; 4.1g Sugars; 1.8g Fiber

INGREDIENTS

2 thick slices bacon, diced
1 pound beef round roast, cut into 1-inch cubes
Sea salt and ground black pepper, to taste

1/2 cup red Burgundy wine
1 onion, thinly sliced
1 carrot, diced
1 celery stalk, diced
2 cloves garlic, minced

1 tablespoon tomato paste
1 thyme sprig
1 bay leaf
1 cup beef broth
1 tablespoon bouquet garni, chopped

DIRECTIONS

Press the "Sauté" button to preheat your Instant Pot. Cook the bacon until it is golden-brown; reserve.

Add the beef to the inner pot; sear the beef until browned or about 3 minutes per side.

Stir in the other ingredients; stir to combine well.

Secure the lid. Choose the "Meat/Stew" mode. Cook for 20 minutes at High pressure. Once cooking is complete, use a quick pressure release; carefully remove the lid.

Serve in individual bowls topped with the reserved bacon. Bon appétit!

373. Mediterranean Pottage with Oats

(Ready in about 15 minutes)

Per serving: 311 Calories; 10.1g Fat; 46g Carbs; 10.3g Protein; 6.2g Sugars; 11g Fiber

INGREDIENTS

1 tablespoon olive oil
1/2 onion, chopped
1 garlic clove, minced
1 carrot, diced
1 parsnip, diced

1/2 turnip, diced
2 cups vegetable broth
1 bay leaf
1 thyme sprig
1 rosemary sprig

Kosher salt and freshly ground black pepper, to taste
2 tablespoons red wine
1/2 cup porridge oats

DIRECTIONS

Press the "Sauté" button and heat the olive oil until sizzling. Now, sauté the onion and garlic until just tender and fragrant.

Add the remaining ingredients to the inner pot; stir to combine.

Secure the lid. Choose the "Manual" mode and cook for 10 minutes at High pressure. Once cooking is complete, use a quick pressure release; carefully remove the lid.

Ladle into individual bowls and serve immediately. Bon appétit!

374. Irish-Style Barley and Cabbage Stew

(Ready in about 35 minutes)

Per serving: 544 Calories; 2.1g Fat; 85g Carbs; 27.1g Protein; 12.4g Sugars; 25g Fiber

INGREDIENTS

3/4 cup white beans, soaked and rinsed
1/3 cup pearled barley
2 cups roasted vegetable broth
1/2 shallot, chopped
1 carrot, chopped
1 rib celery, chopped

1/2 sweet pepper, chopped
1/2 serrano pepper, chopped
2 cloves garlic, minced
1/2 pound cabbage, chopped
1/2 pound potatoes, diced
1 bay leaf
1/2 teaspoon mustard seeds

1/2 teaspoon caraway seeds
1/2 teaspoon cayenne pepper
Sea salt and freshly ground black pepper, to taste
8 ounces canned tomatoes, diced

DIRECTIONS

Place the white beans, barley, and vegetable broth in the inner pot.
Secure the lid. Choose the "Bean/Chili" mode and cook for 25 minutes at High pressure. Once cooking is complete, use a quick pressure release; carefully remove the lid.
Add the remaining ingredients and stir to combine.
Secure the lid. Choose the "Manual" mode and cook for 5 minutes at High pressure. Once cooking is complete, use a quick pressure release; carefully remove the lid.
Serve in individual bowls and enjoy!

375. Almond and Lentil Pottage

(Ready in about 20 minutes)

Per serving: 450 Calories; 23.3g Fat; 47.3g Carbs; 19.4g Protein; 10.7g Sugars; 11.9g Fiber

INGREDIENTS

1/2 tablespoon olive oil
1/2 onion, chopped
1/2 teaspoon fresh garlic, minced
1/2 dried chili pepper, crushed
1/2 pound potatoes, cut into 1-inch pieces
1/2 pound cauliflower, broken into florets

1/2 cup green lentils
1 cup tomato juice
2 cups vegetable broth
Seasoned salt and ground black pepper, to taste
1 teaspoon cayenne pepper

1/4 cup almond butter
1 heaping tablespoon cilantro, roughly chopped
1 heaping tablespoon parsley, roughly chopped

DIRECTIONS

Press the "Sauté" button and heat the olive oil. Now, sauté the onion until it is transparent. Add garlic and continue to sauté an additional minute.
Stir in the chili pepper, potatoes, cauliflower, lentils, tomato juice, vegetable broth, salt, black pepper, and cayenne pepper.
Secure the lid. Choose the "Manual" mode and cook for 10 minutes at High pressure. Once cooking is complete, use a quick pressure release; carefully remove the lid.
Stir in the almond butter. Press the "Sauté" button and simmer for about 3 minutes on the lowest setting. Garnish with cilantro and parsley. Bon appétit!

376. Spanish Zarzuela de Mariscos

(Ready in about 15 minutes)

Per serving: 277 Calories; 9.3g Fat; 26.5g Carbs; 22.3g Protein; 7.8g Sugars; 2.2g Fiber

INGREDIENTS

1 tablespoon olive oil
1/2 onion, finely diced
1 clove garlic, minced
1 thyme sprig, chopped
1 rosemary sprig, chopped
1/2 serrano pepper, deseeded and chopped

1 tomato, pureed
1/2 cup clam juice
1/2 cup chicken stock
3 tablespoons cooking sherry
1/2 pound fresh squid, cleaned and sliced into rings

Sea salt and ground black pepper, to taste
1/2 teaspoon cayenne pepper
1 bay leaf
1/4 teaspoon saffron
1/2 lemon, cut into wedges

DIRECTIONS

Press the "Sauté" button and heat the oil. Now, sauté the onion until tender and translucent.
Now, add the garlic and continue to sauté an additional minute. Add the remaining ingredients, except for the lemon.
Secure the lid. Choose the "Manual" mode. Cook for 10 minutes at High pressure. Once cooking is complete, use a quick pressure release; carefully remove the lid. Serve garnished with lemon wedges. Bon appétit!

377. Indian Lentil Curry

(Ready in about 20 minutes)

Per serving: 420 Calories; 11.4g Fat; 57.6g Carbs; 24.9g Protein; 19g Sugars; 6.3g Fiber

INGREDIENTS

Dahl:
1 tablespoon butter
1/2 brown onion, chopped
2 garlic cloves, minced
1 (1-inch) piece ginger, peeled and grated
1/2 red chili pepper, deseeded and minced
3 fresh curry leaves

1 tomato, chopped
1/4 teaspoon ground cumin
1/4 teaspoon ground cardamom
1 cup dried chana dal, soaked
2 cups vegetable broth
1/2 teaspoon turmeric powder
Kosher salt and ground black pepper, to taste

Tadka (Tempering):
1 tablespoon butter
A pinch of asafetida
1/2 teaspoon cumin seeds
1/2 teaspoon mustard seeds
1/2 onion, sliced
1 bay leaf
1 dried chili pepper, seeded and cut in half

DIRECTIONS

Press the "Sauté" button and melt 2 tablespoons of butter. Once hot, cook the onion until tender and translucent or about 3 minutes.
Then, stir in the garlic and ginger; continue to cook an additional minute or until they are fragrant.
Add the remaining ingredients for the Dal.
Secure the lid. Choose the "Manual" mode and cook for 10 minutes at High pressure. Once cooking is complete, use a quick pressure release; carefully remove the lid.
Clean the inner pot and press the "Sauté" button again. Melt 1 tablespoon of butter.
Now, add a pinch of asafetida, cumin seeds, mustard seeds, onion and bay leaf; sauté for a minute. Stir in the dried chili peppers and cook for 30 seconds longer.
Pour the hot tadka over the hot dal and serve.

378. Spicy Mulligan Stew (Burgoo)

(Ready in about 1 hour)

Per serving: 603 Calories; 18.4g Fat; 39.3g Carbs; 68g Protein; 7.1g Sugars; 7.8g Fiber

INGREDIENTS

1 tablespoon lard, melted
1/2 onion, chopped
1/2 pound pork shank, cubed
1/4 pound beef shank, cubed
1 chicken leg
1/4 cup Kentucky bourbon

2 cups chicken broth
1/2 cup dry lima beans, soaked
1/2 cup tomato puree
1 potato, diced
1 carrot, sliced thickly
1 parsnip, sliced thickly

1/2 celery rib, sliced thickly
1 sweet peppers, seeded and sliced
1/2 jalapeno pepper, seeded and minced
1/2 teaspoon dried sage, crushed
1/2 teaspoon dried basil, crushed
Salt and freshly ground black pepper, to taste

DIRECTIONS

Press the "Sauté" button and melt 1 tablespoon of lard. Once hot, sauté the onion until tender and translucent; reserve.
Add the remaining tablespoon of lard; brown the meat in batches until no longer pink or about 4 minutes.
Add a splash of Kentucky bourbon to deglaze the pot. Pour chicken broth into the inner pot.
Secure the lid. Choose the "Meat/Stew" mode. Cook for 45 minutes at High pressure. Once cooking is complete, use a quick pressure release; carefully remove the lid.
Shred chicken meat and discard the bones; add the chicken back to the inner pot. Next, stir in lima beans and tomato puree.
Secure the lid. Choose the "Manual" mode. Cook for 5 minutes at High pressure. Once cooking is complete, use a quick pressure release; carefully remove the lid.
Then, stir in the remaining ingredients, including the sautéed onion.
Secure the lid. Choose the "Manual" mode. Cook for 5 minutes at High pressure. Once cooking is complete, use a quick pressure release; carefully remove the lid.
Serve with cornbread if desired.

379. Pot-Au-Feu (Traditional French Stew)

(Ready in about 1 hour 10 minutes)

Per serving: 572 Calories; 31.4g Fat; 12.9g Carbs; 59g Protein; 6.2g Sugars; 3g Fiber

INGREDIENTS

1 tablespoon olive oil
1 pound beef pot roast, cut into 2-inch pieces
1/2 onion, chopped
1 carrot, chopped

2 garlic cloves, pressed
1 tomato, pureed
1/2 cup dry red wine
1 ½ cups beef broth
1/2 teaspoon marjoram

1/2 teaspoon sage
Sea salt and ground black pepper, to taste
1/2 shallot, sliced
1/2 pound cremini mushrooms, sliced
1/2 cup chèvres cheese, crumbled

DIRECTIONS

Press the "Sauté" button and heat the olive oil. Cook the beef in batches and transfer to a bowl.
Then, cook the onion in pan drippings. Stir in the carrots and garlic and continue to cook an additional 3 minutes.
Add the tomatoes, wine, broth, marjoram, sage, salt, and black pepper. Add the browned beef.
Secure the lid. Choose the "Meat/Stew" mode. Cook for 45 minutes at High pressure. Once cooking is complete, use a quick pressure release; carefully remove the lid.
Now, add the shallot and mushrooms; continue to simmer on the "Sauté" function for about 10 minutes or until everything is thoroughly heated.
Transfer your stew to a lightly greased casserole dish; top with the cheese and place under a preheated broiler for 10 minutes or until the cheese melts. Serve warm.

380. Vegetable Barley Medley

(Ready in about 25 minutes)

Per serving: 362 Calories; 4.7g Fat; 73.8g Carbs; 9.7g Protein; 5.5g Sugars; 14.3g Fiber

INGREDIENTS

1/2 tablespoon olive oil
1/2 onion, chopped
1 clove garlic, minced
1/2 red chili pepper, minced
1 sweet pepper, seeded and chopped

3/4 cups pearled barley
1 cup water
2 cups vegetable broth
1 stalk celery, chopped
1 carrot, chopped

1 tomato, pureed
1/2 teaspoon red pepper flakes
Sea salt and ground black pepper, to taste

DIRECTIONS

Press the "Sauté" button and heat the olive oil. Now, sauté the onion until tender and translucent.

Then, stir in the garlic and peppers and cook an additional 3 minutes. Stir in the pearled barley. Pour in water and broth.

Secure the lid. Choose the "Manual" mode. Cook for 15 minutes at High pressure. Once cooking is complete, use a quick pressure release; carefully remove the lid.

Add the remaining ingredients to the inner pot.

Secure the lid. Choose the "Manual" mode. Cook for 5 minutes at High pressure. Once cooking is complete, use a quick pressure release; carefully remove the lid. Bon appétit!

381. Olla Podrida Burgalesa

(Ready in about 30 minutes)

Per serving: 545 Calories; 22.1g Fat; 44.6g Carbs; 40.5g Protein; 5.2g Sugars; 8.3g Fiber

INGREDIENTS

1/2 pound meaty pork ribs in adobo
2 ounces Spanish chorizo sausage, sliced
1 tablespoon olive oil
1 onion, chopped

1 carrot, sliced
1 garlic clove, sliced
Salt and black pepper, to taste
1/4 pound alubias de Ibeas beans, soaked overnight

DIRECTIONS

Place the pork and sausage in the inner pot; cover with water.

Add the other ingredients and stir to combine.

Secure the lid. Choose the "Meat/Stew" mode. Cook for 20 minutes at High pressure. Once cooking is complete, use a quick pressure release; carefully remove the lid.

Serve hot with corn tortilla if desired. Enjoy!

382. Thai Coconut and Cauliflower Curry

(Ready in about 50 minutes)

Per serving: 459 Calories; 32.9g Fat; 18.2g Carbs; 28.5g Protein; 7.8g Sugars; 7.3g Fiber

INGREDIENTS

1 tablespoon sesame oil
1/2 pound beef chuck, cubed
1 onion, thinly sliced
1 clove garlic, pressed
1-inch galangal piece, peeled and sliced
1/2 Bird's eye chili pepper, seeded and minced

1/4 cup tomato paste
1 ½ cups chicken bone broth
2 tablespoons Thai red curry paste
1 tablespoon soy sauce
1/2 teaspoon ground cloves
1/2 teaspoon cardamom
1/2 teaspoon cumin

1 cinnamon quill
Sea salt and ground white pepper, to taste
5 ounces canned full-fat coconut milk
1 cup cauliflower florets
1 tablespoon fresh cilantro, roughly chopped

DIRECTIONS

Press the "Sauté" button and heat the sesame oil. When the oil starts to sizzle, cook the meat until browned on all sides.

Add a splash of broth and use a spoon to scrape the brown bits from the bottom of the pot.

Next, stir in the onion, garlic, galangal, chili pepper, tomato paste, broth, curry paste, soy sauce, and spices.

Secure the lid. Choose the "Soup/Broth" mode and cook for 40 minutes at High pressure. Once cooking is complete, use a quick pressure release; carefully remove the lid.

After that, add the coconut milk and cauliflower to the inner pot.

Secure the lid. Choose the "Manual" mode and cook for 4 minutes at High pressure. Once cooking is complete, use a quick pressure release; carefully remove the lid.

Serve garnished with fresh cilantro. Enjoy!

383. Easy Creole Jambalaya

(Ready in about 25 minutes)

Per serving: 427 Calories; 14.8g Fat; 24.8g Carbs; 50g Protein; 6.5g Sugars; 6.8g Fiber

INGREDIENTS

1 tablespoon olive oil
1/2 onion, diced
1/2 teaspoon garlic, minced
1/4 pound chicken breasts, boneless, skinless and cubed
1/4 pound smoked chicken sausage, cut into slices

1 sweet pepper, diced
1 jalapeno pepper, minced
1/2 celery stalk, diced
1 cup chicken bone broth
1 tomato, chopped
1/2 tablespoon Creole seasoning
Sea salt and ground black pepper, to taste

1/2 teaspoon cayenne pepper
1/2 tablespoon oyster sauce
1 bay leaf
1/2 pound shrimp, deveined
1/2 pound okra, frozen
1 stalk green onions, sliced thinly
1/2 tablespoon fresh lemon juice

DIRECTIONS

Press the "Sauté" button and heat the oil. Sweat the onion and garlic until tender and aromatic or about 3 minutes; reserve.

Then, heat the remaining tablespoon of olive oil and cook the chicken and sausage until no longer pink, about 4 minutes. Make sure to stir periodically to ensure even cooking.

Stir in the peppers, celery, broth, tomatoes, Creole seasoning, salt, black pepper, cayenne pepper, oyster sauce, and bay leaf. Add the reserved onion mixture.

Secure the lid. Choose the "Manual" mode. Cook for 7 minutes at High pressure. Once cooking is complete, use a quick pressure release; carefully remove the lid.

Afterwards, stir in the shrimp and okra.

Secure the lid. Choose the "Manual" mode. Cook for 3 minutes at High pressure. Once cooking is complete, use a natural pressure release; carefully remove the lid.

Divide between individual bowls and garnish with green onions. Drizzle lemon juice over each serving. Bon appétit!

384. Jamaican Beef Stew

(Ready in about 35 minutes)

Per serving: 473 Calories; 18.2g Fat; 26.1g Carbs; 54.2g Protein; 11.1g Sugars; 6.1g Fiber

INGREDIENTS

1 tablespoon olive oil
1 pound beef stew meat, cut bite-sized pieces
1/2 red onion, chopped
2 cloves garlic, minced

1 carrot, cut into rounds
1/2 parsnip, cut into rounds
1 stalk celery, diced
Sea salt and ground black pepper, to taste
1/2 teaspoon cayenne pepper

1 ½ cups beef bone broth
1/4 cup tomato paste
1/2 tablespoon fish sauce
1 bay leaf
1/2 cup frozen green peas

DIRECTIONS

Press the "Sauté" button and heat the oil. Once hot, brown the beef stew meat for 4 to 5 minutes; set aside.

Then, cook the onion in pan drippings until tender and translucent; stir in the garlic and cook an additional 30 seconds or until aromatic.

Add the carrots, parsnip, celery, salt, black pepper, cayenne pepper, beef broth, tomato paste, fish sauce, and bay leaves. Stir in the reserved beef stew meat.

Secure the lid. Choose the "Meat/Stew" mode and cook for 20 minutes at High pressure. Once cooking is complete, use a quick pressure release; carefully remove the lid.

Stir in the green peas, cover, and let it sit in the residual heat until warmed through or 5 to 7 minutes. Serve and enjoy!

385. Bosnian Hot Pot

(Ready in about 45 minutes)

Per serving: 496 Calories; 16.6g Fat; 30.5g Carbs; 55.7g Protein; 4.3g Sugars; 5.7g Fiber

INGREDIENTS

1 tablespoon safflower oil
1 pound pork loin roast, cut into cubes
1 garlic clove, chopped
1/2 onion, chopped
1 carrot, cut into chunks

1 celery rib, cut into chunks
1/2 pound potatoes, cut into chunks
Se salt and ground black pepper, to taste
1/2 teaspoon paprika
1 tomato, pureed

1 cup chicken bone broth
1/3 pound green beans, cut into 1-inch pieces
1 tablespoon fresh parsley leaves, roughly chopped

DIRECTIONS

Press the "Sauté" button and heat the oil until sizzling. Once hot, cook the pork until it is no longer pink on all sides.

Add the garlic and onion and cook for a minute or so, stirring frequently.

Stir in the carrots, celery, potatoes, salt, black pepper, paprika, tomatoes, and chicken bone broth.

Secure the lid. Choose the "Meat/Stew" mode and cook for 35 minutes at High pressure. Once cooking is complete, use a quick pressure release; carefully remove the lid.

Add the green beans to the inner pot. Press the "Sauté" button again and let it simmer for a few minutes more. Serve in individual bowls garnished with fresh parsley.

386. Fisherman's Stew with Potatoes

(Ready in about 15 minutes)

Per serving: 619 Calories; 39.5g Fat; 26.2g Carbs; 38.4g Protein; 4.2g Sugars; 3.9g Fiber

INGREDIENTS

1 tablespoon canola oil
1/2 onion, sliced
2 garlic cloves, sliced
1/4 cup Marsala wine
1 cup shellfish stock
1/2 cup water

1/2 pound Yukon Gold potatoes, diced
1 ripe tomato, pureed
Sea salt and ground black pepper, to taste
1 bay leaf
1/2 teaspoon smoked paprika

1/3 teaspoon hot sauce
1 pound halibut, cut into bite-sized pieces
1 tablespoon fresh cilantro, chopped

DIRECTIONS

Press the "Sauté" button and heat the oil. Once hot, cook the onions until softened; stir in the garlic and continue to sauté an additional 30 seconds. Add the wine to deglaze the bottom of the inner pot, scraping up any browned bits.

Add the shellfish stock, water, potatoes, tomatoes, salt, black pepper, bay leaves, paprika, hot sauce, and halibut to the inner pot.

Secure the lid. Choose the "Manual" mode. Cook for 5 minutes at High pressure. Once cooking is complete, use a quick pressure release; carefully remove the lid. Serve with fresh cilantro and enjoy!

387. Traditional Hungarian Gulyás

(Ready in about 30 minutes)

Per serving: 389 Calories; 20g Fat; 5.3g Carbs; 47.1g Protein; 2.5g Sugars; 1.6g Fiber

INGREDIENTS

1 tablespoon olive oil
1 pound beef chuck, cut into bite-sized pieces
2 tablespoons Hungarian red wine
1 onion, sliced

1 garlic clove, crushed
1/2 red chili pepper, minced
Sea salt and freshly ground black pepper, to taste
1/2 tablespoon Hungarian paprika

1 beef stock cube
1 ½ cups water
1 ripe tomato, puréed
1 bay leaf

DIRECTIONS

Press the "Sauté" button and heat the oil. Once hot, cook the beef until no longer pink. Add the red wine and stir with a wooden spoon, scraping up the browned bits on the bottom of the inner pot.

Stir in the remaining ingredients

Secure the lid. Choose the "Meat/Stew" mode. Cook for 20 minutes at High pressure. Once cooking is complete, use a quick pressure release; carefully remove the lid.

Serve in individual bowls and enjoy!

388. Traditional Polish Bigos

(Ready in about 20 minutes)

Per serving: 564 Calories; 28.4g Fat; 32.6g Carbs; 46.1g Protein; 12.5g Sugars; 9g Fiber

INGREDIENTS

1 slice smoked bacon, diced
1/2 pound Kielbasa, sliced
1/3 pound pork stew meat, cubed
1/2 onion, chopped
2 garlic cloves, sliced
1 carrot, trimmed and diced
1/2 pound sauerkraut, drained

1/2 pound fresh cabbage, shredded
1/2 teaspoon dried thyme
1/2 teaspoon dried basil
1 bay leaf
1/2 tablespoon cayenne pepper
1/2 teaspoon mustard seeds
1/2 teaspoon caraway seeds, crushed

Sea salt, to taste
1/2 teaspoon black peppercorns
2 tablespoons dry red wine
1 ½ cups beef stock
1/2 cup tomato puree

DIRECTIONS

Press the "Sauté" button to preheat your Instant Pot. Now, cook the bacon, Kielbasa, and pork stew meat until the bacon is crisp; reserve. Add the onion and garlic, and sauté them until they're softened and starting to brown. Add the remaining ingredients to the inner pot, including the reserved meat mixture.

Secure the lid. Choose the "Manual" mode and cook for 15 minutes at High pressure. Once cooking is complete, use a quick pressure release; carefully remove the lid.

Ladle into individual bowls and serve warm.

389. Winter Pinto Bean and Sausage Stew

(Ready in about 40 minutes)

Per serving: 425 Calories; 31.8g Fat; 21.3g Carbs; 17.2g Protein; 7.1g Sugars; 7g Fiber

INGREDIENTS

1/2 tablespoon olive oil
6 ounces smoked beef sausage, sliced
1 carrot, chopped
1/2 onion, chopped
1 garlic clove, minced

Sea salt and ground black pepper, to taste
1/2 teaspoon fresh rosemary, chopped
1/2 teaspoon fresh basil, chopped
1/2 cup canned tomatoes, crushed

1/2 cup chicken broth
10 ounces pinto beans, soaked overnight
4 ounces kale, torn into pieces

DIRECTIONS

Press the "Sauté" button and heat the oil. Once hot, brown the sausage for 3 to 4 minutes.

Add the remaining ingredients, except for the kale, to the inner pot.

Secure the lid. Choose the "Bean/Chili" mode and cook for 25 minutes at High pressure. Once cooking is complete, use a quick pressure release; carefully remove the lid.

Next, stir in the kale and seal the lid. Let it sit for 5 minutes before serving. Bon appétit!

390. Spanish Stew with Chorizo

(Ready in about 15 minutes)

Per serving: 454 Calories; 38g Fat; 9.3g Carbs; 17.4g Protein; 2.3g Sugars; 1g Fiber

INGREDIENTS

1 tablespoon olive oil
4 ounces Spanish chorizo sausage, sliced
1/2 onion, chopped
1/2 teaspoon ginger-garlic paste

1/2 teaspoon dried rosemary
1/2 teaspoon smoked paprika
1/2 pound fresh oysters, cleaned
Sea salt and freshly ground black pepper, to taste

1 ½ cups chicken broth
1 cup kale leaves, washed
1/2 cup heavy cream

DIRECTIONS

Press the "Sauté" button and heat the sesame oil. When the oil starts to sizzle, cook the sausage until no longer pink.

Add the onion to the inner pot and continue to sauté for a further 3 minutes or until tender and translucent.

Now, stir in the ginger-garlic paste, rosemary, paprika, oysters, salt, pepper, and chicken broth.

Secure the lid. Choose the "Manual" mode and cook for 6 minutes at Low pressure. Once cooking is complete, use a quick pressure release; carefully remove the lid.

Add the kale leaves and heavy cream, seal the lid again, and let it sit in the residual heat until thoroughly warmed. Serve warm and enjoy!

391. Pork Chile Verde

(Ready in about 30 minutes)

Per serving: 467 Calories; 15.3g Fat; 14.4g Carbs; 66g Protein; 7.3g Sugars; 3.4g Fiber

INGREDIENTS

1/2 pound tomatillos, halved
2 garlic cloves, sliced
1 chili pepper, minced
1 heaping tablespoon cilantro, chopped
1 tablespoon olive oil

1 pound pork stew meat, cut into 2-inch cubes
1/2 onion, chopped
1 bell pepper, deveined and sliced
Salt and freshly ground black pepper, to taste
1 cup vegetable broth

DIRECTIONS

Place the tomatillos under a preheated broiler for about 6 minutes. Let cool enough to handle.

Purée the tomatillos with the garlic, chili peppers, and cilantro in your blender; process until everything is finely chopped and mixed.

Press the "Sauté" button and heat the oil. Once hot, cook the pork until no longer pink. Add the onion and cook for a few minutes more or until it is tender and translucent.

Add the remaining ingredients, including tomatillo sauce, to the inner pot.

Secure the lid. Choose the "Meat/Stew" mode. Cook for 20 minutes at High pressure. Once cooking is complete, use a quick pressure release; carefully remove the lid.

Ladle into serving bowls and garnish with tortillas if desired. Bon appétit!

392. Creole Brunswick Stew

(Ready in about 20 minutes)

Per serving: 459 Calories; 19.6g Fat; 35.6g Carbs; 34.3g Protein; 8.3g Sugars; 8.3g Fiber

INGREDIENTS

1 tablespoon lard, melted
1/2 onion, diced
1 clove garlic, minced
1/2 pound chicken breast, cut into 1-inch cubes
1 cup lima beans, soaked
8 ounces canned tomatoes, diced

1 cup chicken broth
1/2 tablespoon Worcestershire sauce
1/2 teaspoon Creole seasoning
Sea salt and ground black pepper, to taste
1/2 teaspoon hot sauce
3/4 cup corn kernels

DIRECTIONS

Press the "Sauté" button and melt the lard. Once hot, cook the onion and garlic until just tender and aromatic.

Now, add the chicken and cook an additional 3 minutes, stirring frequently.

Add the lima beans, tomatoes, broth, Worcestershire sauce, Creole seasoning, salt, black pepper, and hot sauce to the inner pot.

Secure the lid. Choose the "Manual" mode and cook for 12 minutes at High pressure. Once cooking is complete, use a natural pressure release; carefully remove the lid.

Stir in the corn kernels and seal the lid. Let it sit in the residual heat until heated through. Enjoy!

393. Catalan Seafood Stew

(Ready in about 30 minutes)

Per serving: 463 Calories; 19.4g Fat; 34g Carbs; 33.8g Protein; 14g Sugars; 2.1g Fiber

INGREDIENTS

2 tablespoons olive oil
1/2 onion, chopped
2 cloves garlic, minced
2 ounces prosciutto, diced
1/2 pound shrimp
1/2 pound clams

1 Chile de Árbol, minced
1/4 cup dry white wine
1 ½ cups clam juice
1 laurel (bay leaf)
Sea salt and ground black pepper, to taste

1/2 teaspoon guindilla (cayenne pepper)
1 teaspoon rosemary, chopped
1/2 teaspoon basil, chopped
1 tomato, pureed
1/2 fresh lemon, sliced

DIRECTIONS

Press the "Sauté" button and heat the olive oil. Now, sauté the onion until it is transparent. Add the garlic and continue to sauté an additional 1 minute.

Add the prosciutto and cook an additional 3 minutes. Add the remaining ingredients, except for the lemon.

Secure the lid. Choose the "Manual" mode and cook for 10 minutes at High pressure. Once cooking is complete, use a natural pressure release for 10 minutes; carefully remove the lid.

Serve in individual bowls garnished with lemon slices. Enjoy!

394. Authentic Beef Ragout

(Ready in about 20 minutes)

Per serving: 386 Calories; 25.8g Fat; 10.1g Carbs; 27g Protein; 4.3g Sugars; 2.3g Fiber

INGREDIENTS

1 tablespoon butter, melted
1/2 leek, diced
1 carrot, diced
1/2 stalk celery, diced

2 ounces bacon, diced
1/2 pound ground chuck
1/4 cup Italian red wine
1/4 cup tomato puree

1 cup chicken stock
1/2 tablespoon Italian seasoning blend
1/4 teaspoon kosher salt
1/4 teaspoon black pepper

DIRECTIONS

Press the "Sauté" button and melt the butter. Sauté the leek, carrot, celery and garlic for 2 to 3 minutes.

Add the bacon and ground beef to the inner pot; continue to cook an additional 3 minutes, stirring frequently. Add the remaining ingredients to the inner pot.

Secure the lid. Choose the "Manual" mode and cook for 5 minutes at High pressure. Once cooking is complete, use a quick pressure release; carefully remove the lid.

Serve with hot pasta if desired. Bon appétit!

395. Curried Lentil Stew

(Ready in about 20 minutes)

Per serving: 492 Calories; 10.1g Fat; 77.5g Carbs; 24g Protein; 9g Sugars; 9.3g Fiber

INGREDIENTS

1 tablespoon canola oil
1/2 teaspoon cumin seeds
1/2 onion, chopped
1/2 teaspoon garlic paste

1 cup yellow lentils, soaked for 30 minutes and rinsed
1/2 teaspoon tamarind paste
1/2 teaspoon red chili powder

4 curry leaves
1 cup tomato sauce
Kosher salt and white pepper, to taste

DIRECTIONS

Press the "Sauté" button and heat the oil. Then, sauté the cumin seeds for 1 to 2 minutes, stirring frequently.

Then, add the onion and cook an additional 2 minutes. Stir in the remaining ingredients.

Secure the lid. Choose the "Manual" mode. Cook for 5 minutes at High pressure. Once cooking is complete, use a natural pressure release for 10 minutes; carefully remove the lid.

Ladle into individual bowls and serve immediately. Bon appétit!

396. Fricassee De Poulet a L'Ancienne

(Ready in about 30 minutes)

Per serving: 338 Calories; 21.3g Fat; 20.3g Carbs; 17.3g Protein; 6.3g Sugars; 3g Fiber

INGREDIENTS

1 tablespoon canola oil
4 chicken wings
1/2 onion, chopped
1 garlic clove, minced
Kosher salt and ground black pepper, to taste
1/2 teaspoon cayenne pepper
1/2 teaspoon celery seeds

1/2 teaspoon mustard powder
1 carrot, chopped
1 celery stalk, chopped
3/4 cup vegetable broth
1/4 cup cooking sherry
1 tablespoon all-purpose flour
1/2 cup double cream

DIRECTIONS

Press the "Sauté" button and heat 1 tablespoon of olive oil. Now, cook the chicken wings for 2 to 3 minutes per side; set aside. Add a splash of cooking sherry to deglaze the pot.

Then, heat the remaining tablespoon of olive oil; sauté the onion until just tender or about 3 minutes. Stir in the garlic and continue to cook an additional minute, stirring frequently.

Next, add the reserved chicken, salt, black pepper, cayenne pepper, celery seeds, mustard powder, carrots, celery, broth, and sherry to the inner pot.

Secure the lid. Choose the "Poultry" mode. Cook for 15 minutes at High pressure. Once cooking is complete, use a quick pressure release; carefully remove the lid.

Meanwhile, mix the flour with the double cream. Add the flour mixture to the hot cooking liquid; seal the lid and let it sit in the residual heat until thoroughly warmed.

Ladle into individual bowls and serve. Bon appétit!

397. Irish Garden Stew (Slumgullion)

(Ready in about 20 minutes)

Per serving: 546 Calories; 17.9g Fat; 62.3g Carbs; 35.4g Protein; 10.8g Sugars; 6.6g Fiber

INGREDIENTS

1 tablespoon canola oil
1/2 leek, chopped
1 garlic clove, minced
1 carrot, chopped

4 ounces macaroni
1/4 pound ground beef
1/4 pound pork sausage, crumbled
1/2 cup tomato puree

1/2 cup chicken broth
Seasoned salt and black pepper, to taste
1/2 cup canned stewed tomatoes
1 cup green beans, cut into thirds

DIRECTIONS

Press the "Sauté" button and heat the oil. Now, sauté the leek, garlic and carrot until they have softened.

Then, add the macaroni, ground beef, sausage, tomato puree, chicken broth, salt, and black pepper to the inner pot.

Secure the lid. Choose the "Manual" mode. Cook for 10 minutes at High pressure. Once cooking is complete, use a quick pressure release; carefully remove the lid.

After that, add the canned tomatoes and green beans; let it simmer on the "Sauté" function for 2 to 3 minutes more or until everything is heated through. Bon appétit!

398. Spicy Provençal Ratatouille

(Ready in about 25 minutes)

Per serving: 234 Calories; 7.1g Fat; 38.1g Carbs; 5.7g Protein; 15.3g Sugars; 11.5g Fiber

INGREDIENTS

1 pound eggplant, cut into rounds
1/2 tablespoon sea salt
1 tablespoon olive oil
1/2 red onion, sliced
2 cloves garlic, minced

2 sweet peppers, seeded and chopped
1/2 red chili pepper, seeded and minced
Sea salt and ground black pepper, to taste

1/2 teaspoon capers
1/4 teaspoon celery seeds
1 tomato, pureed
1 cup roasted vegetable broth
1 tablespoon coriander, chopped

DIRECTIONS

Toss the eggplant with 1 tablespoon of sea salt; allow it to drain in a colander.

Press the "Sauté" button and heat the olive oil. Sauté the onion until tender and translucent, about 4 minutes.

Add the garlic and continue to sauté for 30 seconds more or until fragrant. Add the remaining ingredients to the inner pot, including the drained eggplant.

Secure the lid. Choose the "Manual" mode. Cook for 7 minutes at High pressure. Once cooking is complete, use a quick pressure release; carefully remove the lid.

Press the "Sauté" button and cook on low setting until the ratatouille has thickened or about 7 minutes. Bon appétit!

399. Traditional Liverpool Scouse

(Ready in about 55 minutes)

Per serving: 492 Calories; 16.1g Fat; 35.1g Carbs; 52g Protein; 8.1g Sugars; 6g Fiber

INGREDIENTS

1 tablespoon olive oil
1 pound beef stew meat, diced
1/2 onion, chopped
1/2 teaspoon garlic, chopped

1 carrot, sliced
1/2 pound potatoes, peeled and diced
1/2 pound rutabaga, peeled and diced
1 bay leaf

Sea salt and ground black pepper, to taste
1 ½ cups beef bone broth

DIRECTIONS

Press the "Sauté" button and heat the oil. Brown the beef stew meat in batches; reserve.

Now, sauté the onion and garlic until just tender and fragrant.

Stir in the remaining ingredients, including the reserved meat.

Secure the lid. Choose the "Meat/Stew" mode. Cook for 45 minutes at High pressure. Once cooking is complete, use a quick pressure release; carefully remove the lid.

Ladle into serving bowls and enjoy!

400. Traditional Indian Rajma

(Ready in about 30 minutes)

Per serving: 472 Calories; 10.4g Fat; 67g Carbs; 25g Protein; 8.1g Sugars; 28.2g Fiber

INGREDIENTS

1 tablespoon sesame oil
1/2 onion, sliced
2 cloves garlic, finely chopped
1 (1-inch) piece fresh ginger root, peeled and grated
1 cup red kidney beans, soaked overnight

1 Bhut jolokia peppers, minced
1/2 teaspoon red curry paste
2 cups vegetable broth
1/2 teaspoon coriander seeds
1/3 teaspoon cumin seeds
1/4 teaspoon ground cinnamon

Seasoned salt and ground black pepper, to taste
1 tomato, pureed
1 tablespoon fresh coriander, chopped

DIRECTIONS

Press the "Sauté" button and heat the oil. Now, sauté the onion until it is transparent. Add the garlic and ginger and continue to sauté an additional 1 minute.

Add the beans, peppers, curry paste, vegetable broth spices, and tomatoes.

Secure the lid. Choose the "Bean/Chili" mode. Cook for 25 minutes at High pressure. Once cooking is complete, use a quick pressure release; carefully remove the lid.

Serve in individual bowls garnished with fresh coriander. Enjoy!

401. Italian Boiled Beef

(Ready in about 35 minutes)

Per serving: 490 Calories; 10.6g Fat; 41g Carbs; 46.7g Protein; 8.9g Sugars; 5.7g Fiber

INGREDIENTS

3/4 pounds beef top round, cut into bite-sized chunks
2 tablespoons all-purpose flour
1/2 tablespoon Italian seasoning
Sea salt and ground black pepper, to taste
1/2 tablespoon lard, at room temperature

1/2 onion, chopped
2 cloves garlic, pressed
2 tablespoons cooking wine
1/4 cup tomato paste
1/2 pound sweet potatoes, diced
1 carrot, sliced into rounds

1 bell pepper, deveined and sliced
1/2 teaspoon fish sauce
1 bay leaf
2 cups beef broth
1 tablespoon fresh Italian parsley, roughly chopped

DIRECTIONS

Toss the beef chunks with the flour, Italian seasoning, salt, and pepper until well coated.

Press the "Sauté" button and melt the lard; brown the beef chunks on all sides, stirring frequently; reserve.

Then, sauté the onion and garlic for a minute or so; add the wine and stir, scraping up any browned bits from the bottom of the inner pot.

Add the beef back into the inner pot. Stir in the tomato paste, sweet potatoes, carrots, bell peppers, fish sauce, bay leaves, and beef broth.

Secure the lid. Choose the "Meat/Stew" mode and cook for 20 minutes at High pressure. Once cooking is complete, use a natural pressure release for 10 minutes; carefully remove the lid. Serve garnished with Italian parsley.

402. Spicy Chickpea Stew

(Ready in about 40 minutes)

Per serving: 560 Calories; 12.1g Fat; 83g Carbs; 21.4g Protein; 15g Sugars; 16.5g Fiber

INGREDIENTS

1 tablespoon olive oil
1/2 leek, chopped
2 cloves garlic, pressed
1 potato, diced
1 carrot, diced

1/2 sweet pepper, seeded and chopped
1/2 jalapeno pepper, seeded and chopped
1/2 cup tomato puree
1/2 teaspoon cumin powder

1/2 teaspoon turmeric powder
1/2 teaspoon mustard seeds
1 cup roasted vegetable broth
3/4 cup chickpeas, soaked overnight

DIRECTIONS

Press the "Sauté" button and heat the oil until sizzling. Once hot, cook the leeks and garlic for 2 to 3 minutes or until they are just tender.

Add the remaining ingredients and stir to combine well.

Secure the lid. Choose the "Meat/Stew" mode and cook for 35 minutes at High pressure. Once cooking is complete, use a quick pressure release; carefully remove the lid.

Serve in individual bowls. Bon appétit!

403. Hearty Squash and Chicken Stew

(Ready in about 35 minutes)

Per serving: 460 Calories; 16.6g Fat; 30.5g Carbs; 44.4g Protein; 10.4g Sugars; 6g Fiber

INGREDIENTS

1 tablespoon olive oil, divided
1 pound chicken thighs
1/2 onion, chopped
1 garlic clove, minced
1 (1-inch) piece fresh ginger, peeled and minced

Kosher salt and freshly ground black pepper, to taste
1/2 teaspoon paprika
1/2 tablespoon fresh sage, chopped
1/2 pound winter squash, peeled and cubed

1 carrot, trimmed and diced
1/4 cup apple cider
3/4 cup chicken stock
1 chopped peeled Granny Smith apple

DIRECTIONS

Press the "Sauté" button and heat the oil. Once hot, sear the chicken thighs for about 2 minutes per side; reserve.

Add the onion, garlic, and ginger and sauté them for 2 to 3 minutes or until just tender. Add the salt, pepper, paprika, sage, winter squash, carrots, apple cider, and chicken stock. Add the reserved chicken thighs.

Secure the lid. Choose the "Manual" mode and cook for 10 minutes at High pressure. Once cooking is complete, use a natural pressure release for 10 minutes; carefully remove the lid.

Remove the chicken thighs and shred with two forks; discard the bones. Add the shredded chicken back into the inner pot.

Afterwards, stir in the apples; cover, press the "Sauté" button on Low and let it simmer for 10 to 12 minutes longer or until the apples are tender.

404. Easy Kentucky Burgoo

(Ready in about 30 minutes)

Per serving: 712 Calories; 25.4g Fat; 42.2g Carbs; 79g Protein; 12.3g Sugars; 5.7g Fiber

INGREDIENTS

1/2 tablespoon lard, melted
1/2 pound pork butt roast, cut into
2-inch pieces
1/2 pound beef stew meat, cut into
2-inch pieces
1 chicken thigh, boneless

1 bell pepper, chopped
1/2 red chili pepper, chopped
1/2 onion, chopped
1 carrot, chopped
2 garlic cloves, chopped
1 cup beef bone broth

1 cup beer
8 ounces canned tomatoes, crushed
Sea salt and ground black pepper, to
taste
1/2 pound frozen corn kernels
1 tablespoon Worcestershire sauce

DIRECTIONS

Press the "Sauté" button and melt the lard. Once hot, brown the meat in batches. Remove the browned meats to a bowl.
Then, sauté the peppers, onion, carrots for about 3 minutes or until tender and fragrant. Add the garlic and continue to cook for 30 seconds more.
Add the meat back to the Instant Pot. Stir in the remaining ingredients, except for the corn kernels.
Secure the lid. Choose the "Meat/Stew" mode and cook for 20 minutes at High pressure. Once cooking is complete, use a quick pressure release; carefully remove the lid.
Lastly, stir in the corn and continue to cook for a few minutes more on the "Sauté" function. Serve immediately.

405. Southern Style Chicken Perlo

(Ready in about 25 minutes)

Per serving: 641 Calories; 21.4g Fat; 80g Carbs; 28.5g Protein; 2.8g Sugars; 2.8g Fiber

INGREDIENTS

1/2 tablespoon olive oil
1/2 onion, chopped
1/2 pound chicken legs, boneless and
skinless
1 garlic clove, minced

2 cups water
1 carrot, diced
1 celery rib, diced
1 bay leaf
1/2 teaspoon mustard seeds

1/4 teaspoon marjoram
Seasoned salt and freshly ground black
pepper, to taste
1/2 teaspoon cayenne pepper
1 cup white long-grain rice

DIRECTIONS

Press the "Sauté" button and heat the olive oil. Now, add the onion and chicken legs; cook until the onion is translucent or about 4 minutes.
Stir in the minced garlic and continue to cook for a minute more. Add the water.
Secure the lid. Choose the "Manual" mode and cook for 10 minutes at High pressure. Once cooking is complete, use a quick pressure release; carefully remove the lid.
Add in the remaining ingredients.
Secure the lid. Choose the "Manual" mode and cook for 5 minutes at High pressure. Once cooking is complete, use a quick pressure release; carefully remove the lid. Serve warm.

406. Harvest Vegetables and Lentil Stew

(Ready in about 15 minutes)

Per serving: 485 Calories; 8.2g Fat; 80.2g Carbs; 26.5g Protein; 9.1g Sugars; 10.8g Fiber

INGREDIENTS

1 tablespoon olive oil
1/2 onion, chopped
1 clove garlic, minced
1 carrot, chopped
1/2 stalk celery, chopped

1 parsnip, chopped
1 cup brown lentils
1 tomato, pureed
1 sprig thyme, chopped
1 sprig rosemary, chopped

1/2 teaspoon basil
Kosher salt and ground black pepper,
to taste
1 cup vegetable broth
2 cups Swiss chard, torn into pieces

DIRECTIONS

Press the "Sauté" button and heat the oil. Sauté the onion until tender and translucent or about 4 minutes.
Then, stir in the garlic and cook an additional 30 seconds or until fragrant.
Now, stir in the carrot, celery, parsnip, lentils, tomatoes, spices, and broth.
Secure the lid. Choose the "Manual" mode. Cook for 10 minutes at High pressure. Once cooking is complete, use a quick pressure release; carefully remove the lid.
Afterwards, add the Swiss chard to the inner pot. Seal the lid and allow it to wilt completely. Bon appétit!

407. Hearty Seafood Cassoulet

(Ready in about 20 minutes)

Per serving: 325 Calories; 11.9g Fat; 16.3g Carbs; 39.4g Protein; 5.8g Sugars; 3.2g Fiber

INGREDIENTS

1 tablespoon olive oil
1/2 shallot, diced
1 carrot, diced
1/2 parsnip, diced
1 teaspoon fresh garlic, minced
1/4 cup dry white wine

1 cup fish stock
1 tomato, pureed
1 bay leaf
1/2 pound shrimp, deveined
1/3 pound scallops
Seasoned salt and freshly ground

pepper, to taste
1/2 tablespoon paprika
1 tablespoon fresh parsley, chopped
1/2 lime, sliced

DIRECTIONS

Press the "Sauté" button and heat the oil. Now, sauté the shallot, carrot, and parsnip for 4 to 5 minutes or until they are tender.
Stir in the garlic and continue to sauté an additional 30 second or until aromatic.
Stir in the white wine, stock, tomato, bay leaf, shrimp, scallops, salt, black pepper, and paprika.
Secure the lid. Choose the "Manual" mode. Cook for 5 minutes at High pressure.
Once cooking is complete, use a natural pressure release for 5 minutes; carefully remove the lid. Serve garnished with fresh parsley and lime slices. Enjoy!

408. Greek-Style Chicken Mélange

(Ready in about 35 minutes)

Per serving: 400 Calories; 27.9g Fat; 11.3g Carbs; 24.6g Protein; 5.1g Sugars; 3.2g Fiber

INGREDIENTS

1 tablespoons olive oil
1/2 onion, chopped
1/2 stalk celery, chopped
1 carrot, chopped
1/2 teaspoon garlic, minced
2 chicken legs, boneless skinless

4 tablespoons dry red wine
1 ripe tomato, pureed
1 cup chicken bone broth
1 bay leaf
Sea salt and ground black pepper, to taste

1/2 teaspoon dried basil
1/2 teaspoon dried oregano
1/4 cup Kalamata olives, pitted and sliced

DIRECTIONS

Press the "Sauté" button and heat the oil. Now, sauté the onion, celery, and carrot for 4 to 5 minutes or until they are tender.
Add the other ingredients, except for the Kalamata olives, and stir to combine.
Secure the lid. Choose the "Manual" mode. Cook for 15 minutes at High pressure. Once cooking is complete, use a natural pressure release for 10 minutes; carefully remove the lid.
Serve warm garnished with Kalamata olives. Bon appétit!

409. Hungarian Famous Paprikás Csirke

(Ready in about 30 minutes)

Per serving: 446 Calories; 10.1g Fat; 31g Carbs; 55.7g Protein; 7.5g Sugars; 4g Fiber

INGREDIENTS

1 tablespoon lard, at room temperature
1 pound chicken, cut into pieces
1 onion, chopped
1 clove garlic, minced

1/2 cup tomato puree
1 Hungarian pepper, diced
1 tablespoon Hungarian paprika
1 cup chicken stock

Kosher salt and cracked ground black pepper
2 tablespoons all-purpose flour
1/2 cup full-fat sour cream

DIRECTIONS

Press the "Sauté" button and melt the lard. Once hot, cook the chicken for about 3 minutes or until no longer pink.
Add the onion to the inner pot; continue sautéing an additional 3 minutes. Now, stir in the garlic and cook for 30 seconds more.
Add the tomato puree, Hungarian pepper, paprika, chicken stock, salt, and black pepper to the inner pot.
Secure the lid. Choose the "Manual" mode. Cook for 15 minutes at High pressure. Once cooking is complete, use a quick pressure release; carefully remove the lid. Remove the chicken from the inner pot; shred the chicken and discard the bones.
In a mixing bowl, stir the flour into the sour cream. Add the flour/cream mixture to the cooking liquid, stirring constantly with a wire whisk. Let it simmer until the sauce is thickened. Return the chicken to your paprikash, stir and press the "Cancel" button. Enjoy!

410. Country-Style Beef and Potato Hash

(Ready in about 30 minutes)

Per serving: 595 Calories; 21.1g Fat; 43g Carbs; 56.1g Protein; 9.9g Sugars; 7.3g Fiber

INGREDIENTS

1 tablespoon lard, melted

1 pound chuck roast, cut into 2-inch cubes

1 onion, chopped

1 clove garlic, minced

1/2 tablespoon Hungarian paprika

2 bell peppers, deveined and chopped

1/2 chili pepper, chopped

1/2 cup tomato puree

2 small potatoes, diced

1 ½ cups beef broth

1 bay leaf

Seasoned salt and ground black pepper, to taste

DIRECTIONS

Press the "Sauté" button and melt the lard. Once hot, cook the beef until no longer pink. Add a splash of broth and stir with a wooden spoon, scraping up the browned bits on the bottom of the inner pot.

Add the onion to the inner pot; continue sautéing an additional 3 minutes. Now, stir in the garlic and cook for 30 seconds more.

Stir in the remaining ingredients

Secure the lid. Choose the "Meat/Stew" mode. Cook for 20 minutes at High pressure. Once cooking is complete, use a quick pressure release; carefully remove the lid.

Discard the bay leaves and serve in individual bowls. Bon appétit!

RICE

411. Spanish Paella with Green Peas

(Ready in about 25 minutes)

Per serving: 503 Calories; 8g Fat; 58.1g Carbs; 46.2g Protein; 9.7g Sugars; 4.8g Fiber

INGREDIENTS

1 tablespoon ghee, at room temperature
1 clove garlic, pressed
1 red bell pepper, cut in strips
1/2 cup basmati rice
1 pound tiger prawns, deveined
Sea salt and ground black pepper, to taste

1 bay leaf
1/2 teaspoon paprika
1/4 teaspoon saffron threads
1/2 tablespoon capers, drained
1 cup chicken broth
1/2 cup green peas, thawed

DIRECTIONS

Press the "Sauté" button and melt the ghee. Once hot, cook the garlic and pepper for about 2 minutes or until just tender and fragrant.
Add the basmati rice, tiger prawns, salt, black pepper, bay leaf, paprika, saffron, capers, and chicken broth to the inner pot.
Secure the lid. Choose the "Manual" mode and cook for 4 minutes at High pressure. Once cooking is complete, use a natural pressure release for 10 minutes; carefully remove the lid.
Add the green peas to the inner pot; press the "Sauté" button one more time and let it simmer until heated through. Enjoy!

412. Winter Sichuan Congee

(Ready in about 35 minutes)

Per serving: 322 Calories; 22.5g Fat; 26.8g Carbs; 16.4g Protein; 3.7g Sugars; 10.2g Fiber

INGREDIENTS

3/4 cup sushi rice, rinsed
3 cups roasted vegetable broth
1 teaspoon fresh ginger, grated
Kosher salt and ground black pepper, to taste

1 tablespoon soy sauce
1 tablespoon chili oil
1/2 cup pao cai

DIRECTIONS

Place the rice, vegetable broth, ginger, and salt in the inner pot of the Instant Pot.
Secure the lid. Choose the "Multigrain" mode and cook for 20 minutes at High pressure. Once cooking is complete, use a natural pressure release for 10 minutes; carefully remove the lid.
Your congee will thicken as it cools. Stir in the black pepper, soy sauce, and chili oil. Serve garnished with pao cai and enjoy!

413. Rice Salad with Fruits and Nuts

(Ready in about 30 minutes)

Per serving: 590 Calories; 23.6g Fat; 86g Carbs; 8.1g Protein; 9.9g Sugars; 2.8g Fiber

INGREDIENTS

1 cup long-grain white rice, rinsed
1 ½ cups water
1/2 teaspoon table salt
2 tablespoons extra-virgin olive oil
1/2 tablespoon orange zest

2 tablespoons orange juice, freshly squeezed
1/2 cup grapes, cut in half
2 tablespoons dried cranberries
1/4 cup pecans
1 tablespoon pomegranate arils

DIRECTIONS

Place the rice, water, and salt in the inner pot of your Instant Pot; stir to combine.
Secure the lid. Choose the "Rice" mode and cook for 10 minutes. Once cooking is complete, use a natural pressure release for 15 minutes; carefully remove the lid.
Fluff the rice with a fork and allow it to cool to room temperature.
Add the remaining ingredients to a nice salad bowl; add the chilled rice. Toss to combine and serve chilled or at room temperature. Bon appétit!

414. Chop Suey Rice Bowls

(Ready in about 15 minutes)

Per serving: 472 Calories; 13.9g Fat; 72g Carbs; 12.3g Protein; 6.6g Sugars; 7.2g Fiber

INGREDIENTS

1 tablespoon butter
1/2 onion, chopped
1 clove garlic, minced
1 celery stalk, chopped
1 carrot, chopped

1/2 pound broccoli, broken into florets
3/4 cup cream of mushroom soup
1/2 cup plain milk
3/4 cup Arborio rice

DIRECTIONS

Press the "Sauté" button and melt the butter. Once hot, cook the onion and garlic for 3 to 4 minutes or until just tender and fragrant. Add the remaining ingredients and gently stir to combine.

Secure the lid. Choose the "Manual" mode and cook for 4 minutes at High pressure. Once cooking is complete, use a quick pressure release; carefully remove the lid.

Serve warm.

415. Smoked Salmon Pilau

(Ready in about 20 minutes)

Per serving: 569 Calories; 15.6g Fat; 60.1g Carbs; 38.2g Protein; 4.6g Sugars; 3.3g Fiber

INGREDIENTS

1 tablespoon butter
1/2 onion, chopped
2 cloves garlic, minced
3/4 cup white rice
1/2 cup vegetable broth

1/2 cup milk
3/4 pound smoked salmon steak
3 ounces green beans
Sea salt and ground black pepper, to season

DIRECTIONS

Press the "Sauté" button and melt the butter. When the butter starts to sizzle, add the onion; sauté the onion until just tender and fragrant. Now, stir in the garlic and continue to sauté an additional minute or until fragrant.

Add the rice, broth, milk, salmon, and green beans; season with salt and black pepper.

Secure the lid. Choose the "Manual" mode and cook for 4 minutes at High pressure. Once cooking is complete, use a natural pressure release for 10 minutes; carefully remove the lid. Bon appétit!

416. Late Summer Risotto

(Ready in about 30 minutes)

Per serving: 463 Calories; 8g Fat; 89.5g Carbs; 15.1g Protein; 19.9g Sugars; 8.4g Fiber

INGREDIENTS

1 tablespoon olive oil
1/2 onion, chopped
1 teaspoon garlic, chopped
3/4 cup long grain white rice
1 cup water
1 carrot, thinly sliced
1/2 green zucchini, cut into thick sliced

10 ounces canned tomato paste
1/2 teaspoon Italian seasoning blend
Sea salt and ground black pepper, to your liking
1 bay leaf
2 cups spinach
1 teaspoon fresh lime juice

DIRECTIONS

Press the "Sauté" button and heat the oil. Once hot, cook the onion and garlic for 2 to 3 minutes or until just tender and aromatic.

Stir in the rice, water, carrots, zucchini, tomato paste, Italian seasoning blend, salt, black pepper, and bay leaf.

Secure the lid. Choose the "Rice" mode and cook for 10 minutes at Low pressure. Once cooking is complete, use a natural pressure release for 15 minutes; carefully remove the lid.

Add the spinach and press the "Sauté" button. Let it simmer on the lowest setting until wilts. Drizzle lime juice over each portion and serve. Bon appétit!

417. Risotto with Petite Peas and Peanuts

(Ready in about 30 minutes)

Per serving: 524 Calories; 16.6g Fat; 83.2g Carbs; 13.5g Protein; 10g Sugars; 8.2g Fiber

INGREDIENTS

3/4 cup white rice
1 tablespoon peanut oil
1 Vidalia onion, chopped
1 clove garlic, minced
1/2 teaspoon cayenne pepper

Sea salt and ground black pepper, to taste
1 tomato, pureed
1 cup vegetable broth
1 bay leaf

1/3 cup frozen petite peas, thawed
1/4 cup peanuts, dry roasted and roughly chopped

DIRECTIONS

Add the white rice, peanut oil, Vidalia onion, garlic, cayenne pepper, salt, black pepper, tomato, vegetable broth, and bay leaf to the inner pot.
Secure the lid. Choose the "Manual" mode and cook for 5 minutes at High pressure. Once cooking is complete, use a natural pressure release for 20 minutes; carefully remove the lid.
Now, stir in the thawed petite peas and seal the lid. Let it sit in the residual heat until everything is heated through.
Serve with roasted peanuts and enjoy!

418. Old-Fashioned Chicken and Rice Soup

(Ready in about 45 minutes)

Per serving: 435 Calories; 16.1g Fat; 51.9g Carbs; 21.7g Protein; 6.6g Sugars; 4.7g Fiber

INGREDIENTS

1 tablespoon olive oil
1/3 pound chicken breast, boneless and cut into small chunks
1/2 onion, chopped
1 clove garlic, minced

1 carrot, peeled and diced
1/2 rib celery, diced
1/2 parsnip, peeled and diced
1/2 teaspoon dried basil
1/2 teaspoon dried thyme

2 cups chicken broth
1/2 cup brown basmati rice
Kosher salt and ground black pepper, to taste
1/4 cup coconut milk

DIRECTIONS

Press the "Sauté" button and heat the oil until sizzling. Then, cook the chicken breast for 3 to 4 minutes or until no longer pink; reserve.
Now, add the onion and garlic and continue sautéing in pan drippings for 2 to 3 minutes more or until they are tender and fragrant.
Add the carrots, celery, parsnip, basil, thyme, broth, rice, salt, and black pepper. Add the chicken breasts back to the inner pot.
Secure the lid. Choose the "Soup/Broth" mode and cook for 20 minutes at High pressure. Once cooking is complete, use a natural pressure release for 15 minutes; carefully remove the lid.
Pour in the coconut milk; seal the lid and let it sit in the residual heat until heated through. Serve in soup bowls and enjoy!

419. Risotto with Shrimp and Peppers

(Ready in about 50 minutes)

Per serving: 442 Calories; 9.3g Fat; 36.1g Carbs; 54g Protein; 3.2g Sugars; 3.6g Fiber

INGREDIENTS

1 tablespoon olive oil
1/2 leek, chopped
1/2 teaspoon garlic, minced
1 bell pepper, chopped
1/2 cup wild rice

1 cup chicken broth
1 rosemary sprig
1 thyme sprig
1/2 teaspoon kosher salt
1/2 teaspoon ground black pepper

1/2 teaspoon cayenne pepper
1 pound shrimp, deveined
1 tablespoon fresh chives

DIRECTIONS

Press the "Sauté" button and heat the olive oil. Once hot, sauté the leek until just tender or about 3 minutes.
Then, stir in the garlic and peppers. Continue to cook for 3 minutes more or until they are tender and fragrant.
Add the wild rice, broth, and seasonings to the inner pot.
Secure the lid. Choose the "Manual" mode and cook for 30 minutes at High pressure. Once cooking is complete, use a natural pressure release for 10 minutes; carefully remove the lid.
Add the shrimp to the inner pot.
Choose the "Manual" mode and cook for 3 minutes at High pressure. Once cooking is complete, use a quick pressure release; carefully remove the lid.
Serve garnished with fresh chives and enjoy!

420. Mexican Cheesy Rice

(Ready in about 35 minutes)

Per serving: 555 Calories; 21.2g Fat; 50.7g Carbs; 31.6g Protein; 3.4g Sugars; 3.6g Fiber

INGREDIENTS

3/4 cup brown rice

1/2 cup chicken broth

1/2 cup chunky salsa

3/4 cup Cotija cheese, shredded

DIRECTIONS

Add the brown rice, chicken broth, salsa, oregano, salt, and black pepper to the inner pot.

Secure the lid. Choose the "Manual" mode and cook for 22 minutes at High pressure. Once cooking is complete, use a natural pressure release for 10 minutes; carefully remove the lid.

Divide between serving bowls and serve with shredded cheese. Enjoy!

421. Spicy Beef Stew with Brown Rice

(Ready in about 30 minutes)

Per serving: 515 Calories; 14g Fat; 66.1g Carbs; 32.1g Protein; 3.5g Sugars; 4.5g Fiber

INGREDIENTS

1 tablespoon lard, at room temperature

1/2 pound beef stew meat, cut into bite-sized chunks

2 cups beef bone broth

1/2 onion, chopped

1 garlic clove, minced

1 sweet pepper, deveined and chopped

1/2 red chili pepper, chopped

1/2 teaspoon dried basil

1/2 teaspoon dried oregano

1/2 teaspoon dried rosemary

Sea salt and ground black pepper, to taste

1 bay leaf

1 tablespoon cornstarch, dissolved in 1/4 cup cold water

3/4 cup brown rice

DIRECTIONS

Press the "Sauté" button and melt the lard. When the lard starts to sizzle, add the beef stew meat and cook until browned on all sides; reserve.

Add a splash of beef broth to the inner pot; use a spoon to scrape the brown bits from the bottom of the pan.

Then, sauté the onion, garlic, and peppers for about 3 minutes or until they are just tender.

Add the other ingredients and stir to combine.

Secure the lid. Choose the "Soup/Broth" mode and cook for 20 minutes at High pressure. Once cooking is complete, use a quick pressure release; carefully remove the lid.

Mix the cornstarch with cold water in a small bowl; stir the slurry into the stew and cook on the "Sauté" function until the cooking liquid has thickened.

Serve warm and enjoy!

422. Chicken, Pea and Rice Bowl

(Ready in about 40 minutes)

Per serving: 437 Calories; 10.7g Fat; 53.1g Carbs; 30.5g Protein; 6.3g Sugars; 6.3g Fiber

INGREDIENTS

1 tablespoon olive oil

1/2 pound chicken fillets, cut into strips

1/2 onion, chopped

1/2 teaspoon garlic, minced

1/2 teaspoon sea salt

1/4 teaspoon black pepper, divided

1/2 teaspoon ground coriander

1/4 teaspoon paprika

1/2 cup white rice

1 cup water

1 red chili peppers, seeded and chopped

3/4 cup green peas, thawed

1/3 cup salsa

DIRECTIONS

Press the "Sauté" button and heat 1 tablespoon of olive oil until sizzling. Then, cook the chicken until no longer pink or about 4 minutes.

Then, heat another tablespoon of olive oil and add the onion and garlic. Cook for 2 to 3 minutes or until fragrant. Now, sauté the garlic until it is aromatic but not browned.

Add the spices, rice, water, and peppers. Add the reserved chicken back to the inner pot.

Secure the lid. Choose the "Rice" mode and cook for 10 minutes. Once cooking is complete, use a natural pressure release for 15 minutes; carefully remove the lid.

Add the green peas and press the "Sauté" button; cook on Less setting until thoroughly heated. Serve with salsa and enjoy!

423. Japanese Rice with Potatoes and Tonkatsu Sauce

(Ready in about 45 minutes)

Per serving: 430 Calories; 3.9g Fat; 80.2g Carbs; 11.2g Protein; 10.3 g Sugars; 8.2g Fiber

INGREDIENTS

3/4 cup brown rice

2 cups water

1/2 pound potatoes, peeled and diced

1 tomato, pureed

1/2 teaspoon sweet paprika

Kosher salt and ground black pepper, to your liking

1/4 cup rice wine

1 tablespoon Tonkatsu sauce

1 bay leaf

1 tablespoon soy sauce

DIRECTIONS

Add all ingredients, except for the soy sauce, to the inner pot.

Secure the lid. Choose the "Manual" mode and cook for 24 minutes at High pressure. Once cooking is complete, use a natural pressure release for 15 minutes; carefully remove the lid.

Ladle into individual bowls; drizzle soy sauce over each serving and enjoy!

424. Thai Rice with Sage and Peppers

(Ready in about 25 minutes)

Per serving: 392 Calories; 5.1g Fat; 60.8g Carbs; 8.3g Protein; 4g Sugars; 5g Fiber

INGREDIENTS

1 teaspoon olive oil

1/2 onion, chopped

1 cup sweet peppers, chopped

1/2 jalapeno pepper, minced

1/2 teaspoon garlic powder

1/2 teaspoon ground bay leaf

1/2 teaspoon dried sage, crushed

1 cup jasmine rice, rinsed

1 cup water

1/2 teaspoon sea salt

DIRECTIONS

Press the "Sauté" button and heat the olive oil. Once hot, cook the onion and peppers until just tender and fragrant.

Now, add the remaining ingredients and stir to combine well.

Secure the lid. Choose the "Manual" mode and cook for 4 minutes at High pressure. Once cooking is complete, use a natural pressure release for 15 minutes; carefully remove the lid.

Serve in individual bowls and enjoy!

425. Chicken and Broccoli Moussaka

(Ready in about 30 minutes)

Per serving: 583 Calories; 21.2g Fat; 55.5g Carbs; 33.5g Protein; 7.1g Sugars; 6.6g Fiber

INGREDIENTS

1 tablespoon butter, melted

1/2 pound chicken breast, skinless

1/2 shallot, sliced

1/2 teaspoon garlic, minced

1/2 pound broccoli florets

1/2 cup white rice

1/2 cup tomato puree

1 cup chicken broth

1/2 teaspoon paprika

1/2 teaspoon Italian seasoning blend

Kosher salt and freshly ground pepper, to taste

2 ounces cheddar cheese, shredded

DIRECTIONS

Press the "Sauté" button and melt 1 tablespoon of butter. Once hot, cook the chicken breast until it is golden brown on both sides.

Shred the chicken with two forks. Add it back to the inner pot. Add the shallots, garlic, broccoli, rice, tomato puree, and chicken broth; stir in the remaining butter.

Season with the paprika, Italian seasonings, salt, and black pepper.

Secure the lid. Choose the "Rice" mode and cook for 10 minutes at Low pressure. Once cooking is complete, use a natural pressure release for 10 minutes; carefully remove the lid.

Top with cheese. Seal the lid again and let it sit in the residual heat until the cheese melts. Serve immediately.

426. Red Fisherman's Risotto

(Ready in about 45 minutes)

Per serving: 442 Calories; 23.5g Fat; 36.2g Carbs; 39.4g Protein; 4.6g Sugars; 13.4g Fiber

INGREDIENTS

1 tablespoon butter, melted
1/2 onion, chopped
1 clove garlic, minced
1/4 cup rice wine

1 cup red rice
1 tablespoon Shoyu sauce
2 cups shellfish stock
1/2 pound shrimp, deveined

Sea salt and ground black pepper, to taste
2 tablespoons goat cheese, crumbled

DIRECTIONS

Press the "Sauté" button and melt the butter. Once hot, cook the onion and garlic for 2 to 3 minutes or until they are just tender.
Add a splash of rice wine; deglaze the bottom of the inner pot with a wooden spoon. Now, stir in the red rice, wine, Shoyu sauce, and shellfish stock to the inner pot.
Secure the lid. Choose the "Multigrain" mode and cook for 20 minutes at High pressure. Once cooking is complete, use a natural pressure release for 10 minutes; carefully remove the lid.
Next, stir in the shrimp, salt, and black pepper.
Secure the lid. Choose the "Manual" mode and cook for 4 minutes at High pressure. Once cooking is complete, use a quick pressure release; carefully remove the lid. Serve garnished with goat cheese and enjoy!

427. Hearty Louisiana-Style Gumbo

(Ready in about 15 minutes)

Per serving: 562 Calories; 18.4g Fat; 53g Carbs; 45g Protein; 5.9g Sugars; 3.5g Fiber

INGREDIENTS

1 tablespoon olive oil
2 ounces Andouille sausage, sliced
1/4 pound chicken cutlets, cut into 1-inch cubes
1/2 onion, chopped
1 bell pepper, seeded and chopped
1 stalk celery, chopped

2 cloves garlic, minced
1/2 tablespoon pimentón de la Vera
1 tablespoon Cajun seasoning
Sea salt and ground black pepper, to taste
1/2 teaspoon cayenne pepper
1 ripe tomato, pureed

1/2 tablespoon fish sauce
1/2 cup white rice
1 cup chicken broth
1/2 pound shrimp, deveined
1 tablespoon fresh parsley, chopped

DIRECTIONS

Press the "Sauté" button and heat the olive oil. Once hot, sauté the Andouille sausage and chicken cutlets for 4 to 5 minutes until they are brown; reserve.
Now, cook the onion in pan drippings; cook until it is tender and translucent.
Add the remaining ingredients, except for the fresh parsley, to the inner pot.
Secure the lid. Choose the "Manual" mode and cook for 4 minutes at High pressure. Once cooking is complete, use a quick pressure release; carefully remove the lid.
Serve garnished with fresh parsley. Enjoy!

428. Spanish Lentejas Caseras

(Ready in about 50 minutes)

Per serving: 464 Calories; 5.1g Fat; 87.7g Carbs; 18.4g Protein; 1.9g Sugars; 8.5g Fiber

INGREDIENTS

3/4 cup brown jasmine rice
7 cups water
1/2 teaspoon sea salt

1 cup kale, torn into pieces
1/2 cup yellow lentils
Salt and ground black pepper, to taste

1 tablespoon pepitas, toasted

DIRECTIONS

Place the rice, water, and salt in the inner pot.
Secure the lid. Choose the "Manual" mode and cook for 25 minutes at High pressure. Once cooking is complete, use a natural pressure release for 20 minutes; carefully remove the lid.
Add the kale, lentils, salt, and black pepper to the inner pot.
Secure the lid. Choose the "Manual" mode and cook for 2 minutes at High pressure. Once cooking is complete, use a quick pressure release; carefully remove the lid.
Serve in individual bowls garnished with toasted pepitas.

429. Pakistani-Style Corn Pilaf

(Ready in about 30 minutes)

Per serving: 441 Calories; 9.3g Fat; 76.2g Carbs; 9.1g Protein; 3.1g Sugars; 5.1g Fiber

INGREDIENTS

1 tablespoon ghee
1/2 shallot, chopped
1 garlic clove, minced
1 cup basmati rice, rinsed
1 cup vegetable broth
Sea salt and white pepper, to taste

1/2 teaspoon coriander seeds
1/2 teaspoon black cardamom
1 tez patta (bay leaf)
1/2 teaspoon turmeric powder
1/2 cup sweet corn kernels, thawed

DIRECTIONS

Press the "Sauté" button and melt the ghee. Once hot, cook the shallot for 4 minutes or until just tender and fragrant. Stir in the garlic and cook an additional minute or until aromatic.

Now, add the basmati rice, broth, and spices.

Secure the lid. Choose the "Manual" mode and cook for 4 minutes at High pressure. Once cooking is complete, use a natural pressure release for 15 minutes; carefully remove the lid.

Add the sweet corn kernels and seal the lid again. Let it sit in the residual heat until thoroughly heated. Enjoy!

430. Mushroom Risotto with Romano Cheese

(Ready in about 30 minutes)

Per serving: 348 Calories; 13.5g Fat; 42.6g Carbs; 10g Protein; 3.7g Sugars; 2.9g Fiber

INGREDIENTS

1 tablespoon olive oil
1/2 onion, chopped
1/2 teaspoon garlic, minced
1 cup Cremini mushrooms, chopped
1/2 teaspoon basil
1/2 teaspoon thyme

Sea salt and ground black pepper, to taste
1/4 cup Sauvignon Blanc
1/2 cup Arborio rice
2 cups vegetable broth
1/4 cup Romano cheese, grated

DIRECTIONS

Press the "Sauté" button and heat the olive oil until sizzling. Then, cook the onion until tender and translucent.

Now, stir in the garlic and mushrooms; cook until they are just tender or about 3 minutes.

Add the basil, thyme, salt, black pepper, Sauvignon Blanc, rice, and vegetable broth.

Secure the lid. Choose the "Manual" mode and cook for 4 minutes at High pressure. Once cooking is complete, use a natural pressure release for 15 minutes; carefully remove the lid.

Divide between individual bowls and serve garnished with Romano cheese. Bon appétit!

431. Rizogalo (Greek Rice Pudding)

(Ready in about 30 minutes)

Per serving: 533 Calories; 14.1g Fat; 87.5g Carbs; 26.7g Protein; 2.5g Sugars; 2.4g Fiber

INGREDIENTS

1 tablespoon butter
3/4 cup white rice
2 cups milk
1 cup water
1 ounce sugar

1 (3-inch strip) of lemon rind
1/2 teaspoon vanilla extract
1/2 teaspoon ground cinnamon
2 tablespoons honey

DIRECTIONS

Place the butter, rice, milk, sugar, lemon rind, and vanilla extract in the inner pot.

Secure the lid. Choose the "Rice" mode and cook for 10 minutes at Low pressure. Once cooking is complete, use a natural pressure release for 15 minutes; carefully remove the lid.

Ladle your rizogalo into four serving bowls; top with cinnamon and honey and serve at room temperature.

432. Pakistani Jeera Rice

(Ready in about 30 minutes)

Per serving: 374 Calories; 11.3g Fat; 60.1g Carbs; 6.9g Protein; 1.7g Sugars; 3.2g Fiber

INGREDIENTS

3/4 cup rice basmati rice, rinsed
1/2 cup water
1 cup cream of celery soup
1/2 green chili deveined and chopped

Sea salt and ground black pepper, to taste
1 bay leaf
1/2 teaspoon Jeera (cumin seeds)
1 tablespoon sesame oil

DIRECTIONS

Place all ingredients in the inner pot. Stir until everything is well combined.
Secure the lid. Choose the "Rice" mode and cook for 10 minutes at Low pressure. Once cooking is complete, use a natural pressure release for 15 minutes; carefully remove the lid.
Serve with Indian main dishes of choice. Enjoy!

433. Authentic Sushi Rice

(Ready in about 30 minutes)

Per serving: 391 Calories; 1.9g Fat; 83g Carbs; 7.1g Protein; 3.5g Sugars; 3g Fiber

INGREDIENTS

1 cup sushi rice, rinsed
1 cup water
2 tablespoons rice vinegar

1/2 tablespoon brown sugar
1/2 teaspoon salt
1 tablespoon soy sauce

DIRECTIONS

Place the sushi rice and water in the inner pot of your Instant Pot.
Secure the lid. Choose the "Rice" mode and cook for 10 minutes at Low pressure. Once cooking is complete, use a natural pressure release for 15 minutes; carefully remove the lid.
Meanwhile, whisk the rice vinegar, sugar, salt and soy sauce in a mixing dish; microwave the sauce for 1 minute.
Pour the sauce over the sushi rice; stir to combine. Assemble your sushi rolls and enjoy!

434. Rice and Chicken Gratin

(Ready in about 50 minutes)

Per serving: 616 Calories; 29.1g Fat; 58g Carbs; 29.3g Protein; 11.2g Sugars; 8.3g Fiber

INGREDIENTS

1 tablespoon butter
1 cup chicken breasts, cut into chunks
1/2 onion, chopped
1 celery rib, chopped
1/2 teaspoon garlic, minced
1/2 cup wild rice

1 cup cream of celery soup
1/2 cup tomato sauce
Sea salt and ground black pepper, to taste
1/2 cup sour cream
1/2 cup goat cheese, crumbled

DIRECTIONS

Press the "Sauté" button and melt the butter. Once hot, cook the chicken until it is no longer pink; reserve.
Now, sauté the onion in the pan drippings until tender. Then, add the celery and garlic; continue to sauté an additional minute or so.
Add the wild rice, cream of celery soup, tomato sauce, salt, and black pepper to the inner pot. Stir in the reserved chicken.
Secure the lid. Choose the "Manual" mode and cook for 30 minutes at High pressure. Once cooking is complete, use a natural pressure release for 15 minutes; carefully remove the lid.
Mix the sour cream with goat cheese; place the cheese mixture over your casserole. Let it sit, covered, for 10 minutes before serving. Bon appétit!

435. Mexican Arroz Rojo with Peppers

(Ready in about 45 minutes)

Per serving: 486 Calories; 4.4g Fat; 96.3g Carbs; 9.7g Protein; 6.5g Sugars; 7.3g Fiber

INGREDIENTS

1/2 tablespoon olive oil
1/2 onion, chopped
1/2 teaspoon garlic paste
1/2 teaspoon ginger, grated
1 sweet pepper, deveined and sliced
1/2 red chili pepper, minced

1 cup red rice
1 cup water
1 cube tomato-chicken bouillon
1/3 cup tomato sauce
1/2 tablespoon taco seasoning
Sea salt, to taste

DIRECTIONS

Press the "Sauté" button and heat the oil until sizzling. Now, sauté the onion until just tender or about 3 minutes.
Add the remaining ingredients and stir to combine.
Secure the lid. Choose the "Manual" mode and cook for 30 minutes at High pressure. Once cooking is complete, use a natural pressure release for 10 minutes; carefully remove the lid.
Taste, adjust the seasonings and serve with salsa on the side. Enjoy!

436. Easy Chicken Feijoada

(Ready in about 40 minutes)

Per serving: 480 Calories; 7.3g Fat; 56g Carbs; 45.6g Protein; 1.8g Sugars; 8.1g Fiber

INGREDIENTS

1/2 cup brown rice
1/2 cup navy beans, drained and rinsed
3/4 cup chicken stock
1/4 cup salsa
1 garlic clove, minced
1 sweet pepper, chopped

1/2 teaspoon cumin
1/2 teaspoon salt
1/2 teaspoon black peppercorns
1 bay leaf
3/4 pound chicken cutlets

DIRECTIONS

Place all ingredients in the inner pot. Stir until everything is well combined.
Secure the lid. Choose the "Bean/Chili" mode and cook for 25 minutes at High pressure. Once cooking is complete, use a natural pressure release for 10 minutes; carefully remove the lid.
Ladle into individual bowls and serve warm. Enjoy!

437. Kidney Beans with Rice and Marinara Sauce

(Ready in about 40 minutes)

Per serving: 384 Calories; 2g Fat; 75g Carbs; 15.8g Protein; 5.6g Sugars; 9.6g Fiber

INGREDIENTS

1/2 cup brown rice
1/2 cup kidney beans
1/2 cup marinara sauce
1 tablespoon fresh parsley, chopped

1 tablespoon fresh scallions, chopped
1/2 tablespoon fresh basil, chopped
1 green garlic stalk, chopped
1 ½ cups vegetable broth

DIRECTIONS

Add all ingredients to the inner pot of your Instant Pot.
Secure the lid. Choose the "Manual" mode and cook for 25 minutes at High pressure. Once cooking is complete, use a natural pressure release for 15 minutes; carefully remove the lid.
Ladle into individual bowls and serve warm. Enjoy!

438. One-Pot Kinoko Gohan

(Ready in about 30 minutes)

Per serving: 426 Calories; 15.3g Fat; 60.5g Carbs; 7.8g Protein; 2.3g Sugars; 3.9g Fiber

INGREDIENTS

2 tablespoons shoyu

1 cup maitake mushrooms, sliced

1 cup shiitake mushrooms, sliced

2 tablespoons mirin

2 tablespoons sake

1 ½ cups water

1 piece dried kombu

2 tablespoons sesame oil

1/2 shallot, chopped

1/2 teaspoon garlic, minced

3/4 cup Kokuho Rose rice

1 cup chicken stock

Kosher salt and ground black pepper, to taste

DIRECTIONS

Press the "Sauté" button to preheat your Instant Pot. Put the shoyu, mushrooms, mirin, sake, water, and dried kombu.
Bring to a simmer on the lowest setting; allow it to cook for 5 to 6 minutes. Discard the kombu and save for another use.
Add the other ingredients to the inner pot.

Secure the lid. Choose the "Manual" mode and cook for 6 minutes at High pressure.

Once cooking is complete, use a natural pressure release for 15 minutes; carefully remove the lid. Serve in individual bowls and enjoy!

439. Classic Spanish Rice Pudding

(Ready in about 25 minutes)

Per serving: 447 Calories; 6.4g Fat; 74.6g Carbs; 10.7g Protein; 24.7g Sugars; 2.5g Fiber

INGREDIENTS

3/4 cup white rice

1 ½ cups milk

2 tablespoons honey

1/2 teaspoon vanilla paste

1/2 teaspoon ground cinnamon

2 (2-inch) strips lemon zest

DIRECTIONS

Place all ingredients in the inner pot.

Secure the lid. Choose the "Manual" mode and cook for 4 minutes at High pressure. Once cooking is complete, use a natural pressure release for 15 minutes; carefully remove the lid.

Fluff the rice with a fork and serve immediately.

440. Easy Egg Drop Soup

(Ready in about 35 minutes)

Per serving: 380 Calories; 12.1g Fat; 56g Carbs; 14.3g Protein; 5.1g Sugars; 5.3g Fiber

INGREDIENTS

3/4 cup wild rice

2 cups chicken bone broth

1/2 onion, chopped

1 clove garlic, pressed

1/2 carrot, chopped

1/2 parsnip, chopped

1 bay leaf

1/2 tablespoon Cajun seasoning

Sea salt and cracked black pepper, to taste

1 tablespoon olive oil

1 tablespoons cornstarch

1 egg, whisked

1 tablespoon fresh cilantro, chopped

DIRECTIONS

Add the wild rice, broth, vegetables, spices, and olive oil to the inner pot of your Instant Pot.

Secure the lid. Choose the "Soup/Broth" mode and cook for 30 minutes at High pressure. Once cooking is complete, use a quick pressure release; carefully remove the lid.

Mix the cornstarch with 4 tablespoons of water and the whisked egg. Stir the mixture into the cooking liquid.

Press the "Sauté" button and let it simmer for 3 to 4 minutes or until heated through.

Ladle into individual bowls. Top each serving with fresh cilantro and serve warm. Bon appétit!

441. One-Pot Indian Khichri

(Ready in about 30 minutes)

Per serving: 481 Calories; 8.4g Fat; 84.3g Carbs; 17.2g Protein; 1.6g Sugars; 7.3g Fiber

INGREDIENTS

1 tablespoon butter
1/2 teaspoon cumin seeds
1 bay leaf
1/2 shallot, sliced

3/4 cup basmati rice
1/2 cup moong dal lentils
1/2 teaspoon ground turmeric
Sea salt and ground black pepper, to taste

DIRECTIONS

Press the "Sauté" button and melt the butter. Once hot, sauté the cumin seeds and bay leaf until they are fragrant.
Now, add the shallot and continue to sauté an additional 3 minute or until it is just tender.
Add the remaining ingredients; stir to combine.
Secure the lid. Choose the "Manual" mode and cook for 4 minutes at High pressure. Once cooking is complete, use a natural pressure release for 15 minutes; carefully remove the lid. Serve warm.

442. Easy Korean Bowl

(Ready in about 45 minutes)

Per serving: 426 Calories; 16.1g Fat; 44g Carbs; 26.3g Protein; 6.3g Sugars; 2g Fiber

INGREDIENTS

1/2 tablespoon lard, melted
1/4 pound ground turkey
1/4 pound ground beef
1 garlic clove, minced
1 tablespoon brown sugar

1 tablespoon Worcestershire sauce
1/2 teaspoon crushed red pepper flakes
Sea salt and ground black pepper, to taste
1/2 cup brown rice

DIRECTIONS

Press the "Sauté" button and melt the lard. Once hot, cook the ground meat until no longer pink or about 3 to 4 minutes.
Then, stir in the garlic and let it cook an additional minute or until it is aromatic.
Add the remaining ingredients; stir to combine.
Secure the lid. Choose the "Manual" mode and cook for 22 minutes at High pressure. Once cooking is complete, use a natural pressure release for 10 minutes; carefully remove the lid.

443. Rice with Cheese and Vegetables

(Ready in about 25 minutes)

Per serving: 417 Calories; 10.1g Fat; 65g Carbs; 14.4g Protein; 4.2g Sugars; 4g Fiber

INGREDIENTS

3/4 cup white rice, rinsed
1/2 onion, chopped
1/2 cup carrots, chopped
1/2 cup celery ribs, chopped
Sea salt and ground black pepper, to taste

1/2 teaspoon dried dill weed
1 cup roasted vegetable broth
1/4 cup Swiss cheese, shredded
1/4 cup Manchego cheese, shredded

DIRECTIONS

Add the rice, onion, carrots, celery, salt, black pepper, dill, and vegetable broth to the inner pot.
Secure the lid. Choose the "Manual" mode and cook for 5 minutes at High pressure. Once cooking is complete, use a natural pressure release for 15 minutes; carefully remove the lid.
After that, stir in the cheese; stir well to combine and seal the lid. Let it sit in the residual heat until the cheese melts. Bon appétit!

444. Spicy Enchilada Rice with Cheese

(Ready in about 35 minutes)

Per serving: 586 Calories; 15.3g Fat; 94g Carbs; 22.1g Protein; 9.1g Sugars; 13g Fiber

INGREDIENTS

1 tablespoon canola oil
1/2 onion, chopped
1 garlic clove, minced
1 sweet pepper, seeded and chopped
1/2 habanero pepper, seeded and minced
1 cup vegetable broth

1/2 cup long grain rice, rinsed
1/2 cup pinto beans, boiled
1/2 cup sweet corn, frozen and thawed
1/2 teaspoon cumin powder
1/4 teaspoon Mexican oregano
Sea salt and ground black pepper, to taste

1/2 cup enchilada sauce
1/3 cup Mexican blend cheese, shredded
1 tablespoon fresh cilantro, roughly chopped

DIRECTIONS

Press the "Sauté" button to preheat your Instant Pot and add the oil. Once hot, cook the onion, garlic, and peppers until they are just tender and fragrant.

Next, add the vegetable broth followed by rice, beans, corn, cumin powder, oregano, salt, black pepper, and enchilada sauce; do not stir.

Secure the lid. Choose the "Manual" mode and cook for 5 minutes at High pressure. Once cooking is complete, use a natural pressure release for 15 minutes; carefully remove the lid.

After that, stir in Mexican blend cheese and seal the lid again. Let it sit in the residual heat for 5 to 10 minutes until the cheese melts. Serve with fresh cilantro and enjoy!

445. Old-Fashioned Pork Pilaf

(Ready in about 30 minutes)

Per serving: 552 Calories; 25.1g Fat; 50.4g Carbs; 29.2g Protein; 3.6g Sugars; 4.1g Fiber

INGREDIENTS

1/4 pound pork sausage, sliced
1/4 pound ground beef
1/2 leek, chopped
1 garlic clove, minced
1/2 celery stalk, chopped

1 carrot, chopped
1 parsnip, chopped
1 sweet pepper, chopped
1/2 poblano pepper, chopped
1/2 tablespoon Old Bay seasoning

1/2 teaspoon dried parsley
1 tablespoon fish sauce
1/2 cup Arborio rice, rinsed
1 cup beef broth

DIRECTIONS

Press the "Sauté" button to preheat your Instant Pot. Once hot, cook the pork sausage and ground beef until they have browned.

Add the leek, garlic, celery, carrots, parsnip, peppers, seasoning, and fish sauce to the inner pot. Continue to cook until the vegetables have softened.

Stir in the rice and beef broth; stir to combine well.

Secure the lid. Choose the "Rice" mode and cook for 10 minutes at Low pressure. Once cooking is complete, use a natural pressure release for 15 minutes; carefully remove the lid. Fluff your rice with a fork before serving. Bon appétit!

446. One-Pot Wild Rice Pilaf

(Ready in about 50 minutes)

Per serving: 277 Calories; 4g Fat; 57.2g Carbs; 6.8g Protein; 22.1g Sugars; 4.1g Fiber

INGREDIENTS

1/2 tablespoon coconut oil
1 carrot, grated
1/4 cup raisins, soaked

2 tablespoons granulated sugar
1/2 cup wild rice
1 cup water

A pinch of salt
A pinch of saffron
1/4 teaspoon cardamom powder

DIRECTIONS

Press the "Sauté" button to preheat your Instant Pot. Once hot, melt the coconut oil. Now, cook the grated carrots for 2 to 3 minutes or until they are tender.

Add the other ingredients to the inner pot.

Secure the lid. Choose the "Manual" mode and cook for 30 minutes at High pressure. Once cooking is complete, use a natural pressure release for 15 minutes; carefully remove the lid. Serve warm.

EGGS & DAIRY

447. Easy Hash Brown Casserole

(Ready in about 30 minutes)

Per serving: 435 Calories; 28.8g Fat; 24.2g Carbs; 21.6g Protein; 3.4g Sugars; 3.2g Fiber

INGREDIENTS

2 ounces bacon, chopped
1/2 onion, chopped
3/4 cup frozen hash browns
4 eggs
1/4 cup milk

1/4 cup Swiss cheese, shredded
1/2 teaspoon garlic powder
1/4 teaspoon turmeric powder
Kosher salt and ground black pepper, to taste

DIRECTIONS

Place 1 cup of water and a metal trivet in the inner pot.

Press the "Sauté" button and cook the bacon until it is crisp and browned. Add in the onions and cook for 3 to 4 minutes, stirring occasionally. Stir in the frozen hash browns and cook until slightly thawed. Grease an oven-proof dish with cooking oil.

In a mixing bowl, whisk the eggs, milk, shredded cheese, garlic powder, turmeric powder, salt and black pepper; now add the bacon/onion mixture to the egg mixture.

Spoon the egg mixture into the prepared dish. Lower the dish onto the trivet.

Secure the lid. Choose the "Manual" mode and cook for 20 minutes at High pressure. Once cooking is complete, use a quick pressure release; carefully remove the lid. Bon appétit!

448. Deviled Eggs with Paprika and Cheese

(Ready in about 10 minutes)

Per serving: 205 Calories; 15.3g Fat; 1.9g Carbs; 14.1g Protein; 1.1g Sugars; 0.3g Fiber

INGREDIENTS

4 eggs
1/4 cup Cottage cheese, crumbled
1 tablespoon butter, softened

1 tablespoon fresh parsley, minced
1/2 teaspoon paprika
Sea salt and ground black pepper, to taste

DIRECTIONS

Place 1 cup of water and a steamer rack in the inner pot. Arrange the eggs on the rack.

Secure the lid. Choose the "Manual" mode and cook for 5 minutes at High pressure. Once cooking is complete, use a quick pressure release; carefully remove the lid.

Peel the eggs and slice them into halves.

In a mixing bowl, thoroughly combine the Cottage cheese, butter, parsley, paprika, sea salt, and black pepper. Stir in the egg yolks. Stir to combine well.

Use a piping bag to fill the egg white halves. Place on a nice serving platter and enjoy!

449. Eggs with Cheese and Chanterelles

(Ready in about 30 minutes)

Per serving: 417 Calories; 33g Fat; 9.6g Carbs; 20.2g Protein; 4.7g Sugars; 1.8g Fiber

INGREDIENTS

1 tablespoon olive oil
1/2 medium onion, chopped
1 clove garlic, minced
1/2 cup Mexican cheese blend, crumbled
3/4 cup Chanterelle mushrooms, chopped

1 bell pepper, sliced
1/2 Poblano pepper, seeded and minced
4 eggs
2 ounces cream cheese
Sea salt and ground black pepper, to taste

DIRECTIONS

Add 1 cup of water and a metal rack to the inner pot of your Instant Pot. Spray a souffle dish and set aside.

Mix all ingredients until well combined. Scrape the mixture into the prepared dish. Lower the souffle dish onto the rack.

Secure the lid. Choose the "Manual" mode and cook for 11 minutes at High pressure. Once cooking is complete, use a natural pressure release for 15 minutes; carefully remove the lid.

Serve with salsa if desired. Enjoy!

450. Queso Fundido Dip

(Ready in about 10 minutes)

Per serving: 226 Calories; 16.2g Fat; 11.1g Carbs; 9.2g Protein; 8.1g Sugars; 0.1g Fiber

INGREDIENTS

1 tablespoon butter
1 tablespoon all-purpose flour
1/2 cup whole milk

2 ounces Monterey Jack, shredded
Kosher salt, to taste
1/2 teaspoon hot sauce

DIRECTIONS

Press the "Sauté" button and melt the butter. Now, add the flour and stir to combine well.
Gradually pour in the milk, stirring continuously to avoid clumps. Bring to a boil and press the "Cancel" button.
Add in the Monterey Jack cheese and stir until cheese has melted; add the salt and hot sauce. Serve warm with tortilla chips if desired. Bon appétit!

451. Silver Dollar Pancakes

(Ready in about 25 minutes)

Per serving: 256 Calories; 3.7g Fat; 47.3g Carbs; 7.7g Protein; 19g Sugars; 1.7g Fiber

INGREDIENTS

1/2 cup all-purpose flour
1 teaspoons baking powder
1/4 teaspoon salt
4 tablespoons milk

1 egg, whisked
1 tablespoon maple syrup
1/4 cup raisins
1 tablespoon almonds, chopped

DIRECTIONS

Add 1 cup of water and a metal trivet to the inner pot.
Mix all ingredients until everything is well combined. Pour the batter into a muffin tin that is previously greased with cooking spray. Lower the muffin tin onto the trivet.
Secure the lid. Choose the "Manual" mode and cook for 8 minutes at High pressure. Once cooking is complete, use a natural pressure release for 10 minutes; carefully remove the lid. Bon appétit!

452. Home-Style Cheese

(Ready in about 20 minutes + chilling time)

Per serving: 223 Calories; 15.1g Fat; 17.1g Carbs; 4.8g Protein; 17g Sugars; 0g Fiber

INGREDIENTS

1 cup whole milk
1/2 cup double cream
1/4 teaspoon kosher salt
1 tablespoon lemon juice

DIRECTIONS

Place the milk, double cream, and salt in the inner pot of your Instant Pot and stir to combine well.
Secure the lid. Choose the "Manual" mode and cook for 5 minutes at Low pressure. Once cooking is complete, use a natural pressure release for 10 minutes; carefully remove the lid.
Add the lemon juice and stir the mixture one more time.
Line a strainer with cheesecloth and pour the mixture into the cheesecloth. Allow the curds to continue to drain in the strainer for about 1 hour. Discard the whey.
Pat your cheese into a ball and remove from the cheesecloth. This cheese will last about a week in your refrigerator. Bon appétit!

453. Dilled Cheese Dip

(Ready in about 15 minutes)

Per serving: 285 Calories; 20.3g Fat; 14.2g Carbs; 10.1g Protein; 9.4g Sugars; 0.5g Fiber

INGREDIENTS

2 tablespoons butter

1/4 teaspoon onion powder

1/4 teaspoon garlic powder

1/4 teaspoon dried dill weed

Sea salt and ground black pepper, to taste

1/2 tablespoon tapioca starch

1/2 cup whole milk

2 ounces Swiss cheese, grated

DIRECTIONS

Press the "Sauté" button and melt the butter. Now, add the onion powder, garlic powder, dill, salt, and black pepper. Stir in the tapioca starch and stir to combine well.

Gradually pour in the milk, stirring continuously to avoid clumps. Bring to a boil and press the "Cancel" button.

Add in the Swiss cheese and stir until the cheese has melted. Serve warm with breadsticks or veggie sticks. Bon appétit!

454. Keto Mac n' Cheese

(Ready in about 12 minutes)

Per serving: 211 Calories; 13.2g Fat; 13.4g Carbs; 11.3g Protein; 6g Sugars; 2.7g Fiber

INGREDIENTS

1/2 pound cauliflower florets

1/4 cup heavy cream

2 ounces Ricotta cheese

1/2 cup Cheddar cheese, shredded

Sea salt and ground white pepper, to taste

1/4 teaspoon garlic powder

1/2 teaspoon shallot powder

1/2 teaspoon celery seeds

1/2 teaspoon red pepper flakes

2 tablespoons Parmesan cheese

DIRECTIONS

Place 1 cup of water and a steamer basket in the inner pot of your Instant Pot. Throw the cauliflower florets into the steamer basket.

Secure the lid. Choose the "Manual" mode and cook for 2 minutes at High pressure. Once cooking is complete, use a quick pressure release; carefully remove the lid. Drain and reserve.

Press the "Sauté" button and use the lowest setting. Now, cook the heavy cream, Ricotta cheese, Cheddar cheese, and spices; let it simmer until the cheeses has melted.

Add in the cauliflower and gently stir to combine. Scatter the Parmesan cheese over the cauliflower and cheese and serve warm. Bon appétit!

455. Macaroni and Cheese

(Ready in about 15 minutes)

Per serving: 544 Calories; 20.1g Fat; 46g Carbs; 22.3g Protein; 9.6g Sugars; 2.8g Fiber

INGREDIENTS

6 ounces elbow macaroni

1 tablespoon butter

1/2 teaspoon celery seeds

Kosher salt, to taste

1 cup water

2 ounces milk

1 cup cheddar cheese, shredded

1/4 cup Parmesan cheese, shredded

DIRECTIONS

Throw the elbow macaroni, butter, celery seeds, salt, and water into the inner pot.

Secure the lid. Choose the "Manual" mode and cook for 10 minutes at High pressure. Once cooking is complete, use a quick pressure release; carefully remove the lid.

Next, stir in the milk and half of the cheeses. Stir until the cheeses has melted; add the second half of the cheeses and stir to combine well. The sauce will thicken as it cools. Bon appétit!

456. Breakfast Muffins with Ham

(Ready in about 13 minutes)

Per serving: 300 Calories; 17.5g Fat; 5.5g Carbs; 24.1g Protein; 1.4g Sugars; 0.6g Fiber

INGREDIENTS

4 eggs
1/4 teaspoon ground black pepper, or more to taste
1/2 teaspoon paprika
Sea salt, to taste
1/2 cup green peppers, seeded and chopped
3 ounces ham, chopped

1/4 cup sour cream
1/4 cup Swiss cheese, shredded
1 tablespoon parsley, chopped
1 tablespoon cilantro, chopped
1 tablespoon scallions, chopped

DIRECTIONS

Mix all ingredients until everything is well combined.
Add 1 cup of water and a metal rack to the inner pot of your Instant Pot.
Spoon the prepared mixture into silicone molds. Lower the molds onto the prepared trivet.
Secure the lid. Choose the "Manual" mode and cook for 6 minutes at High pressure. Once cooking is complete, use a quick pressure release; carefully remove the lid. Bon appétit!

457. Hard-Boiled Eggs

(Ready in about 10 minutes)

Per serving: 126 Calories; 8.3g Fat; 0.7g Carbs; 11.1g Protein; 0.3g Sugars; 0g Fiber

INGREDIENTS

4 eggs
1/4 teaspoon salt
1/4 teaspoon red pepper flakes, crushed
1 tablespoon fresh chives, chopped

DIRECTIONS

Place 1 cup of water and a steamer rack in the inner pot. Arrange the eggs on the rack.
Secure the lid. Choose the "Manual" mode and cook for 5 minutes at High pressure. Once cooking is complete, use a quick pressure release; carefully remove the lid.
Transfer the eggs to icy-cold water. Now, let them sit in the water bath a few minutes until cool.
Peel your eggs and season with salt and red pepper. Serve garnished with freshly chopped chives. Enjoy!

458. Breakfast Cheese and Egg Frittatas

(Ready in about 10 minutes)

Per serving: 274 Calories; 20g Fat; 5.5g Carbs; 14.6g Protein; 4g Sugars; 0.5g Fiber

INGREDIENTS

4 eggs
4 tablespoons milk
1/2 teaspoon cayenne pepper

Sea salt and ground black pepper, to taste
1/4 cup cream cheese

DIRECTIONS

Place 1 cup of water and a metal trivet in the inner pot.
Mix all ingredients until everything is well incorporated. Pour the egg mixture into silicone molds.
Lower the molds onto the prepared trivet.
Secure the lid. Choose the "Manual" mode and cook for 5 minutes at High pressure. Once cooking is complete, use a quick pressure release; carefully remove the lid. Bon appétit!

459. Greek-Style Stuffed Eggs

(Ready in about 10 minutes)

Per serving: 226 Calories; 1.6g Fat; 1.9g Carbs; 11.3g Protein; 0.8g Sugars; 0.3g Fiber

INGREDIENTS

4 eggs

1/4 teaspoon coarse sea salt

1/4 teaspoon black pepper, to taste

1/4 teaspoon turmeric powder

1 teaspoon balsamic vinegar

2 tablespoons Greek-style yogurt

2 tablespoons mayonnaise

1/2 teaspoon fresh dill, chopped

DIRECTIONS

Place 1 cup of water and a steamer rack in the inner pot. Arrange the eggs on the rack.

Secure the lid. Choose the "Manual" mode and cook for 5 minutes at High pressure. Once cooking is complete, use a quick pressure release; carefully remove the lid.

Peel the eggs and slice them into halves.

In a mixing bowl, thoroughly combine the sea salt, black pepper, turmeric powder, vinegar, yogurt, and mayonnaise. Stir in the egg yolks.

Use a piping bag to fill the egg white halves. Garnish with fresh dill. Bon appétit!

460. Spanish Tortilla with Manchego Cheese

(Ready in about 30 minutes)

Per serving: 450 Calories; 29.2g Fat; 26g Carbs; 18.9g Protein; 2.3g Sugars; 2.3g Fiber

INGREDIENTS

4 eggs

4 ounces hash browns

1 tablespoon olive oil

1/2 onion, sliced

Sea salt and ground black pepper, or to taste

1/2 teaspoon taco seasoning mix

1/2 teaspoon fresh garlic, minced

1/4 cup milk

2 ounces Manchego cheese, grated

DIRECTIONS

Add 1 cup of water and a metal rack to the inner pot of your Instant Pot. Spritz a souffle dish with nonstick cooking oil.

In a mixing bowl, thoroughly combine all ingredients, except for the Manchego cheese; mix until everything is well incorporated.

Scrape the mixture into the prepared souffle dish.

Secure the lid. Choose the "Manual" mode and cook for 17 minutes at High pressure. Once cooking is complete, use a natural pressure release for 10 minutes; carefully remove the lid.

Top with Manchego cheese and seal the lid again. Let it sit in the residual heat until the cheese melts. Enjoy!

461. The Best Homemade Yogurt Ever

(Ready in about 9 hours)

Per serving: 112 Calories; 5.9g Fat; 8.7g Carbs; 5.7g Protein; 9.2g Sugars; 0g Fiber

INGREDIENTS

1 ½ cups milk

1 teaspoon prepared yogurt with cultures

A pinch of salt

DIRECTIONS

Pour the milk into the inner pot. Press the "Yogurt" button; adjust the temperature until the screen reads "Boil".

Let it sit for 5 minutes and then remove the inner pot. Allow the milk to cool to about 115 degrees F. Whisk in the prepared yogurt with the cultures; add a pinch of salt.

Add the inner pot back to the Instant Pot.

Secure the lid. Choose the "Yogurt" mode and adjust until the screen reads 8:00. Once the cycle is complete, remove the lid.

Transfer the prepared yogurt to your refrigerator until ready to use. Bon appétit!

462. Frittata with Mushrooms and Asiago Cheese

(Ready in about 15 minutes)

Per serving: 309 Calories; 26g Fat; 5.2g Carbs; 14.1g Protein; 2.3g Sugars; 1g Fiber

INGREDIENTS

3 eggs

1/4 cup double cream

1/4 cup Asiago cheese, shredded

Sea salt and freshly ground black pepper, to taste

1/2 teaspoon cayenne pepper

1 tablespoon olive oil

1/2 yellow onion, finely chopped

1 clove garlic, minced

2ounces Italian brown mushrooms, sliced

1 cup spinach, torn into pieces

1/2 tablespoon Italian seasoning mix

DIRECTIONS

In a mixing bowl, thoroughly combine the eggs, double cream, Asiago cheese, salt, black pepper, and cayenne pepper.

Grease a baking dish with olive oil. Add the remaining ingredients; stir in the egg mixture. Spoon the mixture into the prepared baking dish.

Place 1 cup of water and a metal trivet in the inner pot. Lower the baking dish onto the prepared trivet.

Secure the lid. Choose the "Manual" mode and cook for 5 minutes at High pressure. Once cooking is complete, use a quick pressure release; carefully remove the lid. Bon appétit!

SNACKS & APPETIZERS

463. Sticky Little Smokies

(Ready in about 10 minutes)

Per serving: 206 Calories; 5g Fat; 21.5g Carbs; 7g Protein; 10.2g Sugars; 2.9g Fiber

INGREDIENTS

3 ounces little smokies

1/2 cup roasted vegetable broth

1/4 cup light beer

2 ounces grape jelly

1 tablespoon white vinegar

1/4 cup chili sauce

2 tablespoons brown sugar

1/4 teaspoon jalapeno pepper, minced

DIRECTIONS

Place all ingredients in the inner pot of your Instant Pot.

Secure the lid. Choose the "Manual" mode and cook for 2 minutes at High pressure. Once cooking is complete, use a quick pressure release; carefully remove the lid.

Serve hot or keep on warm in your Instant Pot until ready to serve.

464. Tangy Chicken Wings with Cilantro

(Ready in about 30 minutes)

Per serving: 119 Calories; 4.5g Fat; 4.3g Carbs; 14.1g Protein; 1.9g Sugars; 0.8g Fiber

INGREDIENTS

1 teaspoon butter

4 chicken wings

2 cloves garlic, minced

1/2 teaspoon cayenne pepper

1/2 teaspoon smoked paprika

Sea salt and ground black pepper, to taste

1/2 cup chicken broth

1/2 lime, freshly squeezed

2 tablespoons fresh cilantro, chopped

DIRECTIONS

Press the "Sauté" button and heat the olive oil until sizzling. Once hot, brown the chicken wings for 2 to 3 minutes per side.

Add in the remaining ingredients and toss to coat well.

Secure the lid. Choose the "Manual" mode and cook for 10 minutes at High pressure. Once cooking is complete, use a natural pressure release for 10 minutes; carefully remove the lid.

Broil the chicken wings for about 5 minutes or until they are golden brown. Bon appétit!

465. Chinese-Style Baby Carrots

(Ready in about 10 minutes)

Per serving: 110 Calories; 4.5g Fat; 15.2g Carbs; 2.3g Protein; 7.5g Sugars; 4.2g Fiber

INGREDIENTS

1/2 pound baby carrots, trimmed and scrubbed

1/4 cup orange juice

1/2 cup water

1 tablespoon raisins

1/2 tablespoon soy sauce

1 tablespoon Shaoxing wine

1/2 teaspoon garlic powder

1/2 teaspoon shallot powder

1/2 teaspoon mustard powder

1/4 teaspoon cumin seeds

1 teaspoon butter, at room temperature

1 tablespoon sesame seeds, toasted

DIRECTIONS

Place all ingredients, except for the sesame seeds, in the inner pot of your Instant Pot.

Secure the lid. Choose the "Manual" mode and cook for 2 minutes at High pressure. Once cooking is complete, use a quick pressure release; carefully remove the lid.

Serve in a nice bowl, sprinkle the sesame seeds over the top and enjoy!

466. Cocktail Mushrooms with Herbs

(Ready in about 10 minutes)

Per serving: 92 Calories; 6.2g Fat; 8g Carbs; 3.8g Protein; 2g Sugars; 2g Fiber

INGREDIENTS

6 ounces button mushrooms, brushed clean
1 clove garlic, minced
1/2 teaspoon onion powder
1/2 teaspoon dried basil
1/2 teaspoon dried oregano
1/3 teaspoon dried rosemary

1/2 teaspoon smoked paprika
Coarse sea salt and ground black pepper, to taste
1/2 cup vegetable broth
1 tablespoon butter
1 tablespoon tomato paste

DIRECTIONS

Place the mushrooms, garlic, spices, and broth in the inner pot.
Secure the lid. Choose the "Manual" mode and cook for 4 minutes at High pressure. Once cooking is complete, use a quick pressure release; carefully remove the lid.
Now, stir in the butter and tomato paste. Serve with cocktail sticks or toothpicks. Enjoy!

467. Herby Ribs with Port Wine

(Ready in about 1 hour 45 minutes)

Per serving: 276 Calories; 16.6g Fat; 11g Carbs; 9.7g Protein; 9g Sugars; 0.5g Fiber

INGREDIENTS

1/2 tablespoon lard
1 pound short ribs
Sea salt and ground black pepper, to season
1/4 cup port wine
1/2 teaspoon cayenne pepper
1 tablespoon molasses

1 tablespoon rice vinegar
1 clove of garlic
1 rosemary sprig
1 thyme sprig
1/2 cup beef bone broth

DIRECTIONS

Press the "Sauté" button and melt the lard. Once hot, cook the short ribs for 4 to 5 minutes, turning them periodically to ensure even cooking.
Add the other ingredients.
Secure the lid. Choose the "Manual" mode and cook for 90 minutes at High pressure. Once cooking is complete, use a natural pressure release; carefully remove the lid.
Afterwards, place the short ribs under the broiler until the outside is crisp or about 10 minutes. Transfer the ribs to a platter and serve immediately.

468. Greek-Style Dipping Sauce

(Ready in about 20 minutes)

Per serving: 143 Calories; 11.1g Fat; 9.4g Carbs; 3.4g Protein; 1.6g Sugars; 4.5g Fiber

INGREDIENTS

1 artichoke
2 tablespoons mayonnaise
2 tablespoons Greek yogurt
1 teaspoon Dijon mustard
1/2 teaspoon tzatziki spice mix

DIRECTIONS

Place 1 cup of water and a steamer basket in the inner pot of your Instant Pot.
Place the artichokes in the steamer basket.
Secure the lid. Choose the "Manual" mode and cook for 11 minutes at High pressure. Once cooking is complete, use a quick pressure release; carefully remove the lid.
Meanwhile, whisk the remaining ingredients to prepare the sauce. Serve the artichokes with the Greek sauce on the side. Bon appétit!

469. Candied Nuts, Seeds and Chickpeas

(Ready in about 25 minutes)

Per serving: 395 Calories; 17.5g Fat; 46g Carbs; 10g Protein; 21g Sugars; 5.6g Fiber

INGREDIENTS

2 tablespoons pecans halves

2 tablespoons almonds

1/4 cup canned chickpeas

1 tablespoon sunflower seeds

1 tablespoon pumpkin seeds

1 tablespoon butter

2 tablespoons maple syrup

1/4 teaspoon grated nutmeg

1/4 teaspoon ground ginger

1/4 teaspoon kosher salt

1/4 cup Sultanas

DIRECTIONS

Place all ingredients, except for the Sultanas, in the inner pot of your Instant Pot. Stir to combine well.

Press the "Sauté" button and cook until the butter has melted and the nuts are well coated.

Secure the lid. Choose the "Manual" mode and cook for 10 minutes at High pressure. Once cooking is complete, use a quick pressure release; carefully remove the lid.

Bake on a roasting pan at 370 degrees F for about 8 minutes. Add the Sultanas and stir to combine. Bon appétit!

470. Easy Buffalo Dip

(Ready in about 25 minutes)

Per serving: 237 Calories; 17g Fat; 2g Carbs; 14g Protein; 1.3g Sugars; 0.3g Fiber

INGREDIENTS

1/4 pound chicken breasts, chopped

1 ounce hot sauce

1 tablespoon butter

1 ounce cream cheese, softened

Salt to taste

1 ounce cheddar cheese, shredded

1 tablespoon fresh parsley, chopped

1/2 tablespoon fresh chives, chopped

DIRECTIONS

Add the chicken breasts to the inner pot of your Instant Pot; add in the hot sauce and butter.

Secure the lid. Choose the "Manual" mode and cook for 8 minutes at High pressure. Once cooking is complete, use a quick pressure release; carefully remove the lid.

Stir in the cream cheese and salt. Spoon chicken dip into a baking dish; top with the cheddar cheese and bake at 395 degrees F for about 8 minutes or until cheese is bubbling.

Scatter fresh parsley and chives over the top and serve warm.

471. Light Lettuce Wraps

(Ready in about 20 minutes)

Per serving: 224 Calories; 10.3g Fat; 14g Carbs; 18.6g Protein; 8.4g Sugars; 3.2g Fiber

INGREDIENTS

1/3 pound chicken breasts

1 teaspoon sesame oil

1/2 small onion, finely diced

1 garlic clove, minced

1/2 teaspoon ginger, minced

Kosher salt and ground black pepper, to taste

1 tablespoon hoisin sauce

1/2 tablespoon soy sauce

1 tablespoon rice vinegar

1/2 head butter lettuce, leaves separated

DIRECTIONS

Add the chicken breasts and 1 cup of water to the inner pot of your Instant Pot.

Secure the lid. Choose the "Manual" mode and cook for 8 minutes at High pressure. Once cooking is complete, use a quick pressure release; carefully remove the lid. Shred your chicken with two forks.

Press the "Sauté" button and heat the oil. Once hot, cook the onion and garlic for 3 to 4 minutes or until they are softened.

Now, add the chicken and cook for 2 to 3 minutes more. Add the ginger, salt, black pepper, hoisin sauce, soy sauce, and rice vinegar; let it cook for a few minutes more.

Spoon the chicken mixture into the lettuce leaves, wrap them and serve immediately. Bon appétit!

472. Mediterranean-Style Polenta Bites

(Ready in about 20 minutes)

Per serving: 381 Calories; 22g Fat; 31.1g Carbs; 7.1g Protein; 4.7g Sugars; 2.5g Fiber

INGREDIENTS

1/2 cup cornmeal

1 ½ cups water

1/2 cup milk

1/2 teaspoon kosher salt

1/2 tablespoon butter

1/3 cup cream cheese

1 tablespoon cilantro, finely chopped

1 tablespoon chives, finely chopped

1/2 tablespoon thyme

1/2 teaspoon rosemary

1/2 teaspoon basil

1/3 cup bread crumbs

1 tablespoon olive oil

DIRECTIONS

Add the polenta, water, milk. and salt to the inner pot of your Instant Pot. Press the "Sauté" button and bring the mixture to a simmer. Press the "Cancel" button.

Secure the lid. Choose the "Manual" mode and cook for 8 minutes at High pressure. Once cooking is complete, use a quick pressure release; carefully remove the lid.

Grease a baking pan with butter. Add the cream cheese and herbs to your polenta.

Scoop the hot polenta into the prepared baking pan and refrigerate until firm. Cut into small squares. Spread the breadcrumbs on a large plate; coat each side of the polenta squares with breadcrumbs.

Heat the olive oil in a nonstick pan over medium heat; cook the polenta squares approximately 3 minutes per side or until golden brown. Bon appétit!

473. Italian Pizza Dipping Sauce

(Ready in about 25 minutes)

Per serving: 271 Calories; 16.5g Fat; 15g Carbs; 13.2g Protein; 8.4g Sugars; 4.4g Fiber

INGREDIENTS

2 ounces cream cheese

1/2 cup tomato sauce

1/4 cup mozzarella cheese, shredded

1/3 cup green olives, pitted and sliced

1/3 teaspoon oregano

1/2 teaspoon basil

1/3 teaspoon garlic salt

1/3 cup Romano cheese, shredded

DIRECTIONS

Add 1 ½ cups of water and metal trivet to the inner pot. Spritz a souffle dish with cooking spray.

Place the cream cheese on the bottom of the souffle dish. Add the tomato sauce and mozzarella cheese. Scatter sliced olives over the top.

Add the oregano, basil, and garlic salt. Top with Romano cheese. Lower the dish onto the prepared trivet.

Secure the lid. Choose the "Manual" mode and cook for 18 minutes at High pressure. Once cooking is complete, use a quick pressure release; carefully remove the lid.

Serve with chips or breadsticks if desired. Enjoy!

474. Mexican Nacho Dip

(Ready in about 35 minutes)

Per serving: 246 Calories; 13g Fat; 22.3g Carbs; 12.1g Protein; 5.3g Sugars; 5.4g Fiber

INGREDIENTS

1/2 tablespoon olive oil

1/2 onion, chopped

1 clove garlic, minced

1/2 red chili pepper, finely chopped

1/2 cup pinto beans, rinsed

1/4 cup chunky salsa

1 cup vegetable broth

1/2 teaspoon ground cumin

Kosher salt and ground black pepper, to taste

1/2 ounce package taco seasoning mix

1/2 cup Cheddar cheese, shredded

1/2 cup queso fresco cheese, crumbled

1 tablespoon fresh cilantro, chopped

DIRECTIONS

Press the "Sauté" button and heat the olive oil until sizzling. Once hot, cook the onion for 3 to 4 minutes or until tender and fragrant.

After that, stir in the garlic and chili pepper; continue sautéing an additional 30 to 40 seconds.

Stir in the beans, salsa, broth, cumin, salt, black pepper, and taco seasoning mix.

Secure the lid. Choose the "Bean/Chili" mode and cook for 25 minutes at High pressure. Once cooking is complete, use a quick pressure release; carefully remove the lid.

Then, mash your beans with a potato masher or use your blender. Return to the Instant Pot and press the "Sauté" button; stir in the cheese and let it melt on the lowest setting. Serve garnished with cilantro and enjoy!

475. Sticky Cocktail Meatballs

(Ready in about 20 minutes)

Per serving: 350 Calories; 14.1g Fat; 27.2g Carbs; 25.1g Protein; 14.2g Sugars; 1.8g Fiber

INGREDIENTS

1/4 pound ground chicken
1/4 pound ground turkey
1 egg
1/2 cup tortilla chips, crumbled
1/2 onion, finely chopped

1 garlic clove, minced
1/2 teaspoon basil
Sea salt and ground black pepper, to taste
1/2 tablespoon olive oil
2 ounces grape jelly

DIRECTIONS

In a mixing bowl, thoroughly combine all ingredients, except for the olive oil and grape jelly. Shape the mixture into 24 meatballs.
Press the "Sauté" button and heat the olive oil. Once hot, brown meatballs for 3 to 4 minutes.
Add the grape jelly to the inner pot.
Secure the lid. Choose the "Manual" mode and cook for 6 minutes at High pressure. Once cooking is complete, use a natural pressure release for 5 minutes; carefully remove the lid.
Serve with cocktail sticks and enjoy!

476. Coconut Cinnamon Popcorn

(Ready in about 10 minutes)

Per serving: 235 Calories; 9.5g Fat; 34.2g Carbs; 3.6g Protein; 9.6g Sugars; 5.1g Fiber

INGREDIENTS

1 tablespoon coconut oil
1/4 cup popcorn kernels
3 tablespoons icing sugar
1/2 tablespoon ground cinnamon

DIRECTIONS

Press the "Sauté" button and melt the coconut oil. Stir until it begins to simmer.
Stir in the popcorn kernels and cover. When the popping slows down, press the "Cancel" button.
Toss the freshly popped corn with icing sugar and cinnamon. Toss to evenly coat the popcorn and serve immediately.

477. Fava Dip with Olives

(Ready in about 50 minutes)

Per serving: 138 Calories; 5.5g Fat; 19.1g Carbs; 6.9g Protein; 9.4g Sugars; 7.1g Fiber

INGREDIENTS

1/2 tablespoon olive oil
1/2 red onion, finely chopped
1/2 teaspoon garlic, minced
Sea salt and ground black pepper, to taste
1/3 pound fava beans, rinsed

1/2 teaspoon basil
1/2 teaspoon oregano
1 tablespoon lemon juice
1/4 cup Kalamata olives, pitted
1/2 tablespoon fresh mint leaves, roughly chopped

DIRECTIONS

Press the "Sauté" button and heat the oil. Once hot, cook the onion until tender and translucent.
Now, stir in the garlic and let it cook for 30 seconds more, stirring frequently. Then, add the salt, pepper, fava beans, basil, and oregano. Add enough water to fully submerge the beans.
Secure the lid. Choose the "Bean/Chili" mode and cook for 40 minutes at High pressure. Once cooking is complete, use a natural pressure release for 5 minutes; carefully remove the lid.
Add the lemon juice and puree the mixture with an immersion blender, Transfer to a nice serving bowl and serve garnished with Kalamata olives and mint leaves. Enjoy!

478. Garlicky Party Shrimp

(Ready in about 10 minutes)

Per serving: 210 Calories; 12.2g Fat; 2.8g Carbs; 23.5g Protein; 1.3g Sugars; 0.4g Fiber

INGREDIENTS

1/2 pound shrimp, deveined

2 tablespoons butter

2 tablespoons soy sauce

1 garlic clove, minced

Sea salt and ground black pepper, to taste

1 tablespoon fresh scallions, chopped

DIRECTIONS

Throw all ingredients, except for the scallions, into the inner pot of your Instant Pot.

Secure the lid. Choose the "Manual" mode and cook for 4 minutes at High pressure. Once cooking is complete, use a quick pressure release; carefully remove the lid.

Transfer your shrimp to a nice serving bowl. The sauce will thicken as it cools. Garnish with fresh scallions and serve with toothpicks.

479. Taco Stuffed Pepper Bites

(Ready in about 20 minutes)

Per serving: 204 Calories; 13.7g Fat; 11.2g Carbs; 10.3g Protein; 5.7g Sugars; 1.7g Fiber

INGREDIENTS

1 ounce bacon, chopped

2 tablespoons onion, chopped

1 garlic clove, minced

2 ounces Mexican cheese blend, crumbled

1/2 teaspoon Worcestershire sauce

1/2 teaspoon Taco seasoning mix

4 mini sweet bell peppers, seeds and membranes removed

1 tablespoon fresh cilantro, finely chopped

DIRECTIONS

Press the "Sauté" button to preheat your Instant Pot. Now, cook the bacon until it is crisp; crumble with a spatula and reserve.

Now, cook the onion and garlic in pan drippings until just tender and fragrant. Add the cheese, Worcestershire sauce, and Taco seasoning mix. Stir in the reserved bacon.

Evenly divide the bacon/cheese mixture among the peppers.

Place a metal trivet and 1 cup of water in your Instant Pot. Arrange the stuffed peppers onto the trivet.

Secure the lid. Choose the "Manual" mode and cook for 5 minutes at High pressure. Once cooking is complete, use a natural pressure release for 5 minutes; carefully remove the lid.

Serve on a platter garnished with fresh cilantro. Enjoy!

STOCKS & SAUCES

480. French Court-Bouillon

(Ready in about 2 hours 10 minutes)

Per serving: 148 Calories; 12.1g Fat; 6.3g Carbs; 4g Protein; 2.5g Sugars; 1.4g Fiber

INGREDIENTS

1/2 pound meaty pork bones
1 carrot, chopped
1/2 celery stalk, chopped

1/2 brown onion, quartered
1/2 tablespoon olive oil

DIRECTIONS

Add all ingredients to the inner pot of your Instant Pot.
Secure the lid. Choose the "Soup/Broth" mode and cook for 120 minutes at Low pressure. Once cooking is complete, use a natural pressure release for 10 minutes; carefully remove the lid.
Remove the bones and vegetables using a metal spoon with holes and discard. Pour the liquid through the sieve into the bowl.
Use immediately or store in your refrigerator. Bon appétit!

481. Mediterranean Tomato Sauce

(Ready in about 45 minutes)

Per serving: 97 Calories; 7.1g Fat; 8.2g Carbs; 1.6g Protein; 4.8g Sugars; 3.3g Fiber

INGREDIENTS

10 ounces canned tomatoes, crushed
1 tablespoon olive oil
1 clove garlic, minced
1/4 teaspoon dried rosemary
1/4 teaspoon dried basil

1/4 tablespoon dried oregano
1/2 onion, quartered
Kosher salt and freshly ground black pepper, to taste
1/2 teaspoon tamari sauce
1 tablespoon fresh parsley leaves, finely chopped

DIRECTIONS

Reserve 1 cup of the crushed tomatoes.
Press the "Sauté" button and heat olive oil. Once hot, cook the garlic for a minute or so or until it is fragrant but not browned.
Now, stir in the rosemary, basil, and oregano; continue to sauté for 30 seconds more. Stir in the tomatoes, onion, salt, and pepper.
Secure the lid. Choose the "Soup/Broth" mode and cook for 40 minutes at High pressure. Once cooking is complete, use a quick pressure release; carefully remove the lid.
Add the reserved tomatoes, tamari sauce and parsley to your tomato sauce. Bon appétit!

482. Grandma's Berry Sauce

(Ready in about 25 minutes)

Per serving: 168 Calories; 5g Fat; 30.4g Carbs; 1.4g Protein; 24g Sugars; 3g Fiber

INGREDIENTS

1/2 cup frozen blueberries, thawed
1/4 cup frozen raspberries, thawed
1/4 cup frozen strawberries, thawed
1/4 cup granulated sugar

1 teaspoon cornstarch
3/4 cup water
1 tablespoon orange juice
1 ounce cream cheese, at room temperature

DIRECTIONS

Add the berries, sugar, and cornstarch, and water to the inner pot; stir to combine.
Secure the lid. Choose the "Manual" mode and cook for 10 minutes at High pressure. Once cooking is complete, use a natural pressure release for 10 minutes; carefully remove the lid.
Stir in the orange juice and cream cheese; stir to combine and serve with waffles or pancakes.

483. Sicilian Sauce with Pork and Wine

(Ready in about 55 minutes)

Per serving: 211 Calories; 13.6g Fat; 6.5g Carbs; 15.2g Protein; 2.9g Sugars; 1.6g Fiber

INGREDIENTS

1/2 tablespoon olive oil
1/4 pound pork butt
1/2 onion, chopped
1 garlic clove, pressed
2 tablespoons Malvasia wine, or other
Sicilian wine

1 fresh tomato, pureed
1 ounce tomato paste
1 bay leaf
1 tablespoon fresh cilantro, chopped
1/2 teaspoon dried basil
1/2 teaspoon dried rosemary

1/4 teaspoon cayenne pepper
1/4 teaspoon black pepper, freshly
cracked
1/4 teaspoon salt
1 cup chicken broth

DIRECTIONS

Press the "Sauté" button and heat the oil. When the oil starts to sizzle, cook the pork until no longer pink.

Add the onion and garlic and continue to cook for a few minutes more or until they are tender and fragrant. Add a splash of wine to deglaze the pot.

Stir in the other ingredients.

Secure the lid. Choose the "Meat/Stew" mode and cook for 35 minutes at High pressure. Once cooking is complete, use a natural pressure release for 15 minutes; carefully remove the lid.

Next, remove the meat from the inner pot; shred the meat, discarding the bones. Return the meat to your sauce and serve over pasta if desired.

484. Classic French Bouillon

(Ready in about 45 minutes)

Per serving: 83 Calories; 6.4g Fat; 5.4g Carbs; 0.2g Protein; 2.6g Sugars; 1.4g Fiber

INGREDIENTS

1/2 teaspoon salt
1/2 teaspoon mixed peppercorns
1/4 cup white wine
1 onion, sliced

1 celery rib, sliced
1 carrot, sliced
1 bay leaf
1 sprig fresh rosemary

A bunch of fresh parsley
1/2 lemon, sliced
1 tablespoon olive oil

DIRECTIONS

Add all ingredients to the inner pot of your Instant Pot. Add cold water until the inner pot is 2/3 full.

Secure the lid. Choose the "Soup/Broth" mode and cook for 30 minutes at High pressure. Once cooking is complete, use a natural pressure release for 10 minutes; carefully remove the lid.

Discard the vegetables. Bon appétit!

485. Vegetable Stock with White Wine

(Ready in about 1 hour 15 minutes)

Per serving: 137 Calories; 9.3g Fat; 8.2g Carbs; 3.3g Protein; 5.2g Sugars; 1.8g Fiber

INGREDIENTS

1 carrot, cut into 2-inch pieces
1 medium celery rib, cut into 2-inch pieces
1/2 onion, peeled and quartered
1 sprig fresh rosemary
1 sprig fresh thyme

1 tablespoon olive oil
Kosher salt and black peppercorns, to taste
1/4 cup dry white wine
1 cup water

DIRECTIONS

Start by preheating your oven to 400 degrees F. Grease a large roasting pan with cooking spray

Place the carrots, celery, onions, and herbs in the prepared roasting pan. Roast, tossing halfway through the cooking time, until the vegetables are tender about 35 minutes.

Transfer the vegetables to the inner pot. Add the remaining ingredients.

Secure the lid. Choose the "Soup/Broth" mode and cook for 30 minutes at High pressure. Once cooking is complete, use a natural pressure release for 10 minutes; carefully remove the lid.

Strain the broth through a fine-mesh sieve and discard the solids. Let it cool completely before storing.

486. Fall Applesauce with Cinnamon and Dates

(Ready in about 25 minutes)

Per serving: 137 Calories; 0.3g Fat; 35.7g Carbs; 0.8g Protein; 28g Sugars; 5.8g Fiber

INGREDIENTS

2 Honeycrisp apples, peeled, cored and chopped
1 cup water
1/2 tablespoon fresh lemon juice

1/4 teaspoon ground cloves
1/2 teaspoon cinnamon powder
4 dates, pitted and chopped

DIRECTIONS

Add all ingredients to the inner pot; stir to combine.

Secure the lid. Choose the "Manual" mode and cook for 10 minutes at High pressure. Once cooking is complete, use a natural pressure release for 10 minutes; carefully remove the lid.

Mash the apple mixture to the desired consistency. Serve warm or cold.

487. Pork Bone Broth

(Ready in about 55 minutes)

Per serving: 82 Calories; 4.1g Fat; 3.3g Carbs; 9.9g Protein; 1.5g Sugars; 1.6g Fiber

INGREDIENTS

1 pork bone
1 celery stalk, cut into large chunks
1 carrot, cut into large chunks
1/2 onion, quartered

1 garlic clove, smashed
1 bay leaf
Sea salt and black peppercorns, to taste
2 cups water, divided in half

DIRECTIONS

Preheat your oven to 400 degrees F. Coat a roasting pan with a piece of aluminum foil; brush with a little oil.

Arrange the pork bones and vegetables on the prepared roasting pan. Roast in the preheated oven for 25 to 30 minutes.

Transfer the roasted pork bones and vegetables to the inner pot of your Instant Pot. Now, stir in the bay leaves, salt, black peppercorns, and water.

Secure the lid. Choose the "Manual" mode and cook for 25 minutes at High pressure. Once cooking is complete, use a quick pressure release; carefully remove the lid.

Strain the stock and discard the solids. Keep in your refrigerator or freezer if desired. Enjoy!

488. Classic Chicken and Veggie Stock

(Ready in about 1 hour 10 minutes)

Per serving: 80 Calories; 1.9g Fat; 6g Carbs;10.9g Protein; 2g Sugars; 1.8g Fiber

INGREDIENTS

1 cup chicken carcass
1 carrot, cut into 2-inch pieces
1/2 celery rib, cut into 2-inch pieces
1/2 large onion, quartered
Sea salt, to taste

1/2 teaspoon mixed peppercorns
1 bay leaf
1 tablespoon parsley
2 cups cold water

DIRECTIONS

Place all ingredients in the inner pot.

Secure the lid. Choose the "Soup/Broth" mode and cook for 40 minutes at High pressure. Once cooking is complete, use a natural pressure release for 20 minutes; carefully remove the lid.

Remove the bones and vegetables with a slotted spoon. Use immediately or store for later use.

Bon appétit!

489. Easy Shrimp Consommé

(Ready in about 55 minutes)

Per serving: 72 Calories; 2.7g Fat; 4.9g Carbs; 10.3g Protein; 1.3g Sugars; 0.8g Fiber

INGREDIENTS

Shrimp shells from 1 pound shrimp
2 cups water
2 tablespoons cilantro, chopped
1 celery stalk, diced

4 clove garlic
1/2 onion, quartered
1/2 teaspoon mixed peppercorns
1/2 tablespoon sea salt

1 bay leaf
2 tablespoons olive oil

DIRECTIONS

Add all ingredients to the inner pot.

Secure the lid. Choose the "Soup/Broth" mode and cook for 30 minutes at High pressure. Once cooking is complete, use a natural pressure release for 10 minutes; carefully remove the lid.

Strain the shrimp shells and vegetables using a colander. Bon appétit!

490. Tikka Masala Sauce

(Ready in about 30 minutes)

Per serving: 103 Calories; 4.5g Fat; 13.2g Carbs; 4g Protein; 8.1g Sugars; 2.2g Fiber

INGREDIENTS

1 teaspoon olive oil
1/2 onion, chopped
1 clove garlic, chopped
1/2 inch fresh ginger, peeled and grated
1/2 teaspoon bird's eye chili, minced

1 bell pepper, seeded and chopped
Sea salt and ground black pepper, to taste
1/2 teaspoon cayenne pepper
1/2 teaspoon coriander powder
1/2 teaspoon turmeric powder

1/2 teaspoon Garam Masala
1 ripe tomato, pureed
1/2 cup vegetable broth
1/2 cup plain coconut yogurt

DIRECTIONS

Press the "Sauté" button to preheat your Instant Pot. Add the oil and sauté the onion for about 3 minutes or until tender and fragrant.

Now, add the garlic, ginger and peppers; continue to sauté an additional minute or until they are aromatic.

Add the spices, tomatoes, and broth.

Secure the lid. Choose the "Manual" mode and cook for 11 minutes at High pressure. Once cooking is complete, use a natural pressure release for 10 minutes; carefully remove the lid.

Afterwards, add the coconut yogurt to the inner pot and stir to combine. Serve with chickpeas or roasted vegetables. Enjoy!

491. Spaghetti Meat Sauce

(Ready in about 20 minutes)

Per serving: 233 Calories; 15.7g Fat; 9.5g Carbs; 14.1g Protein; 5.2g Sugars; 2.2g Fiber

INGREDIENTS

1 tablespoon olive oil
1/3 pound ground beef
1/2 onion, chopped
1/2 teaspoon fresh garlic, minced
Sea salt and ground black pepper, to taste

1/2 teaspoon brown sugar
1/2 teaspoon dried sage
1/2 teaspoon dried oregano
1/2 teaspoon dried basil
1/2 teaspoon cayenne pepper, or to taste

1 cup beef broth
1 ripe tomato, pureed
1 tablespoon tomato ketchup

DIRECTIONS

Press the "Sauté" button and heat the oil. When the oil starts to sizzle, cook the ground beef until no longer pink; crumble it with a wooden spatula.

Add the onion and garlic and continue to cook for a few minutes more or until they are tender and fragrant. Add a splash of beef broth to deglaze the pot.

Stir in the remaining ingredients; stir to combine well.

Secure the lid. Choose the "Manual" mode and cook for 6 minutes at High pressure. Once cooking is complete, use a natural pressure release for 5 minutes; carefully remove the lid.

Serve over pasta if desired. Bon appétit!

492. Velvety Caramel Sauce

(Ready in about 20 minutes)

Per serving: 291 Calories; 11.4g Fat; 50g Carbs; 0.3g Protein; 50.1g Sugars; 0g Fiber

INGREDIENTS

1/2 cup water

1/2 cup granulated sugar

1 tablespoon butter, cut into small pieces

1/4 cup heavy whipping cream

1/4 teaspoon coarse sea salt

1/2 teaspoon vanilla

A pinch of cardamom

DIRECTIONS

Press the "Sauté" button to preheat the Instant Pot; now, cook the sugar and water, stirring frequently, until the sugar has dissolved.

Let the mixture boiling until it turns an amber color or about 10 minutes.

Then, whisk in the butter, followed by the remaining ingredients.

Allow your sauce to cool. It will thicken up once it's cooled in your refrigerator. Bon appétit!

493. Classic Marinara Sauce

(Ready in about 25 minutes)

Per serving: 87 Calories; 7g Fat; 6.1g Carbs; 1.3g Protein; 3.8g Sugars; 2.6g Fiber

INGREDIENTS

1 tablespoon olive oil

1 garlic clove, minced

1 tablespoon tomato paste

8 ounces crushed tomatoes with juice

1/2 cup water

Sea salt to taste

1 tablespoon fresh basil, minced

1/2 tablespoon fresh parsley, minced

DIRECTIONS

Press the "Sauté" button and heat olive oil. Once hot, cook the garlic for a minute or so or until it is fragrant but not browned.

Now, stir in the remaining ingredients.

Secure the lid. Choose the "Soup/Broth" mode and cook for 40 minutes at High pressure. Once cooking is complete, use a quick pressure release; carefully remove the lid. Bon appétit!

494. Vanilla Cranberry Sauce

(Ready in about 20 minutes)

Per serving: 122 Calories; 0.2g Fat; 28.4g Carbs; 0.5g Protein; 18g Sugars; 5.3g Fiber

INGREDIENTS

1/2 pound fresh cranberries, rinsed

1/2 blood oranges, juiced

1/2 tablespoon blood orange zest

1/4 cup sugar

2 tablespoons golden cane syrup

1 clove

1 cinnamon stick

1/2 teaspoon vanilla extract

DIRECTIONS

Add the cranberries to the inner pot of your Instant Pot.

Add the remaining ingredients to the inner pot; stir to combine well.

Secure the lid. Choose the "Manual" mode and cook for 3 minutes at High pressure. Once cooking is complete, use a natural pressure release for 10 minutes; carefully remove the lid. Bon appétit!

Let it cool. Serve your sauce chilled or at room temperature. Bon appétit!

495. Harvest Pear Butter

(Ready in about 25 minutes)

Per serving: 114 Calories; 0.1g Fat; 29.2g Carbs; 0.4g Protein; 24g Sugars; 3.5g Fiber

INGREDIENTS

1/2 pound cup pears, cored, peeled and chopped

1 teaspoon freshly squeezed lemon juice

1/4 cup sugar

1/2 teaspoon ground cinnamon

1/4 teaspoon ground cardamom

1/2 teaspoon vanilla essence

DIRECTIONS

Add all ingredients to the inner pot; stir to combine.

Secure the lid. Choose the "Manual" mode and cook for 10 minutes at High pressure. Once cooking is complete, use a natural pressure release for 10 minutes; carefully remove the lid.

Mash the pear mixture to the desired consistency. Serve at room temperature or cold. Bon appétit!

496. Hot Peppery Sauce

(Ready in about 40 minutes)

Per serving: 60 Calories; 3g Fat; 6.8g Carbs; 1.2g Protein; 4.4g Sugars; 1.3g Fiber

INGREDIENTS

1/2 tablespoon butter, melted

1/2 banana shallot, chopped

1/2 teaspoon garlic, minced

1 jalapeño pepper, seeded and chopped

1 serrano pepper, seeded and chopped

1 tomato, chopped

1/4 cup white vinegar

1/2 cup water

1 teaspoon white sugar

Sea salt and ground black pepper, to taste

DIRECTIONS

Press the "Sauté" button and melt the butter. Once hot, cook the shallot for 3 to 4 minute or until it is tender and fragrant.

Now, add the garlic and continue to cook an additional 30 seconds or until aromatic.

Add the remaining ingredients.

Secure the lid. Choose the "Manual" mode and cook for 25 minutes at High pressure. Once cooking is complete, use a natural pressure release for 10 minutes; carefully remove the lid.

Let it cool. Serve your sauce hot or at room temperature. Bon appétit!

497. Classic Beef Bone Stock

(Ready in about 3 hours 5 minutes)

Per serving: 65 Calories; 2.4g Fat; 4.6g Carbs; 6.7g Protein; 1.9g Sugars; 1.1g Fiber

INGREDIENTS

1/2 pound frozen beef bones

1/2 onion, halved

1/2 stalk celery, chopped

1/2 carrot, chopped

1 clove garlic, whole

1 bay leaf

1 tablespoon apple cider vinegar

1/2 teaspoon sea salt

1/4 teaspoon black pepper

2 ½ cups water

DIRECTIONS

Start by preheating your oven to 390 degrees F. Line a baking pan with aluminum foil.

Place the beef bones, onions, celery, carrots, and garlic on the baking pan. Roast for 40 to 45 minutes.

Transfer the roasted beef bones and vegetables to the inner pot of your Instant Pot. Add the bay leaves, apple cider vinegar, sea salt, pepper, and boiling water to the inner pot.

Secure the lid. Choose the "Manual" mode and cook for 120 minutes at High pressure. Once cooking is complete, use a natural pressure release for 20 minutes; carefully remove the lid.

Remove the beef bones and vegetables and discard. Pour the broth through a strainer. Enjoy!

498. Easy Festive Gravy

(Ready in about 15 minutes)

Per serving: 89 Calories; 0.1g Fat; 21.9g Carbs; 0.2g Protein; 13.3g Sugars; 0.3g Fiber

INGREDIENTS

1 cup pan juices
2 tablespoons cornstarch
1/ cup cold water

Salt and ground black pepper, to taste
1/2 teaspoon cayenne pepper

DIRECTIONS

Press the "Sauté" button to preheat the Instant Pot; then, cook the pan juices for about 3 minutes, bringing it to a boil.
Whisk the cornstarch with cold water until the cornstarch has dissolved; then whisk the cornstarch slurry into the pan juices.
Add the salt, black pepper, and cayenne pepper; continue cooking on the lowest setting until your sauce has reduced slightly and the flavors have concentrated.
Use the "Keep Warm" function to keep your sauce warm until ready to serve.

499. Home-Style Mexican Salsa

(Ready in about 40 minutes)

Per serving: 90 Calories; 0.5g Fat; 19.8g Carbs; 3.2g Protein; 9.4g Sugars; 3.6g Fiber

INGREDIENTS

1/2 onion, chopped
1 garlic clove, pressed
1 ripe tomato, crushed
2 ounces canned tomato paste
1 sweet pepper, chopped

1 chili peppers, chopped
1/4 cup rice vinegar
1/2 tablespoon brown sugar
Sea salt and red pepper, to taste
1/2 teaspoon dried Mexican oregano

DIRECTIONS

Put all ingredients into the inner pot of your Instant Pot.
Secure the lid. Choose the "Manual" mode and cook for 25 minutes at High pressure. Once cooking is complete, use a natural pressure release for 10 minutes; carefully remove the lid.
Allow your salsa to cool completely; store in your refrigerator or freezer. Bon appétit!

500. American-Style BBQ Sauce

(Ready in about 20 minutes)

Per serving: 155 Calories; 3.2g Fat; 27.5g Carbs; 2.4g Protein; 18.5g Sugars; 4.7g Fiber

INGREDIENTS

1/2 tablespoon butter
1/2 shallot, chopped
1 clove garlic, minced
1/2 cup tomato sauce
2 tablespoons cider vinegar
1/2 tablespoon coconut sugar
1 tablespoon molasses

1/2 tablespoon Worcestershire sauce
1/2 teaspoon yellow mustard
1/2 teaspoon hot sauce
Kosher salt and ground black pepper
1/3 teaspoon paprika
1/2 cup vegetable broth

DIRECTIONS

Press the "Sauté" button and melt the butter. Then, sauté the shallot until tender and translucent, about 4 minutes. Add the garlic and cook for a further 30 seconds.
Stir in the remaining ingredients.
Secure the lid. Choose the "Manual" mode and cook for 5 minutes at High pressure. Once cooking is complete, use a natural pressure release for 5 minutes; carefully remove the lid. Bon appétit!

501. Black Bean Dipping Sauce

(Ready in about 35 minutes)

Per serving: 128 Calories; 3.7g Fat; 19.3g Carbs; 4.8g Protein; 4.9g Sugars; 4.6g Fiber

INGREDIENTS

1/2 tablespoon olive oil
1/4 brown onion, chopped
1 garlic clove, chopped
1/2 jalapeño pepper, seeded and minced
1/3 teaspoon dried Mexican oregano
1/4 teaspoon ground cumin

Sea salt and ground black pepper, to taste
1/2 cup black beans, rinsed, drained
1/2 cup chicken broth
2 tablespoons fresh cilantro, chopped
1/3 cup Pico de Gallo

DIRECTIONS

Press the "Sauté" button and heat the olive oil until sizzling. Once hot, cook the onion for 3 to 4 minutes or until tender and fragrant. After that, stir in the garlic; continue sautéing an additional 30 to 40 seconds.
Add the jalapeño pepper, oregano, cumin, salt, black pepper, beans, and broth to the inner pot.
Secure the lid. Choose the "Bean/Chili" mode and cook for 25 minutes at High pressure. Once cooking is complete, use a quick pressure release; carefully remove the lid.
Then, mash your beans with potato masher or use your blender. Serve garnished with cilantro and Pico de Gallo. Bon appétit!

502. Herbed Chicken Broth

(Ready in about 2 hours 15 minutes)

Per serving: 59 Calories; 2g Fat; 1.6g Carbs; 3.5g Protein; 0g Sugars; 0.6g Fiber

INGREDIENTS

Chicken bones from 1/2 pound roast chicken
1/2 parsnip
1/2 celery
1 tablespoon fresh parsley
1 teaspoon fresh thyme

1 teaspoon fresh coriander
1/2 teaspoon fresh dill
1 tablespoon cider vinegar
1/3 teaspoon sea salt
1/4 teaspoon ground black pepper

DIRECTIONS

Place all ingredients in the inner pot. Add cold water until the pot is 2/3 full.
Secure the lid. Choose the "Soup/Broth" mode and cook for 120 minutes at Low pressure. Once cooking is complete, use a natural pressure release for 10 minutes; carefully remove the lid.
Remove the bones and vegetables using a metal spoon with holes and discard. Pour the liquid through the sieve into the bowl.
Use immediately or store in your refrigerator. Bon appétit!

503. Chicken Ragù with Wine

(Ready in about 20 minutes)

Per serving: 288 Calories; 13g Fat; 20.4g Carbs; 22.1g Protein; 10.1g Sugars; 5.3g Fiber

INGREDIENTS

1/2 tablespoon olive oil
1/2 pound ground chicken
1/2 onion, chopped
1 clove garlic, minced
1/4 cup dry red wine

1/2 stalk celery, chopped
1/2 bell pepper, chopped
1/2 teaspoon fresh basil, chopped
1/2 teaspoon fresh rosemary, chopped
1/2 teaspoon cayenne pepper

Salt and fresh ground pepper to taste
1/2 cup tomato sauce
1/3 cup chicken bone broth

DIRECTIONS

Press the "Sauté" button and heat the oil. When the oil starts to sizzle, cook the ground chicken until no longer pink; crumble it with a wooden spatula.
Add the onion and garlic to the browned chicken; let it cook for a minute or so. Add a splash of wine to deglaze the pan.
Stir in the remaining ingredients.
Secure the lid. Choose the "Manual" mode and cook for 6 minutes at High pressure. Once cooking is complete, use a natural pressure release for 10 minutes; carefully remove the lid. Bon appétit!

504. Spicy Chorizo Sauce

(Ready in about 20 minutes)

Per serving: 344 Calories; 23.9g Fat; 15.2g Carbs; 19.1g Protein; 8.1g Sugars; 3.3g Fiber

INGREDIENTS

1/2 tablespoon olive oil
1/2 pound Chorizo sausage, sliced
1/2 onion, chopped
1/2 teaspoon garlic, minced
1/2 sweet pepper, seeded and finely chopped
1/2 habanero pepper, seeded and minced
1 teaspoon sugar

1/2 teaspoon dried basil
1/2 teaspoon dried rosemary
1/2 teaspoon red pepper flakes
Sea salt and freshly ground black pepper, to taste
8 ounces canned diced tomatoes, with juice
1/2 cup chicken broth

DIRECTIONS

Press the "Sauté" button and heat the oil. When the oil starts to sizzle, cook the Chorizo until no longer pink; crumble it with a wooden spatula.

Add the onion, garlic, and peppers and cook for a minute or so. Add a splash of chicken broth to deglaze the pan.

Stir in the remaining ingredients.

Secure the lid. Choose the "Manual" mode and cook for 6 minutes at High pressure. Once cooking is complete, use a natural pressure release for 10 minutes; carefully remove the lid. Bon appétit!

505. Nana's Raspberry Coulis

(Ready in about 20 minutes)

Per serving: 130 Calories; 0.4g Fat; 34g Carbs; 0.9g Protein; 30.3g Sugars; 3.8g Fiber

INGREDIENTS

4 ounces fresh or frozen raspberries
1/4 cup brown sugar
1/2 cup water

1/4 cup fresh orange juice
1/2 tablespoon fresh ginger root, peeled and finely grated
1 teaspoon zest from an organic orange

DIRECTIONS

Add all the ingredients to the inner pot of your Instant Pot.

Secure the lid. Choose the "Manual" mode and cook for 3 minutes at High pressure. Once cooking is complete, use a natural pressure release for 10 minutes; carefully remove the lid.

Let it cool. Serve your sauce chilled or at room temperature. Bon appétit!

506. Mediterranean Eggplant Sauce

(Ready in about 10 minutes)

Per serving: 190 Calories; 12.4g Fat; 14.2g Carbs; 7.2g Protein; 7.5g Sugars; 5.3g Fiber

INGREDIENTS

1/2 tablespoon olive oil
1/2 pound eggplants, sliced
1 garlic clove, minced
1 tomato, chopped
1/2 cup white wine
1/2 teaspoon oregano

1/4 teaspoon rosemary
1/4 teaspoon basil
Sea salt and ground black pepper, to taste
1 tablespoons tahini (sesame butter)
1/4 cup Romano cheese, freshly grated

DIRECTIONS

Press the "Sauté" button and heat the olive oil. Then, cook the eggplant slices until they are charred at the bottom. Work with batches.

Add the garlic, tomatoes, wine, and spices.

Secure the lid. Choose the "Bean/Chili" mode and cook for 3 minutes at High pressure. Once cooking is complete, use a quick pressure release; carefully remove the lid.

Press the "Sauté" button again to thicken the cooking liquid. Add the tahini paste and stir to combine. Top with Romano cheese and serve.

507. Two-Cheese and Bacon Sauce

(Ready in about 15 minutes)

Per serving: 195 Calories; 12.5g Fat; 10.1g Carbs; 11.1g Protein; 5.5g Sugars; 1.3g Fiber

INGREDIENTS

1 ounce bacon, diced
1/2 onion, chopped
1/2 red chili pepper, seeded and minced
1 clove garlic, pressed
1 ripe tomato, chopped
1/4 teaspoon ground cumin

1/4 teaspoon turmeric powder
Kosher salt and ground black pepper, to taste
3/4 cup vegetable broth
2 ounces Cottage cheese, at room temperature
1/3 cup Pepper Jack cheese, grated

DIRECTIONS

Press the "Sauté" button to preheat your Instant Pot. Then, cook the bacon for 2 to 3 minutes. Reserve.

Add the onion and pepper to the inner pot and continue to cook until they are fragrant. Stir in the garlic and continue to sauté for 30 seconds more.

Now, add the tomatoes, spices, and broth.

Secure the lid. Choose the "Manual" mode and cook for 5 minutes at High pressure. Once cooking is complete, use a quick pressure release; carefully remove the lid.

Lastly, stir in the cheese. Seal the lid again and let it sit in the residual heat until the cheese melts.

Ladle into a nice serving bowl, top with the reserved bacon, and serve.

508. Goat Cheese and Artichoke Dip

(Ready in about 15 minutes)

Per serving: 262 Calories; 18.4g Fat; 16g Carbs; 12.1g Protein; 3.4g Sugars; 7.3g Fiber

INGREDIENTS

1 tablespoon butter
1/2 onion, chopped
1 clove garlic, minced
5 ounces artichoke hearts
1/2 cup chicken broth

Sea salt and freshly ground black pepper, to taste
1/4 teaspoon red pepper flakes
1/2 pound fresh or frozen spinach leaves
2 ounces cream cheese
1 ounce goat cheese, crumbled

DIRECTIONS

Press the "Sauté" button and melt the butter. Then, sauté the onion and garlic until just tender and fragrant.

Then, add the artichoke hearts, broth, salt, black pepper, and red pepper flakes.

Secure the lid. Choose the "Manual" mode and cook for 5 minutes at High pressure. Once cooking is complete, use a quick pressure release; carefully remove the lid.

Add the spinach and cheese to the inner pot; seal the lid and let it sit in the residual heat until thoroughly warmed. Enjoy!

509. Classic Chicken and Leek Stock

(Ready in about 1 hour)

Per serving: 70 Calories; 1.8g Fat; 14g Carbs; 2.7g Protein; 4g Sugars; 2.5g Fiber

INGREDIENTS

1/2 pound chicken white meat
1/2 white onion, quartered
1/2 small leek, white parts
1/2 parsnip, sliced thickly
1/2 celery rib, sliced thickly

1 bay leaf
1 stalk flat-leaf parsley
1/4 teaspoon dried dill weed
1/4 teaspoon mixed peppercorns

DIRECTIONS

Add all ingredients to the inner pot.

Secure the lid. Choose the "Soup/Broth" mode and cook for 40 minutes at High pressure. Once cooking is complete, use a natural pressure release for 20 minutes; carefully remove the lid.

Discard the vegetables and bones; save the chicken meat for later use. Bon appétit!

510. Home-Style Fumet

(Ready in about 55 minutes)

Per serving: 93 Calories; 8.1g Fat; 2.7g Carbs; 2.2g Protein; 1.4g Sugars; 0.9g Fiber

INGREDIENTS

1/2 pound meaty bones and heads of halibut, washed

1 lemongrass stalk, chopped

1 carrot, chopped

1/2 parsnip, chopped

1/3 onion, quartered

1 sprig rosemary

1 sprig thyme

1 tablespoon olive oil

DIRECTIONS

Place all ingredients in the inner pot. Add cold water until the pot is 2/3 full.

Secure the lid. Choose the "Soup/Broth" mode and cook for 40 minutes at High pressure. Once cooking is complete, use a natural pressure release for 10 minutes; carefully remove the lid.

Strain the vegetables and fish. Bon appétit!

DESSERTS & DRINKS

511. Cinnamon Stewed Apples

(Ready in about 10 minutes)

Per serving: 149 Calories; 0.3g Fat; 34.3g Carbs; 0.6g Protein; 31.5g Sugars; 5.7g Fiber

INGREDIENTS

2 large apples
1/2 teaspoon ground cinnamon
1/3 teaspoon ground cloves
1 tablespoon honey

DIRECTIONS

Add all ingredients to the inner pot. Now, pour in 1/2 cup of water.
Secure the lid. Choose the "Manual" mode and cook for 2 minutes at High pressure. Once cooking is complete, use a quick pressure release; carefully remove the lid.
Serve in individual bowls. Bon appétit!

512. Easy Dulce de Leche

(Ready in about 35 minutes)

Per serving: 295 Calories; 16.4g Fat; 22.1g Carbs; 15g Protein; 0.7g Sugars; 0g Fiber

INGREDIENTS

1 can (14-ounce) sweetened condensed milk

DIRECTIONS

Place a trivet and steamer basket in the inner pot. Place the can of milk in the steamer basket.
Add water until the can is covered.
Secure the lid. Choose the "Manual" mode and cook for 20 minutes at High pressure. Once cooking is complete, use a natural pressure release for 10 minutes; carefully remove the lid.
Don't open the can until it is completely cooled. Bon appétit!

513. Coconut Banana Bread

(Ready in about 50 minutes)

Per serving: 281 Calories; 11.1g Fat; 37.1g Carbs; 5.3g Protein; 13.1g Sugars; 1.2g Fiber

INGREDIENTS

1/4 stick butter, melted
1 egg
1/2 teaspoon vanilla extract
1/4 cup sugar
1/2 teaspoon baking soda
1 banana, mashed
1/2 cups all-purpose flour
1/4 cup coconut flaked

DIRECTIONS

Mix all ingredients in a bowl until everything is well incorporated.
Add 1 cup of water and metal trivet to the bottom of the inner pot. Spritz a baking pan with nonstick cooking oil.
Scrape the batter into the prepared pan. Lower the pan onto the trivet.
Secure the lid. Choose the "Manual" mode and cook for 45 minutes at High pressure. Once cooking is complete, use a quick pressure release; carefully remove the lid.
Allow the banana bread to cool slightly before slicing and serving. Enjoy!

514. Lemon Pound Cake

(Ready in about 35 minutes)

Per serving: 360 Calories; 20.1g Fat; 35.6g Carbs; 9.3g Protein; 30.9g Sugars; 0.2g Fiber

INGREDIENTS

1/2 cup butter cookies, crumbled

1 tablespoon butter, melted

1 egg

1 egg yolk

2 tablespoons lemon juice

7 ounces canned sweetened condensed milk

1 tablespoon honey

1/4 cup heavy cream

4 tablespoons sugar

DIRECTIONS

Place a metal trivet and 1 cup of water in your Instant Pot. Spritz a baking pan with nonstick cooking spray.

Next, mix the cookies and butter until well combined. Press the crust into the prepared baking pan.

Then, thoroughly combine the eggs, lemon juice, condensed milk, and honey with a hand mixer.

Pour this mixture on top of the prepared crust. Lower the baking pan onto the trivet and cover with a piece of foil.

Secure the lid. Choose the "Manual" mode and cook for 15 minutes at High pressure. Once cooking is complete, use a natural pressure release for 15 minutes; carefully remove the lid.

Afterwards, whip the heavy cream with sugar until the cream becomes stiff. Frost your cake and serve well chilled. Bon appétit!

515. Molten Lava Cake

(Ready in about 30 minutes)

Per serving: 404 Calories; 14.4g Fat; 61g Carbs; 7.6g Protein; 31.5g Sugars; 3g Fiber

INGREDIENTS

1/4 stick butter

1/3 cup sugar

1 egg

1 tablespoon coconut milk

1/2 teaspoon vanilla

1/2 cup self-rising flour

1 tablespoon cocoa powder

1/2 tablespoon carob powder

1 ounce bittersweet chocolate

1 ounce semisweet chocolate

DIRECTIONS

Place a metal trivet and 1 cup of water in your Instant Pot. Butter custard cups and set aside.

Then, beat the butter and sugar until creamy. Fold in the eggs, one at a time, and mix until everything is well combined.

Add the milk and vanilla and mix again. Then, stir in the flour, cocoa powder, and carob powder. Fold in the chocolate and stir to combine. Divide the mixture between the prepared custard cups.

Lower the cups onto the trivet.

Secure the lid. Choose the "Steam" mode and cook for 15 minutes at High pressure. Once cooking is complete, use a natural pressure release for 10 minutes; carefully remove the lid. Enjoy!

516. Stuffed Apples with Walnuts and Currants

(Ready in about 25 minutes)

Per serving: 321 Calories; 13.6g Fat; 53g Carbs; 2.2g Protein; 44.6g Sugars; 5.3g Fiber

INGREDIENTS

2 baking apples

1/4 cup granulated sugar

1/4 teaspoon cardamom

1/3 teaspoon cinnamon

1/4 cup walnuts, chopped

2 tablespoons currants

1 tablespoon coconut oil

DIRECTIONS

Add 1 ½ cups of water and a metal rack to the bottom of the inner pot.

Core the apples and use a melon baller to scoop out a bit of the flesh. Mix the remaining ingredients. Divide the filling between your apples.

Secure the lid. Choose the "Steam" mode and cook for 15 minutes at High pressure. Once cooking is complete, use a quick pressure release; carefully remove the lid.

Serve with ice cream, if desired. Bon appétit!

517. Old-Fashioned Mixed Berry Jam

(Ready in about 25 minutes)

Per serving: 150 Calories; 0.3g Fat; 37.1g Carbs; 0.8g Protein; 30.1g Sugars; 2.3g Fiber

INGREDIENTS

1/2 pound fresh mixed berries

1/2 cup granulated sugar

1 tablespoon fresh lemon juice

1 tablespoon cornstarch

DIRECTIONS

Add the fresh mixed berries, sugar, and lemon juice to the inner pot.

Secure the lid. Choose the "Manual" mode and cook for 2 minutes at High pressure. Once cooking is complete, use a natural pressure release for 15 minutes; carefully remove the lid.

Whisk the cornstarch with 3 tablespoons of water until well combined. Stir in the cornstarch slurry.

Press the "Sauté" button and bring the mixture to a rolling boil. Let it boil for about 5 minutes, stirring continuously, until your jam has thickened. Bon appétit!

518. Double Chocolate Fudge

(Ready in about 15 minutes + chilling time)

Per serving: 401 Calories; 27.1g Fat; 31.3g Carbs; 6.8g Protein; 18.1g Sugars; 6.6g Fiber

INGREDIENTS

4 ounces canned condensed milk

1 tablespoon peanut butter

1/4 teaspoon ground cardamom

1/4 teaspoon ground cinnamon

1/2 teaspoon vanilla extract

2 ounces bittersweet chocolate chips

2 ounces semisweet chocolate chips

DIRECTIONS

Line the bottom of a baking sheet with a piece of foil.

Add the milk, peanut butter, cardamom, cinnamon, and vanilla to the inner pot of your Instant Pot; stir until everything is well incorporated.

Next, press the "Sauté" button and use the lowest setting to cook the mixture until thoroughly warmed. Now, fold in the chocolate chips and stir again to combine well.

Lastly, pour the mixture into the prepared baking sheet and transfer to your refrigerator; let it sit until solid.

Cut into squares and serve. Bon appétit!

519. New York-Style Cheesecake

(Ready in about 45 minutes)

Per serving: 465 Calories; 28.1g Fat; 45.4g Carbs; 8.5g Protein; 28.1g Sugars; 2g Fiber

INGREDIENTS

1 tablespoon granulated sugar

1 tablespoon butter

5 large graham crackers, crumbled

2 tablespoons almonds, ground

1/4 teaspoon cinnamon

2 ounces Philadelphia cheese

1/2 teaspoon vanilla extract

1/2 tablespoon lemon zest

1/2 tablespoon arrowroot powder

1/4 cup golden caster sugar

1 egg

1/4 cup creme fraiche

1 tablespoon golden caster sugar

DIRECTIONS

Place a metal trivet and 1 cup of water in your Instant Pot. Spritz a baking pan with nonstick cooking spray.

Next, mix granulated sugar, butter, crackers, almonds, and cinnamon into a sticky crust. Press the crust into the prepared baking pan.

In a mixing bowl, combine the Philadelphia cheese, vanilla extract, lemon zest, arrowroot powder, 1/4 of golden caster sugar, and eggs. Pour the filling mixture over the crust and cover it with a piece of foil.

Lower the baking pan onto the trivet.

Secure the lid. Choose the "Manual" mode and cook for 25 minutes at High pressure. Once cooking is complete, use a natural pressure release for 15 minutes; carefully remove the lid.

Lastly, beat the creme fraiche with 2 tablespoons of golden caster sugar. Spread this topping over the cheesecake right to the edges. Cover loosely with foil and refrigerate overnight. Bon appétit!

520. Butternut and Coconut Pudding

(Ready in about 20 minutes)

Per serving: 355 Calories; 21.1g Fat; 42.5g Carbs; 4.1g Protein; 18.1g Sugars; 3.9g Fiber

INGREDIENTS

3/4 pound butternut squash, peeled, seeded, and diced

1/2 cup coconut cream

3 tablespoons maple syrup

A pinch of kosher salt

1/2 teaspoon pumpkin pie spice mix

2 tablespoons almond milk

DIRECTIONS

Add 1 cup of water and a metal rack to the bottom of the inner pot. Place your squash in a steamer basket; lower the basket onto the rack.

Secure the lid. Choose the "Steam" mode and cook for 10 minutes at High pressure. Once cooking is complete, use a quick pressure release; carefully remove the lid.

Stir the remaining ingredients into the cooked squash; combine all ingredients with a potato masher.

Let it cook on the "Sauté" function until everything is thoroughly heated or about 4 minutes. Serve immediately.

521. Greek Hosafi (Stewed Dried Fruits)

(Ready in about 20 minutes)

Per serving: 327 Calories; 7.3g Fat; 66.4g Carbs; 4.8g Protein; 45.8g Sugars; 4.7g Fiber

INGREDIENTS

2 ounces dried figs

2 ounces dried apricots

1 ounce sultana raisins

1 ounce prunes, pitted

1 ounce almonds

1/4 cup sugar

1 cinnamon stick

1 vanilla bean

1/4 teaspoon whole cloves

1/4 teaspoon whole star anise

1 cup water

1 tablespoon Greek honey

DIRECTIONS

Place all ingredients in the inner pot of your Instant Pot.

Secure the lid. Choose the "Manual" mode and cook for 2 minutes at High pressure. Once cooking is complete, use a natural pressure release for 10 minutes; carefully remove the lid.

Serve with Greek yogurt or ice cream, if desired.

522. Nut Butter Brownies

(Ready in about 40 minutes)

Per serving: 456 Calories; 38.1g Fat; 25.1g Carbs; 7.5g Protein; 17.9g Sugars; 3.5g Fiber

INGREDIENTS

1/4 cup walnut butter

2 tablespoons sunflower seed butter

1/4 cup coconut sugar

2 tablespoons cocoa powder

1 egg

A pinch of grated nutmeg

A pinch of salt

1/4 cardamom powder

1/4 teaspoon cinnamon powder

1/2 teaspoon baking soda

1/2 teaspoon vanilla extract

1/4 cup dark chocolate, cut into chunks

DIRECTIONS

Place a metal trivet and 1 cup of water in your Instant Pot. Spritz a baking pan with nonstick cooking spray.

In a mixing bowl, combine all ingredients, except for the chocolate; stir well to create a thick batter.

Spoon the batter into the prepared pan. Sprinkle the chocolate chunks over the top; gently press the chocolate chunks into the batter.

Lower the baking pan onto the trivet.

Secure the lid. Choose the "Manual" mode and cook for 20 minutes at High pressure. Once cooking is complete, use a natural pressure release for 10 minutes; carefully remove the lid.

Place your brownies on a cooling rack before slicing and serving. Bon appétit!

523. Hot Mulled Apple Cider

(Ready in about 1 hour 35 minutes)

Per serving: 139 Calories; 0.4g Fat; 26.2g Carbs; 0.5g Protein; 18.9g Sugars; 1.9g Fiber

INGREDIENTS

1 ½ cups apple cider

1/2-inch piece fresh ginger, peeled and sliced

1 cinnamon stick

1 vanilla bean

1/2 teaspoon whole cloves

1/2 teaspoon allspice berries

1/4 orange, sliced into thin rounds

1/4 cups brandy

DIRECTIONS

Place all ingredients, except for the brandy, in the inner pot of your Instant Pot.

Secure the lid. Choose the "Slow Cook" mode and cook for 1 hour 30 minutes at the lowest temperature.

Strain the cider mixture and stir in the brandy. Serve immediately.

524. Hungarian Golden Dumpling Cake (Aranygaluska)

(Ready in about 35 minutes)

Per serving: 464 Calories; 23.5g Fat; 58.8g Carbs; 6.6g Protein; 33.3g Sugars; 2.6g Fiber

INGREDIENTS

1/4 cup granulated sugar

1 ounce walnuts, ground

1/2 teaspoon grated lemon peel

1 tablespoon butter, at room temperature

1 teaspoon fresh lemon juice

4 ounces refrigerated buttermilk biscuits

1 tablespoon cream cheese, at room temperature

4 tablespoons powdered sugar

1/2 teaspoon vanilla extract

DIRECTIONS

Place 1 cup of water and a metal trivet in the inner pot of your Instant Pot. Lightly grease a loaf pan with shortening of choice.

In a shallow bowl mix the granulated sugar, walnuts, and lemon peel. Mix the melted butter and lemon juice in another shallow bowl.

Cut each biscuit in half. Dip your biscuits into the butter mixture; then, roll them in the walnut/sugar mixture.

Arrange them in the loaf pan.

Secure the lid. Choose the "Manual" mode and cook for 25 minutes at High pressure. Once cooking is complete, use a natural pressure release for 5 minutes; carefully remove the lid.

In the meantime, whip the cream cheese with the powdered sugar, and vanilla extract. Drizzle over the hot cake and serve.

525. Dutch Baby

(Ready in about 40 minutes)

Per serving: 451 Calories; 19.3g Fat; 52.3g Carbs; 13.1g Protein; 18.1g Sugars; 2.5g Fiber

INGREDIENTS

2 tablespoons butter, melted

2 eggs

3/4 cup milk

3/4 cup all-purpose flour

1/4 teaspoon kosher salt

1/4 teaspoon cinnamon powder

1/2 teaspoon vanilla extract

1/2 cup canned blueberries with syrup

DIRECTIONS

Place 1 cup of water and a metal trivet in your Instant Pot. Line the bottom of a springform pan with parchment paper; grease the bottom and sides of the pan with melted butter.

Mix the eggs, milk, flour, salt, cinnamon, and vanilla until everything is well combined. Now, spoon the batter into the prepared pan. Lower the pan onto the trivet.

Secure the lid. Choose the "Manual" mode and cook for 30 minutes at High pressure. Once cooking is complete, use a quick pressure release; carefully remove the lid.

Serve garnished with fresh blueberries and enjoy!

526. White Hot Chocolate with Chai Syrup

(Ready in about 10 minutes)

Per serving: 364 Calories; 14.5g Fat; 53g Carbs; 8.7g Protein; 50g Sugars; 1.7g Fiber

INGREDIENTS

1 ½ cups whole milk
2 tablespoons almond butter
2 tablespoons honey
1 tablespoon Masala Chai Syrup

1/2 teaspoon vanilla extract
A pinch of sea salt
A pinch of grated nutmeg
1/2 tablespoon gelatin

DIRECTIONS

Add the milk, almond butter, honey, Masala Chai Syrup, vanilla extract, sea salt, and grated nutmeg to the inner to of your Instant Pot.
Secure the lid. Choose the "Manual" mode and cook for 6 minutes at Low pressure. Once cooking is complete, use a quick pressure release; carefully remove the lid.
Add the gelatin and mix with an immersion blender until your hot chocolate is frothy and smooth. Enjoy!

527. Rice Pudding with Cranberries

(Ready in about 20 minutes)

Per serving: 358 Calories; 6.6g Fat; 63.6g Carbs; 9.8g Protein; 22.2g Sugars; 1.5g Fiber

INGREDIENTS

1/2 cup white rice
1 cup water
A pinch of salt
1 cup milk
2 tablespoons maple syrup

1 egg, beaten
1/2 teaspoon vanilla extract
1/4 teaspoon cardamom
A pinch of grated nutmeg
1/4 cup dried cranberries

DIRECTIONS

Place the rice, water, and salt in the inner pot of your Instant Pot.
Secure the lid. Choose the "Manual" mode and cook for 3 minutes at High pressure. Once cooking is complete, use a natural pressure release for 10 minutes; carefully remove the lid.
Add in the milk, maple syrup, eggs, vanilla extract, cardamom, and nutmeg; stir to combine well.
Press the "Sauté" button and cook, stirring frequently, until your pudding starts to boil. Press the "Cancel' button. Stir in the dried cranberries.
Pudding will thicken as it cools. Bon appétit!

528. Home-Style Horchata

(Ready in about 20 minutes)

Per serving: 271 Calories; 16.4g Fat; 27.2g Carbs; 8.6g Protein; 22.4g Sugars; 3.6g Fiber

INGREDIENTS

6 ounces rice milk, unsweetened
2 ounces almond milk, unsweetened
2 tablespoons agave syrup
1 cinnamon stick
1 vanilla bean

DIRECTIONS

Combine all ingredients in the inner pot of your Instant Pot.
Secure the lid. Choose the "Manual" mode and cook for 5 minutes at High pressure. Once cooking is complete, use a natural pressure release for 10 minutes; carefully remove the lid.
Serve garnished with a few sprinkles of ground cinnamon if desired. Enjoy!

529. Summer Blueberry Sauce

(Ready in about 25 minutes)

Per serving: 269 Calories; 0.4g Fat; 68g Carbs; 0.9g Protein; 62.1g Sugars; 2.8g Fiber

INGREDIENTS

1/2 pound fresh blueberries
1/2 cup granulated sugar
1/2 teaspoon vanilla extract
1/2 tablespoon freshly grated lemon zest
1/4 cup fresh lemon juice

DIRECTIONS

Place the blueberries, sugar, and vanilla in the inner pot of your Instant Pot.
Secure the lid. Choose the "Manual" mode and cook for 2 minutes at High pressure. Once cooking is complete, use a natural pressure release for 15 minutes; carefully remove the lid.
Stir in the lemon zest and juice. Puree in a food processor; then, strain and push the mixture through a sieve before storing. Enjoy!

530. Jamaican Hibiscus Tea

(Ready in about 20 minutes)

Per serving: 110 Calories; 0.2g Fat; 29.8g Carbs; 0.2g Protein; 28.5g Sugars; 0.1g Fiber

INGREDIENTS

2 cups water
1/4 cup dried hibiscus flowers
1/4 cup brown sugar
1/2 teaspoon fresh ginger, peeled and minced
1 tablespoon lime juice

DIRECTIONS

Combine all ingredients, except for the lime juice, in the inner pot of your Instant Pot.
Secure the lid. Choose the "Manual" mode and cook for 5 minutes at High pressure. Once cooking is complete, use a natural pressure release for 10 minutes; carefully remove the lid.
Stir in the lime juice and serve well chilled.

531. Skinny Mini Cheesecakes

(Ready in about 45 minutes)

Per serving: 431 Calories; 36.5g Fat; 23.2g Carbs; 9.8g Protein; 14.5g Sugars; 6.1g Fiber

INGREDIENTS

1/4 cup almonds
1/4 cup sunflower kernels
4 dates, chopped
6 ounces coconut milk
1/3 cup coconut yogurt

DIRECTIONS

Spritz four ramekins with nonstick cooking spray.
Process the almonds, sunflower kernels, and dates in your blender until it turns into a sticky mixture.
Press the crust mixture into the prepared ramekins.
Thoroughly combine the coconut milk and yogurt in a mixing bowl. Pour this mixture into the ramekins and cover them with a piece of foil.
Place a metal trivet and 1 cup of water in your Instant Pot. Lower the ramekins onto the trivet.
Secure the lid. Choose the "Manual" mode and cook for 25 minutes at High pressure. Once cooking is complete, use a natural pressure release for 15 minutes; carefully remove the lid. Bon appétit!

532. Mixed Berry Compote

(Ready in about 30 minutes)

Per serving: 182 Calories; 0.7g Fat; 45.5g Carbs; 1.6g Protein; 38.2g Sugars; 5.6g Fiber

INGREDIENTS

1/4 pound blueberries
1/4 pound blackberries
1/4 pound strawberries
1/4 cup brown sugar

1/2 tablespoon orange juice
1/4 teaspoon ground cloves
1 vanilla bean

DIRECTIONS

Place your berries in the inner pot. Add the sugar and let sit for 15 minutes. Add in the orange juice, ground cloves, and vanilla bean.

Secure the lid. Choose the "Manual" mode and cook for 2 minutes at High pressure. Once cooking is complete, use a natural pressure release for 10 minutes; carefully remove the lid.

As your compote cools, it will thicken. Bon appétit!

533. Cinnamon Coffee Cake

(Ready in about 40 minutes)

Per serving: 485 Calories; 27.1g Fat; 57.4g Carbs; 2.1g Protein; 23.3g Sugars; 1.2g Fiber

INGREDIENTS

6 ounces refrigerated biscuits
2 tablespoons granulated sugar
1/2 teaspoon ground cinnamon
1/4 teaspoon nutmeg, preferably freshly grated

1/4 cup raisins, if desired
2 tablespoons butter, melted
1 ounce firmly packed brown sugar

DIRECTIONS

Place 1 cup of water and a metal trivet in the inner pot of your Instant Pot. Lightly grease 12-cup fluted tube pan with cooking spray.

In a food bag, mix the granulated sugar, cinnamon, and nutmeg.

Separate the dough into biscuits and cut each into quarters. Place them in the food bag and shake to coat on all sides. Place them in the prepared pan, adding raisins among the biscuit pieces.

In a small mixing bowl, whisk the melted butter with brown sugar; pour the butter mixture over the biscuit pieces.

Secure the lid. Choose the "Manual" mode and cook for 25 minutes at High pressure. Bake until no longer doughy in the center.

Once cooking is complete, use a natural pressure release for 10 minutes; carefully remove the lid.

Turn upside down onto serving plate and serve warm. Bon appétit!

534. Rum Caramel Pudding

(Ready in about 40 minutes)

Per serving: 445 Calories; 26.3g Fat; 36.4g Carbs; 10.9g Protein; 21.1g Sugars; 1.3g Fiber

INGREDIENTS

2 stale croissants, cut into chunks
1/4 cup granulated sugar
1/2 cup milk
1/2 cup heavy cream

1 tablespoon rum
1/4 teaspoon ground cinnamon
1 egg, whisked

DIRECTIONS

Place 1 cup of water and a metal trivet in the inner pot of your Instant Pot. Place the croissants in the lightly greased casserole dish.

Press the "Sauté" button and use the lowest setting. Then, place the granulated sugar and water and let it cook until the mixture turns a deep amber color.

Now, add the milk and heavy cream, and cook until heated through. Stir in the rum, cinnamon, and eggs; stir to combine.

Secure the lid. Choose the "Manual" mode and cook for 25 minutes at High pressure. Once cooking is complete, use a natural pressure release for 10 minutes; carefully remove the lid. Bon appétit!

535. Autumn Pear and Pecan Pie

(Ready in about 35 minutes)

Per serving: 372 Calories; 14.8g Fat; 57.5g Carbs; 7.4g Protein; 21.4g Sugars; 10.2g Fiber

INGREDIENTS

4 refrigerated cinnamon rolls
2 tablespoons all-purpose flour
2 tablespoons brown sugar
1/4 teaspoon cinnamon

1/2 tablespoon butter
1/4 cup pecans, chopped
2 pears, cored and sliced

DIRECTIONS

Press and flatten the rolls into a lightly greased pie plate. Make sure there are no holes between the flattened rolls.
In a mixing bowl, mix the flour, brown sugar, cinnamon, butter, and pecans. Place the slices of pears on the prepared cinnamon roll crust. Spoon the streusel onto the pear slices.
Add 1 cup of water and a metal rack to the bottom of the inner pot. Lower the pie plate onto the rack.
Secure the lid. Choose the "Manual" mode and cook for 25 minutes at High pressure. Once cooking is complete, use a natural pressure release for 5 minutes; carefully remove the lid. Bon appétit!

536. Classic Vanilla Cupcakes

(Ready in about 40 minutes)

Per serving: 504 Calories; 24.6g Fat; 73.1g Carbs; 10.1g Protein; 50.5g Sugars; 3.5g Fiber

INGREDIENTS

1/2 cup cake flour
1/2 teaspoon baking powder
A pinch of salt
1/8 teaspoon ground cardamom
1/4 teaspoon ground cinnamon
1/2 teaspoon vanilla extract

1 egg
1/4 cup honey
4 tablespoons almond milk
2 ounces cream cheese
1/4 cup powdered sugar
1/2 cup heavy cream, cold

DIRECTIONS

In a mixing bowl, thoroughly combine the flour, baking powder, salt, cardamom, cinnamon, and vanilla.
Then, gradually add in the egg, honey, and milk. Mix to combine well. Now, spoon the batter into silicone cupcake liners and cover them with foil.
Place 1 cup of water and a metal trivet in your Instant Pot. Lower your cupcakes onto the trivet.
Secure the lid. Choose the "Manual" mode and cook for 25 minutes at High pressure. Once cooking is complete, use a natural pressure release for 10 minutes; carefully remove the lid.
While the cupcakes are cooking, prepare the frosting by mixing the remaining ingredients. Frost your cupcakes and enjoy!

537. Winter Hot Apple Cider

(Ready in about 55 minutes)

Per serving: 173 Calories; 0.4g Fat; 39.5g Carbs; 0.6g Protein; 32.6g Sugars; 5g Fiber

INGREDIENTS

2 apples, cored and diced
1/2 cup brown sugar
1 cinnamon sticks
1 vanilla bean

1 teaspoon whole cloves
1/2 small naval orange
2 tablespoons rum
2 cups water

DIRECTIONS

Place the ingredients in the inner pot of your Instant Pot.
Secure the lid. Choose the "Manual" mode and cook for 50 minutes at High pressure. Once cooking is complete, use a quick pressure release; carefully remove the lid.
Mash the apples with a fork or a potato masher. Pour the mixture over a mesh strainer and serve hot. Bon appétit!

538. Easter Chocolate Cake with Apricots

(Ready in about 55 minutes)

Per serving: 490 Calories; 16g Fat; 70.2g Carbs; 10.2g Protein; 41.2g Sugars; 4.7g Fiber

INGREDIENTS

2 ounces instant pudding mix

1 cup milk

2 ounces vanilla cake mix

4 tablespoons peanut butter

1 ounce chocolate chips

2 tablespoons dried apricots, chopped

DIRECTIONS

In a mixing bowl, thoroughly combine the pudding mix and milk. Por the mixture into a lightly greased inner pot.

Prepare the cake mix according to the manufacturer's instructions, gradually adding in the peanut butter. Pour the batter over the pudding.

Secure the lid. Choose the "Manual" mode and cook for 30 minutes at High pressure. Once cooking is complete, use a natural pressure release for 10 minutes; carefully remove the lid.

Sprinkle the chocolate chips and dried apricots on top. Seal the lid and let it stand for 10 to 15 minutes until the chocolate melts. Enjoy!

539. Greek Compote with Honey Yogurt

(Ready in about 20 minutes)

Per serving: 216 Calories; 0.2g Fat; 56.4g Carbs; 0.7g Protein; 51.2g Sugars; 2.9g Fiber

INGREDIENTS

1/2 cup rhubarb

1/4 cup plums

1/2 cup apples

1/2 cup pears

1/2 teaspoon ground ginger

1 vanilla bean

1 cinnamon stick

1/4 cup caster sugar

1/2 cup Greek yoghurt

2 tablespoons honey

DIRECTIONS

Place the fruits, ginger, vanilla, cinnamon, and caster sugar in the inner pot of your Instant Pot.

Secure the lid. Choose the "Manual" mode and cook for 2 minutes at High pressure. Once cooking is complete, use a natural pressure release for 10 minutes; carefully remove the lid.

Meanwhile, whisk the yogurt with honey.

Serve your compote in individual bowls with a dollop of honeyed Greek yogurt. Enjoy!

540. Traditional Polish Szarlotka

(Ready in about 1 hour 25 minutes)

Per serving: 551 Calories; 24.1g Fat; 85.7g Carbs; 4.8g Protein; 58.2g Sugars; 7.9g Fiber

INGREDIENTS

2 apples, peeled, cored and chopped

1/4 teaspoon ground cloves

1/4 teaspoon ground cardamom

1/4 teaspoon ground cinnamon

1 tablespoon sugar

1/2 cup flour

1/2 teaspoon baking powder

A pinch of salt

4 tablespoons butter, melted

1/4 cup honey

1/2 tablespoon orange juice

1/2 teaspoon vanilla paste

DIRECTIONS

Grease and flour a cake pan and set it aside. Toss the apples with the ground cloves, cardamom. cinnamon and sugar.

In a mixing bowl, thoroughly combine the flour, baking powder and salt.

In another mixing bowl, mix the butter, honey, orange juice, and vanilla paste. Stir the wet ingredients into the dry ones; spoon 1/2 of the batter into the prepared cake pan.

Spread half of the apples on top of the batter. Pour in the remaining batter covering the apple chunks. Spread the remaining apples on top. Cover the cake pan with a paper towel.

Add 1 cup of water and a metal rack to your Instant Pot. Lower the cake pan onto the rack.

Secure the lid. Choose the "Manual" mode and cook for 55 minutes at High pressure. Once cooking is complete, use a natural pressure release for 10 minutes; carefully remove the lid.

Transfer the cake to a cooling rack and allow it to sit for about 15 minutes before slicing and serving.

541. Classic French Souffle

(Ready in about 1 hour)

Per serving: 425 Calories; 33.1g Fat; 28.1g Carbs; 5.2g Protein; 18.8g Sugars; 3.5g Fiber

INGREDIENTS

1/2 pound carrots, trimmed and cut into chunks
1/4 cup sugar
1/2 teaspoon baking powder

1/2 teaspoon vanilla paste
1/4 teaspoon ground cardamom
1/4 teaspoon ground cinnamon
1 tablespoon flour

1 egg
4 tablespoons cream cheese, room temperature
4 tablespoons butter, softened

DIRECTIONS

Place 1 cup of water and a steamer basket in the bottom of your Instant Pot. Place the carrots in the steamer basket.
Secure the lid. Choose the "Steam" mode and cook for 10 minutes at High pressure. Once cooking is complete, use a quick pressure release; carefully remove the lid.
Process the mashed carrots, sugar, baking powder, vanilla, cardamom, cinnamon, and flour in your food processor until creamy, uniform, and smooth.
Add the eggs one at a time and mix to combine well. Stir in the cream cheese and butter; mix to combine well.
Spritz a baking pan with cooking spray; spoon the carrot mixture into the baking dish.
Add 1 cup of water and metal trivet to the bottom of the inner pot; cover with a paper towel.
Secure the lid. Choose the "Manual" mode and cook for 35 minutes at High pressure. Once cooking is complete, use a natural pressure release for 10 minutes; carefully remove the lid. Bon appétit!

542. Almond Cream Pie

(Ready in about 45 minutes)

Per serving: 455 Calories; 34g Fat; 30.3g Carbs; 8.3g Protein; 21.2g Sugars; 0.7g Fiber

INGREDIENTS

1/3 cup cookies, crushed
1 tablespoon coconut oil, melted
4 ounces cream cheese

1/4 cup granulated sugar
1 egg
1/4 cup sour cream

1/8 teaspoon grated nutmeg
1/3 teaspoon pure vanilla extract
1/4 cup almonds, slivered

DIRECTIONS

Place a metal trivet and 1 cup of water in your Instant Pot. Spritz a baking pan with nonstick cooking spray.
Next, mix the cookies and coconut oil into a sticky crust. Press the crust into the prepared baking pan.
Thoroughly combine the cream cheese, sugar, eggs, sour cream, nutmeg, and vanilla extract in a mixing bowl. Pour this mixture over the crust and cover it with a piece of foil.
Lower the baking pan onto the trivet.
Secure the lid. Choose the "Manual" mode and cook for 25 minutes at High pressure. Once cooking is complete, use a natural pressure release for 15 minutes; carefully remove the lid.
Top with slivered almonds and serve well chilled. Bon appétit!

543. Chocolate Mini Clafoutis

(Ready in about 40 minutes)

Per serving: 429 Calories; 17.5g Fat; 56.6g Carbs; 7.6g Protein; 24.8g Sugars; 2.1g Fiber

INGREDIENTS

1/4 cup all-purpose flour
1/4 cup rice flour
1/2 teaspoon baking powder
1/2 teaspoon vanilla paste

1/4 teaspoon ground cinnamon
A pinch of salt
1 tablespoon granulated sugar
1 egg, whisked

1/3 cup milk
2 tablespoons coconut oil
1/4 cup chocolate syrup

DIRECTIONS

Add 1 cup of water and a metal rack to the bottom of the inner pot. Lightly grease a mini muffin tin with shortening of choice.
Mix the flour, baking powder, vanilla, cinnamon, salt, sugar, eggs, milk, and coconut oil until thoroughly combined and smooth.
Pour the batter into the muffin tin and lower it onto the rack.
Secure the lid. Choose the "Manual" mode and cook for 25 minutes at High pressure. Once cooking is complete, use a natural pressure release for 10 minutes; carefully remove the lid.
Serve with chocolate syrup and enjoy!

544. Orange Spritzer with Cranberries

(Ready in about 25 minutes)

Per serving: 103 Calories; 0g Fat; 25.6g Carbs; 0.8g Protein; 24.7g Sugars; 0.1g Fiber

INGREDIENTS

2 ounces fresh cranberries
2 tablespoons granulated sugar
1 cup pulp-free orange juice
3/4 cup water

DIRECTIONS

Place all ingredients in the inner pot.

Secure the lid. Choose the "Manual" mode and cook for 5 minutes at High pressure. Once cooking is complete, use a natural pressure release for 15 minutes; carefully remove the lid.

Divide between eight glasses and fill with club soda. Enjoy!

545. Traditional Budín Puertorriqueño

(Ready in about 1 hour)

Per serving: 484 Calories; 23.3g Fat; 51.7g Carbs; 15.5g Protein; 24.5g Sugars; 3.9g Fiber

INGREDIENTS

1/4 pound Puerto Rican sweet bread, torn into pieces
1/4 cup water
1/4 teaspoon cinnamon powder
1/4 teaspoon ground cloves
1/2 teaspoon vanilla essence
1/4 cup brown sugar

2 cups coconut milk
1/2 tablespoon rum
1 egg, beaten
A pinch of salt
2 tablespoons butter, melted

DIRECTIONS

Place 1 cup of water and a metal trivet in the inner pot of your Instant Pot. Place the pieces of sweet bread in a lightly greased casserole dish. Now, mix the remaining ingredients; stir to combine well and pour the mixture over the pieces of sweet bread. Let it stand for 20 minutes, pressing down with a wide spatula until the bread is covered.

Secure the lid. Choose the "Manual" mode and cook for 25 minutes at High pressure. Once cooking is complete, use a natural pressure release for 10 minutes; carefully remove the lid. Bon appétit!

546. Hazelnut Jumble Bread

(Ready in about 35 minutes)

Per serving: 494 Calories; 30g Fat; 51.4g Carbs; 5.7g Protein; 23.3g Sugars; 1.2g Fiber

INGREDIENTS

1/4 cup granulated sugar
1 tablespoon hazelnuts, ground
3 refrigerated biscuits
2 tablespoons butter, melted

2 ounces cream cheese, at room temperature
2 tablespoons powdered sugar
1 tablespoon apple juice
1/2 teaspoon vanilla extract

DIRECTIONS

Place 1 cup of water and a metal trivet in the inner pot of your Instant Pot. Lightly grease 10-inch fluted tube pan with cooking spray.

In a shallow bowl, mix the granulated sugar and ground hazelnuts.

Cut each biscuit in half. Dip your biscuits into the melted butter; then, roll them in the hazelnut/sugar mixture.

Arrange them in the fluted tube pan.

Secure the lid. Choose the "Manual" mode and cook for 25 minutes at High pressure. Once cooking is complete, use a natural pressure release for 5 minutes; carefully remove the lid.

In the meantime, whip the cream cheese with the powdered sugar, apple juice, and vanilla extract. Drizzle over the hot cake and serve.

547. Granny's Pinch-Me Cake

(Ready in about 40 minutes)

Per serving: 485 Calories; 22.8g Fat; 62.4g Carbs; 8.7g Protein; 27g Sugars; 3.5g Fiber

INGREDIENTS

4 frozen egg dinner rolls, thawed

3 tablespoons brown sugar

1/2 teaspoon ground cinnamon

2 tablespoons walnuts, ground

2 tablespoons coconut oil, melted

1/4 cup powdered sugar

1 tablespoon coconut milk

DIRECTIONS

Place 1 cup of water and a metal trivet in the inner pot of your Instant Pot. Spray a Bundt pan with cooking spray and set aside.
Cut each dinner roll in half.

In a mixing bowl, thoroughly combine the brown sugar, cinnamon, and walnuts. In another bowl, place the melted coconut oil. Dip the rolls halves in the coconut oil and roll them in the brown sugar mixture.

Arrange the rolls in the prepared Bundt pan. Cover the pan with a piece of aluminum foil; allow it to rise overnight at room temperature. On the next day, lower the pan onto the trivet.

Secure the lid. Choose the "Manual" mode and cook for 25 minutes at High pressure. Once cooking is complete, use a natural pressure release for 10 minutes; carefully remove the lid.

After that, invert the bread onto a serving plate.

In a mixing bowl, whisk the powdered sugar and coconut milk until smooth. Drizzle the glaze over the top and sides of your cake. Bon appétit!

548. French Pots de Créme au Chocolate

(Ready in about 25 minutes)

Per serving: 460 Calories; 23.3g Fat; 53g Carbs; 7.2g Protein; 42.1g Sugars; 1.5g Fiber

INGREDIENTS

3/4 cup double cream

1/4 cup whole milk

2 egg yolks

1/4 cup sugar

1/2 teaspoon instant coffee

A pinch of pink salt

4 ounces chocolate chips

DIRECTIONS

Place a metal trivet and 1 cup of water in your Instant Pot.

In a saucepan, bring the cream and milk to a simmer.

Then, thoroughly combine the egg yolks, sugar, instant coffee, and salt. Slowly and gradually whisk in the hot cream mixture.

Whisk in the chocolate chips and blend again. Pour the mixture into mason jars. Lower the jars onto the trivet.

Secure the lid. Choose the "Manual" mode and cook for 6 minutes at High pressure. Once cooking is complete, use a natural pressure release for 10 minutes; carefully remove the lid.

Serve well chilled and enjoy!

549. Traditional Arroz Con Leche

(Ready in about 25 minutes)

Per serving: 370 Calories; 4.4g Fat; 72.4g Carbs; 7.6g Protein; 32.2g Sugars; 1.7g Fiber

INGREDIENTS

1/2 cup white pearl rice

1/2 cup water

A pinch of salt

1 ¼ cups milk

1/4 cup sugar

1/4 teaspoon grated nutmeg

1/2 teaspoon vanilla extract

1/2 teaspoon cinnamon

1 teaspoon lemon zest

DIRECTIONS

Place the rice, water, and salt in the inner pot of your Instant Pot.

Secure the lid. Choose the "Rice" mode and cook for 10 minutes at Low pressure. Once cooking is complete, use a natural pressure release for 10 minutes; carefully remove the lid.

Add in the milk, sugar, nutmeg, vanilla, cinnamon, and lemon peel; stir to combine well.

Press the "Sauté" button and cook, stirring continuously, until your pudding starts to boil. Press the "Cancel' button. Enjoy!